THE COWBOY'S TRAIL GUIDE

TO

WESTERNS

by

DAVID F. MATUSZAK

PACIFIC SUNSET PUBLISHING
2003

To Wrangler Bob and Doc Steve, my first saddlemates.

CENTENNIAL EDITION

Published by
Pacific Sunset Enterprises, Inc.
RR3 Box 668-A
Redlands, CA 92373-8710

http://www.pacificsunset.com/

ISBN 0-9633582-5-1
Library of Congress Control Number: 2003095590

Printed in the United States

10 9 8 7 6 5 4 3 2

CONTENTS.

FOREWORD.
ACKNOWLEDGMENTS.
PREFACE.

THE FIRST 100 YEARS.

APPENDICES.

—I was just thinking that of all the trails in this life there is one that matters most. It is the trail of a true human being.

—Graham Greene
Dances With Wolves

FOREWORD.

I was born and raised in the West. I've played in it. Made my livin' in it. Loved in it. Raised my family in it. I figure I'll die in it. Yes Sir, the American West.

Guess I had a hand at shaping the world's image of the West. No doubt it had a hand at shaping me. Ya see, I grew up in L.A. during the transitional period between silent and sound pictures. My earliest recollections of Hollywood's West were silents. By the time I was nine, the feature-length talking Western had come along. Youngsters my age couldn't help but be influenced by the cowboys of the "silver screen." So it should come as no surprise that at the age of seventeen I broke into films as a stunt man and began rodeoin'. You might say, I was a third generation Californian who became a first generation stunt man—right on the heels of the Gower Gulch boys.

I feel very fortunate to have been a part of what some say was the golden age of the Western. Of the roughly three hundred Westerns that I've had a part in, I'm most proud of my work in *The Grey Fox* which earned Canada's Genie Awards for Best Picture, Best Director, Best Screenplay, and Best Foreign Actor.

In *The Grey Fox,* I had the opportunity to portray the West as it really was. Not only is the story a true one, but every effort was made to assure that it was historically accurate. As we all know, Westerns have not always done that. The history of the West has always fascinated me. The more I discovered about the real West, the more I realized that we in Hollywood did not always deliver an authentic view of the West.

So it is my pleasure to introduce a book that sets the record straight—*The Cowboy's Trail Guide to Westerns.* In it David Matuszak carefully guides us through the Western genre. His own love of the West leads the way in portraying the true spirit of the West. I hope you find it as enjoyable as I did.

Sincerely,

Richard Farnsworth

Diamond D Ranch
Lincoln, New Mexico

Note: On October 6, 2000, shortly after an Academy award nomination for best actor,
Dick left us. He died on the Diamond D Ranch in the heart of the West that he loved.

ACKNOWLEDGMENTS.

Trail guides will always be indebted to the trail blazers who passed before them. My special thanks to the genre's pioneer trail blazers Les Adams and Buck Rainey, Thomas Weisser, Phil Hardy and Michael R. Pitts.

One person more than any other was responsible for ensuring the completion of this guide. He is my computer mentor, Grant Kirkwood. His technical advice and programming contributions are deeply appreciated.

Special thanks to Charlton Heston who understands the precious value of time, yet gave it so freely in supplying me with background information. I am much obliged to Richard Farnsworth for the foreword. I am particularly grateful to both Jack Elam and Harry Carey, Jr. for our thought provoking conversations regarding Western filmmaking. The contributions of Mele Peltz, Ellen Wald, and Scott Kennedy are appreciated as well.

Among the many archivists and librarians whose assistance contributed to this guide the American Film Institute's Jennifer Nolan deserves special thanks. It would be impossible to thank all the others, but they know who they are and to each of them my sincere gratitude.

Final thanks to Jack Rainey not only for his review of the manuscript and advice, but in particular for his encouragement. His own enthusiasm for the Old West combined with his interest in my work became an inspiration. During the final stages of this manuscript he was instrumental on keeping me focused at a time when this project seemed like riding a tireless pitching bronc. Now that I've got this guide bucked out, my sincere thanks.

PREFACE.

So, Yer Headed West. Well, I've been there. Permit me to be your guide. For nearly forty years, I've roamed about the West both on land and by film. I am as much a product of both the real West and the Western genre as any man alive. For much of my life has been spent searching for the essence of the American West.

I was six years old in 1959 and riding with the "Ardendale Kids." We were a tough bunch. Riding Schwinn ponies with our Mattel "Fanner Fifties" strapped to our sides, we roamed the length of Ardendale Avenue in the Los Angeles suburbs every afternoon from three to five. We knew what had to be done. We learned from the best—Wyatt Earp, Paladin, Lucas McCain, Cheyenne Bodie, The Lone Ranger.

Forty-seven TV Westerns were in production that year. Eleven of the top twenty programs according to Neilson were Westerns including such classics as: *Gunsmoke, Have Gun--Will Travel, The Life and Legend of Wyatt Earp, Cheyenne, Wagon Train, Wanted: Dead or Alive, Maverick, The Rifleman,* and *Tales of Wells Fargo.* Together with feature-length films they assured that the next generation of Americans would enjoy the myth of the Old West as much as their fathers before them.

Every afternoon we acted out the episodes that we had watched the night before. And we had every weapon necessary to do it. Hugh O'Brian's buntline Colt, Nick Adams' pistol-grip shotgun, Gene Barry's cane and derringer—we had them all. Roger was armed with Steve McQueen's sawed-off Winchester and custom holster while Ed carried Chuck Connors' rapid-fire Winchester. At ten years old, "Big Dave" was one of the old timers of the gang. He never did like those newfangled weapons and always stuck with his Fess Parker-era muzzleloader. Brother Bob wore his black double-rigged holster with matching pearl-handled Colts, but I favored Jack Kelly's plain single holster and .45—it seemed more realistic to me.

At precisely the same time my folks invested in a ranch in the Oregon Cascades. It was located nearly an hour from the nearest town. Across the back fence lie a hundred miles of Cascade wilderness. There were no utilities. Our only neighbor lit their house with kerosene and coleman lanterns. We lit our cabins each night for a couple of hours with an old gasoline generator. But, there was no television and there were no Westerns. It was time to begin living the real West.

Each of the next twelve years I spent nearly three months, the entire summer, on "the ranch." It was there that I learned to shoot, ride, fish and prospect. Although I didn't realize it until years later, it was there that I developed my love of the West.

During a two-hundred mile pack trip across the Cascades in 1981, I stumbled upon gold dredges working the waters that I had prospected for fun as a child. My interest in mining was renewed—particularly when I discovered that gold sold that day for more than $800.00 an ounce. The following summer I found myself prospecting the bone-chilling waters of both the Cascades and the Sierra Nevadas. The early days of that modern rush were wild times. There were shootings nearly every week. Makeshift gold camps dotted the riverbanks replacing the '49ers canvas tents with nylon. In the Sierra Nevadas I spent summers for more than a decade digging for gold by daylight. At night I dug through every piece of local history researching the miners who came before me. What began as a search for better diggin's resulted in a quest to understand the pioneer spirit.

My winters in those days were spent teaching school and building a small ranch on a few acres of badlands near the San Bernardino Mountains where I now raise horses. After a long day of digging fence-post holes, I occasionally stumbled on a Western movie on the television. But, they somehow looked different than I remembered them as a child. I had recently begun riding in an Old West show specializing in historical authenticity which led me to become even more critical of Hollywood's version of the West. Soon I found myself rating each film on a piece of paper and then throwing it into a box. It was the humble beginnings of this guide.

From that unmarked trailhead I've spent nearly two decades preparing this guide. It's a journey that has taken me all over the West. From Little Big Horn to Deadwood. From the Rockies to the Wallowa Valley. I've explored every essential aspect of the genre both from personal experience and by academic research. I've had a hell of a good time along the way, largely as a result of exploring the differences between both the Western myth and its spirit. Some say that the Old West died long ago. In many ways it never did. You just have to know where to look for it and be able to recognize it when you find it. Allow me to guide you through the Western genre.

THE FIRST 100 YEARS.

The first 100 years of Western filmmaking left the indelible mark of a hot brand on our culture. From the *Great Train Robbery* to *The Outsider*, tens of thousands of Westerns of all types were made. Amongst them nearly 2100 feature-length films were produced during the sound era. The centennial edition of this guide addresses them all. The good ones, the bad ones—even the ugly ones.

The Western genre evolved during its first century. The Western was foaled in the silent era, green broke on "Bs" and rode hard through the '40s and '50s. The Western was lathered and put away wet by the '60s. Went lame in the '70s. Was put out to pasture in the '80s, but became sound again by the '90s. At the close of the first century, the Western proved its heart by demonstrating that there is plenty of life left in the genre.

The centennial edition of this guide has undergone significant revision. The accuracy of the first edition proved to be excellent. However, as might be expected with a volume of this magnitude a handful of inaccuracies were discovered. They have been corrected. The most noticeable change is the addition of hundreds of new photographs, illustrations and quotes. During the past several years, I reviewed well over a hundred additional Westerns. These include new releases since the printing of the first edition. While travelling in "uncharted territory," I discovered that many films listed in the first edition were not true Westerns. They have been deleted from the log and added to Appendix I. Many requests were received to add filming locations to the film log. It has been done. Many story credits and production notes have been added as well. Academy Awards and nominations are included. "The Next 100 Years" section was added to predict the future of the genre and to discuss the making of the first perfect Western. My top 20 list of Westerns has been expanded to the "100 Best of the West" of the first century. That section was also expanded to include my picks for best actors, actresses, character actors, Native American actors, and directors . And finally, several of the film industry's most noted organizations have recently released their own top film lists. They have been noted in the film log. Among those lists is the Lone Pine Film Festival's Top 10 "A" Westerns. Their list was developed during a round table discussion that I chaired at the 2002 festival. These revisions make *The Centennial Edition of the Cowboy's Trail Guide to Westerns* a complete and thorough examination of the Western genre during its first century of filmmaking.

CHAPTER I.

INTRODUCTION.

Preparing for the Journey requires setting some parameters. Otherwise, you'd never fit this guide into your saddlebags. As many as ten thousand true Westerns of all types were produced making it impractical to do justice to all forms of the genre in any one volume. Further complicating the matter is my predecessors' reluctance to set parameters thereby establishing a working definition of the genre. The result has been collections of films which unreasonably stretch the Western's boundaries. Without specific criteria, far too many films have been unjustly included in the genre. Many films share elements of the Western, but let's face it, isn't *Star Wars* really a Western set in outer space?

With this in mind, the first consideration in defining the Western is the setting. The story must be set in the West. A true Western is set in the trans-Mississippi frontier, territory west of the Mississippi which I have extended to include the border territories of both Mexico and Canada. Those who include stories set in South America or Australia, for example, simply don't understand the unique concept of the American West. The second consideration is the time period.

The opening and closing of the Old West has long been argued by scholars. The opening of the West will be defined here as beginning in 1803 with the Louisiana Purchase. The closing of the West is more difficult to determine. Historians like Frederick Jackson Turner pointed to the results of the Census of 1890. Others say it was much later pointing to the disappearance of the horse culture and its replacement with the automobile as the primary mode of transportation. I tend to agree. What is clear is that it closed at different times in different places. By the turn of the century, generally speaking, the Wild West was closed. Pockets of the Wild West remained, however, in remote regions of the north, southwest and in Mexico until as late as 1915.

With setting and time restrictions firmly in place, this work will focus on "feature-length" films of the sound era. Because feature-length films have never been adequately defined, establishing a working definition may appear arbitrary. However, keep in mind the objective of this work: to guide you through Westerns that you will most likely encounter along the trail. The accessibility of Westerns on commercial, cable and satellite TV, videos, and in the theatre, make it more than likely that you will primarily encounter full-length films of the sound era. Distinguishing silent from sound pictures is relatively easy, but within the sound era clear cut definitions distinguishing shorts, "Bs", serials and full-length films from one and other is more difficult. Consequently, full-length or "feature-length," films are defined here as those with editing or with the addition of commercials can be aired in no less than a ninety minute time slot. Westerns with real running times of approximately seventy minutes or longer are aired most often.

There are a few other considerations when defining true Westerns. A fine line exists between lighthearted humor and comedy. I have been careful not to cross it. Good-natured humor often made frontier life more bearable. Comedies, on the other hand, focus primarily on the punch line rather than the story. For this reason they have been excluded. Music was a popular past time in the West. Cowboys, for example, often sang on night watch over the herd. However, true Westerns are not Broadway productions. Consequently, musicals must not be given serious consideration in the genre. And finally, the "B" Western. Even though series "B" Westerns meet many of the previous criteria, they are a distinctly separate art form within the genre thus deserving a guide of their own.

Prior to your departure through the Western genre, prepare thoroughly. Supply yourself with a fundamental understanding of the relationship between the real West and the Western myth. The following portion of this guide is intended not only to prepare you for your journey, but also as additional guidance should you become lost along the way.

———————

*—There are no **old** movies really—only movies you have already seen and ones you haven't.*
—Peter Bogdanovich
Director and filmographer

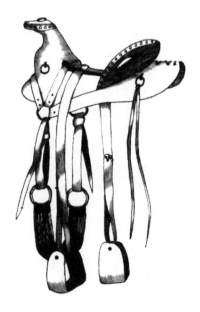

CHAPTER II.

HISTORY.

The History of Western movies is the history of the motion picture industry. When Thomas Edison patented a projector that allowed audiences instead of individuals to view films, his company immediately set out to quench the country's seemingly insatiable thirst for Old West entertainment. At the time, Wild West shows could be found around every corner and the public was ripe for a new venue for their passion. In 1894, the same year that Wild West show superstar, Annie Oaklie made her film debut, Edison's company produced three noteworthy shorts: *Sioux Indian Ghost Dance, Indian War Council,* and *Bucking Bronco*. In 1898, Edison produced a Western movie, *Cripple Creek Bar-Room*. Representative of early silents, it was a series of film sequences lacking any story.

Edwin S. Porter, an Edison engineer, became the father of story telling on film with the first commercial success of a film that told a story. In just ten minutes, *The Great Train Robbery* (1903) became not only an industry landmark, but changed the way the world saw the West forever. It was the first Western to compete favorably with the Wild West shows. In fact, the decline of the Wild West show coincided directly with the evolution of the Western movie.

Broncho Billy Anderson (right) in *The Golden Trail.*

The forty or more actors in *The Great Train Robbery* received no credit for their work as was customary with films of those times. Playing as many as four different roles in that film and receiving credit for none of them, was an aspiring actor named Gilbert M. Anderson— Broncho Billy. Anderson developed the concept of a central character in Westerns. By casting himself as the hero in his own productions, Broncho Billy became the first cowboy star and the first to be given screen credit. Between 1908 and 1915 Anderson produced nearly 400 one and two-reel films, the first Western serials. Westerns of that period reflected the public's desire for dime-novel heroes and Wild West show theatrics.

Bucking the trend, William S. Hart believed the public would appreciate authenticity in Westerns. From 1915 to 1921, Hart dominated the genre by introducing realism to his productions. Like Anderson, Hart chose the cowboy as his central character developing him into a legendary loner, a formula duplicated countless times in the genre. When Hart dropped the reins of popularity in the mid-twenties, they were grabbed by Tom Mix.

Like Anderson and Hart before him, Tom Mix developed a cowboy persona. However, Mix abandoned Hart's formula of authenticity in favor of pure fantasy. He became the quintessential dime-store cowboy. Drawing from his experiences performing in Wild West shows, his films during the twenties and early thirties offered the public a mythical look at the West. Together with such notables as Hoot Gibson, Ken Maynard, Jack Holt, and Harry Carey, he defined the genre during the silent era.

The silent era, however, was not entirely lost to serial Westerns. The first epic Western, *The Covered Wagon* (1923) was responsible for the commercial success of the feature-length Western. It resulted in Hollywood tripling its production of Westerns the following year including films like John Ford's, *The Iron Horse* and Irving Willat's, *North of '36.* These films further established the direction the genre would run.

The Sound Era was not created overnight. Instead, Hollywood gradually made the transition to sound between the years 1928 and 1932. The transition was particularly difficult for Westerns because the primitive microphone technology restricted outdoor recording. By 1932, however, most of the technical problems had been sufficiently resolved. During those formative years, a transition took place from silent pictures to full-sound films with dialogue. By introducing sound effects to the original production, *The Big Hop* (1928) became the first Western to employ sound. However, it lacked dialogue and musical score. For a time, films utilizing sound effects and musical scores were often produced in both silent and sound versions in order to accommodate theatres unequipped for sound.

The studios continued to experiment with new technologies and techniques for outdoor shooting resulting in the gradual viability of clear dialogue. In 1929, Paramount released their first sound Western, *The Virginian,* staring Gary Cooper. It is generally regarded as the first feature-length sound Western with dialogue. Thus begins our story...

Gary Cooper and Mary Brian in *The Virginian.*

CHAPTER III.

"B" WESTERNS.

B **Westerns** began with the first talkies and ended in 1954 with the filming of the last "B", *Two Guns and a Badge.* For nearly three decades thousands of these Westerns were produced. Before giving way to the Western TV series of the fifties, Bs offered a generation of movie goers a mythical look at the Old West. Yet, "B" Westerns have never been adequately defined. Early theatres advertised programs on their marquees in the following fashion:

> A: Red River
> B: Dead Man's Gold

The "A" listing advertised the feature film and the "B" listed the second attraction. As time passed, the studios assumed the nomenclature considering "A" pictures as big money productions and "Bs" as low "B"udget films. Low budgets usually resulted in poor quality productions. Needless to say, however, large budgets were no guarantee of quality. Clearly, there is far more to consider when differentiating between As and Bs than production costs.

Film length more than any other characteristic identifies a Western as a "B" film. Most Bs lasted 65 minutes or less making them suitable for inclusion in double-feature programs. Beyond film length, Bs can best be distinguished by their unique look and feel. This look and feel was often characterized by a one-dimensional "dime-novel" singing hero accompanied by a comic sidekick. The settings were often a peculiar mix of the Old West and depression era technology. These lighthearted and good-natured action films offered much needed escapism to depression and war-era audiences. Though Roy Rogers, Hopalong Cassidy, Charles Starrett and Rex Allen films are all classic examples of series "B" Westerns, the quintessential Bs were made by Gene Autry. Autry developed the "B" formula of action, music and comedy into an art form. Weaving characteristics of Broncho Billy and Tom Mix together with his own persona, Autry developed himself into a matinee idol and American icon. Gene delivered the music. Smiley Burnette or Pat Buttram supplied the comedy and the writers and stunt men created the action. The stories were so simple and straightforward that the writers often obtained their ideas from the morning newspaper. Consequently, the plots reflected the characteristic mixing of the Old West with contemporary themes.

The combination of Old West and contemporary technology was characteristic of Roy Rogers films as well. Like Autry, Rogers produced feature-length "B" films. *Susanna Pass* (1949) begins as a true feature film set in the Old West, but suddenly a 1940s forestry station sounds its electric alarm bell, along comes a truck, electric lights and a seismograph. Then it's right back to the Old West. In *Spoilers of the Plains* (1951), Rogers is the singing cowboy who together with his comic sidekick become involved with a 1940s government rocket project.

The overwhelming popularity of Bs led to the production of films for specific target audiences. Most noteworthy were the Black Westerns. Filmed at a Black dude ranch near Victorville, California, the appeal of *Harlem on the Prairie* (1935), spawned a series of successful African American "B" Westerns released only in the ghettos. George Randall and Herbert Jeffries led an all-Black cast. Unlike the "Black-pride" Westerns of the 1970s which reflected the themes of the civil rights movement, the early Black

Westerns simply replaced white actors with African Americans and duplicated the popular "B" formula.

In the final analysis, it would be unfair to judge "B" Westerns on the criteria established in this guide. They deserve a category of their own within the genre.

Gene Autry, Hollywood's singing cowboy.

New Mexico cowpunchers pick a tune.

CHAPTER IV.

SPAGHETTI WESTERNS.

Spaghetti Westerns are the most recognizable examples of foreign films. Hundreds of Westerns were shot on foreign soil. Unlike films such as *Villa Rides* (1968) and *Valdez Is Coming* (1971) which were American productions shot over seas, spaghetti Westerns were foreign productions. The first significant European Western was the German production, *The Emperor of California* (1936). The story revolves around Sutter's gold discovery, but from a very different perspective. Germany's contemporary views regarding U.S. imperialism are clearly reflected in the theme. Foreign films often reflected the country's own national character or became a propaganda vehicle comparing their politics to the United States.

During the early 1960s, the Italians began to ride the coat tails of the slumping Hollywood Western. They produced small budget films which often featured American stars attempting to revive their sliding careers. We know them today as "Spaghetti Westerns." Production companies from all over Europe followed. Not until 1964 with the introduction of Sergio Leone's, *A Fistful of Dollars*, did the Spaghetti Western gain prominence. Launching Clint Eastwood's career, it was the first of the "Leone trilogy." *For a Few Dollars More* (1965) and *The Good, the Bad, and the Ugly* (1966) followed. Together they defined the Spaghetti Western and cast the mold for nearly 500 foreign productions filmed until the late 1970s.

The Spaghetti Western developed a distinctive style differing from earlier foreign films which had simply duplicated the Hollywood Western formula. Spaghetti Westerns were characterized by revenge resulting in excessive violence. The themes reflected a society with firsthand experience of the atrocities of World War II. Graphic violence became a trademark of these films. Contemporary audiences were desensitized by a common plot formula intended to temper the violence with revenge. The introduction of a violent rape and/or murder scene early in the film instilled rage and a sense of revenge in the minds of the audience. When the on-screen revenge followed, the graphic violence seemed justified. The European preoccupation with violence can perhaps only be explained by those who experienced two world wars on their homeland. It is interesting to note that many of the Spaghetti Western directors also directed significant numbers of European horror films which also featured graphic violence.

The motives of Spaghetti Western heroes differed significantly from their American production counterparts. Spaghetti Western heroes were often the surviving victims of a murdered family and, consequently, their actions were motivated by revenge. Whereas, Hollywood heroes reflected one of America's contemporary national characteristics: the strong helping the weak.

Another distinctive characteristic of the Spaghetti Western was the European brand of sex. Spaghetti Westerns were often

—As long as I have a face, you'll always have a place to sit.
—Gianrico Tondinelli
China 9, Liberty 37

8

Clint Eastwood

—For me, and I say this with a smile, the greatest screenwriter of Western films was Homer, because Achilles, Ajex, Hector and the others are the archetypes of Western characters.
—Sergio Leone

Lee Van Cleef

The Good,

the Bad,

and the Ugly

Eli Wallach

racy by 1960s, American standards. Perhaps the Victorian influence in Hollywood productions more accurately portrayed the sexual attitudes of the American settler. If so, Spaghetti Westerns better portrayed behavior inside frontier brothels.

The last characteristic worthy of mention is the Spaghetti Western's utter disregard for historical accuracy. Though the apparel and props generally appear better than average, the facts are often so distorted that they demonstrate complete ignorance of Western history. For example, in *Charge of the Seventh Cavalry* (1964) Indians counterattack the Union army as a result of among other distortions Arkansas and Texas requesting to withdraw from the Civil War??? In *Man Who Killed Billy the Kid* (1967) Billy is depicted as a martyr killing only in self-defense. In the end Pat Garrett is unable to shoot the Kid. Consequently, Billy is killed instead by his arch enemy, Mark Liston.

With few exceptions, Spaghetti Westerns rank side by side with the poorest Hollywood "B" Westerns. They were often released under multiple titles and the foreign actors and directors took American sounding pseudonyms in order to gain greater appeal. Nearly 500 Spaghetti Westerns are included here. The majority of them are rarely seen in America. They represent a vast uncharted territory which is best left as wilderness.

—This is the West, Sir. When the legend becomes fact, print the legend.
—Carleton Young
The Man Who Shot Liberty Valance

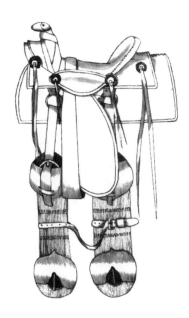

CHAPTER V.

THE MYTH OF THE WEST.

The Myth of the West was responsible for creating the Western genre as we know it. Even though reality is far more interesting than myth, Hollywood followed a clearly blazed trail of sensationalizing the Old West. Along that trail teams of showmen quickly discovered that the Western myth could be very profitable. They developed "showmanship economics." Showmanship economics is the process of sensationalizing reality for profit.

The West enjoyed a long tradition of creating its own legends. Whether it be mountainmen spinning yarns around the campfire or cowboys boasting in a frontier saloon, creating mythical reputations amongst themselves was a common form of entertainment in the Old West. It was storytelling, but seldom was the tale confused with reality. They knew the reality of the West. They were living it. It wasn't until the arrival of Eastern newspaper correspondents and dime novelists that the stories about the West became profitable. In order to sell the West, they created a myth overshadowing the unique Western spirit.

The industrial revolution created dull and complacent life-styles for many Eastern city dwellers. Their humdrum lives created a demand for escapism that was satisfied by the steady supply of fascinating stories from the Western

—To buy the legend...for the people back East, a piece of the American West they can believe in...the lies they need—we all need.
—Dime novelist, Wilbur Olsen (Sam Peckinpah)
China 9, Liberty 37

frontier. As the stories became more exciting, the appeal widened resulting in greater sales. Consequently, the Western myth was created by sensationalizing history. Dime novels and Wild West shows delivered the mythical West to cities all over the world.

The advent of the steam-powered, high-speed rotary press and the increased literacy rate of late 19th century Easterners created both the means and the market for showmanship economics to flourish. "Dime novel" publishing became a highly competitive industry led by Erastus F. Beadle. Beadle dominated dime publishing until his retirement in 1889. Early dime novels sensationalized the Old West with tall tales of imaginary frontiersman like "Duke Darrall" and "Moccasin Mat." Later, real frontiersman such as Kit Carson, George A. Custer, and Buffalo Bill Cody were immortalized by their publications. Whether it was a factual character like Buffalo Bill or pure fantasy like Deadwood Dick, the result was the same. The myth of the West was developed on those pages supplying Hollywood with

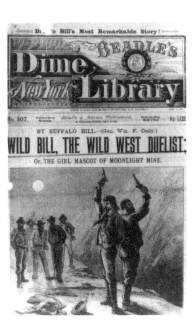

12

a well-seasoned audience with preconceived notions about how the West was won.

Perhaps Hollywood's best attempt at explaining the country's love affair with the dime novel is the film, *From Noon Til Three* (1976). Charles Bronson is a third-rate outlaw who following an afternoon affair with a rich widow is mistaken for dead. The widow (Jill Ireland) exaggerates his rather pathetic life in

—Hee, hee, hee…That's all bullshit!
—Charles Bronson
From Noon Till Three

a dime novel developing Bronson into a larger than life worldwide hero. The myth created by the dime novel makes it impossible for Bronson to convince anyone that he's not dead.

The dime novel came to life in 1883 with the opening of Buffalo Bill Cody's first Wild West Show. Buffalo Bill developed showmanship economics into an art form. By assembling the characters of dime novels for an "authentic" shoot-em-up exhibition, he offered the world his own mythical version of the Old West—one that he took a personal hand in creating.

Buffalo Bill understood very early that the myth of the West could be manipulated for profit. Between the days of his adventures as a frontier scout and the development of his Wild West show he honed his theatrical skills on the eastern stage. In the summer of 1876, following Custer's defeat, Cody returned west to rejoin his old regiment. Seeking the adventure of what most believed would be the last great Indian war, he led a scouting party of Fifth Regiment cavalry along War Bonnet Creek. There they stumbled on an advance party of Cheyenne en route to join Sitting Bull in the north. A brief skirmish

Charles M. Russell's *Cody's Fight with Yellowhand*

ensued resulting in one Indian casualty. Dressed in one of his stage costumes, Buffalo Bill downed a warrior by the name of Yellow Hair (Yellowhand). He promptly scalped the man claiming it as, "the first scalp for Custer!" Within five weeks he returned east to exploit his deeds in a new play, *The Red Right Hand*. Soon his legendary deed moved from the stage to the arena.

Cody's first scalp for Custer remained a standard attraction as his Wild West show traveled the world for thirty years entertaining an estimated fifty million people. So successful was he that at the turn of the century, just as the film industry was blossoming, nearly a hundred imitations of his show toured the East. Posters were plastered on shop and barn walls throughout the East advertising such shows as: Tompkins Real Wild West and Frontier Exhibition, Buffalo Ranch, and Miller Brothers 101 Ranch Wild West. For fifty years Wild West shows entertained the world. During the last thirty they competed with the movie Western by offering the public what Hollywood could not—the sounds of the Old West. Within but a few years of the perfection of Westerns with sound, however, the last of the Wild West shows went belly up.

Buffalo Bill Cody

Cody must also be recognized for his early attempts at utilizing the development of motion pictures to portray the West. He declared, "My object of desire has been to preserve history by the aid of the camera with as many living participants in the closing Indian wars of North America as could be procured." As early as 1894 his Wild West show was filmed for the peepshow circuit. Kinetoscope parlors appeared that year first in New York City then in Europe. Bankruptcy in 1913 forced him to collaborate in the Colonel W. F. Cody (Buffalo Bill) Historical Pictures Company.

The company produced *Buffalo Bill's Indian Wars* (1913). Cody joined with other actual participants including retired General Nelson Miles in creating their version of the Indian wars. The film may have been considered too authentic by the military who had supplied cavalrymen for the film. Cody's truthful portrayal of the massacre at Wounded Knee apparently motivated the government to delay releasing the film for more than a year. The film was re-released following Cody's death in 1917 never being widely distributed. No known copies exist today. Buffalo Bill is rarely credited for his contributions to the genre perhaps because the film industry had gone west.

By 1910, "Gower Gulch" was established in the vicinity of Sunset Boulevard and Gower Street in Hollywood. It was a colony of real cowboys who had

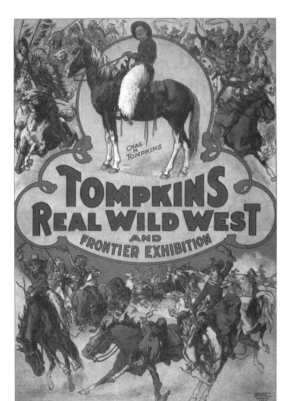

congregated for the purpose of supplying stunt men, extras, and so forth for the hundreds of Westerns in production. Stray cowboys from the days of the Old West first found refuge in Wild West shows. However, five dollars a day and a box lunch lured many of them to Hollywood. As many as nine of every ten Western actors during this time were real cowboys. Real cowboys created very real film sequences. In many ways, the authenticity in Westerns was never better than in those early silents.

In addition to the real cowboys, early silents were actually produced by real lawmen and outlaws. *"The Bank Robbery"* (1908), for example, was produced by the Oklahoma Mutoscene Company which was formed by Bill Tilghman and Al Jennings. Jennings was a former train robber and Tilghman was the lawman who captured him. *The Bank Robbery* was based on one of Jennings' attempted holdups and filmed at the actual locations. The film was not well received.

Charles Goodnight

One of the West's most famous frontiersman tried his hand at filmmaking. Cowpuncher-turned-cattlebaron, Charles Goodnight, attempted to portray an authentic West. At the age of eighty, his Goodnight Films company produced in five parts *Old Texas* (1916). However, it too failed commercially.

Others attempted to deliver authenticity to the young genre. Wyatt Earp and Emmett Dalton became technical directors and William S. Hart rode point on a drive to make the Western an authentic portrayal of the Old West. Realism experienced significant commercial success—particularly with Hart, but it was short lived. Growing in popularity was a new Western hero, one who personified Hollywood's Western myth.

Tom Mix turned the dime-novel hero into a celluloid icon. Everything about Mix was a myth. Even his own persona paralleled the myth he portrayed on film. Mix fabricated wild tales of his own exploits including having served with the Texas Rangers and as a U.S. Marshal in Montana, scouting for General Chafee in the Spanish-American War, etc. He was in fact an accomplished horseman who rose to fame in Wild West shows. Mix broke into films with nearly a hundred early Western shorts. In 1917, an ex-nickelodeon operator named William Fox hired him for feature films. Mix's characters were choir boys on horseback. They were flawless good guys complete with the symbolic white hat. Everything about them from their dress to their deeds was pure myth. Yet, by the mid-twenties Mix overtook William S. Hart in popularity outlasting his career by a decade. Once

Tom Mix (center) in *My Pal the King.*

again, the myth prevailed.

Wyatt Earp's attempt to enter motion pictures further illustrates the importance of myth. Hoping to promote his life story, Wyatt traveled to Hollywood. Upon his arrival, he befriended William S. Hart and Tom Mix. Even though Earp represented the quintessential Westerner and had become a legend in his own time, Hart and Mix were unable to convince any producer to portray Earp's life on film. The problem was Earp's story was based in reality without sufficient exaggeration. That is to say, the "mythmakers" had not developed Earp's life into a commercial commodity. It wasn't until 1931, two years after his death, that his biography was published. Hollywood developed his myth, thereafter, with countless films portraying his deeds.

Among the earliest Wyatt Earp films was *Frontier Marshal* (1939) staring Randolph Scott. But, according to Allan Dwan, a director well versed in the development of the myth from his work in early silents, the film wasn't about Earp's life at all. Instead of portraying Earp's authentic life on film, his name was used to represent a mythical version of any frontier marshal—myth sold better than reality.

The myth of the West developed primarily around three legendary figures: cowboys, Indians and gunfighters. All three evolved from authentic figures of the Old West into near mystical legends. Most Westerns revolved around one or more of these characters. Separating the myth from reality is often difficult because their myth is so deeply rooted in our culture.

The Cowboy Myth was responsible for immortalizing the West. No other historical figure commanded such universal appeal as did this legendary horseman. Sitting tall in the saddle, the brim of his hat tipped low over his brow and his silhouette against the setting sun, he remains today an unmistakable icon of the West. Was the American cowboy the independent, self-reliant manifestation of the Western spirit? Or, was he simply a laborer for the cattle industry?

Montana cowpunchers in 1886.

The term "cowboy" referred originally to members of Tory bands who rustled in New York state, but following the Civil War cowboy took on a different connotation describing members of the growing work force responsible for driving Texas cattle to northern markets. By the 1880s, the term "cowpuncher," which described the men who went alongside trains with a pole to prod cattle that went down inside, became synonymous with cowboy. The word cowboy, however, stuck with the public becoming the term around which the myth gradually developed.

The earliest dime novels rarely featured cowboys. Instead, the heroes were developed from scouts, hunters and the like. Cowboys were relegated to supporting roles. It wasn't until the great cattle drives and the arrival of the wild cattle towns like Dodge and Abilene that Easterners took note of the West's version of an industrial worker. The cowboy myth developed around a rugged breed of laborers willing to endure hardships never imagined by Eastern factory workers. The myth was based on real frontiersmen, men like Teddy Blue.

—I must of swallowed a pound of dirt today. This cattle driving's more work than I remember it.

—Alan Hale, Jr.
Canyon River

"Teddy Blue," Edward C. Abbott, drove Texas longhorns north during the 1870s and 1880s. Unlike most cowpunchers who migrated to Texas from the South following the war, Teddy was born in England and was transplanted by his parents in 1871 to Nebraska. They raised him to be a farmer, but Teddy grew up surrounded by cowboys and their Texas herds. To a boy the lure of the open range was far more appealing than the toil of a plow. So, in the summer of 1878 when his father requested he "...take old Morgan and Kit and Charlie and plow the west ridge tomorrow.", Teddy Blue ran off to Texas to become a full-time cowboy. His own coming of age paralleled the golden age of the cowboy.

From Texas to Alberta, Teddy drove cattle. All along the trail he worked hard, slept little, and had a hell of a good time. His nickname was given to him as the result of an episode in Miles City, Montana. At Turner's Theatre he was propositioned by a whore who led him backstage down a long dark hall. Remembering the $700. in his gun belt and fearing foul play, he turned around. In doing so, his spur caught on the carpet and he fell through a thin partition onto the stage. Teddy quickly recovered by grabbing a musician's chair and straddling it. He bucked around the stage yelling, "Whoa Blue! Whoa Blue!"—a cowboy expression at the time. By the time they dragged him off the stage, the audience howling with laughter had branded him "Blue."

Though Teddy was a cowpuncher all his life, he made but four drives north from Texas. Nearly a third of all cowboys never repeated their first. His work was well respected commanding as much as $75. a month at a time when others were offered $30. to $45. He earned every penny. Teddy was a hell-raising, hard-working company man. Like his counterparts, he was

—In fact there was only two things the old-time cowpuncher was afraid of, a decent woman and being set afoot.

—Teddy Blue

loyal, tireless and never complained. He rode point, swing, flank and drag by sunlight then rode night watch by starlight. Teddy paused at day's end long enough to wash out and spit up the day's trail dust and down his grub before climbing into the saddle again to calm the herd with a verse of "The Little Black Bull" on his turn at night watch. Sleep was often in short supply.

The cowboy myth was based on this difficult, but carefree life-style. Easterners began to take note and by the 1880s the cowboy was well on his way to becoming an American legend.

Dime novels, Wild West shows, the artistry of Charles Russell and Frederic Remington, and Owen Wister's novel, *The Virginian,* all contributed to developing his myth. The 1880s became the golden age of the cowboy. Thousands of cowboys, like Teddy Blue, raised and drove herds to cattle towns like Abilene where they were subsequently shipped by rail to beef-hungry Easterners. They faced drought, disease, hostile Indians, rustlers and the hardships of frontier life. They seldom faced it alone.

The cowboy as a self-reliant range rider is based more in myth than in reality. His coffee came from South America. Much of his gear, clothing and tack was manufactured in the East. His food, with the obvious exception of beef, was grown and often prepared by someone else. Cowboys were the indispensable work force of the cattle industry. The cattle industry in turn was one component of the economic development of the West and in collaboration with the mining, fur, farming and transportation industries the economic growth of an entire nation was assured.

Teddy Blue, 1879

Rod Cameron in *Panhandle.*

Yul Brynner in *Invitation to a Gunfighter.*

The Gunfighter became a mythical symbol of frontier justice. Right or wrong, he dispensed his own brand of law and order. With self-determination he took matters into his own hands. In those hands was the great equalizer, the Colt .45, so called because with the squeeze of a finger it made all men equal. The Colt itself became part of the myth. Though it was far and above the most prevalent handgun on the frontier, many preferred the action of

Clint Eastwood in *Hang 'Em High.*

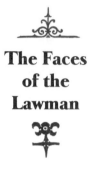

**The Faces
of the
Lawman**

Texas Rangers

John Wayne as Rooster Cogburn

other popular revolvers like the Remington or Smith & Wesson. All of the six-guns shared the same mystique.

Hollywood developed the myth of the gunfighter into a classic struggle between good and evil. Rarely were the sides confused. After all, the good guys wore white hats and the bad guys wore black resulting in the easy identification of heroes. As Hollywood developed the Western into an art form it did so significantly influenced by two world wars. More than ever America needed heroes—particularly recognizable heroes. However, in the real West good and evil were not so easily distinguished. So fine was the line separating outlaws from lawmen that often they crossed over it from both directions. Consequently, lawmen were often nothing more than thugs with a tin star.

—Ryan, I never drew first on a man in my life. That's the only way to stay clean—you play it by the rules. Without the rules you're nothing!
—Burt Lancaster
Lawman

The Lawman on film was associated with strong character and unquestionable virtue. The "John Wayne ethic" symbolized Hollywood's code of the West. The lawman protected the weak often at great personal expense. And he upheld the law even in the face of public ridicule. In short, the myth of the lawman reflected in many ways America's national character—both as we viewed ourselves and in the eyes of the world.

Early in the 20th century, America established itself as a dominant world power and at precisely the same time the film industry evolved. Consequently, Western lawmen reflected how Americans viewed themselves as the world's protector of freedom and justice. This concept of the strong helping the weak became a popular theme for Hollywood lawmen. Hollywood lawmen, however, seldom reflected the true character of 19th century frontiersmen.

Wyatt Earp provides a case study in real lawmanship. Law enforcement was seldom steady work. Wyatt like most lawmen looked to other sources of income to supplement his meager salary. He and his brothers mined, operated saloons, gambling halls, and brothels. Much of his time was spent in the company of drunks, addicts and whores. Wyatt was a man of conviction, strong-willed and often strong-armed. Today he'd be the ACLU's worst nightmare. Yet, this is precisely the kind of man required to control frontier cattle and mining towns. He did so with remarkable efficiency and often without gunplay.

The law, the honest ones carry it hard and clean all their lives. Behind their backs the others buy it, sell it, dirty it, tie it into knots.
—Robert Ryan
Lawman

Ronald Reagan

**The Many Faces
of
Wyatt Earp**

Randolph Scott

Joel McCrea

Wyatt Earp

James Garner

Kevin Costner

Kurt Russell

Wyatt was an early advocate of gun control. By striking first with a good old-fashioned pistol whipping, he regularly ended a confrontation before it escalated into a gunfight. When this failed to resolve the issue, Wyatt utilized the barrel of his gun with deadly results. In the most famous shoot out of all, the gunfight at the OK Corral, Wyatt's confidence and decisiveness was instrumental in producing a lopsided victory for the Earps. Hollywood acted out many mythical versions of this event. So many different eyewitness accounts were recorded that no one will ever know precisely what occurred. What is clear is that the entire episode lasted approximately thirty seconds. It was the classic Western showdown, face to face within spittin' distance. Not on main street, but in a back alley. The gunfighter myth was developed largely from this single event. It evolved into the Hollywood main street showdown climaxing hundreds of Westerns.

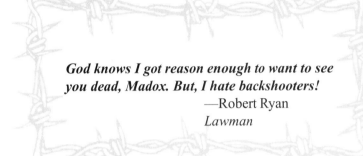

God knows I got reason enough to want to see you dead, Madox. But, I hate backshooters!
—Robert Ryan
Lawman

Hollywood developed the gunfight into a melodramatic art form complete with its own technique, protocol and code of honor. The Hollywood code of honor prevented heroes from ever backshooting or ambushing their adversaries. If the hero did surprise the villain, he was obligated to offer a warning and an opportunity to draw first.

In a Hollywood showdown two gunmen faced off on main street at high noon, the townspeople scattered to safety. The gunfighters stared into each other's eyes then paused to tie down their low-slung holsters. Their eyes met again. Perhaps a last warning was uttered. Another pause. The hero waited for the villain to make the first move. When he did, like lightening the hero drew and shot from the hip often fanning the hammer of his .45. Evil laid dead on main street.

Variations of this shoot-out provided the final scene of countless Westerns. Fact is, it was all myth. The gunfighter showdown was quite rare in the Old West. The tie-down, low-slung holster was a Hollywood invention as was the fast-draw technique. In reality, the Colt was accurately fired at arms length after taking careful aim. Cocking the hammer on the draw or fanning it was just as likely to result in its owner being shot. And had they really allowed the villain to draw first, there would have been a disproportionate number of outlaws roaming the West.

The Outlaw in motion pictures seldom conveyed any redeeming qualities. He was most often portrayed as a one dimensional celluloid version of a vaudevillian villain complete with boos and hisses. His motives were clearly evil. The myth was derived largely from the likes of outlaws such as William H. Bonney—alias Billy the Kid.

—I'm the best shot there is…I killed people who needed killin'.
—Val Kilmer
Billy the Kid (1989)

22

Buster Crabbe (center) in *Billy the Kid Trapped.*

John Mack Brown (left) in *Billy the Kid* (1930).

The Many Faces
of
Billy the Kid

Robert Taylor in
Billy the Kid (1941)

William H. Bonney

Michael Pollard in
Dirty Little Billy.

Kris Kristofferson in *Pat
Garrett and Billy the Kid.*

Billy the Kid's legend was primarily the result of exaggerated newspaper accounts and dime novels. He was in fact a rather insignificant outlaw. Yet, showmanship economics produced a mythical badman who's exploits have been exaggerated on film more often than any other Western figure. More than fifty films spanning more than half a century have been produced about Bonney. Wallace Berry was among the first of the sound-era Kids. The story's ending was altered to reflect his mythical friendship with Pat Garrett who instead of ambushing the Kid allowed him to escape. It is interesting to note that the European release of the same film ended with the Kid's death. It was not only more accurate, but reflected a pattern of violence utilized decades later by Spaghetti Westerns. Buster Crabbe, Bob Steele, Robert Taylor, Jack Buetel, Audie Murphy, Paul Newman, Michael J. Pollard and Kris Kristofferson were but a few of the dozens of Billy the Kids. The Kid even played opposite of Roy Rogers which is not surprising given that in real-life he was often reported to be in places where he'd never been.

A Las Vegas journalist coined the phrase, "Billy the Kid." He reported that the Kid led fifty outlaws who were rustling in the Fort Sumner vicinity. Truth was, Bonney was nowhere near there at the

—Motion pictures have spread the legend, and because an audience is educated, they know from the films that Billy the Kid was a handsome, dashing outlaw, and if somebody would make him today as he really was, it would probably be so much against the grain of an audience that it couldn't be a success.

—Fritz Lang, director

—Dear Governor Axtell,
...Send three men and instruct them not to shoot, as I am unarmed. In short, Sir, I surrender.
Your Obedient Servent,
William H. Bonney
P.S. I changed my mind. Kiss my ass!
—Emilio Estevez
Young Guns

—...I am afraid to give up because my enemies would kill me. If it is in your power to annul these indictments I hope you will do so, so as to give me a chance to explain. I have no wish to fight any more.
Your obedient Servent,
W. H. Bonney
—W. H. Bonney

24

Red Cloud   Standing Buffalo

Captured Crow warriors and their guards in 1887.

time. Accounts like those sold newspapers in the East much the same way that the tabloid media made a fortune selling the O.J. Simpson story.

The real Billy the Kid, like most outlaws, was a far cry from the myth. Though the man himself was not significant, the legend he produced certainly was. It is the importance we place on legends like his and the manner in which we develop their myth that reflect our own values.

The Western myth remained profitable through the early 1960s when our own values began to significantly change. The Vietnam War, race relations, the assassinations of the Kennedys, and other elements of social unrest all contributed to changing the way we viewed our country and ourselves. For the first time we questioned traditional American values, heroes, and the myth of the West. Consequently, the Western entered its darkest period. Hollywood responded in 1980 with *Heaven's Gate,* a film short on myth and long on authenticity. It proved a monumental box office disaster setting the genre back yet another decade. Not until the tremendous box office success of *Dances With Wolves* (1990) would the genre be given new life.

Indian culture was rarely portrayed on film through the eyes of Native Americans. Instead, the myth of the West developed largely around the adversarial relationship between Indians and settlers from the settlers' perspective. The early film industry produced Westerns designed to cater to its primary audience— the predominantly white society of the early 20th century. Consequently, motion pictures developed the western myth by telling a very one-sided story. It must be noted that Indians were not singled out in this respect. For example, Hispanics and African-Americans together accounted for as many as half of all American cowboys, yet, Hollywood rarely offered their perspective.

From the settlers' perspective Indians represented a significant obstacle to westward expansionism. White settlers believed the American West was theirs for the taking. In order to justify their encroachment of Indian lands, they armed themselves with the notion of "Manifest Destiny" which gave them divine authority to conquer the West. The first pioneers enjoyed relatively peaceful relations with Indians. Trappers routinely traded with them and were able to coexist in vast areas of wilderness. Even during the great mass migration west to the California gold fields, life-threatening encounters with "hostile" Indians were rare. Glenda Riley's sample of 150 diaries, journals, memoirs, and letters assembled from all major overland trails, 1830-1900, cited:

113 recorded no difficulties with hostiles
 22 encountered minor problems
 15 experienced major difficulties, but not extensive loss of life

However, the fear of Indians was very real. Exaggerated reports of Indian attacks became popular reading in the East. These reports generated a hysterical fear of Indians among many settlers. For example, one woman traveler prepared for suicide with a locket full of poison in the event she was captured by hostiles. In 1849, The U.S. War

—You gotta remember Indians ain't people. They're wild animals. When they get a taste of blood you gotta kill 'em!

—Lon Chaney, Jr.
The Indian Fighter

Department offered to sell guns and ammunition at cost to California emigrants and many of those traveling overland armed themselves like army battalions. As competition for Indian lands intensified violent encounters became more common.

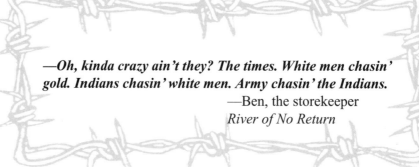

—Oh, kinda crazy ain't they? The times. White men chasin' gold. Indians chasin' white men. Army chasin' the Indians.
—Ben, the storekeeper
River of No Return

The relationship between white settlers and the American Indian changed significantly during the later part of the 19th century. Three factors account for this change: the settlers' European concept of the individual ownership of land, the mining industry and the buffalo trade. The concept of individual land ownership was foreign to the American Indian. For hundreds of years tribes roamed freely throughout their native regions following the hunt or seasons. They often fought and died to preserve tribal "ownership" of regions large enough to support the group. By the early 1870s, homesteaders had settled in numbers sufficient to threaten this way of life.

The mining industry accelerated this process. Because mining was an industry reliant on the contributions of a community and not merely the work of independent prospectors as was so often depicted on film, gold strikes flooded thousands onto Indian lands often already protected by treaty. As the infrastructure developed to support the mines, ranching and farming most threatened the Indians. When the gold played out the miners, gamblers and prostitutes moved on, but farmers and ranchers often set roots claiming the land as their own.

Perhaps no one understood this threat to the Indian way of life better than General George Armstrong Custer. During his military campaign of 1874, he brought along prospectors in the hopes that gold would be discovered in the Black Hills. Already protected by the Fort Laramie Treaty, the Black Hills were sacred land and prime hunting grounds for the Lakota Indians. Gold was indeed discovered. By the winter of 1875, fifteen thousand miners rushed onto Indian lands. What Custer failed to accomplish with military tactics, he succeeded in part by forever destroying the Indians' lifestyles in the Black Hills.

The buffalo trade ultimately put an end to the plains Indians' way of life. Entire cultures relied on the

Buffalo bones mark a culture's gravesite.

buffalo as their primary source of food, shelter, clothing and tools. So when the fur trade slaughtered millions of bison nearly rendering the specie extinct, the life-style of the nomadic plains Indian came to an end. Tribes not reliant on the buffalo experienced similar fates for essentially the same reasons. As the number of settlers multiplied, the area that Indians historically relied on for hunting or foraging shrunk until they no longer supported the tribe. No Indian understood the relationship between white encroachment and the survival of his life-style better than the legendary Apache renegade—Geronimo.

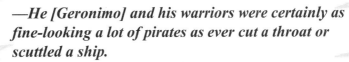

—He [Geronimo] and his warriors were certainly as fine-looking a lot of pirates as ever cut a throat or scuttled a ship.
—Captain John Gregory Bourke

Geronimo continued to raid the Southwest long after most western tribes were forced onto reservations. The story of his pursuit and final surrender provides a case study of the conflict between Indian and white culture. Most of what we know of Geronimo was written by his enemies. The white culture recorded its history on paper, in this case primarily military records. Indians, on the other hand, relied on oral histories when they were not scratching stories into rocks or hides. Consequently, Geronimo's myth developed from detailed and often exaggerated white accounts of his deeds with little explanation or understanding of his motives.

From the acquisition of Apache territory in 1848 to Geronimo's final surrender in 1886, the U.S. Government had no consistent Indian policy. Policies fluctuated between annihilation to pacification to "civilization." The opening of Apache territory as a result of the 1848 Treaty of Guadalupe-Hidalgo and the Gadsden Purchase of 1853, created little friction between the two cultures. Not until 1858, when the transcontinental Butterfield Overland stage line cut right through Apache lands, did Cochise become alarmed. Cochise, chief of the Chiricahuas the most formidable of the dozen or so bands of Apaches, attempted to coexist with the new culture by contracting to cut firewood for one of the stage stations. However, misunderstandings led to hostilities eventually resulting in the 1862 battle at Apache Pass. The Apaches openly confronted the cavalry only to be shelled by howitzer field cannons. Geronimo and his fellow Chiricahuas discovered then and there that the only way to fight off this intruder was to employ the tactics of guerrilla warfare.

For a decade the Chiricahuas successfully raided on both sides of the Mexican border. The attempts

—A fool sees only today. It is because I respect you [Cochise] as a leader of your people, that I think of tomorrow.
—James Stewart (Thomas Jeffords)
Broken Arrow

Chuck Connors in *Geronimo* (1962).

**The Faces
of
Geronimo**

Geronimo

Jay Silverheels in *Broken Arrow.*

of both the U.S. and Mexican armies to control them proved unsuccessful. Hostilities continued until 1871, when a scout named Thomas Jeffords negotiated with Cochise to allow his mail riders through Apache territory. A year later, the Chiricahua Reservation was formed with Jeffords appointed as agent.

The peace was short-lived, however. In 1874, Cochise became ill and died. Without him the Chiricahuas grew restless. For generations they had marauded freely living by this Apache virtue: "Steal without being caught. Kill without being killed." For many the confinement of a reservation was no better than being imprisoned. Among the most restless of them was a fierce warrior named Gokhlayeh. Gokhlayeh's wife and family had been slaughtered by the Mexican cavalry. He was bitter and vengeful. He was Geronimo.

Geronimo was not a chief. That distinction was a birthright. Instead, he became a leader of renegade Apaches who refused to give up their freedom.

Geronimo began his own version of "assimilation" by utilizing the reservation as a sanctuary for his raids into Mexico. Each time he returned, he brought stolen horses and cattle to sell on the reservation. These "break outs" became his trademark. It was the best of both worlds: the shelter and rations of the reservation in the winter and the life of an Apache warrior in the spring and summer. U.S. officials were not at all amused by Geronimo's ingenuity. And, needless to say, neither were the Mexicans.

Apache scout, "Peaches"

Settlers horrified at the mere thought of raiding Apaches petitioned the military for protection. The situation further escalated when an Arizona rancher was killed during a raid. That incident led to the closing of the Chiricahua Reservation in 1876. The same year Al Sieber, Chief of Scouts, dropped off a sixteen-year-old apprentice named Tom Horn to live with Chief Pedro in order that the young scout learn the ways of the Apache. A decade later, Horn would sit face to face with Geronimo to arrange his final surrender. The Chiricahuas were relocated to the San Carlos Reservation, but Geronimo refused to go slipping back instead into Mexico. Thus begins the greatest holdout to the Indian way of life in Western history.

Returning from Mexico with stolen cattle, Geronimo crossed the border at Warm Springs, New Mexico. There he was trapped by Indian agent, John Clum, and taken to San Carlos. From the

—You'll have to remember that you're Apache and be proud of it. But, you must learn much of the white man's way. It's his world now and you must learn to live with it.
—Audie Murphy (John P. Clum)
Walk the Proud Land

reservation he continued his break-out pattern utterly frustrating the military. The myth of Geronimo grew terrorizing the settlers. His exploits had become so exaggerated that if a raid resulted in the deaths of two settlers, the papers reported a dozen casualties. Public pressure resulted in the reassignment of General George Crook to Arizona in 1882.

Upon his arrival at San Carlos, Crook realized that the vast majority of the 4000 Apaches were willing to live a peaceful farming existence. He pleaded with Washington to supply him with tools and seed sufficient to allow the Apaches to successfully farm. "I could not, in spite of the most strenuous efforts, secure for them agricultural implements, except perhaps a few hoes and shovels. Even seed was denied, and to furnish this, I had to give them the grain saved in making issues to my pack trains and troop horses. The ground was cultivated with these few hoes and shovels, which did not average one to each family, and in many, perhaps most, instances, with pointed sticks hardened by fire. I saw long extent of irrigating ditches

Chato

the entire labor on which had been performed with such implements, the loose earth being carried on baskets and flour sacks and deposited at needed points." Crook failed to note that the Apaches were attempting to irrigate a desert. The Apache failure at farming resulted in their reliance on a welfare system of rations to survive, a system utterly corrupt.

Corruption on reservations throughout the West became institutionalized. San Carlos was no exception. Even Crook's most trusted scout and longtime friend, Archie McIntosh, became a corrupt reservation agent. The agents often cheated the Indians in the following manner. The agent held back issuing some bacon, vinegar, and soap, thereby creating a credit at the reservation commissary. This credit should have been used to purchase flour and sugar for the Indians. Instead, the agent took the unissued bacon and used the money on account to purchase other supplies which he took home and sold pocketing the profit. It was a shell game designed to deceive government officials. The Indians, on the other hand, were led to believe that this was business as usual. To insure they would not complain, the Indian leaders were kept particularly well supplied. Consequently, when agents were fired for corruption, it was not unusual for the Indians to side with the agent. Such was the case when McIntosh was fired and

—[The] old man in there tells me they're gettin' short-weighed on beef, Dutch…Just don't water the beef before you weigh 'em! You'd be surprised how many steaks there are in two gallons of river water.
—Burt Lancaster
Ulzana's Raid

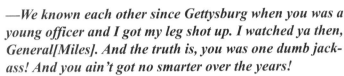

—We known each other since Gettysburg when you was a young officer and I got my leg shot up. I watched ya then, General[Miles]. And the truth is, you was one dumb jackass! And you ain't got no smarter over the years!
—Richard Widmark (Al Sieber)
Mr. Horn

Geronimo himself petitioned Crook to have him reinstated.

Even with sufficient rations, Geronimo was not content. By now he was a man of significant prominence with a corresponding ego. Not only was his ego nourished by each successful raid, he had a genuine love of the life-style of an Apache warrior which the military had thus far been unable to suppress. To the military, it became clear that the solution to resolving the Apache dissatisfaction for the reservation was to destroy the remaining symbols of the old life. Captain Crawford noted, "If we could only get rid of Geronimo, Chatto & this man Ka-e-ten-nae the rest of them would be all right & could easily be managed."

General Crook orchestrated the Arizona Apache campaign and General Miles took full credit for its conclusion. But, the men actually responsible for its success were the civilian and Indian scouts. Al Sieber, Tom Horn and their Tonto Apache scouts wore Geronimo into submission by their relentless tracking.

General Crook introduced the tactic of using Indians to fight Indians. Whether it was tribal rivalries or just relishing the opportunity to become a warrior again, reservation Apaches agreed to fight their own kind. They were successfully led by Chief of Scouts, Al Sieber, and his assistant, Tom Horn. Together they utilized the same guerrilla tactics successfully employed by Geronimo. Traveling as lightly as Geronimo in the rugged Sierra Madres enabled the scouts to wear Geronimo down little by little. In March of 1886, Geronimo surrendered to Crook. Before crossing back into the U.S., however, Geronimo led a band of 38 into the darkness of the night. Upon his return, Crook was admonished by his superior, General Philip Sheridan. Crook resigned and was replaced by General Nelson Miles.

General Miles immediately restructured the campaign by demoting Tom Horn, who had recently replaced Sieber as Chief of Scouts, to interpreter.

Al Sieber (seated), Apache scouts and an unidentified Washington official in 1883.

32

Horn quit in disgust and went mining. Miles reassigned the Indian scouts in groups of five to each cavalry troop. Each troop in turn was dispatched throughout the Sierra Madres connected by a system of heliographs flashing Morse code from ridge top to ridge top. The idea was simple. Miles spread five thousand American troops—a fourth of the country's standing army—all over the Sierra Madres. By coordinating their movements by helio, Geronimo would soon realize that he could run, but he could no longer hide. Good idea, but it failed miserably. Without Horn or Sieber to translate the Apache scouts, the troop commanders were unable to coordinate the essential component of the chase—the trackers. Furthermore, Geronimo's guerrilla tactics were once again no match for the cavalry. Consequently, in August, Miles requested that Horn rejoin him as Chief of Scouts.

—There's only one way to beat the Apache. Fight the way he fights. Hit and run until he can't run anymore.
—Charlton Heston (Ed Bannon based on Al Sieber)
Arrowhead

—Geronimo's a man so great that [Gentleman Jim] Corbett there'd have to stand on his mother's shoulders to kiss his ass!
—Steve McQeen
Tom Horn

Horn reorganized the search utilizing the helios. By leaving the cavalry behind and traveling with just thirty Apache scouts, Horn was able to communicate by helio, drop his trail, and cut in ahead of Geronimo. Horn's intent was to run Geronimo until he dropped. It worked. Geronimo sent word that he was forty-five miles away and requested the soldiers stop the chase long enough to allow him to speak with Horn.

Geronimo and Horn shared a mutual respect for each other. Most importantly, Geronimo trusted that Horn would not lie to him. To an Apache truthfulness was an essential aspect of honor. Horn was accompanied by Lieutenant Charles B. Gatewood. Tom negotiated a meeting of surrender between Geronimo and Miles. Military protocol and Miles' ego produced a last minute complication resulting in

—Nothing a man does is wrong if he tells the truth.
—Geronimo

—...because it is easier to die in a world you understand than to live in one that makes no sense.
—Jimmie Herman
Geronimo (1993)

Apache scouts and their prisoners.

—Apaches like to sneak up and pick off strays.
—John Wayne
Stagecoach

34

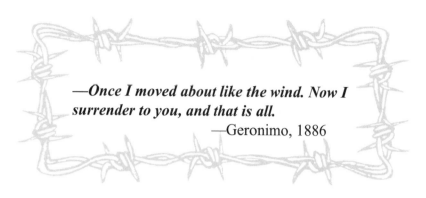

Geronimo running off and Horn quitting. The next day Miles granted Horn full authority in the matter which resulted in Geronimo's final surrender to Miles.

The relationships between both Geronimo and Horn and between Cochise and Jeffords illustrates the importance placed on truth between the two cultures. Unfortunately for the Apache, the integrity of individuals like Jeffords and Horn was not representative of their culture. During the negotiations of his surrender, Geronimo discovered what Miles had done to deceive him and to insure the end of traditional Apache life. The San Carlos Apaches had already been relocated by train to Florida. Instead of being returned to San Carlos, on September 3, 1886, Geronimo agreed to the same fate.

Within a year a significant number of Apaches died in Florida. Lacking their traditional herbs and exposed to malaria, they succumbed to disease. Were it not for women socialites who petitioned Washington to relocate the Indians to the Fort Sill Military Reservation in Indian Territory, Oklahoma, complete genocide may have occurred. Geronimo and his tribe were moved to Fort Sill where more died of disease and despair.

Geronimo was never allowed to return to his native land. He spent his last years satisfying the white culture's curiosity. The once fearless Apache renegade became part celebrity and part oddity. Whether in Roosevelt's 1901 inauguration parade, appearing in the 1904 St. Louis World's Fair, or selling souvenirs on the reservation, Geronimo promoted not only his own myth, but the myth of the American Indian.

Throughout the West, the military protected the settlers' interests creating the many conflicts immortalized on film by Hollywood. By the turn of the century, most Indians had been forced onto reservations where if they didn't die of malnutrition or disease they died of a broken heart. In the wake of the Wounded Knee Massacre, the American Indian was forced to choose between life on the reservation or cultural extermination.

The struggle over land between Native Americans and settlers supplied the script for hundreds of Westerns. Even though there were isolated exceptions dating back as far as *The Vanishing American* (1925), the vast majority of films unfairly represented the clash between the cultures. *Broken Arrow* (1950) is

Wounded Knee, 1890

Jeff Chandler and James Stewart in *Cheyenne Autumn.*

generally recognized as becoming the first major motion picture to set the record straight. In it the relationship between Thomas Jeffords (James Stewart) and Cochise (Jeff Chandler) is portrayed.

John Ford's *Cheyenne Autumn* (1964) also made a significant contribution in this regard. Ford noted, "Let's face it, we've treated [Indians] very badly; its a blot on our shield. We've cheated and robbed, killed, murdered, massacred and everything else…But, they kill one white man and, God, out come the troops! There are two sides to every story, but I wanted to show [in *Cheyenne Autumn*] their point of view for a change. I had wanted to make it for a long time [because in my Westerns] I've killed more Indians than Custer, Beecher and Chivington put together."

Hollywood's Indians were most often portrayed as "savage" villains or occasionally as defenseless victims of white European culture. In fact, they were neither. They were the last of North America's primitive cultures. Vastly out numbered by an industrialized society, their fate was inevitable. The process by which this occurred in the American West provides one of the most fascinating, but certainly not unique, chapters in history.

Hollywood developed the Western genre by promoting the myth of the West. In far too many instances it focused on mythical relationships between cowboys and Indians, lawmen and outlaws, creating thousands of shoot-'em-up action films. Seldom portrayed was the true nature of frontier conflicts between native peoples struggling to maintain their life-style and an industrialized nation expanding west. Though the spirit of the West was evident on both sides in their daily struggle to survive on the frontier, in the end the myth prevailed.

—If we didn't have Indians in an Indian picture and they weren't shooting arrows at us, what would we put in there? Ya know, that's the way they were written…I don't want to make a documentary about Indians. I want to make a picture that was exciting about that period.
—Budd Boetticher, director

Byington family, Utah, 1870.

Nebraska sodbusters

—That's what I like about this country. There's always greener grass over the next hill.
—George Peppard
How the West Was Won

Nebraskan pioneers, circa 1887

A Mormon farmer, his five wives and their children.

CHAPTER VI.

THE SPIRIT OF THE WEST.

The Spirit of the West is rooted deeply within the human spirit where from the beginning mankind has demonstrated an inherent desire to be free. The search for freedom is the foundation of Western expansionism. By the early 19th century, life east of the Mississippi began to develop social and economic restraints that for many became intolerable. To them the western frontier represented social and economic opportunity. It became a symbol of freedom for generations to come.

Pioneers came from all walks of life representing a diverse cross-section of Easterners. However, Easterners were not the only ones venturing to the West. They in fact came from all over the world. The California Gold Rush was largely responsible for settling the West. It created the largest mass migration in world history. Pioneers came from Europe, South America, China—from all corners of the earth. For them the West represented economic opportunity. Clearly, the appeal of the American West has long been a worldwide phenomena.

—Better'n dyin' behind a plow. I tried it. Settled down for a year once. Took ten years off my life!
—Henry Fonda, mountainman
How the West Was Won

What was it about those western pioneers that defined their spirit and created a legacy which has fascinated and entertained the world for more than a century? First and foremost was that pioneers were risk takers—gamblers of sort. They were often willing to risk everything, their very lives if necessary, to fulfill their goals in the West. In doing so, pioneers faced every hardship the western frontier had to offer. Among those hardships developed two significant conflicts: man vs. nature and man vs. evil. They provided the themes of countless Westerns. The conflict between man and nature is inherent to his attempt to adapt to a frontier environment. The western frontier offered settlers every conceivable environmental hardship. From extreme cold to squeltering heat, from drought to floods, the West challenged the limits of the human spirit. The search for prosperity often became a mere struggle to survive.

—There's right and there's wrong. You've got to do one or the other.
—John Wayne
The Alamo

Evil on the frontier was often reduced to simple black and white ideologies regarding survival. In other words, evil was manifested in any threat to their survival. In the absence of a formal judicial system, man vs. evil often became an individual conflict between the frontiersman and his antagonists.

Often the most distasteful aspect of conflict resolution for a frontiersman was compromise. To compromise an issue meant to compromise one's ideals. And to compromise one's ideals often meant destroying your own personal spirit. In the minds of many frontiersmen, any compromise involving the simple distinction between right and wrong led ultimately to a loss of personal freedom—which was the very thing they most sought in the West.

As the West became more populated, the struggle to survive became synonymous with the struggle to control land and natural resources. Settlers were pitted against economic forces such as the cattle and railroad industries, all of whom were threatened by the Indians' desire to maintain control of their native lands. Westerners seldom understood the complexities regarding these forces. Instead, they merely confronted them as threats to their survival and freedom.

> *—Love me, love my land. Seems simple enough to me. You can't compromise on those things.*
>
> —Jeff Richards
> *The Marauders*

Hollywood too often developed the spirit of the West around frontier legends without crediting those most responsible for taming the West, the common settler. They too refused to allow failure to deter them from their goals. Even in the face of repeated failures they persevered. They never quit. Without these traits many were swallowed by the West one piece at a time. In essence, what separated pioneers from most of us was their willingness to endure hardship and risk their lives in the search for freedom in the West.

William S. Hart changed the way that Hollywood portrayed the West. The earliest Westerns often failed to portray the primitive conditions on the frontier. As I mentioned earlier in the "History" section, Hart became obsessed with depicting the West as an authentic frontier. By creating the look and feel of the Old West and depicting every detail of frontier life, Hart portrayed the spirit of the West. He employed authentic dress and props. Frontier towns were portrayed with dusty main streets, makeshift buildings and raggedy-ass inhabitants.

Hart was a successful stage actor before embarking on a film career at the age of forty-four. Though he was an Easterner, as a boy Hart lived for a time in the West. His childhood memories of cattle drives, the Sioux, and the Dakota Territory shaped his passion for portraying an authentic West on film. Between 1914 and 1925 Hart delivered his version of the real West to the screen. Were it not for his Shakespearean background resulting in silent melodramas, many of his films would compare favorably with the best contemporary Westerns.

By 1925, Hart was too old to remain a convincing romantic lead. His final effort, *Tumbleweed* (1925), was among the earliest epic

William S. Hart

Westerns, but resulted in box-office failure. Hart's spirit of the West was rejected by the public who instead favored the myth. A new Western star emerged who by commercially packaging the myth overtook Hart in popularity—Tom Mix.

—The truth of the West meant more to me than a job.
—William S. Hart

Were it not for showmanship economics, it is quite possible that the spirit of the West may not have been overshadowed from the beginning by the myth of the West. Had 19th century newspaper correspondents and dime novelists not sensationalized the West, Wild West shows and movie Westerns would never have discovered profit in the further development of the myth. There is plenty of evidence, such as the popularity of the artwork of Russell and Remington, to suggest that an accurate portrayal of the spirit of the West by newspapers, novelists, and Wild West shows would have resulted in a similar evolution of the West's universal appeal. Regardless, the time has come to balance the appeal of the myth of the West with the intrigue of the spirit of the West. In order to experience the spirit of the West through motion pictures, a thorough appreciation for frontier life is necessary. This is best obtained when films authentically portray the Old West.

—Lookin' back, we had in the person of Teddy Roosevelt the finest president in the history of this country. He had the spirit and determination that matched the times and the land. Then the women got the vote and everything went to hell.
—Ned Beatty
The Life and Times of Judge Roy Bean

—People don't care why the stagecoach goes over the cliff as long as it goes over.
—Broncho Billy Anderson

CHAPTER VII.

AUTHENTICITY.

Authenticity in a Western offers the viewer a firsthand experience of the Old West. It comes largely as a result of careful attention to every detail of frontier life. The accuracy of the story, acting, set, props and so forth, all play vital roles in delivering a believable view of the West. You will discover in the trail guide that each film includes not only an overall rating, but separate ratings for authenticity, story and acting. The primary focus of the authenticity evaluation is the details of every day life in the West and adherence to historical detail.

Life in the West can be accurately portrayed only when special attention is paid to details. Filmmakers must create authentic sets, props, clothing and life-styles in order to offer the viewer an authentic experience of the West. In this regard, myth and reality are easily distinguished. The romantic and often glorified portrayal of life as a cowboy is perhaps the best example of perpetuating a myth on film. Seldom are the details of the daily existence of a cowboy depicted. The demand for cattle following the Civil War was overwhelming creating a booming industry reliant on a new work force comprised of cowboys. This work force consisted of men from all walks of life: veterans, farmers, Eastern city dwellers, former slaves—all venturing west in search of opportunity. What they found was hard work, long hours and primitive conditions for a dollar a day.

Seldom has Hollywood depicted the long hours of mending fences in the biting cold of Montana winters or in the blistering heat of a Texas sun. Life on the frontier was spent mostly working and surviving. Repairing saddles and tack, washing and mending clothes, cooking, hunting for meals all consumed time outside the regular work of mining, trapping, or ranching. Little glamour is associated with these tasks and, consequently, in order to perpetuate the myth little attention was paid to them on film. Yet, it is the independence associated with this life-style that best reflects the spirit of the West.

Many details of Western life escaped the eye of Hollywood demonstrating the film industry's lack of understanding of frontier life. Perhaps the most obvious mistakes involved the mythical performance of the Colt .45 revolver. Of the three most common barrel lengths available in the "Peacemaker," the longest and most accurate was seven and a half inches. I can assure you that a good shot at fifty feet is something to be proud of. Yet, Hollywood transformed the .45 into a long-range, shot-from-the-hip sniper's weapon capable of shooting the gun out of your hand across town. And just how many shots, without reloading, can a "six-gun" fire?

Not only did Hollywood exaggerate the capabilities of the Peacemaker, but it often displayed complete ignorance regarding when it was used. The Peacemaker was Colt's revolver New Model Army 1873. Yet, far too often Hollywood armed its heroes with a weapon that would not be invented until years after the story took place. For example, Audie Murphy and the cast of *Kansas Raiders* (1950) shot at each other with Peacemakers a decade before its invention. Because the Peacemaker became an essential element of the gunfighter myth, it became the most inappropriately used prop of the genre.

Other more subtle errors were common as well. For example, a lawman in *The Sacketts* (1979) wore chaps in town while carrying on his civil duties. Chaps? They're worn by working cowboys! Ever walk in the southwest heat for any length of time in chaps? It gets a bit hot and awkward. Hollywood saloon fights require little discussion. They've been replaced today by WWE wrestling.

Military Life on the frontier was seldom depicted on film as it really was. Hollywood often painted a romantic picture full of daily encounters with hostiles in which the "good guys" seldom suffered casualties and always got the girl. In reality, military life was difficult, often tedious, and seldom romantic. Drinking, target shooting, gambling and whores often provided the only diversions to the drudgery of a remote frontier outpost. The bitter cold winters on the plains or the scorching heat of the Southwest was but one more factor contributing to a significant desertion and suicide rate. Yet, Hollywood desertions were motivated by cowardice and the only suicide that comes to mind was that of the outpost commander in *Dances With Wolves* (1990).

It was the harsh reality of life on the frontier that today intrigues us. The character of the men and women that endured that life-style is what set them apart. Their demonstration of the upper limits of the human spirit tamed the Wild West. Never is there a need to exaggerate their deeds. There lives defined the spirit of the West which we can best understand when it is realistically portrayed.

Rest and Relaxation often made life on the frontier bearable if not down right enjoyable. In other words, it wasn't all work on the frontier. Much of the work in the West was seasonal. Mining and farming were often reliant on good weather. Ranching was intermittent. Trail drives ended in rip-roaring boom towns like Abilene. And military responsibilities often depended on periodic outbursts of hostility which left much free time to be spent carousing. Consequently, the pioneers looked to many forms of recreation to pass the time.

Faro players

Drinking and gambling were far and above the most popular of pass times. The first arrivals in a frontier town were likely to be whiskey, faro and whores. The early frontier was populated by nearly ninety percent men. As towns and cities developed more and more women appeared. Along with the women came religion and culture. Circuit preachers, traveling minstrels, theatrical groups and circuses all provided diversions from the hardships of frontier life.

A variety of sports were evident as well. Of these only billiards has been fairly represented on film. Yet, bowling alleys were prevalent. Wrestling and boxing were popular. Even baseball crossed the plains on its inventor's way to the California gold fields. Baseball became even more popular following the Civil War

—I don't mean to argue with an officer on the Sabbath, but that one [pitch] sure as spit looked good to me!
—trooper catching the pitcher
Ulzana's Raid

when Union and Confederate veterans who had learned to play during the war spread the game throughout the West. Yet, baseball's popularity on the frontier was not proportionately represented on film. The following examples are the only films that come to mind in which the game is played.

In *The Great Northfield Minnesota Raid* (1972), Cole Younger (Cliff Robertson) becomes intrigued by a well organized game played by the townspeople. A spectator explains to him, "It's the national pastime." Cole responds by blasting the next fly ball to pieces like a clay pigeon and commenting, "Our national pastime is shooting and always will be." Bruce Dern watches outlaws playing at their hideout in *Posse* (1975). In the opening of *Ulzana's Raid* (1972), soldiers are playing at a frontier cavalry outpost. Cavalrymen are also playing during the late 1870s on an Arizona reservation in *Geronimo* (1993).

Clothing and Props which are authentic replicas of the time period lend credibility to a Western and often they reflect a film's overall authenticity. Motion pictures that pay careful attention to these details offer the viewer a better appreciation for the primitive conditions of frontier life. Western apparel in films of the 1930s and 1940s often reflected the influence of the Gower Gulch cowboys of the silent era led by the likes of William S. Hart. However, by the early 1950s a distinctive style of gunfighter attire had developed influenced by such "B" and serial stars as Gene Autry, William Boyd (Hopalong Cassidy) and Roy Rogers. The low profile "telescope" crown hats and the low-slung, tie-down holster became standard accessories. Hollywood gunfighters, cowboys, gamblers, miners, farmers and trappers of the 1950s apparently all shopped the same clothier. This mythical costuming was further perpetuated by the decade's stampede of TV serial Westerns.

Many stars developed a public image to further their screen persona. Apparel such as Guy Madison's denim jacket in films like *Reprisal!* (1956) and *The Hard Man* (1957) assisted in defining Madison's

—If you've never, or rarely, played men from other centuries, the clothes feel funny. You walk differently in chain mail than in cowboy boots and chaps. A sword rides on your hip differently from a .45...
—Charlton Heston

commercial appeal, but it did nothing for authenticity. Although Levi Strauss patented Jacob Davis's "waist overalls" in 1873, blue jeans as we know them are a product of the 20th century. The denim jacket that Madison wore was a contemporary pattern. Madison himself was an avid outdoorsman personifying the Westerner of the 1950s, but unfortunately he projected a contemporary image of himself into films portraying characters from the past century. It would take Hollywood nearly two decades to come to its senses. By the early 1970s, Western apparel returned to some resemblance of what was actually worn on the frontier.

Too often Westerns portray authentic themes only to have the feeling of real frontier life spoiled by the use of phony props. Even the smallest details such as period furnishings, tack, weapons, etc., reflect on a films authenticity. For instance, watch closely the next time you see *Broken Arrow* (1950). A close resemblance to an authentic Indian arrow would have been sufficient in order to make the prop believable. What you will notice, however, are arrows with white plastic knocks. Little details like this ruin the impression of authentic frontier life.

The Sets of a Western must first convey a unique aspect of the West—the land. The magnificence of the frontier is often difficult to capture on film. At the turn of the century, pioneer film studios were located in New York, Chicago and New Jersey. Universal was among a number of companies located in New York. The American Film Company in Chicago. And Edison produced his films in New Jersey. Consequently, The earliest Westerns were in fact made in the East. The first Western, for example, *The Great Train Robbery* (1903) was shot in the forests of New Jersey.

By 1909, film companies were sending their crews to the West for several reasons. Authentic western mainstreets were still in operation in places like Tuscon, Arizona. Southern California offered both weather conducive to year-round outdoor shooting and the countryside settings of the San Fernando Valley, San Juan Capistrano, Lakeside and La Mesa. Soon the studios would set up shop in Hollywood to take full advantage of these opportunities. But, the weather and settings were not the only reasons they came West.

Film Crews were hiding from henchmen hired by the Motion Picture Patents Company. The Patents Company was a trust formed by major film companies. Not only did they limit film length to one or two reelers and refuse to grant screen credit for actors, they enforced their Latham Loop Patent. The Latham Loop was the loop of film formed in order to thread film into a camera. Without it film could not be run through a camera rendering filmmaking impossible. By regulating the use of the Latham Loop, a handful of powerful film companies sought to control the entire industry. The Patents Company hired "regulators" to prevent crews from shooting—even resorting to sniping with rifles to destroy the cameras. Consequently, film crews sought refuge in remote locations in the West. However, The Patents Company henchmen followed.

Pioneer film director, Allan Dwan, described one encounter with a Patents Company enforcer. While filming a Western in La Mesa near San Diego, Dwan was located by one of their henchman. Instead of complying with his orders to halt filming, Dwan who recently finished college at Notre Dame where he played football, took the Patents man for a walk up the road intending to "beat his brains out." They stopped at a bridge over an arroyo in which there were tin cans lying about. Attempting to intimidate Dwan, the Patents man pulled a gun out of his shoulder holster and fired at the shiniest can missing it by some five yards. Dwan responded by drawing and firing his own revolver hitting the can twice. The Patents man left that afternoon accompanied to the train depot by Dwan's well-armed cowboys.

Early Westerns were filmed entirely outdoors often capturing the essence of the frontier—the land. However, the development of the film industry in Hollywood created two obstacles to set authenticity. First, because of its proximity to the studios, the San Fernando Valley became the West. That is to say, southern California offered very little scenic contrast. As the San Fernando Valley became more populated, the studios discovered the Alabama Hills located outside Lone Pine. More feature-length Westerns were filmed there than any other location. The Alabama Hills offered magnificent rock formations set at the foot of the snow-capped Sierra Nevadas. However, again because of its proximity to Hollywood the film industry relied too heavily on this location. The result was Westerns prior to 1960 lacked sufficient diversity in their landscapes. Fortunately, some Hollywood directors like John Ford and Kevin Costner insisted on other frontier locations to film the West.

Ford captured the essence of the frontier with his brilliant portraitures of the western landscape. In films like *Stagecoach* (1939) and *The Searchers* (1956) his favorite location, Monument Valley, Utah, offered the public a very different and majestic view of the frontier. In many ways, Ford's stylized portrayals of the western landscape define the genre.

Costner's success in reviving the genre with *Dances With Wolves* (1990) came largely as a result of his majestic depiction of the frontier prairie.

The second obstacle to set authenticity came as a result of the development of Hollywood's studio system resulting in factory-like mass production of Westerns. Indoor shooting in the sound studios seldom conveyed the spirit of the frontier. No actor riding a stuffed horse with its head bobbing up and down while the landscape rolled by him in the background ever was convincing.

The Alabama Hills

Authentic locations for shooting became increasingly difficult to find as the country evolved. When filmmakers used locations that appeared like the Old West they occasionally neglected to edit out obvious reminders of their own era. One such error in *The Nevadan* (1950) illustrates this point. While Randolph Scott is pitching atop "Thunder" at what is depicted as an Old West ranch, the modern high-power electric lines and pole are blatantly obvious in the background. Mistakes like these ruin the illusion the setting can create of portraying an authentic Old West.

What the public accepted from Hollywood as authentic clothing, props and sets was the result of their own knowledge and expectations of the West. Westerns during the 1950s say as much about the audience as the filmmakers themselves. Authenticity in Westerns was at an all-time low. Television Western series during the '50s saturated the public with the Old West. The authenticity of Western movies paralleled that of TV Westerns. By the early 1960s, the myth came crashing down and along with it—the genre.

Stagecoach (1939) filmed in Monument Valley.

The social revolution of the '60s and the Vietnam War's influence on patriotism combined to affect contemporary opinions regarding American heroes and institutions. This manifested itself in a significant reduction in the number of Westerns produced during that period. The myth was out. Historical revisionists were in. Audiences once entertained by the shoot-'em-up action of Hollywood stunt men were offered a fresh look at the West from a new source—gunfighter re-enactor groups.

Re-enactors became the Wild West shows of the '70s and '80s. Most of the nations hundreds of groups offered little in the way of historical authenticity because they did little but act out Hollywood's myth. However, a significant number of them payed close attention to every detail of period dress and props. Most noteworthy of them was the California Bounty Hunters which was formed in 1967. They were the first to become recognized by California as a state historic educational organization. By carefully studying museum artifacts, old photographs, the paintings of artists like Russell and Remington, and by incorporating original clothing, weapons, and artifacts from their personal collections into their shows, these hobbyists carefully corrected many of Hollywood's inaccuracies. Madison's denim jacket was replaced with dusters, frock and buffalo coats. Audie Murphy's neck scarf became a functional bandana. Authentic replica holsters were worn in place of fast-draw holsters. From the top of their hats to the heels of their boots every detail, even their buttons were original or exact copies of the real thing. Their performances at frontier-day celebrations, schools and living history demonstrations offered more and more people an authentic look at the Old West. As the public became better informed, Hollywood responded with a keener eye for historical detail enabling us to experience the true spirit of the West.

Historical Authenticity on film is the product of two eras: the time period represented in the story and the period in which it was filmed. In other words, history reflects the attitudes of the original recorders and later it may be revised by contemporary filmmakers. Because

—And don't forget the Western is... the history of this country…
—Fritz Lang, director

Westerns reflect in part the society in which they are produced, too often Hollywood distorted the authentic West. Contemporary cultural values often replaced not only the historical facts, but the underlying themes of frontier life. For example, *They Died With Their Boots On* (1942) is plagued by World War II-era patriotism. In *A Man Called Horse* (1970), the Yellow Hand Indian drug induced religious visions are too heavily influenced by the '60s drug culture.

Hollywood's reluctance to cast its own heroes as villains led to many historically inaccurate films such as *The Cimarron Kid* (1952). Audie Murphy was cast as Bill Doolin—alias the Cimarron Kid. In real life, Murphy was a genuine World War II hero, America's most decorated soldier. Casting him as a villain meant tarnishing the hero image that Hollywood was fostering. Consequently, Murphy's version of Doolin became a whitewash of a ruthless outlaw. In fact, nearly every aspect of the film was inaccurate—particularly Doolin's participation in the Coffeyville fiasco.

—He [Joseph Lewis] seemed genuinely embarassed, even humiliated, that his film, **Seventh Cavalry,** *was historically false—as though Hollywood's historical pictures were ever accurate…*
—Peter Bogdanovich
Director and filmographer

The most disappointing inaccuracies, however, appear in a contemporary film—*Dances With Wolves* (1990). Costner produced a near perfect Western were it not for two inexcusable errors. First was his portrayal of the Lakota Indians as '60s vintage communal dwellers—particularly in contrast to the Pawnee. Even though the story was written from Dances With Wolves' perspective, it was void of any of the brutal cultural traditions of the Lakota. Only the Pawnee were harshly depicted. The two tribes adversarial relationship was

Sgt. Wylyams mutilated by Sioux, Arapaho and Cheyenne, 1867.

portrayed no better than that of two Hollywood gunfighters facing off with their black and white hats. Costner's depiction of the Pawnee as a bloodthirsty waring tribe and the Sioux as a peace-loving people was grossly inaccurate. In fact, the tribes had been fighting over that land for generations. The Pawnee were stealing back the land previously stolen from them by the Lakota. The Pawnee were no more brutal than the Sioux. For example, Costner failed to mention the routine mutilation of captives by the Sioux.

Authenticity would better have been served if Costner had painted an even picture of both tribes. Costner took pride in delivering what he claimed was an authentic portrayal of Sioux life, which for the most part it was. However, his adaptation of Michael Blake's novel could easily have resulted in a balanced view of the Sioux. Given the extensive research to produce an authentic story, it is unclear what motivated him to present history in that fashion. Costner should have allowed us to determine whether the "savage" traits of the plains Indians played a role in their religion and struggle for survival. It is up to us to avoid placing our cultural values on their ways.

The second inexcusable flaw was Costner's one-sided portrayal of the frontier military. Aside from his own character, the soldiers were completely void of any humanity towards the Indians. And they were cast as bumbling idiots! A more sensible approach would have been to portray the enlisted men as often short on brains and long on bravado. With little education, they were more likely to have been insensitive, even bigoted

Cavalrymen inside the tent of Lieutenant Brown, Pine Ridge Agency circa 1890.

towards the hostiles. The sergeant, the backbone of the military, would likely have been a battle-seasoned and rigid enforcer of military regulations—a competent soldier. The commissioned officers of the frontier cavalry were often intelligent West Point graduates who were trained to pragmatically approach their assignments. Instead, Costner delivered a genocidal version of the Three Stooges.

Revisionist History has often been responsible for improving our understanding of the Old West. On the other hand, revisionists, as we have seen from Oliver Stone, have the power to distort history as well. Hollywood can

> —*We're sure that you'll finally realize that realism untempered by sentiment and humanity is really just a mean, hard, cold outlook on life—a frightening outlook.*
> —Irene Rich
> *Angel and the Badman*

hardly be blamed for presenting what was historically accurate at the time of filming if the facts were later revised. For example, when Paul Newman portrayed Billy the Kid in *The Left Handed Gun* (1958), history believed William Bonney to be left-handed. This conception was based on the only known full-length photograph of the Kid. In it Billy posed with his holster on his left side. Decades past before someone noticed that the buttons on his shirt and vest were reversed like those on women's apparel. Suddenly historians realized that the photo had been reversed during its development and, henceforth, films have depicted the Kid accurately as right-handed.

A far more significant historical development was discovered in the 1970s with the translation of the de la Peña diary. Lieutenant Colonel José de la Peña was a member of an elite unit of Santa Anna's Army responsible for the carnage at the Alamo. He described Davy Crockett's capture. According to de la Peña, Crockett and a handful of his Tennesseans surrendered during the final minutes of the siege. De la Peña's eyewitness account told of Crockett's subsequent torture and execution. This directly conflicts with the myth perpetuated by Texans in their famous battle cry, "Remember the Alamo!" It was based on the images of their dying comrades fighting to the last man. For this reason the Alamo has been often compared to the battle of Goliad. The results at Goliad were similar to those at the Alamo except for one significant difference. At Goliad a significant number of Texans surrendered

> —[The Man Who Shot Liberty Valance] *is a deceptively simple Western which concludes, metaphorically, with a U.S. that has buried its heroes in legends that are false, that has built out of the wilderness an illusory garden and left us tragically longing for the open frontiers and ideals we have lost.*
> —Peter Bogdanovich
> Director and filmographer

Fess Parker in *Davy Crockett,
King of the Wild Frontier.*

**The Faces
of
Davy Crockett**

Davy Crockett

John Wayne in *The Alamo.*

before being executed. Surely, the Texans at Goliad fought and died with the same bravery and honor as their brothers at the Alamo. Yet, today only the Alamo is remembered largely as a result of Hollywood's portrayal of Fess Parker wildly swinging "Betsy" from atop the Alamo walls or John Wayne throwing himself torch-in-hand on powder kegs. In either scenario the symbolism is clear, that at the Alamo the last Texans fought to the death. Whether Hollywood will confront the Alamo with historical revision will be determined by the contemporary demand for myth vs. reality.

The most serious consequence of historical inaccuracies on film is that over a period of time the public believes the Hollywood version *is* history. Even the filmmakers believe they have produced an accurate portrayal of the West. In the end, we lose any chance of experiencing an authentic West through film.

A film's authenticity is evaluated here on its ability to create an authentic experience of the frontier. If the story is fiction, it must be accurate. If it is a true story—don't distort the facts! Only when films are authentic can we gain real insight into the true spirit of the West.

*—Half the people in the world are women.
Why does it have to be **you** that stirs me!*
—John Wayne
McLintock!

CHAPTER VIII.

THE STORY.

The Story of the West defines the Western film as America's only true art form. Because the Old West became a worldwide experience, America's art form gained universal appeal. This appeal is not so much a result of a reflection of the themes of Western expansionism as it is an examination of American values. Those who equate the essence of the West with cattle empires, railroads, cowboys and Indians, lawmen and outlaws, and so forth, fail to understand the underlying uniqueness of the story of the West. Once again, Western films reflect American values during two time periods: when the story took place and during the time period it was produced.

Hollywood has showcased American values by focusing on relatively few themes characterizing the Western spirit. Most Westerns employ at least one of the foundational themes of the West: Individualism, man vs. nature, and man vs. evil. They are thoroughly discussed in the Spirit section of this guide. The remaining themes also reflect the spirit and myth of the West. For example, that morality is not always popular is a theme portrayed in films such as *High Noon* (1952) and *The Proud Ones* (1956). Themes like the strong helping the weak were often featured by Hollywood. Noteworthy examples are *The Man Who Shot Liberty Valance* (1962), *The Magnificent Seven* (1960) and *Shane* (1953). In *The Man Who Shot Liberty Valance,* John Wayne helps Jimmy Stewart rid his town of a bully (Lee Marvin). Yul Brynner and his all-star cast of American mercenaries protect Mexican peons from outlaws in *The Magnificent Seven.* The story was actually adapted from Akira Kurosawa's *The Seven Samurai.* And Shane (Alan Ladd) is a retired gunfighter who protects a settler (Van Heflin) from a professional gunfighter played by Jack Palance. Films like *Rio Bravo* (1959) and *Warlock* (1959) employed a variation of this theme: that because society is weak, it must be protected by the strong.

A thorough understanding of American values is necessary in order to explain the Western's fixation with the strong helping the weak. The reasons lie deep within the national character originating in part with John Winthrop's "city upon a hill" concept. Winthrop professed that the eyes of the world were upon the American colonists and that they had a Christian responsibility to protect the weak among them. This national attitude was strengthened during both world wars—precisely the same time that the Western evolved.

Shane is also noteworthy for being the most celebrated example of numerous stories depicting the retired gunfighter who can not avoid strapping on his guns for one last showdown. The frontiersman experiencing

—But I've learned somethin', son. I've learned that what a man thinks either makes or destroys him. And there's nothin' any more harmful than thinkin' about revenge. It poisons your mind and rots your guts and leaves a brand on you that never fades.
—Walter Brennan
The Showdown

52

difficulty coping with the passing of the Old West, is a popular theme depicted in such Westerns as *Tom Horn* (1980) and *The Good Old Boys* (1995). Other films, like *Will Penny* (1968), focused instead on the passing of the individual's frontier life-style. Revenge for revenge's sake is a trademark of foreign productions, whereas American productions employ revenge as a vehicle for producing some other result, i.e., justice, personal safety and so forth. Variations of these few themes continue to supply Western screenwriters with the bulk of their material.

Because the Western is a male dominated genre, the underlying themes of many stories reflect men's relationships with women. A man's motives for venturing west were often influenced by a woman—particularly one who had broken his heart. Whether his heart had been broken by a romance gone sour or as a result of her untimely death, the West became a refuge for broken hearts. *Red River, Davy Crockett, King of the Wild Frontier* (1955) and *Wyatt Earp* (1994) are but a few examples depicting men whose lives were forever altered by broken hearts often motivating them to undertake Herculean tasks against insurmountable odds in the West.

Because the early frontier was inhabited primarily by men, often men grew accustomed to the carefree life-style of the frontier bachelor. A serious relationship with a woman was often the most feared threat to a mountainman's freedom. In *How the West Was Won* (1963), for example, Jimmy Stewart portrays a trapper accustomed to relationships with whores and whiskey. He looks forward to his trading trips to the city referring to his behavior as, "goin' to see the varmit." When a good woman happens along, she threatens his very way of life.

> —*The development of this country is unimaginable without the days of the Wild West—when a dancehall girl was the only woman among one hundred gold miners.*
> —Fritz Lang

> —*I'll always be goin' to see the varmit, Eve! I...I just ain't cut out to be a farmer or a husband.*
> —James Stewart
> *How the West Was Won*

A good woman confronts a cowboy in *Will Penny* as well. The cowboy (Charlton Heston) faces Stewart's same dilemma regarding his way of life—his freedom. Women offer both Stewart and Heston the opportunity to settle down. One chooses a family, the other his freedom.

And finally, women often attempted to reform Western outlaws. Occasionally, they were successful. In *Jesse James* (1939) Tyrone Power is on the verge of going straight for the sake of his wife and family when he is bushwacked by Bob Ford. Perhaps the most noteworthy example is *Angel and the Badman*. The angel (Gail Russell) is a young Quaker girl who upon falling instantly in love with a badman (John Wayne) is hellbent on reforming him.

The story of the West is a diverse collection of episodes of trapping, ranching, farming, mining, hunting, logging, frontier justice, and Indians which define America's national character. Although many films authentically represent Western themes, too often Hollywood offered us stories in which any conflict had but one resolution—through the sights of a Colt .45. Hollywood's "shoot 'em up" mentality ruled the genre for too many years. The challenge to future filmmakers is to produce stories that allow the Western myth to create expectations in our minds much the same as our ancestors were enticed to go West by dime novelists. With our dreams firmly in hand, the story must take us West on an authentic frontier adventure.

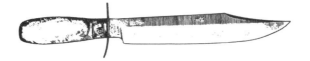

Burt Lancaster in *Apache*

Chief Joseph

The Faces
of the
American Indian

Jack Palance in *Arrowhead*

CHAPTER IX.

ACTING.

A cting in a Western film became for many a dream come true. Professional actors, athletes, politicians and so forth were all lured to the Western screen. In fact, the genre's credits reads like a *Who's Who*. Familiar names such as Humphrey Bogart, Marilyn Monroe, Ronald Reagan, Bill Cosby, Shirley Temple, Edward G. Robinson, James Cagney, Jim Thorpe, Leroy "Satchel" Paige and Elvis Presley are but a few of the hundreds of prominent personalities that appeared on the Western screen. Together with the standards of the genre, they formed a cast who assumed the responsibility of communicating the legacy of the West to future generations.

When evaluating their performances one criteria is paramount. The essence of portraying a Western character on film is to be convincing. Quality performances have been rendered by actors who convinced us that their role was an accurate portrayal of an Old West character. Whether the role was fictional or historical, the role must bring to life the personality of the character. Actors that project their own personalities into historical figures should be staked out on an ant hill. There is plenty of opportunity for artistic license in fiction, but don't screw with history!

Humphry Bogart (right) as a gunfighter.

The genre has produced many fine performances, but too often they came from the supporting cast and not the stars. Character actors like Walter Brennan rarely turned out anything but outstanding performances. Slim Pickens, Chill Wills, Ben Johnson and Jack Elam are but a few of the many character actors that often made an otherwise mediocre Western a film worth watching. Few character actors successfully made the crossover to a quality staring role. Perhaps the finest exception was Richard Farnsworth. As a character actor, Farnsworth lent a touch of authenticity to each of his films. In his staring role as Bill Miner in *The Grey Fox* (1983), he was superb.

No other star commanded "presence" on film as did John Wayne. John Wayne was the 20th century embodiment of the Western myth often conveying the spirit of the West just as well. Good or bad, his

Marilyn Monoe, Robert Mitchum and Tommy Rettig in *River of No Return*.

films will define the genre for generations to come. Whole volumes are devoted to his films, yet two stand above the rest. *Red River* (1948) is the finest Western ever made. Wayne along with the entire cast gave convincing performances resulting in an outstanding blend of the Western myth and spirit. *The Shootist* (1976), his last film in which he gave his finest performance, is an outstanding fictional account of the closing of the Wild West symbolized by the dignified death of an aging gunfighter.

Slim Pickens

Other stars such as Clint Eastwood, Randolph Scott, Henry Fonda, James Stewart, Gregory Peck and Burt Lancaster developed unmistakable stylized film personas which characterized both the myth and spirit of the West. Perhaps America's greatest actor, Charlton Heston, turned out hit or miss performances. Occasionally, his characters appeared Shakespearian and were simply not convincing. However, most often he was excellent—particularly his performance in *Will Penny*. This was in part a result of his devotion to his craft. Heston, like many of the finest character actors, learned pioneer skills such as riding and shooting resulting in convincing roles. Too often other stars failed to do their homework turning legendary frontiersmen into dime-store cowboys.

Hollywood's casting of whites to play Indians may have been our culture's final injustice forced upon Native Americans. With the possible exception of Jack Palance in *Arrowhead* (1953), white actors have not given convincing performances in Indian roles. Cases in point, Burt Lancaster in *Apache* (1954) and Chuck Connors in *Geronimo* (1962). *The Indian Fighter* (1955) is a perfect example of how Hollywood cast white actors in the speaking Indian roles then surrounded them with authentic Native American extras. The results would have been humorous if they weren't in fact so pathetic! Were it

Richard Farnsworth in *The Grey Fox.*

not for the limited contributions of a small band of Native American actors who delivered dignity to the genre like Jay Silverheels, Chief Dan George, Will Sampson and Graham Greene, Indians never would have been convincingly portrayed on the silver screen.

Contemporary Westerns have wisely cast Native Americans as Indians. *Dances With Wolves* in particular deserves credit for this trend. Costner successfully gambled not only on the casting , but on using the native Lakota language with subtitles. Use of Native American languages only enhance the authenticity of a Western. Any difficulty that the audience experiences in understanding the dialogue is

John Wayne in *The Shootist*

—All actors want to make Westerns. They grew up on them and they don't make enough of them.
—Tom Selleck

Chief Dan George

Will Sampson

Jay Silverheels

insignificant when compared to the difficulty experienced by pioneer frontiersmen whose very lives often were dependent upon accurate translations of Indian dialects. The success of *Dances With Wolves* resulted not only in Hollywood casting virtually all subsequent Indian roles with Native Americans, but it convinced the industry of the marketability of Indian films.

In this guide you will find listed the principle players of each film together with noteworthy supporting cast. The rating for acting is an overall evaluation of all the players intended to offer the viewer some expectation of what they will encounter along the way. You will likely notice that more often than not the quality of the acting coincides with the overall quality of the film.

—I never knew an actor who didn't like making Westerns.
—Charlton Heston

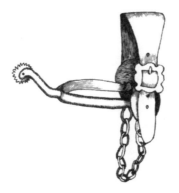

CHAPTER X.

DIRECTORS.

The **Director** ultimately determines the quality of a Western. No other single influence within the genre has been as responsible for shaping our image of the West. Too often that image has been distorted in order to produce commercially successful films. In a way, Hollywood was built by distorting the real West.

The driving force behind all directors was money. Simply stated, directors who failed to produce commercially successful Westerns found themselves out of work. Consequently, it became the director's responsibility to give the public what they wanted—entertainment.

—Make pictures that make money.
—Howard Hawks

Film directors were often as intrigued with the Old West as their audience. Pioneer director, Raoul Walsh, for example, worked a turn-of-the-century Texas cattle drive at the age of seventeen. He dreamed of being a Texas cattleman, but found himself instead a motion picture cowboy in New Jersey. Eventually, he worked his way out of the saddle and into the director's chair.

Walsh was among the first directors to research the West. Prior to filming *The Life of General Villa* (1914), he spent nearly five months filming the real Pancho Villa in Mexico. He was even allowed to film Villa's executions. Often in the morning Villa's men lined up fifteen to twenty Federales against a wall to be shot. Standing off to the side were more of Villa's men, some with rocks in their hands and others with knives. According to Walsh, no sooner had the bullet-ridden corpses collapsed to the ground than, "the bastards with rocks ran in, opened the guys' mouths and knocked the gold teeth out. And the others with the knives went in and started to cut their pants and take their boots off." Though many aspects of the film were very authentic, Walsh fabricated Villa's entire life story.

Pioneer directors discovered that the real West had a difficult time living up to its own myth which was created by dime novels and Wild West shows. Fritz Lang, who seriously researched the history of his Westerns before shooting them, prepared for *Western Union* (1941). His investigation of the construction of the famous telegraph line revealed very little drama worthy of a Hollywood production. The closest thing he found to drama was that the builders ran out of wood for poles forcing them to locate canyons with timber. According to Lang, "The only other thing that disturbed the laying of the line was the ticks on the buffaloes: the buffaloes got itchy and rubbed themselves against the poles, and the poles tumbled."

Conscious of the public's desire for the Western myth, Lang concocted a mythical version of the Western Union development. Though the story is credited to Zane Grey, according to Lang, nothing but Grey's title was ever used in the film. Lang admitted to "directorial touches" on his Westerns. In *Western Union*, for example, the covered wagons were colored yellow and violet which he patterned after the colors of the Western Union telegraph forms. The man who actually built the telegraph line was married and had seven children—Randolph Scott was depicted in the film as a bachelor.

Perhaps the most significant pioneer director was Allan Dwan. He directed hundreds of Westerns beginning with one-reel silents at the turn of the century. Dwan viewed filmmaking as entertainment—

60

not history. He directed, no, mass produced Westerns at a time when a film was often shot in just six days.

Allan Dwan approached directing much the same as a football coach prepares for Saturday's game. In fact, following his football playing

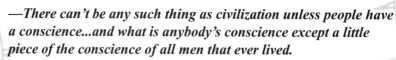

—There can't be any such thing as civilization unless people have a conscience...and what is anybody's conscience except a little piece of the conscience of all men that ever lived.
—Henry Fonda
The Ox-Bow Incident

days at Notre Dame, he remained briefly as a coach. It appears all good directors operate with the efficiency of a good coach. Like a team reflects their coach in every way, so does a film reflect its director.

Few directors demonstrated the personal integrity of Joseph H. Lewis—particularly in relation to their own awareness of the historical inaccuracies of their own films. "Wagon Wheel Joe," as he was often referred to because of his early technique of shooting a scene through the spokes of a wagon wheel, extensively researched the authenticity of every Western he directed. When faced with reality concerning the role that the myth of the West played in selling to the public a film like *7th Cavalry* (1956), Lewis struggled with his conscience. "I became terribly confused because I found out what kind of a horrible man Colonel Custer was. Jiminy Cricket! This was really a maniac—despicable man. And *that* truly interfered with my work: because I couldn't tell a true story. And I couldn't make a hero out of this man because of what I knew about him, and you *had* to in this film." Often under contract, directors were forced to make pictures they didn't like.

Westerns were a business—a factory of films. Don Siegel was pushed by his producer to turn out *Duel at Silver Creek* (1952) on schedule. At the time, it was not unusual for a feature-length Western to be shot in three weeks. But, Siegel thought it unfair to expect the director to film without a completed script. He felt it only reasonable to be informed which of the leading men would in the end get the girl—Steve McNally or Audie Murphy. Ultimately, Siegel would later say, "I couldn't take the film seriously." Two decades later Siegel directed one of the finest Westerns of all time—*The Shootist.*

—I'm John Ford. I make Westerns.
—John Ford

Too often directors used the West only as a backdrop to portray their personal views of the world. William Wellman did this in *The Ox-Bow Incident* (1943). The film is not about the West at all. Instead, Wellman utilizes the West as a vehicle to promote his dark view of mankind.

On the other hand, directors like John Ford understood the essential focus of a Western backdrop—the land. Ford displayed many shortcomings in other areas of authenticity. However, he more than made up for it by his ability to use the land as a canvass to paint an authentic celluloid portrait of the American frontier.

Critics have often knocked Ford for being preoccupied with style. This may have been. However, his style was developed not only as the result of authentically depicting the Western landscape, but by defining American values on film in unforgettable classics such as *Stagecoach* (1939)*, Fort Apache (1948) She Wore a Yellow Ribbon* (1949) and *The Searchers* (1956).

—I don't see how a person can make a Western without being influenced by John Ford.
—Howard Hawks

Ford must receive full credit for his commercial success as well. His films directly promoted the genre making it possible for studios to produce more Westerns. *Stagecoach*, for example, has often been credited with reestablishing the commercial viability of the feature-length Western. In the final analysis, Ford created epic Westerns that will define the genre to the world for generations to come.

Directors of the genre became the storytellers of the West. No other director told that story any better than Howard Hawks. Hawks made relatively few Westerns, but among them is the classic—*Red River* (1948). In it Hawks created an authentic look and feel of the West which he blended with perhaps the most powerful story the genre has ever produced. Hawks created very real and very powerful emotions which he wove throughout his themes. Those themes focused on men who relied on their own inner strength when faced with crisis.

—The director's the storyteller and should have his own method of telling it.
—Howard Hawks

Yet, the key to Hawks' success was simplicity. "I just use the simplest camera in the world. Let the audience see exactly as they would if they were there." He also noted, "It [the plot] didn't matter at all. All we were trying to do was to make every scene entertain." That may have been, but the result was that by keeping it simple Hawks often conveyed the spirit of the West better than any other filmmaker.

Many other directors made significant contributions to the genre. Thus far, however, no one has consistently woven all the essential elements of directing a Western into their films. By combining Dwan's efficiency, Walsh's preparation, Lang's research, Lewis' integrity together with Hawks' simplicity and Ford's style, a director could create a Western with a perfect blend of the myth and spirit of the West.

Directors are identified in this guide with the "D" following the cast. Their evaluation is reflected in the authenticity, story and overall ratings.

—For me the best drama is the one that deals with a man in danger.
—Howard Hawks

*—I loved a woman once. There isn't a day
goes by I don't think of her. That's the way it is.*
—Henry Fonda
Stranger on the Run

CONCLUSION.

At last, the Western is a unique examination of both man and his environment together with a view of his relationships with one another. It is a diverse collection of episodes representing the social and economic development of the American frontier. This American art form defines the national character by reflecting its cultural values.

Future Westerns will continue to reflect contemporary American values. As researchers continue to sort out the history of the West, we will be confronted with more accurate accounts of the deeds of our pioneer ancestors. Our responsibility will be to judge them fairly. Fair judgement will largely rely on an evaluation of their motives based on cultural values of their time and not our own.

If the Western is a window peering into the soul of American culture, then the responsibility to produce outstanding Westerns lies within two elements of the film industry. First of all, it lies with us the viewers. We create the demand for Westerns that authentically portray the spirit of the West. Directors will in turn respond to more sophisticated audiences by better balancing the spirit and myth of the West. It comes down to simple showmanship economics.

In the final analysis, the Western portrays the myth and spirit of the West to us much the same as the frontier did to our ancestors. The challenge those pioneers faced remains for us today—to preserve our culture as one that is constantly exploring for a better life for its children. And it often challenges us further. Because the West symbolizes all of our hopes and dreams, at times it represents nothing more than a personal challenge to live and love with a broken heart.

As the world changes and we step further into the "Information Age," it becomes increasingly more important to produce Westerns. This new world economy is yet another obstacle to human dignity and individualism. Consequently, filmmakers must celebrate the human spirit by taking us West. Hollywood's challenge will be to weave the myth and spirit of the West into a perfect Western—which has yet to be made. Be assured that I will continue to roam the genre searching for that Western.

64

TRAIL GUIDE.

✦ THE RATING SYSTEM. ✦

The **Rating System** developed for this guide is intended for Westerners. This is not a book for cinematic connoisseurs. Film style, cinematography, editing and so forth are concerns for the likes of Ebert and Roeper. Films are evaluated here on their ability to weave together the myth and spirit of the West into an authentic and entertaining experience. There are difficulties inherent to evaluating so many films during a span of more than twenty years. Most films received multiple viewings, often years apart, which I believe has resulted in a fair and consistent evaluation of each film in relation to others.

Pictures are rated on a five-star system, five being best. Films receiving a full five-star rating are rare finds. A gold strike or an hour with the finest St. Louis "dove" are the only acceptable reasons to miss these. Movies receiving a four-star rating are a must see. They favorably compare with bucking the tiger at a high stakes faro game. Three-star films are solid examples of the genre. They are best suited for a fire-warmed cabin in the company of the one you love. Two-star pictures should only be considered to break the monotony of a week-long blizzard in a Montana line shack. And finally, one-star films should not be given any consideration at all. I'd rather be stretching barbed wire bare-handed in the snow.

Uncharted Territory is likely to be encountered during your journey through the genre. Most of the genre, in fact, will remain a wilderness due to the vast number of Westerns produced. No one will ever know precisely how many Westerns were made for two reasons. Film manufactured prior to 1950 was backed with silver nitrate, thus the term "silver screen." An unknown number of Westerns were melted for their silver content during World War II. Secondly, an uncertain number of films were lost to "nitrate deterioration." Hollywood's pioneer filmmakers were unaware of this process which would over time turn their film first to goo then to powder. Experts estimate as many as seventy-five percent of silents and half of all motion pictures filmed before 1950 were lost to this phenomena. Thousands of films in Hollywood's storage facilities self destructed. Many of those were uncataloged or were stored in unmarked canisters. So it is impossible to know exactly what was lost.

The vast majority of these losses were films of the silent era. Consequently, it is safe to say that this guide includes a complete collection of all feature-length Westerns. Of the nearly 2100 Westerns presented here, fewer than three hundred are readily accessible on video or TV and perhaps less than a hundred of those receive ninety percent of the air time. Nearly 900 Westerns have received ratings here. All other films are identified as "Uncharted Territory." They are identified in this guide by the following icon:

Beware! Even though all of these trails have been identified as Westerns by pioneer guides of the genre, many of them may not be true Westerns at all. (See Appendix I. for an abbreviated list of films that do not meet my criteria.) When you stumble on an unrated trail, I hope the basic information I have supplied will assist you in determining if it is a direction you wish to explore.

In addition to an overall rating, each film has been assigned three additional ratings: authenticity, story and acting. They serve two purposes. First, they offer the viewer some insight regarding the assignment of the overall rating. And second, they can be utilized to select films for their strengths in these specific areas which I believe are the essential elements to producing a top-notch Western.

Films are often strong in one area and weak in another. For example, many Westerns produced in the '80s and '90s are strong in the area of authenticity. *The Return of Josey Wales* (1986) and *Brotherhood of the Gun* (1991) received favorable ratings for authenticity. However, because the acting and story are poor they fail to convey the myth or spirit of the West. Even a respectable three-star rating for authenticity did not save *The Return of Josey Wales*. It is the worst domestic Western I've ever seen!

———————————————

ABBREVIATIONS AND EXPLANATIONS OF TERMS.

AA	Allied Artists
AAC	The Associates and Aldrich Co.
ABC	American Broadcasting Corporation
ABCCF	ABC Circle Films
AC	Artists Creation
Action Int.	Action International
Action Pict.	Action Pictures
Admiral	
Admiral Films	
AE	Avco Embassy
AF	Alive Films
AFP	Agamennon Film Productions
AFL	Atlantis Films Ltd.
AFRC	Associated Film Releasing Corp.
AFR Co.	Associated Film Releasing Company
AJCP	A.J.C. Productions
AI	American International
A-I	American-International
AIDV	A.I.D. Variety
AL	Allarcom Ltd.
Alco	
Allied	
Alp.	Alperson
ALP	Alan Landsburg Productions
Ambassador	
Amblin E.	Amblin Entertainment
ANE	American National Enterprises
AP	Alaska Pictures
APC	Arcola Pictures Corp.
Apex	
APr	Alson Productions
ARC	American Releasing Corp.
Argosy	
Armada	
Artclass	
ASP	Aaron Spelling Productions
ASRP	Albert S. Ruddy Productions
Assoc.	Associated
Astor	
Atherton	
Aywan	
BAMP	B.A.M. Productions
BAP	Bad Axe Prod.
Batjac	
BBCF	BBC Films
BCP	Bing Crosby Productions
Beaumont	
Beckman	
Bel-Air	
B-H	Batjac-Hagging
BI	Boxoffice International
B-KP	Bennett-Katleman Productions
BLP	Bruce Lansbury Productions
Bonanza V.	Bonanza Ventures
BP	Bryna Productions
Brentwood I.	Brentwood International
BRI	Bruder Releasing, Inc.
Brigade P.	
Broder	
Bryanston	
Bryna	
B-TP	Burroughs-Tarzan Pictures
BV	Buena Vista
Canyon	
CAP	Craig Anderson Productions
Catalina P.	Catalina Productions
CBPP	Charles B. Pierce Productions
CBS-TV	Columbia Broadcasting Systems-TV
C-CR	Cal-Com Releasing
CE	Carmel Enterprises
CESJP	Charles E. Seillers, Jr. Productions
CF	Cannon Films
CFE	Cabin Fever Entertainment
CFL	
CF Ltd.	Cougar Films Ltd.
CFP	Charles Fries Productions
Cherokee P.	Cherokee Productions
Chevron	
CI	Calendary International
Cinergi P.	Cinergi Productions
CIP	Crown International Pictures
Citation	
Clover	
C-NHC	Concord-New Horizons Corp.
CO	Cineplex Odeon
Columbia	
Comworld P.	Comworld Pictures
Corinth F.	Corinth Films
Cosmos	
Cougar	
Cougar Prod.	Cougar Productions
Cowboy P.	Cowboy Productions
CP-TV	Columbia Pictures TV
CP	Crown Productions
CRC	Cinerama Releasing Corp.
Crescent	
C/RP	Chris/Rose Production
CS	Cinema Shares
CSTF	CST Featurization
CVW	C.V. Whitney
DC	Dove Cinema
D-D	Doty-Dayton
D-DP	Doty-Dayton Productions
Deputy Corp.	
DF	Dimension Films
DFC	Dalton Film Co.
DGP	David Gerber Productions
DHF	Double Helix Films
Disney	Walt Disney
DN	Douglas Netter
DP	Dalia Productions
dPE	de Passe Entertainment
D Prod.	Dimensions Productions
DRMP	DRM Productions
DTP	Danny Thomas Productions
DWP	David Wolper Productions
EAF	Eagle American Films
Earlmar Prod.	Earlmar Productions
EE	Ellman Enterprises
EFP	Ed Friendly Productions
EL	Eagle Lion
ELP	Evan Lloyd Productions
ELC	Eagle Lion Classic
Embassy	
Ember	
Emerson	
Emirau	
EMLP	Edward and Mildred Lewis Productions
Empire	
Enterprise	
ESP	Ed Stabile Prod.
ES Prod.	Edward Small Productions
FA	First American
Fairway	
Fame Pict.	Fame Pictures
FB/JP	Fred Berner/JoCo Productions
FCOC	Film Consortium of Canada
Fenady	
Fenedy A.	Fenedy Assoc.
FF	Fantasy Films
FFCA	Feature Films Corp. of America
Fidelity	
Film Classics	Film Classics
Film Ctr.	Film Center
Filmhaus	
Filmmakers	
Filmways	
Fipco P.	Fipco Productions
First National	
F-MC	Film-Makers Cooperative
FMEI	FM Entertainment International
FN	
Fonda F.	Fonda Films
Fox	
FR	Fox Run
Fulvia	
FV	Film Ventures
FVI	Film Ventures International
Gamalex Prod.	Gamalex Productions
Gaumont-TV	Gaumont Television
Gaylord P.	Gaylord Productions
GC	Golden Circl
GCP	Glen Cove Productions
GE	Globe Enterprises
G Eag.	Golden Eagle
GKE	Gold Key Entertainment
Globe	
Globel	
Gold C.	Gold Coast
GP	Goldstein Productions
GRC	Globe Releasing Corp.
GrP	Grand Productions
GS	Golden State
G.S.F.	
Gulf CP	Gulf Coast Productions
Guild	
Guamont	
Guardian	
GTHV	Good Times Home Video
Hallmark E.	Hallmark Entertainment
HBO	Home Box Office
H-BP	Hanna-Barbara Productions
HCF	Hispano Continental Films
HE	Heritage Entertainment
Hemdale Prod.	
Hercules	
HF	Huntington Films
HFC	Hemdale Film Corp.
HHE	Hallmark Home Entertainment
HHFP	Hallmark Hall of Fame Prods.
HHP	Howard Hughs Productions
H-L	Hecht-Lancaster
HMP	Harvey Matofsky Productions
HN	Hirschman Northern
Howco	
Howco Prod.	Howco Productions
IF	Imagery Films

I-I	Independent-International
IMC-I	IMC-Isram
Int.	International
ITCEG	ITC Entertainment Group
JADFI	JAD Films International
JBP	Jack Broder Productions
JCC	Joseph Cates Company
JCP	Joseph Cates Productions
JDGP	J.D. Geigelson Productions
JF	Jensen Farley
JHP	Jack Hilton Prod.
JHHE	Jack H. Harris Enterprises
JP	Joshua Prod.
J-W	Joyce-Werker
Kain P.	Kain Productions
Kanob	
K-B	
KBP	Kunz Bros. Productions
K&C	Kragen & Co.
KFE	King Features Entertainment
KI	Key International
King Bros.	
KP	King Prod.
K-S	Konigsburg-Sanitsky
Laurel	
LBSC	LBS Communications
LEP	Lazy "E" Prod.
LHP	Lance Hool Prod.
Libra P.	Libra Pictures
Lion S.P.	Lion Share Productions
Lippert	
LMG	Lincoln Media Group
Lorimar Prod.	
LP	Levinson Productions
L-P	Levitt-Pickman
LSP	Lone Star Productions
L-SP	Lou-Steodutions
L-T	Lemay-Templeton
Macco P.	Macco Prod.
Madrid	
Mark IV P.	Mark IV Pictures
MBSC	M.B. Scott Productions
MC	Mirisch Company
MCA	Music Corp. of America
MCP	Morgan Creek Productions
MDAAI	M.D.A. Associates, Inc.
M-DP	Mad-Dog Productions
Melroy	
MF	Miramax Films
MGM	Metro-Goldwyn-Mayer
Mirisch	
MLGP	MLG Properties, Inc.
MMF	Movie Mongrel Films
Mono.	Monogram
Monterey	
MP	Montgomery Productions
MPP	Mary Pickford Productions
M Prod.	Manson Productions
MS	Marvin Schwartz
Mulberry Sq.	Mulberry Square
Multi	
Nassour	
NBC Prod.	National Broadcasting Corp. Productions
NBC-TV	
NG	National General
N-H	Nassour-Hartford
NRP	Norman Rosemont Productions
N-RP	Newland-Raynor Productions
NW	New World
NWP	New World Pictures
OFI	Onyx Films Inc.
Ogiens	
OP	Omnibus Productions
Orion	
P-A	Pathe-American
Palomar	
Pando	
Pan. Prod.	Panoramic Productions
Parade	
Parallel	
Paramount	
Pathe P.	Pathe Pictures
PCP	Plaster City Productions
PCR	
PDC	Producers Distributing Corp.
Peakviewing P.	Peakviewing Productions
Peerless	
PF	Premier Films
PFLC	Paramount Famous Lasky Corp.
PGF	Poly Gram Films
PI	Pacific International
Plantation P.	Plantation Productions
Pleaeau	
P.M. Films	
PP	Penland Productions
Proteus F.	Proteus Films
PSME	
Puritan	
QEI	Quintex Entertainment, Inc.
QMP	Quinn Martin Productions
Realart	
Realert	
Reargard Prod.	
Regal	
Rel.	Reliable
Reliance	
Republic	
Resolute	
RF	Regal Films
R-F-C	Russ-Field-Gabco
RHIE	RHI Entertainment
RHP	Roy Huggins Productions
R-HP	Rackin-Hayes Productions
RKO	
RKO-Radio	RKO-Radio
RKP	Raymond Katz Productions
R-LP	Rich-Ludwig Productions
RMI	Reel Movies International
Romina	
Romson	
Rorvic	
RP	Raven Pictures
RPP	Robert Papazian Productions
Santa Clara	
Satori	
SC	Sun Classic
S-B	Scott-Brown
Schwartz	
Screen Guild	
SE	Shapiro Entertainment
Sebastian Int.	Sebastian International
Sentinal	
7 Arts	
SFI	Saga Films International
SG	Screen Gems
SGC	Samuel Goldwyn Company
SGP	Spelling/Goldberg Productions
Shalako E.	Shalako Enterprises
Showtime	
SI	Sun International
Silvermine	
Silverstein Int.	Silverstein International
Siringo P.	Siringo Productions
SJCP	Stephen J. Cannell Productions
SLP	Savage Land Productions
Small	
SP	Sun Productions
SRO	Selznick Releasing Organization
S&S	Stage and Screen
SSC	Schick Sun Classics
S-SF	Six-Shooter Films
SSP	Silver Screen Partners
Starfire	
Sunset	
Superior	
SW	Sterling World
Syndicate	
Tacar	Tacar Productions
TBG	The Beacon Group
TBS-TV	Turner
TCF	
TCR	
TEG	Tribune Entertainment Co.
Telepictures P.	Telepictures Productions
TF	Trebol Film
TGP	12-Gauge Productions
Tiffany	
Tig P.	Tig Productions
THE	Turner Home Entertainment
Tiger	
Times Pict.	Times Pictures
T-LP	Taylor-Laughlin Productions
TNT	Turner Network Television
TP	Tejas Productions
TPC	Top Pictures Corp.
Transcona	
Trimark Pict.	Trimark Pictures
Tri-Star	
TWE	Trans World Entertainment
20th C. Fox	20th Century Fox
UA	United Artists
UAC	United Artists Classics
U-I	Universal-International
Universal	
UP	Unicorn Prod.
USA	United Screen Arts
USAN	USA Network
US Pict.	United States Pictures
VAP	Victor Adamson Production
VD	Visual Drama
Ventura	
Ventura Pict.	Ventura Pictures
Vidmark	
vonZ	von Zernack-Samuels Productions
Warner	
WB	Warner Brothers
WB-7 Arts	Warner Bros.-7 Arts
WC	Wrather Corp.
WCP	Wheeler Company Productions
Western Adventure	
Westwood	
WF	Willow Films
W-G-W	
WHPI	Wild Horse Prod., Inc.
Win.	Winchester
Windsor Prod.	
W-K	Wald-Krasna
WNP	Willie Nelson Productions
Wrather	
WS	William Steiner

WW   World Wide
W-W   World-Wide
WWP   Wilderness Women Prod.
XITP   XIT Prods.
Zukor

FOREIGN FILMS.

Austr.   Australia
Brit.   British
Can.   Canada
Czech.   Czechoslovakia
Fr.   French
Ger.   Germany
HK   Hong Kong
Isr.   Israel
Ital.   Italian
Mex.   Mexico
Neth.   Netherlands
Nor.   Norway
Phil.   Philippines
Pol.   Poland
Rus.   Russia
S.A.   South Africa
Slov.   Slovakia
Sp.   Spanish
Swed.   Sweden
Yug.   Yugoslavia

TOP MOVIE LISTS.

Best of the West   100 Best of the West
AFI GM   AFI's 100 Greatest American
                    Movies of the First Century
                    of Filmmaking
AFI MHPM   AFI's 100 Most Thrilling
                    American Films: Most Heart-
                    Pounding Movies
IMDb   International Movie Data
                    Base's Top 50 Western
                    Movies
LPFF   Lone Pine Film Festival's
                    Top 10 "A" Westerns

Abilene Town (1946) UA ★★◖

Randolph Scott
Ann Dvorak
Edgar Buchanan
Rhonda Fleming
Lloyd Bridges
Jack Lambert
D: Edwin L. Marin

A gunman delivers law and order to a cattle town.
Based on Ernest Haycox's *Trail Town*.

Au ★★★

S ★★◖

A ★★◖

Abilene cowpunchers circa 1870.

Above All Laws see Adventures in Silverado

Ace High (1967) FF—Ital./Sp.

Eli Wallach
Terence Hill
Bud Spencer
D: Giuseppe Colizzi

Gunmen plot to retrieve their losings from a gambling house.

> *—What chance have ya got against a woman like that? What chance have ya got against any woman?*
> —Edgar Buchannan
> *Abiline Town*

Across the Great Divide (1976) PI

Robert Logan
George "Buck" Flower
Heather Rattray
Mark Hall
D: Stewart Raffill

Two orphans and a drifter travel to Oregon.
Filmed in Alberta, Canada.

Across the Wide Missouri (1951) MGM ★★★◖

Clark Gable
Ricardo Montalban
John Hodiak
Adolphe Menjou
James Whitmore
D: William Wellman

A trapper discovers happiness with an Indian wife. Filmed in Colorado.

Au ★★★★

S ★★★◖

A ★★★◖

> *—You're full of magic. The one woman in the world for me. I love you, Pigeon. Maybe I didn't know it when I found you, but I know it now.*
> —Clark Gable
> *Across the Wide Missouri*

Adios see The Lash

Adios Cjamango (1969) FF—Ital./Sp.

Mark Rivers
Dianik Zuraowska
D: Harry Freeman (Josè Maria Zabalza)

A bounty hunter helps a widow during a range war.
Sequel to *Cjamango*.

Adios Gringo (1965) FF—Ital./Sp./Fr.

Giuliano Gemma
Evelyn Stewart (Ida Galli)
D: George Finley

A man tricked into buying stolen cattle tracks down the thieves.

Adios Hombre (1966) FF—Ital./Sp.

Craig Hill
Eduardo Fajardo
D: Mario Caiano

Outlaws hide out in a saloon while waiting for a gold shipment.

Adiòs, Sabata (The Bounty Hunters) (Indio Black) (1970) FF—Ital.

Yul Brynner
Dean Reed
D: Frank Kramer (Gianfranco Parolini)

A gunfighter teams with a young man to
steal a Mexican government gold reserve.

Au ★

S ★

A ⭐

*—Hey, fellows, are you gonna let me help pick
up that gold or not? You sons of ....!!*
—Dean Reed
Adiòs, Sabata

Adventures in Silverado (Above All Laws) (1948) Columbia

William Bishop
Gloria Henry
Edgar Buchanan
Forrest Tucker
D: Phil Karlson

A stagecoach driver clears himself by capturing a highwayman.
Story by Robert Luis Stevenson.

The Adventures of Bullwhip Griffin (1967) BV

Roddy McDowell
Suzanne Pleshette
Karl Malden
Harry Guardino
D: James Neilson

A young Boston boy and his butler head for the California gold fields.
A Disney production.

The Adventures of Frontier Fremont (1976) SC

Dan Haggerty
Denver Pyle
Tony Mirrati
Norman Goodman
D: Richard Friedenberg

The Adventures of Starbird (1978) Cougar

A. Martinez
Don Haggerty
Louise Fitch
Skip Homeier
D: Jack Hively

Against a Crooked Sky (1975) D-D

Richard Boone
Stewart Petersen
Henry Wilcoxon
Clint Richie
D: Earl Bellamy

An old trapper helps a boy search for his kidnapped sister.
Filmed at Professor Valley, CO River, Castle Valley,
Arches National Park, Dead Horse Point St. Park, UT.

The Alamo (1960) UA

John Wayne
Richard Widmark
Laurence Harvey
Richard Boone
Frankie Avalon
Patrick Wayne
Chill Wills
Ken Curtis
D: John Wayne

Legendary Texans defend a makeshift fort from a Mexican siege.
As an unannounced and unwanted guest, John Ford directed a short
second unit sequence. Oscar nominations for best picture, supporting
actor (Wills), cinematography: color, film editing, and scoring:
drama/comedy. Oscar for best sound. Filmed in Bracketville, TX.

Au ★★★
S ★★★★
A ★★★★

John Wayne in the Alamo.

*—There's right and there's wrong.
You gotta do one or the other...*
—John Wayne
The Alamo

The Alamo: 13 Days to Glory (1987) NBC-TV ★★★★

James Arness
Brian Keith
Alec Baldwin
Raul Julia

Lorne Greene
D: Burt Kennedy

Legendary Texans endure the siege at the Alamo. From J. Lon
Tinkle's book. Filmed at the Duke's Alamo set in Bracketville, TX.

Au
S
A

Alaska (1944) Mono.

Kent Taylor
Margaret Lindsey
John Carradine
D: George Archainbaud

A Klondike prospector is falsely accused of murder.
Based on Jack London's *Flush of Gold.*

Albuquerque (1948) Paramount

Randolph Scott
Barbara Britton
George Hayes
Lon Chaney, Jr.
D: Ray Enright

The son of a town boss protects a wagon train line from
his father. Based on a Luke Short (Frederick D. Glidden)
story. Filmed in Sedona, AZ, and the Iverson Movie Ranch.

Alias Smith and Jones (The Day They Hanged Kid Curry) (1971) ABC-TV/Universal

Peter Deuel
Ben Murphy
Forrest Tucker
Susan Saint James
James Drury
D: Gene Levitt

Two notorious outlaws accept the governor's offer of amnesty with
strings attached. Pilot for the TV series. Filmed at Castle Valley,
Professor Valley, La Sal Mountains., Potash Plant, UT.

Au
S
A

Alien Thunder (Dan Candy's Law) (1973) OFI

Donald Sutherland
George Tootoosis
Chief Dan George
Kevin McCarthy
D: Claude Fournier

A Saskatchewan Mountie tracks an Indian who
stole a cow to feed his starving family.

Kid Curry

*—It's not about land or money. It's about the
one thing that no man should ever be able to
take from another man—the freedom to make
his own choices about his life…*
—Alec Baldwin
Alamo: 13 Days to Glory

Alive or Preferably Dead (1969) (Sundance Cassidy and Butch the Kid) (1975) (Sundance and the Kid) (1976) FF—Ital./Sp.

John Wade
Karen Blake
Robert Neuman
D: Arthur Pitt

Two estranged brothers will inherit their uncle's fortune if they can live together for six months.

Al Jennings of Oklahoma (1951) Columbia

Dan Duryea
Gale Storm
Dick Foran
D: Ray Nazzaro

A lawyer and his brother turn outlaws. Very loosly based on the exploits of Al Jennings. Filmed at the Iverson Movie Location Ranch.

Au ★

S ★★

A ★★

—There's an old saying about juries. The longer they're out, the better your chances.
—Dan Duryea
Al Jennings of Oklahoma

All Out (1968) FF—Ital./Sp.

John Ireland
Mark Damon
D: Umberto Lenzi

A bounty hunter and an outlaw search for buried treasure.

Along Came Jones (1945) Int./RKO ★★★⯪

Gary Cooper
Lorreta Young
Dan Duryea
William Demarest
D: Stuart Heisler

A cowboy is mistaken for an outlaw. Story by Alan Lemay. Filmed at the Iverson Movie Location Ranch.

Au ★★★⯪

S ★★★⯪

A ★★★★

William Demarest and Gary Cooper

Along the Great Divide (1951) WB ★★★

Kirk Douglas
Virginia Mayo
John Agar

76

Walter Brennan
D: Raoul Walsh

A marshal leads a lynch mob survivor and others across the desert. Filmed in the Alabama Hills

Au ★★★

S ★★★

A ★★★★◣

Ambush (1950) MGM ★

Robert Taylor
John Hodiak
Arlene Dahl
Don Taylor
Chief Thunder Cloud
D: Marguerite Roberts

A scout searches for the sister of an Army officer's girl. From the Luke Short novel. Filmed at Corriganville.

Au ★

S ★

A ★

Ambush at Cimarron Pass (1958) RF/TCF ★

Scott Brady
Margia Dean
Clint Eastwood
D: Jodie Copelan

Ex-Confederates accompany a Seventh Cavalry prisoner escort through hostile Apache country. Eastwood's first significant role in a Western.

Au ★◣

S ★

A ★

Ambush at Tomahawk Gap (1953) Columbia ★ ★

John Hodiak
John Derell
David Brian
D: Fred Sears

Four badmen search a ghost town for buried loot.

Au ★★★

S ★★

A ★★

American Empire (My Son Alone) (1942) UA

Richard Dix
Leo Carrillo
Preston Foster
Frances Gifford

> *—You're all guilty! You'll all pay!*
> —Kirk Douglas
> *Along the Great Divide*

> *—What are we supposed to do now, just sit around and let 'em pick us off one by one?*
> —Clint Eastwood
> *Ambush at Cimarron Pass*

D: William McGann

A rancher builds a cattle empire in postwar Texas.

American Outlaws (2001) WB ★ ★

Colin Farrell
Scott Caan
Ali Larter
Gabriel Macht
Timothy Dalton
D: Les Mayfield

Jesse James and his gang seek justice
against the railroad. Filmed in Texas.

Au ★ ★ ◖

S ★ ★

A ★ ★

Among Vultures (1964) FF—Ger./Ital./Fr./Yug.

Stewart Granger
Pierre Brice
Elke Summer
D: Alfred Vohrer

An Apache chief helps settlers crossing the Rockies.
Based on the Karl May novel.

And God Said to Cain (1969) FF—Ital.

Klaus Kinski
Peter Carsten
D: Anthony Dawson (Antonio Margheriti)

When a man wrongfully imprisoned is pardoned, he seeks revenge.

...And Now Miguel (1966) Universal

Guy Stockwell
Pat Cardi
Michael Ansara
Clu Gulager
D: James B. Clark

An artist teaches a boy the virtue of patience.

And the Crows Will Dig Your Grave (1971) FF—Ital./Sp.

Craig Hill
Fernando Sancho
Frank Baña
D: John Wood

Wells Fargo hires bounty hunters to stop gold thieves.

Wells Fargo gold wagon.

78

And They Smelled the Strange, Exciting, Dangerous Scent of Dollars (1973) FF—Ital.

Robert Malcom
Pierro Vida
D: Italo Alfaro (Pierro Regnoli)

An outlaw and a bounty hunter join forces to stop a robbery.

Angel and the Badman (1947) Republic

John Wayne
Gail Russell
Harry Carey
D: James E. Grant

An outlaw is reformed by a Quaker's daughter.
Filmed in Sedona, AZ.

John Wayne and Gail Russell

The Animals (Five Savage Men) (1971) L-P

Henry Silva
Keenan Wynn
Michael Carey
D: Ron Joy

A school teacher avenges her own rape.

Animal Called Man (1973) FF—Ital.

Vassili Karis (Wassilli Karamensinis)
Lillian Bray
Craig Hill
D: Roberto Mauri

A bandit tangles with the town boss over a shooting contest.

—Only a man that carries a gun ever needs one.
—Harry Carey
Angel and the Badman

Another Man, Another Woman (1977) FF—Fr.

James Caan
Geneviève Bujold
Jennifer Warren
D: Claude Lelouch

A French widow meets a New Mexican widower.
Remake of *A Man and a Woman.*

Another Pair of Aces (1991) CBS-TV

Willie Nelson
Kris Kristofferson
Joan Severance

Rip Torn
D: Bill Bixby

Any Gun Can Play (1968) FF—Ital.

George Hilton
Edd Byrnes
Gilbert Roland
D: Enzo G. Castellari

Three men join forces to divide a fortune in stolen gold.

Anything for a Friend (1973) FF—Ital.

Gordon Mitchell
Red Carter (Lionel Stander)
D: Miles Deem (Demofilo Fidani)

Two bandits expose a crooked casino operator.

Apache (1954) UA ★★◗

Burt Lancaster
Jean Peters
John McIntire
Charles Buchinsky (Bronson)
D: Robert Aldrich

One of Geronimo's braves refuses to surrender to
reservation life. Based on a Paul Wellman story.
Filmed in Sedona, AZ.

Au ★★◗

S ★★★

A ★◗

Apache Ambush (1955) Columbia ★ ★

Bill Williams
Richard Jaeckel
Alex Montoya
Movita
Tex Ritter
Ray "Crash" Corrigan
D: Fred F. Sears

Civil War veterans preparing for a cattle drive discover
Henry repeating rifles. Filmed near Jamestown, CA.

Au ★★◗

S ★★

A ★★

Apache Drums (1951) U-I ★ ★ ★

Stephen McNally

Apache War Chief, Al-Che-Say.

80

Coleen Gray
Willard Parker
D: Hugo Fregonese

An exiled gambler returns to help a town defend itself
against Indians. Filmed at Red Rock Canyon, CA.

Au ★★★

S ★★★

A ★★✦

Apache Gold see Winnetou the Warrior

Apache's Last Battle (Old Shatterhand) (1964) FF—Ger./Yug./Fr./Ital.

Lex Barker
Guy Madison
Pierre Brice
D: Hugo Fregonese

A cavalry officer stirs up trouble between the Comanches and the Apaches.
Third in a series of "Winnetou" films.

Apaches Rifles (1964) 20ᵗʰ C. Fox

Audie Murphy
Michael Dante
Linda Lawson
D: William H. Witney

A frontiersman prevents an Indian war.
Filmed in Mojave, California.

Apache Trail (1942) MGM ★✦

Lloyd Nolan
Donna Reed
William Lundigan
Chill Wills
D: Richard Thorpe

The theft of a peace pipe results in an Apache uprising.
Story by Ernest Haycox.

Au ★✦

S ★✦

A ★✦

Apache Territory (1958) Rorvic/Columbia ★★

Rory Calhoun
Barbara Bates
John Dehner
D: Ray Nazarro

A drifter helps settlers fight Indians. From
Louie L'Amour's, *The Last Stand at Papago Wells*.

The Apache Kid

Au
S
A

Apache Uprising (1969) Paramount

Rory Calhoun
Corinne Calvet
John Russell
Lon Chaney, Jr.
D: R.G. Springsteen

A West Point officer learns that traditional military tactics are ineffective against the Apache. Filmed at Vasquez Rocks, Agua Dulce, CA.

Au
S
A

Apache Warrior (1957) RF/20th C. Fox

Keith Larson
Jim Davis
Rodolfo Acosta
D: Elmo Williams

An Indian scout is tracked by the cavalry for avenging his brother's murder. Based on the Apache Kid.

Au
S
A

Apache War Smoke (1952) MGM

Gilbert Roland
Glenda Farrell
Robert Horton
Barbara Ruick
Henry Morgan
D: Harold Kress

A stagecoach manager refuses to hand over a suspected killer to Indians threatening his way station. Remake of *Apache Trail* (1943). Story by Ernest Haycox.

UNCHARTED
TERRITORY

Apache Woman (1955) GS/ARC

Lloyd Bridges
Joan Taylor
Lance Fuller
D: Roger Corman

A gunman investigates the brother of the half-breed Apache woman that he loves.

UNCHARTED
TERRITORY

—I told you once, Jen, I…I didn't like to be tied down. I like to keep movin'. What kind of life is that for a woman?

—Rory Calhoun
Apache Territory

Naiche, son of Cochise and his wife, Ha-o-zinne.

Apache Woman (1976) FF—Ital.

Al Cliver (Pier Luigi Conti)
Yara Kewa
D: George McRoots

A cavalryman rescues the Apache woman he loves from gunrunners.

Apocalypse Joe (1970) FF—Ital./Sp.

Anthony Steffen
Eduardo Fajardo
D: Leopoldo Savona

A gunman inherits a gold mine possessed by outlaws.

The Appaloosa (Southwest to Sonora) (1966) Universal ★★★

Marlon Brando
Anjanette Comer
John Saxon
Emilio Fernandez
D: Sidney J. Furie

An Appaloosa stallion is stolen by a Mexican bandit.

Au ★★★★
S ★★✦
A ★★★

Arizona (1940) Columbia ★★★

Jean Arthur
William Holden
Warren William
Porter Hall
Edgar Buchanan
D: Wesley Ruggles

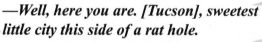

—Well, here you are. [Tucson], sweetest little city this side of a rat hole.
Arizona

A pioneer woman struggles to keep her freight line operating.
Oscar nominations for art direction: B&W and original score.
Old Tucson was built to shoot this film.

Au ★★★★
S ★★★
A ★★★

Arizona (1970) FF—Ital./Sp.

Anthony Steffen
Rosalba Neri
D: Sergio Martino

An outlaw released from prison seeks revenge on a retired gunfighter.

Arizona Bill see The Road to Fort Alamo

"An Arizona Type."

Arizona Bushwackers (1968) Paramount

Howard Keel
Yvonne De Carlo
John Ireland
Marilyn Maxwell
Brian Donlevy
Montie Montana
D: Lesley Selander

When a Confederate officer becomes sheriff of a small Arizona town, he investigates gunrunners.

Arizona Colt (1965) FF—Ital./Fr.

Guiliani Gemma
Fernando Sancho
D: Michele Lupo

An Arizona gunfighter and a Mexican bandit face off.

The Arizona Kid (1930) Fox

Warner Baxter
Carole Lombard
Theodore von Eltz
Hank Mann
D: Alfred Santell

A gunman pursues the outlaw who stole his gold. Story by O. Henry. Sequel to *In Old Arizona* (1929).

Arizona Kid (1974) FF—Phil./Ital.

Mamie Van Doran
Gordon Mitchell
D: Luciano Carlos

The Arizona Kid protects a town from bandits.

Arizona Raiders (1965) Columbia

Audie Murphy
Michael Dante
Ben Cooper
Buster Crabbe
D: William Witney

Two reformed Quantrill's raiders help an Arizona Ranger track raiders still at large. Story by Frank Gruber and R. Schayer. Filmed at Old Tucson.

Au ★
S ★
A ★★

—I shoulda killed him when I had a chance.
—Audie Murphy
Arizona Raiders

Audie Murphy in *Arizona Raiders*.

The Arizonian (1935) RKO

Richard Dix
Preston Foster
Margot Grahame
Louis Calhern
Jim Thorpe
D: Charles Vidor

A reforming lawman delivers law and order to Silver City.
From *The Peacemaker* novel. Story by Dudley Nichols.

Armed and Dangerous: Time and Heroes of Bret Harte (1977) FF—Rus.

Donatas Banionis
Ludmilla Senchina
Vsevolod Abdulov
D: Vladimir Vainsok

Bret Harte helps farmers fight a land baron.

Arrowhead (1953) Paramount

Charlton Heston
Jack Palance
Katy Jurado
Brian Keith
D: Charles Marquis Warren

An Indian scout becomes suspicious of the Apache's peaceful intentions. Brien Keith's first appearance in a feature since he was 3 years old. Based on the character Al Sieber, chief of scouts and a W.R. Burnett story. Filmed at Fort Clark in Bracketville, TX. #58 Best of the West.

Au ★★★★
S ★★★★
A ★★★★★

—*You were that high learning arithmatic. I was that high learning how to cut a man's throat so it takes him nearly a day to die.*
—Charlton Heston
Arrowhead

Arrow in the Dust (1954) AA ★★

Sterling Hayden
Coleen Gray
Keith Larson
Lee Van Cleef
Iron Eyes Cody
D: Lesley Selander

A deserter impersonates an officer in order to lead a wagon train to safety.

Au ★★
S ★★
A ★★

—*When the stakes are my neck, I play it my way!*
—Sterling Hayden
Arrow in the Dust

The Assassin see The Gunfighters

At Gunpoint (1955) AA ★ ★ ◖

Fred MacMurray
Dorothy Malone
Walter Brennan
Skip Homeier
D: Alfred L. Werker

A storekeeper's life changes when he shoots a bankrobber.

Au ★ ★

S ★ ★

A ★ ★ ★

Aurora Encounter (1986) NWP

Jack Elam
Peter Brown
Carol Bagdararian
Dottie West
D: Jim McCullough, Sr.

At the turn of the century an alien lands in the wild West.

The Avenger see Texas Adios

The Avenging (Two Against the Wind) (1981) Comworld P.

Michael Horse
Sherry Hersey
Efrem Zimbalist, Jr.
Taylor Lacher
D: Lyman Dayton

A half-breed experiences prejudice.

Brigham Young

The Avenging Angel (1995) THE ★ ★ ★ ◖

Tom Berenger
James Coburn
Charlton Heston
D: Craig R. Baxly

A Mormon gunfighter uncovers a
plot to assassinate Brigham Young.
From the Gary Stewart (III) novel.

*—Better one man sacrifice for the kingdom of
God on earth. Prepare yourself for paradise.*
—Tom Berenger
The Avenging Angel

Au ★ ★ ★ ★

S ★ ★ ★ ◖

A ★ ★ ★ ◖

Awkward Hands (1968) FF—Sp./Ital.

Peter Lee Lawrence
Alberto de Mendoza
D: Rafael Romero Marchent

A ranch hand seeks revenge against a Mexican land baron.

UNCHARTED
TERRITORY

Backlash (1956) U-I ★ ★ ★

Richard Widmark
Donna Reed
William Campbell
Edward C. Platt
Harry Morgan
D: John Sturges

A gunman confronts his outlaw father. Screenplay by Borden Chase. Filmed at Old Tucson.

Au ★ ★ ⯪

S ★ ★ ★

A ★ ★ ★ ⯪

—You know, it's a funny thing about your father. You begin to wonder about him— what he was like, what he was doing.
—Richard Widmark
Backlash

Back to God's Country (1953) U-I ★ ⯪

Rock Hudson
Marcia Henderson
Steve Cochran
Hugh O'Brian
D: Joseph Penny

A sea captain and his wife mush a dog sled across the Canadian wilderness. Based on a James O. Curwood story.

Au ★ ⯪

S ★ ⯪

A ★ ★

Backtrack! (1969) Universal/ABC-TV ★

James Drury
Rhonda Fleming
Neville Brand
Doug McClure
Philip Carey
D: Earl Bellamy

Ramrod sends Trampas to Mexico where he teams up with the Texas Rangers. From the "Virginian" and "Laredo" TV series. Screenplay by Borden Chase. Working title, *The Godchild*. ABC-TV Movie of the Week. Filmed at Old Tucson.

Au ★

S ★

A ★ ⯪

Marlene Dietrich in *Rancho Notorious.*

Eleanore Dumont aka "Madame Moustache"
was a saloon operator in Nevada City.

Bad Girls of the West

 Our 21st century ideal of beauty was often
much different than that of the 19th century.

Rosa May was a gold rush prostitute.

Diana Barrymore as a saloon girl in *Frontier Badman.*

Bad Bascom (1946) MGM

Wallace Berry
Margaret O'Brien
Marjorie Main
D: S. Sylvan Simon

A bankrobber hides out in a Mormon wagon train.

Bad Company (1972) Paramount

Jeff Bridges
Barry Brown
Jim Davis
John Savage
D: Robert Benton

Two draft dodgers head west to become outlaws.

The Badge of Marshal Brennan (1957) AA

Jim Davis
Arleen Whelan
Lee Van Cleef
Marty Robbins
D: Albert C. Gannaway

An outlaw assumes the identity of a dying lawman.

Au ★
S ★
A ★

Bad Girls (1994) 20th C. Fox ★★★

Madeleine Stowe
Mary Stuart Masterson
Drew Barrymore
D: Jonathan Kaplan

Four prostitutes search for a new life.
Filmed at Alamo Village, TX, Red Hills Ranch,
Sonora, Sierra Railroad, Jamestown, CA.

Au ★★★
S ★★
A ★★★

—Pick it up. Put it in. Die like a man!
—Madeleine Stowe
Bad Girls

Bad Jim (1990)

James Brolin
Richard Roundtree
John Clark Gable
Harry Carey, Jr.
Rory Calhoun
D: Clyde Ware

Bad Kids of the West (1967) FF—Ital.

Andrea Balestri
Mirko Ellis
D: Tony Good (Bruno Corbucci and Tonino Ricci)

Two killers take refuge in a town inhabited only by children.

The Badlanders (1958) APC/MGM

Alan ladd
Ernest Borgnine
Katy Jurado
D: Delmer Daves

Two men attempt to outsmart each other in a gold heist.
Based on W.R. Burnett's, *The Asphalt Jungle.* Filmed at Old Tucson.

Au ★ ★
S ★ ★
A ★ ★

Bad Lands (1939) RKO

Robert Barrat
Douglas Walton
Robert Coote
Noah Berry, Jr.
Jack (John) Payne
D: Lew Landers

A lawman leads his posse into the desert after hostiles.

Badlands of Dakota (1941) Universal

Robert Stack
Ann Rutherford
Richard Dix
Frances Farmer
Broderick Crawford
Lon Chaney, Jr.
Andy Devine
D: Alfred E. Greene

A sheriff and his girl encounter Wild Bill Hickok,
Calamity Jane and George Custer.

Au ★
S ★
A ★

Badlands of Montana (1957) 20th C. Fox ★

Rex Reason
Margia Dean
Beverly Garland
D: Daniel B. Ullman

A local politician works on both sides of the law.

Kaiar, a Paiute in Nevada. Taken
during the Powell Survey, 1873.

—This time we won't need a buttonhook.
—Alan Ladd
The Badlanders

Au

S ⚑

A ★⚑

The Bad Man (1930) FN

Walter Huston
Drothy Revier
Sidney Blackmer
Guinn Williams
D: Clarence Badger

An outlaw helps a man and his grandfather save their ranch.
Remake of the 1923 silent version.

UNCHARTED
TERRITORY

The Bad Man (1941) MGM

Wallace Beery
Lionel Barrymore
Laraine Day
Ronald Reagan
Chill Wills
D: Richard Thorpe

Remake of the 1930 version.

UNCHARTED
TERRITORY

The Bad Man of Brimstone (1937) MGM

Wallace Beery
Virginia Bruce
Dennis O'Keefe
Noah Beery
D: J. Walter Reuben

An outlaw reforms himself in the process of saving
his son from a life of prizefighting.

UNCHARTED
TERRITORY

Bad Man of Wyoming see Wyoming

Badman's Country (1958) Peerless/WB

George Montgomery
Neville Brand
Buster Crabbe
D: Fred F. Sears

Pat Garrett, Wyatt Earp, Buffalo Bill and Bat Masterson
team to fight Butch Cassidy.

Au ★⚑

S ★⚑

A ★⚑

*—When a mad dog comes at you,
you've got to kill it ot be killed!*
—George Montgomery
Badman's Country

Bad Man's River (1971) FF—Ital./Fr./Sp.

Lee Van Cleef
James Mason

Gina Lollobrigida
Eduardo Fajardo
D: Eugenio Martin

A bank robbers wife steals his loot.

Bad Man's Territory (1946) RKO

Randolph Scott
Ann Richards
George Hayes
Chief Thunder Cloud
Ben Johnson
D: Tim Whelan

A gunman faces off against a host of legendary badmen.

The Bad Men of Missouri (1941) WB

Dennis Morgan
Jane Wyman
Wayne Morris
Arhtur Kennedy
D: Ray Enright

The Younger brothers fight northern carpetbaggers.

Bad Men of Tombstone (1949) AA

Barry Sullivan
Marjorie Reynolds
Broderick Crawford
D: Kurt Neumann

A gunfighter faces an outlaw gang in Tombstone.
From the Jay Monaghan novel.

The Younger brothers

Baker's Hawk (1976) D-D ★ ★

Clint Walker
Burl Ives
Diane Baker
Lee H. Montgomery
D: Lyman D. Dayton

A frontier family defends a lone frontiersman from vigilantes.
From the Jack M. Brickham novel. Filmed in Utah.

Au ★★★
S ★★
A ★★★

—Ah, red tail, eh. Kinda runty though, ain't he?
—Burl Ives
Baker's Hawk

Ballad of a Bounty Hunter (I Do Not Forgive…I Kill!) (1979) UA/TF

James Philbrook
Norma Bengell
Simon Andrew
Luis Induni

D: Joaquin L. Marchent

A gunfighter must hunt the brother of his lover. Foreign film originally released as *I Do Not Forgive...I Kill!* (1968).

Ballad of a Gunfighter (1964) Parade

Marty Robbins
Joyce Redd
Bob Barron
D: Bill Ward

Two bandits fall for the same woman.

Ballad of a Gunman (1967) FF—Ital./Ger.

Anthony Ghidra
Angelo Infanti
Anthony Freeman
D: Alfio Caltabiano

Two outlaws track the same Mexican bandit.

—He wasn't really a good man—he wasn't really a bad man. But Lord, he was a man!
—David Warner
Ballad of Cable Hogue

The Ballad of Cable Hogue (1970) WB ★★⬩

Jason Robards
Stella Stevens
David Warner
Strother Martin
Slim Pickens
D: Sam Peckinpah

At a desert watering hole a prospector demonstrates the pioneer spirit and the futility of life on the frontier. Filmed around Apache Junction, AZ

Au ★★⬩
S ★★★
A ★★★

Stella Stevens and Jason Robard in *The Ballad of Cable Hogue*.

The Ballad of Gavilan see Gavilan

The Ballad of Gregorio Cortez (Gregorio Cortez) (1983) Embassy

Edward James Olmos
Tom Bower
James Gamon
Bruce McGill
D: Robert M. Young

Texas Rangers pursue a Mexican-American who mistakenly killed a sheriff in 1901. First aired on PBS-TV in 1982.

The Ballad of Jose (1968) Universal ★★⬩

Doris Day

Peter Graves
George Kennedy
Andy Devine
D: Andrew V. McLaglen

A frontier widow decides to raise
sheep in Wyoming cattle country.

Au ★★◖

S ★★

A ★★★

The Ballad of Little Jo (1993) FB/JP ★★★◖

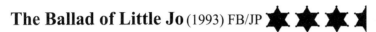

Suzy Amis
Bo Hopkins
Ian McKellen
David Chung
Carrie Snodgrass
D: Maggie Greenwald

When a well-to-do New Yorker is shunned for delivering a bastard
child, she heads west for a fresh start. Based on a true story.
Filmed in Red Lodge and Carbon County, Montana.

Au ★★★★◖

S ★★★

A ★★★◖

—My God, Little Jo!
—Bo Hopkins
The Ballad of Little Jo

The Ballad of Lucy Whipple (2001) CBS-TV ★★

Glenn Close
Jena Malone
Bruce McGill
"Meat Loaf" Aday
Wilford Brimley
Robert Pastorelli
D: Jeremy Kagan

A 13 year old girl, her mother and two
younger siblings seek a new life in the
California goldfields. Based on the Karen
Cushman novel. Filmed at Park City UT.

Au ★★★★◖

S ★★★

A ★★★★

*—The jury's hung higher than a dead
pig at Christmas time!*
—Wilford Brimley
The Ballad of Lucy Whipple

Bandera Bandits (1973) FF—Ital./Sp./Ger.

Tomàs Milian
Susan George
Telly Savalas
Eduardo Fajardo
D: Sergio Corbucci

A Western "Bonnie and Clyde" duo run from the law.

UNCHARTED
TERRITORY

Bandido! (1956) UA

Robert Mitchum
Ursula Thiess
Gilbert Roland
D: Richard Fleischer

An American mercenary steals a shipment of guns and
the wife of the soldier guarding them. Filmed in Mexico.

Au

S ★★★

A ★★★★

Bandidos (1967) FF—Ital./Sp.

Terry Jenkins
Enrico Maria Salerno
D: Max Dillman (Massimo Dallamano)

A gunfighter seeks revenge against the outlaw that mamed his hands.

UNCHARTED
TERRITORY

Bandit Queen (1950) Lippert

Barbara Britton
Willard Parker
Philip Reed
D: William Berke

A young woman becomes a masked crusader to avenge her family's murder.

UNCHARTED
TERRITORY

The Bandits (1979) LSP

Robert Conrad
Jan Michael Vincent
D: Robert Conrad & Alfredo Zacarias

Three "gringos" and three Mexican patriots compete
with Mexican army in a search for buried gold.
Filmed in Mexico in 1966 as *Los Bandidos*,
but apparently not released until 1979.

Au ★★★

S ★★★

A ★★★

Bandolero! (1968) 20ᵗʰ C. Fox ★★★

James Stewart
Dean Martin
Raquel Welch
George Kennedy
Will Geer
Harry Carey, Jr.
D: Anrew V. McLaglen

A lawman and his posse track escaped convicts.
Filmed at Alamo Village, Texas.

Dean Martin in *Bandolero*.

Au ★★★
S ★★★
A ★★★

Bang, Bang (1968)

Tom Bosley
Guy Madison
D: Stanley Prager (Giorgio Gentili) and Luciano Lelli

An inventor promises to clean up a frontier
town with his mechanical gunfighter.

> —There's three things a man ought never do:
> spit in church, scratch hisself in front of his
> ma, ahhh, pick his nose...
> —Will Geer
> *Bandolero*

Banjo Hackett: Roamin' Free (Banjo Hackett) (1976) NBC-TV/BLP/Columbia ★

Don Meredith
Ike Eisenmann
Jennifer Warren
Chuck Connors
Anne Francis
Slim Pickens
D: Andrew V. McLaglen

A horse trader and his nephew
search for the boy's stolen horse.
Filmed in the Los Padres National
Forest, California.

> —You know, you and me are lucky if we can remember
> our grandfather's face or his father's name. But, the
> blood of fine horses runs back through man's history.
> —Don Meredith
> *Banjo Hackett*

Au ★
S ★
A ★

Barbarosa (1982) Universal

Willie Nelson
Gary Busey
Denny De La Paz
Gilbert Roland
D: Fred Schepisi

A Texas gunman avoids the fury of his in-laws dating
back thirty years to his wedding day.

Barbary Coast (1935) UA

Miriam Hopkins
Edward G. Robinson
Joel McCrea
Walter Brennan
Brian Donlevy
David Niven
D: Howard Hawks

A San Francisco dancehall queen falls for an honest and broke young man.

Barbary Coast (1975) ABC-TV

William Shatner

Dennis Cole
Charles Aidman
Michael Ansara
Neville Brand
Bill Bixby
D: Bill Bixby

A government agent and a San Francisco casino owner team up to investigate an extorsion plot. Pilot for the TV series.

Barbary Coast Gent (1944) MGM

Wallace Berry
Binnie Barnes
John Carradine
Bruce Kellogg
Chill Wills
D: Roy Del Ruth

A reformed conman fights outlaws in the Nevada gold fields.

Baree (Northern Passage) (1994)

Jeff Fahey
Jacques Weber
Lorne Brass
Neve Campbell
D: Arnaud Sélignac

An Indian woman is tracked across the frontier by an obsessive fur trader. Made for TV movie. From the James O. Curwood novel.

Wife of Spotted Tail, 1872.

The Baron of Arizona (1950) Deputy Corp./Lippert

Vincent Price
Ellen Drew
Beulah Bondi
D: Samuel Fuller

A land office clerk devises a scheme to "repossess" Arizona from the U.S. government.

Barquero (1970) UA ★ ★

Lee Van Cleef
Ellen Drew
Beulah Bondi
Marriet Hartley
D: Samuel Fuller

A land office clerk devises a scheme to "repossess" Arizona from the U.S. government in order to create his own country.

Au ★ ★ ★

S ★

A ★ ★

—Back in the East I read books about men who were taming the wilderness. I dreamed about those men.

—Marriet Hartley
Barquero

Barricade (1950) WB

Dane Clark
Raymond Massey
Ruth Roman
D: Peter Godfrey

A sadistic mine operator is challenged by an outlaw.

The Barrier (1937) Paramount

Leo Carrillo
Jean Parker
James Ellison
D: Lesley Selander

A man kidnaps a girl and raises her to believe that
she's a half-breed Indian. Based on a Rex Beach story.

Bastard, Go and Kill (1971) FF—Ital.

George Eastman
Scilla Gabel
D: Gino Mangini

A homesteader seeks revenge for the murder of his family.

Battle at Apache Pass (1952) U-I

John Lund
Jeff Chandler
Beverly Tyler
Hugh O'Brian
Jay Silverheels
Jack Elam
D: George Sherman

Cochise teams with the U.S. Cavalry to fight Geronimo.
Filmed in Professor Valley, Courthouse Wash, Ida Gulch,
CO River, Sand Flats and Arches, UT.

Au ★

S ★

A ★★

Battle at Powder River see Tomahawk

Battle at Rogue River (1954) Columbia

George Montgomery
Richard Denning
Martha Hyer
D: William Castle

"Boots and saddles."

A cavalry officer attempts to make peace with Oregon Indians.
Filmed at Newhall Ranch, CA.

Au

S

A

The Bear (L'Ours) (1989) FF—Fr.

Youk (bear cub)
Bart (Kodiak bear)
Jack Wallace
Tscheky Karyo
D: Jean-Jacques Annaud

British Columbian hunters track Kodiak bears in 1885.
Based on James O. Curwood's *The Grizzly King*.
Oscar nomination for film editing. #32 Best of the West.

Au

S

A

Beast (1970) FF—Ital.

Klaus Kinski
Steven Tedd
D: Mario Costa

An outlaw rapes and ravages his way west.

Beau Bandit (1930) RKO

Rod La Rocque
Doris Kenyon
George Duryea (Tom Keene)
D: Lambert Hillyer

A smooth talking bandit is distracted by a pretty
school teacher when he plans to rob a bank.

The Beautiful Blonde From Bashful Bend (1949) 20th C. Fox

Betty Grable
Cesar Romero
Rudy Vallee
Olga San Juan
Sterling Holloway
D: Preston Sturges

A saloon singer poses as a school teacher after she accidently shoots a judge.

Beauty and the Bandit (1946) Mono.

Gilbert Roland
Martin Garralaga
Frank Yaconelli

D: William Nigh

In old California the Cisco Kid intercepts silver bound for San Marino. Based on O'Henry's character.

Behind the Mask of Zorro (Oath of Zorro) (1965) FF—Ital./Sp.

Tony Russell
Jesus Puente
D: Ricardo Blasco

Zorro protects a count and the governor from a revolutionary bandit. Sequel to *Three Swords of Zorro*.

Belle Le Grande (1951) Republic

Vera Ralston
John Carroll
William Ching
Henry Morgan
D: Allan Dwan

A San Francisco gambling queen falls for a silver miner.

Au ★

S ★

A ★

Gypsy Rose Lee and Randolph Scott in *Belle of the Yukon*.

Belle of the Yukon (1944) Int./RKO ★

Randolph Scott
Gypsy Rose Lee
Dinah Shore
D: William A. Seiter

When a conman abandons her, a dancer discovers him operating a Klondike saloon.

Au ★

S ★

A ★

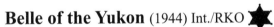

—*When you turn platonic, wolves will be vegetarians.*
—Gypsy Rose Lee
Belle of the Yukon

Belle Starr (1941) 20th C. Fox

Randolph Scott
Gene Tierney
Dana Andrews
Chill Wills
D: Irving Cummings

Starr marries a Confederate guerilla and fights Yankee carpetbaggers.

Belle Starr (1980) CBS-TV ★ ★

Elizabeth Montgomery

Randolph Scott and Gene Tierney in *Belle Starr*.

Cliff Potts
Michael Cavanaugh
D: John A. Alonzo

The infamous gunwoman joins the
James, Dalton and Younger brothers.

Au

S

A

Belle Starr's Daughter (1947) APr/20ᵗʰ C. Fox

George Montgomery
Rod Cameron
Ruth Roman
D: Lesley Selander

A marshal reforms the daughter of the legendary outlaw.
Sequel to *Belle Starr* (1941). Screenplay and story by W.R. Burnett.

UNCHARTED TERRITORY

Belle Starr Story (1968) FF—Ital.

Elsa Martinelli
Robert Woods
D: Nathan Wich (Lina Wertmuller)

The infamous female outlaw pursues a life of crime.

UNCHARTED TERRITORY

Bells of San Fernando (1947) Screen Guild

Donald Woods
Gloria Warren
Monte Blue
D: Terry Morse

An Irish immigrant opposes a town boss in old California.

UNCHARTED TERRITORY

Ben and Charlie (1970) FF—Ital.

Giuliano Gemma
George Eastman
D: Michele Lupo

Two friends are mistaken for outlaws.

UNCHARTED TERRITORY

Arthur Kennedy and James Stewart in *Bend of the River.*

Bend of the River (Where the River Bends) (1952) U-I

James Stewart
Arthur Kennedy
Julia Adams
Rock Hudson
Henry Morgan
D: Anthony Mann

Two men lead a wagon train to Oregon.
Based on Bill Gulick's, *Bend of the Snake.*

Screenplay by Borden Chase.
Filmed at Mt. Hood, Oregon.

Au

S

A ★★★★

Best Man Wins (1948) Columbia

Edgar Buchanan
Anna Lee
Robert Shayne
Gary Gray
D: John Sturges

From Mark Twain's "The Celebrated
Jumping Frog of Calavaras County."

—You'll be seein' me, you'll be seein' me. Every time you bed down for the night you'll look into the darkness and wonder if I'm there. And some night I will be there—you'll be seein' me.
—Jimmy Stewart
Bend of the River

Best of the Bad Men (1951) RKO ✦ ✦

Robert Ryan
Claire Trevor
Jack Beutel
Robert Preston
Walter Brennan
D: William D. Russell

Confederate guerillas turn outlaws.

Au

S ✦✦

A ✦✦

—Freeze, you oversized polecats!
—Walter Brennan
Best of the Badmen

Between God, the Devil and a Winchester (1968) FF—Ital./Sp.

Gilbert Roland
Richard Harrison
D: Dario Silvestri

Bob Ford leads a band of outlaws after stolen treasure.

Beyond the Frontiers of Hate see Four Came to Kill Sartana

Beyond the Law (1968) FF—Ital./Ger. ✦ ✦ ⬧

Lee Van Cleef
Antonio Sabàto
Gordon Mitchell
Bud Spencer
D: Giorgio Stegani

A gunfighter attempts to steal a mining company's payroll.

Au ★★★

S ★★⬧

A

102

Beyond the Prairie: The True Story of Laura Ingalls Wilder (2000) CBS-TV ★ ★

Richard Thomas
Meredith Monroe
Lindsay Crouse
D: Marcus Cole

The author of the *Little House on the Prairie* book series recounts life in 1880s Dakota territory. First Western of the 21st century.

Au ★★★★
S ★★
A ★★★◗

—A writer's life begins long before the first words are set down on the tablet. It begins with a sense of anticipation. A sense that one's own life is a story that must somehow find a way to be told.
—Meredith Monroe (Laura Ingalls Wilder)
Beyond the Prairie: The True Story of Laura Ingalls Wilder

Beyond the Prairie II: The True Story of Laura Ingalls Wilder Continues (2002)

CBS-TV ★ ★

Meredith Monroe
Walton Goggins
Lindsay Crouse
Richard Thomas
D: Marcus Cole

The Wilders leave their South Dakota home and travel to Missouri where they attempt to make a small farm profitable.

Au ★★★★
S ★★
A ★◗

Walton Goggins and Meredith Monroe in *Beyond the Prairie II.*

The Big Bonanza (1944) Republic ◗

Richard Arlen
Robert Livingston
Jane Frazee
George Hayes
D: George Archainbaud

An unjustly court-martialled officer confronts a childhood friend turned outlaw.

Au ◗
S ◗
A ◗

—Why, dad-blame-it! I'll hamstring any coyote that calls you a coward!
—George "Gabby" Hayes
The Big Bonanza

The Big Cat (1949) EL

Lon McCallister
Peggy Anne Garner
Preston Foster
Sara Hayden
Skip Homeier
Forrest Tucker
D: Phil Karlson

—Mary dear, listen to me! I've got a hand of cards here that comes to a man once in a lifetime!
—Henry Fonda
A Big Hand for the Little Lady

UNCHARTED TERRITORY

The Big Country (1958) WW/UA ★ ★ ★ ◗

Gregory Peck
Jean Simmons
Carroll Baker
Charlton Heston
Burle Ives
Chuck Connors
D: William Wyler

A gentleman becomes entangled in a feud between cattle barons. Oscar nomination for scoring drama/comedy. Best supporting actor Oscar for Ives. Filmed at Canyon de Chelly National Monument. #36 IMDb.

Au ★ ★ ★
S ★ ★ ★ ◗
A ★ ★ ★ ★

Burle Ives in *The Big Country.*

Big Deal at Dodge City see A Big Hand for the Little Lady

The Big Gundown (1966) FF—Ital./Sp. ★ ◗

Lee Van Cleef
Tomàs Milian
Walter Barnes
D: Sergio Sollima

A Texas lawman tracks a Mexican bandit who raped and murdered a 12 year old girl.

Au ★ ★ ◗
S ★ ◗
A ★

—I'll hunt you down and kill you like the rotten beast you are!
—Lee Van Cleef
The Big Gundown

A Big Hand for the Little Lady (Big Deal at Dodge City) (1966) WB ★ ★ ◗

Henry Fonda
Joanne Woodward
Jason Robards
Charles Bickford
Burgess Meredith
D: Fielder Cook

When a woman's husband dies in the middle of a high-stakes poker game, she assumes his hand.

Au ★ ◗
S ★ ★
A ★ ★ ★ ◗

Jason Robards, Henry Fonda and Charles Bickford in *A Big Hand for a Little Lady.*

Big Jack (1949)

Wallace berry
Richard Conte
Marjorie Main
Edward Arnold
D: Richard Thorpe

Big Jake (1971) NG ★★★★

John Wayne
Richard Boone
Maureen O'Hara
Patrick Wayne
Bobby Vinton
Harry Carey, Jr.
Jim Davis
John Agar
John Ethan Wayne
D: George Sherman

A gunman tracks his grandson's kidnappers.
#59 Best of the West.

Au ★★★⚊

S ★★★★

A ★★★★

John Ethan Wayne and John Wayne in *Big Jake*.

The Big Land (Stampeded) (1957) WB ★★

Alan Ladd
Virginia Mayo
Edmond O'Brien
D: Gordon Douglas

A Texan convinces cattleman and farmers
to build a railroad. Story by Frank Gruber.

Au ★★

S ★★

A ★★⚊

*—I've been eatin' so much rabbit, when I sleep
at night I keep dreamin' about carrots!*
—Edmond O'Brien
The Big Land

The Big North see The Wild North

The Big Race see The Texan

Big Ripoff (1967) FF—Sp./Ital.

Chip Gorman (Andrea Giordana)
Rosemarie Dexter
D: Franco Rosseti

A bandit searches for gold coins.

The Big Showdown (Storm Rider) (1972) (The Grand Duel) (1974) FF—Ital./Fr. ★★

Lee Van Cleef
Horst Frank
Peter O'Brien
Marc Mazza
D: Giancarlo Santi

A lawman protects a falsely accused murderer from bounty hunters.

Au ★★⚊

S ★

A

The Big Silence see The Great Silence

The Big Sky (1952) Win./RKO ★★★✦

Kirk Douglas
Dewey Martin
Elizabeth Threatt
Arthur Hunnicutt
Jim Davis
D: Howard Harks

Kentucky mountainmen join a keelboat
expedition through Indian country.
Technical advice by Joe De Yong.

Au ★★★✦
S ★★★✦
A ★★★★

*—Sure is big country. Only thing bigger is
the sky. Looks like God made it, forgot to
put people in it.*

—Kirk Douglas
The Big Sky

The Big Trail (1930) Fox ★★★✦

John Wayne
Marguerite Churchill
Ian Keith
Tyrone Power, Sr.
Ward Bond
Chief Big Tree
Iron Eyes Cody
D: Raoul Walsh

While leading the first wagon train on the Oregon Trail, a
scout avenges a murder. The Duke's first leading
role under his film name, "John Wayne".
From the Hal G. Evarts serial first appearing in the Saturday
Evening Post (Nov.-Jan. 1929-30). Filmed in Jackson, WY.

Au ★★★★
S ★★★✦
A ★★

Marguerite Churchill and John Wayne in *The Big Trail.*

The Big Trees (1952) WB ★★★★

Kirk Douglas
Eva Miller
Patrice Wymore
Edgar Buchanan
Alan Hale, Jr.
D: Felix Feist

A religious homesteader prevents a timber boss
from clear-cutting the California redwoods.
Remake of *Valley of the Giants.*

Au ★★★✦
S ★★★★
A ★★★★

*—No great trail was ever blazed without
hardship. And ya gotta fight! That's life.
When ya stop fighten', that's death.*

—John Wayne
The Big Trail

Billy the Kid (The Highwayman Rides) (1930) MGM

> John Mack Brown
> Wallace Beery
> Kay Johnson
> Karl Dane
> D: King Vidor

Billy the Kid and his bride are hunted by Pat Garrett.

> *—Lose, you're nothing. Win, you're somebody.*
> *—Ben Johnson*
> *Bite the Bullet*

Billy the Kid (1941) MGM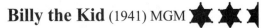

> Robert Taylor
> Brian Donlevy
> Ian Hunter
> Mary Howard
> Lon Chaney, Jr.
> Chill Wills
> D: David Miller

The Kid faces a childhood friend—the town marshal. Remake of the 1930 version. Oscar nomination for cinematography: color. Filmed in Monument Valley, UT and Sedona, AZ.

Au ★★
S ★★★
A ★★★

Brian Donlevy
in Billy the Kid.

Billy the Kid (1962) FF—Sp.

> George Martin
> Jack Taylor
> D: Leon Klimovsky

The Kid pursues a life of crime.

Billy the Kid (Gore Vidal's Billy the Kid) (1989) TNT

> Val Kilmer
> Duncan Regher
> Patrick Massett
> Ned Vaughn
> D: William A. Graham

The Kid becomes entangled in the Lincoln County Wars. Gore Vidal's version of Billy's life. Filmed in Old Tucson. #71 Best of the West.

Au ★★★★★
S ★★★★
A ★★★★

Billy Two Hats (1973) UA/Algonquin ★★★★

> Gregory Peck
> Jack Warden
> Desi Arnez, Jr.
> Sian Barbara Allen
> D: Ted Kotcheff

A lawman tracks down two men in the southwest.
#82 Best of the West.

Au

S ★★★★

A ★★★★

Bite the Bullet (1975) Columbia

Gene Hackman
Candice Bergen
James Coburn
Ben Johnson
Jan-Michael Vincent
D: Richard Brooks

Riders compete in a marathon horse race across
the desert. Oscar nominations for sound and
scoring: original music. Filmed near Durango,
Colorado and White Sands National Monument.

Au

S ★★★★

A ★★★★

Bitter Creek (1954) Westwood/AA

Bill Elliot
Carlton Young
Beverly Garland
D: Thomas Carr

A gunman forces a confrontation with the
man he suspects of killing his brother.

Dan Duryea as Black Bart

Black Bart

Black Bart (Black Bart, Highwayman) (1948) U-I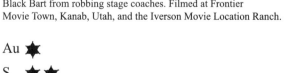

Yvonne De Carlo
Dan Duryea
Jeffrey Lynn
Frank Lovejoy
Chief Many Treaties
D: George Sherman

Gold rush dancer, Lola Montez, attempts to discourage
Black Bart from robbing stage coaches. Filmed at Frontier
Movie Town, Kanab, Utah, and the Iverson Movie Location Ranch.

Au ★

S ★★

A ★★

The Black Bounty Killer see Boss Nigger

The Black Dakotas (1954) Columbia ★ ★

Gary Merrill
Wanda Hendrix

Lola Montez

John Broomfield
Noah Beery, Jr.
John War Eagle
Jay Silverheels
Clayton Moore
D: Ray Nazarro

A Confederate spy attempts to steal gold promised by Dakota Indians to the Union.

Au ★⬥

S ★★

A ★★

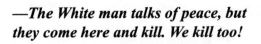

—The White man talks of peace, but they come here and kill. We kill too!
—Jay Silverheels
The Black Dakotas

Black Eagle (1948) Columbia

William Bishop
Virginia Patton
Gordon Jones
D: Robert Gordon

A young man becomes involved with a crooked livestock agent. Based on O'Henry's *The Passing of Black Eagle*.

UNCHARTED TERRITORY

Black Eagle of Santa Fe (1964) FF—Ger./Ital./Fr.

Brad Harris
Horst Frank
D: Ernst Hofbauer

A federal agent investigates an Indian uprising.

UNCHARTED TERRITORY

Black Fox (1994) RHIE ★★★

Christopher Reeve
Raoul Trujillo
Tony Todd
D: Steven H. Stern

Two friends mediate a dispute between Indians and settlers in 1861 Texas. First of a trilogy.

Au ★★★

S ★★★

A ★★★

—The only thing I'm slave to is my family and my word.
—Tony Todd
Black Fox

Black Fox: The Price of Peace (1994) RHIE ★★⬥

Christopher Reeve
Raoul Trujillo
Tony Todd
D: Steven H. Stern

An ex-slave defends Kiowas from a white hunting party in 1862 Texas. Second of a trilogy.

Au ★★★

—Man can't live worryin' about dyin', brother.
—Tony Todd
Black Fox: The Price of Peace

S

A

Black Fox: Good Men and Bad (1994) RHIE

Christopher Reeve
Kim Coates
Tony Todd
D: Steven H. Stern

A homesteader avenges his wife's murder in 1865 Texas.
Third of a trilogy. Filmed in Alberta, Canada.

Au

S

A

—Son, I got one rule in life—
I only shoot people that need killin'.
—Christopher Reeve
Black Fox: Good Men and Bad

The Black Ghost (1932)

Lon Chaney, Jr.
Dorothy Gulliver
Richard Neill
Yakima Canutt
D: ?

Black Horse Canyon (1954) U-I

Joel McCrea
Mari Blanchard
Murvyn Vye
D: Jesse Hibbs

A black stallion eludes mustangers.

Black Jack (1968) FF—Ital.

Robert Woods
LucienneBridou
D: Gianfranco Baldanello

An outlaw and his gang fight over their loot.

Thomas "Black Jack" Ketchum mistakenly
decapitated during his hanging.

Blackjack Ketchum, Desperado (1956) Clover/Columbia

Howard Duff
Victor Jory
Maggie Mahoney
D: Earl Bellamy

A reluctant gunfighter must strap on his guns one last time.
Story by Louis L'Amour.

Black Killer (1971) FF—Ital./Ger.

Klaus Kinski

110

Fred Robsahm
D: Lucky Moore (Carlo Croccolo)

A new sheriff and a gunfighter attempt to restore order to Tombstone.

Black Patch (1957) MP/WB

George Montgomery
Diane Brewster
Tom Pittman
Sebastian Cabot
Strother Martin
D: Allen H. Miner

A marshal is accused of murder.

Au
S
A

—Unbuckle your gunbelts and drop 'em!
—George Montgomery
Black Patch

Black Spurs (1965) Paramount

Rory Calhoun
Terry Moore
Linda Darnell
Scott Brady
Lon Chaney
D: R.G. Springsteen

A cowboy schemes to ruin a town's image
so that the railroad will bypass it.

Black Stallion see Return of Wildfire

Black Tigress (1967) FF—Ital.

Peter Martell
Lola Falana
D: Siro Marcellini

A "soiled dove" entices information regarding
missing treasure from her clients.

The Black Whip (1956) Regal/20ᵗʰ C. Fox

Hugh Marlowe
Coleen Gray
Richard Gilden
Angie Dickinson
Strother Martin
D: Charles Marquis Warren

A way station manager protects four stranded
women and the governor from outlaws.

Au

*—It doesn't make any difference which
side you're on. Pick up your sword or gun
and you turn back a thousand years.*
—Hugh Marlowe
The Black Whip

S
A

Blade Rider, Revenge of the Indian Nations (1966)

Chuck Connors
Burt Reynolds
Greg Morris
Lee Van Cleef
Noah Beery, Jr.
D: Harry Harris, Vincent McEveety and Allen Reisner

Compilation of three episodes of the "Branded" TV series.

Blake's Marauders (Payment in Blood) (Winchester for Hire) (1968) FF—Ital.

Edd Byrnes
Guy Madison
D: E.G. Rowland (Enzo G. Castellari)

A Confederate raider refuses to accept the outcome of the war.

UNCHARTED
TERRITORY

Blazing Arrows see Fighting Caravans

Blazing Guns (1943) Mono.

Ken Maynard
Hoot Gibson
Kay Forrester
D: Robert Tansey

Two U.S. Marshals investigate a town boss and his gang.
Filmed at Corriganville Ranch and Monogram Ranch, CA.

Au
S
A

Blind Justice (1994)

Armond Assante
Elizabeth Shue
Robert Davi
D: Richard Spence

A nearly blind Civil War veteran protects a baby.

Blindman (1971) FF—Ital.

Tony Anthony
Ringo Starr
Agneta Eckemyr
D: Ferdinando Baldi

A blind gunman searches for a wagon load of whores stolen by bandidos.

Blood Arrow (1958) Emirau/RF

Scott Brady
Paul Richards
Phyllis Coates
D: Charles Marquis Warren

Three frontiersman help a girl deliver small pox serum through hostile country.

Au
S
A

Blood at Sundown (1967) FF—Sp./Ital.

Anthony Steffen
Evelyn Stewart
D: Jose Antonio and Edward Muller (Eduardo Mulargia)

An Army deserter seeks revenge against the man who crippled him.

Blood at Sundown (reissued title 1969) (One Thousand Dollars on the Black) (original title 1967) FF—Ital./Ger.

Anthony Steffen
Gianni Garko
D: Albert Cardiff (Albert Cardone)

A man and his brother face off.

Blood Calls to Blood (1968) FF—Ital./Sp.

Fernando Sancho
Stephen Forsyte
D: Lewis King

A gunfighter seeks revenge against a bandit who robbed a monestery.

Blood Church (1985) FF—Ital.

Gaithor Brownne
Carmella N. Hall
Buxx Banner
D: Tom Vacca

Pancho Villa attempts to return a bell to a church in New Mexico.

Blood for a Silver Dollar (1965) FF—Ital./Fr.

Montgomery Wood (Guiliano Gemma)
Evelyn Stewart

D: Calvin J. Padget (Giorgio Ferroni)

An ex-Confederate travels to Yellowstone to begin a new life.

Blood Money (1974) FF—HK/Ital.

Lee Van Cleef
Lo Leigh
Karen Yeh (Yeh Ling Chih)
Julian Ugarte
D: Anthony M. Dawson (Antonio Margheriti)

A gunman attempts to assemble the pieces of a treasure map
tattooed on different people. The first Hong Kong-Italian Western.

Blood on the Arrow (1964) AA

Dale Robertson
Martha Hyer
Wendell Corey
Dandy Coran
D: Sidney Salko

The lone survivor of an Indian attack takes refuge at a trading post.

Chief Gall, a Hunkpapa Dakota

Blood on the Moon (1948) RKO-Radio ★★★★

Robert Mitchum
Barbara Bell Geddes
Robert Preston
Walter Brennan
Harry Carey, Jr.
Iron Eyes Cody
D: Robert Wise

A gunman fights the injustice done to homesteaders
by cattlemen. From Luke Short's, *Gunman's Choice*.
Filmed in Sedona and the Iverson Movie Location Ranch.
#90 Best of the West.

Au ★★★★
S ★★★★
A ★★★★

Blood Red (1989) HFC ★★★

Giancarlo Giannini
Dennis Hopper
Eric Roberts
D: Peter Masterson

A Sicilian family refuses to sell its
California vineyards to the railroad.

Au ★★★★
S ★★★
A ★★

—You're all a pack of fools!
—Dennis Hopper
Blood Red

Blood River (1974) FF—Ital.

Fabio Testi
John Ireland
Rosalba Neri
D: Gianfranco Baldenello

Very obscure.

Blood River (1991) CBS-TV

Rick Schroder
Wilford Brimley
John P. Ryan
Adrienne Barbeau
D: Mel Damski

A frontiersman aides a fugitive in escaping a corrupt land baron.
Filmed in Calgary, Alberta, and at Ft. Steele, B.C., Canada.

Au ★★★
S ★★✦
A ★★★✦

—*...Once in a while the gentle touch of a woman helps soothe the savage beast within a man.*

—Wilford Brimley
Blood River

Blue (1968) Paramount

Terence Stanp
Jeanne Pettet
Karl Malden
Ricardo Montalban
D: Silvio Narizzano and Yakima Canutt

The adopted son of a bandido learns the ways of civilized life.
Filmed in Professor Valley, CO River, Sevenmile Canyon, La Sal,
Sand Flats, Redd's Ranch, Wood's ranch, UT.

The Bold Caballero (1936) Republic

Bob Livingston
Heather Angel
Sig Rumann
Ian Wolf
Chief Thunder Cloud
D: Wells Root

Zorro opposes corrupt government officials.
Based on a Johnston McCulley story.

Boldest Job in the West (1969) FF—Ital./Sp./Fr.

Mark Edwards
Fernando Sancho
D: Josè Antonio De La Loma

A Sun Valley bank robbery goes wrong.

Bonanza: The Next Generation (1988) Gaylord/LBSC/Bonanza V. ★ ★

John Ireland
Robert Fuller
Barbara Anderson
Michael Landon, Jr.
Gillian Greene
D: Wilam Claxton

The Cartwrights continue their saga at the turn of the century. Based on the TV series.

Au ★ ★

S ★ ⬧

A ★ ⬧

Bonanza: The Return (1993)

Ben Johnson
Michael Landon, Jr.
Emily Warfield
Jack Elam
Dirk Blocker
D: Jerry Jameson

A gunman seeks revenge against the late Little Joe by attempting to take the Ponderosa from the Cartwrights. Made for TV movie.

UNCHARTED TERRITORY

Bonanza: Under Attack (1995) R-LP ★ ★ ⬧

Leonard Nimroy
Dennis Farina
Ben Johnson
Jack Elam
D: Mark Tinker

At the turn of the century, Frank James takes refuge from Pinkertons on the Ponderosa.

Au ★ ★ ★

S ★ ★

A ★ ★

Boot Hill (1969) FF—Ital./Sp.

Terence Hill
Bud Spencer
Lionel Stander
Woody Strode
D: Giuseppe Colizzi

A gunfighter attempts to retire by joining the circus.

UNCHARTED TERRITORY

Boot Hill Mamas see Outlaw Women

Border Cafe (1937) RKO

Harry Carey

John Beal
Armida
D: Lew Landers

A young man goes west and saves a town.

Border Devils (1932)

Harry Carey
Kathleen Collins
George "Gabby" Hayes
D: William Nigh

A gunman assumes a deadman's identity to track a gang.

Border Fence (1951) Gulf C.P./Astor

Walter Wayne
Lee Morgan
Mary Nord
D: Norman Sheldo (Sheldon), H. W. Kier

A paroled rancher is accused of rustling.
Filmed in San Antonio, Texas.

Border Guns (1934) Aywon

Bill Cody
Blanche Mehaffey
Bill Cody, Jr.
D: Jack Nelson

A drifter becomes entangled in an Arizona
border town fight with bandidos.

The Border Legion (1930) Paramount

Richard Arlen
Jack Holt
Fay Wray
D: Edwin H. Knopf and Otto Brower

An outlaw sacrifices himself for the woman
he loves. Based on the Zane Grey novel.

Border River (1954) U-I

Joel McCrea
Yvonne De Carlo
Pedro Armendariz
Alfonso Bedoya
D: George Sherman

A Confederate officer takes Union gold to Mexico
to exchange for arms. Filmed at Professor Valley,
CO River, White's ranch and Courthouse Wash, UT.

—You know, tonight I drink tequila. Tomorrow champaaaagne. Heh, heh—(belch)—heh, heh, heh.

—Alfonso Bedoya
Border River

Au

S ★★

A ★★

Border Saddlemates (1952) Republic

RexAllen
Mary Ellen Kay
Slim Pickens
D: William Witney

A veterinarian uncovers
Montana counterfeiters.

Au

S ★

A ★

Border Shootout (1990)

Michael Ansara
Bruce Paul Barbour
Glenn Ford
D: Chris McIntyre

A young rancher is appointed deputy to face the town bully.

Born to Fight see The Kid and the Gunfighter

Born to Kill (1967) FF—Ital.

Gordon Mitchell (Charles Pendleton)
Femi Benussi
D: Tony Mulligan

A stranger is convinced by a prostitute to protect
her town from a land baron.

Born to the Saddle (1953) Astor

Chuck Courtney
Donald Woods
Leif Erickson
D: William Beaudine

A crooked gambler hires a boy to train a racehorse.

Boss Nigger (The Black Bounty Killer) (1974) D Prod.

Fred Williamson
D'Urville Martin
William Smith
Barbara Leigh
Don "Red" Barry
D: Jack Arnold

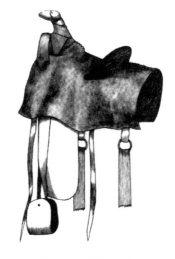

Texas mochila saddle.

Two gunmen terrorize a town in which outlaws have taken refuge.

The Bounty Hunter (1954) Transcona/WB ★ ★ ★ ★

Randolph Scott
Dolores Dorn
Marie Windsor
Ernest Borgnine
Fess Parker
D: Andrè de Toth

A bounty hunter is hired by Pinkertons to track
trainrobbers. Filmed at the Iverson Movie
Location Ranch. #93 Best of the West.

Au ★ ★ ★ ✦

S ★ ★ ★ ★

A ★ ★ ★ ★

*—Might as well give up, Williams.
This is the end of the line!*
—Randolph Scott
The Bounty Hunter

The Bounty Hunter (1989) Action Int.

Robert Ginty
Bo Hopkins
Leota Waterdown
Melvin Holt
D: Robert Ginty

The Bounty Hunter in Trinity (1972) FF—Ital.

Jeff Cameron
Paul McCren
D: Oskar Faradine

The town of Trinity hires a bounty hunter for protection from bandidos.

The Bounty Killer (1965) Embassy ★

Dan Duryea
Rod Cameron
Audrey Dalton
Richard Arlen
Buster Crabbe
Bob Steele
Bronco Billy Anderson
D: Spencer G. Bennet

A mild mannered Easterner turns bounty hunter
after accidently wiping out an outlaw gang.
Filmed at Corriganville Ranch, California.

Au ★

S ★

A ★

*—You know why I'm a bounty hunter?
Because you good people pay me to do it!*
—Dan Duryea
The Bounty Killer

The Bounty Killer (1966) (Ugly Ones) (1968) FF—Sp./Ital.

Tomàs Milian

Richard Wyler
D: Eugenio Martin

A bounty hunter and an outlaw compete
for a woman's affections. Based on the
Marvin Albert story.

The Bounty Man (1972) ABC-TV/CF

Clint Walker
Richard Basehart
John Ericson
Margot Kidder
Arthur Hunnicutt
D: John Llewellyn Moxey

A bounty hunter and his rival pursue the same outlaw.

The Boy From Oklahoma (1954) WB ★★

Will Rogers, Jr.
Nancy Olsen
Lon Chaney, Jr.
Slim Pickens
D: Michael Curtiz

A law student becomes town sheriff.
Filmed at Warner Ranch, Calabasas, CA.

Au ★

S ★★

A ★★

—Everybody's heard of Billy the Kid, I guess. Howdy!
—Will Rogers, Jr.
The Boy From Oklahoma

Boy of the West (1943) FF—Ital.

Giovanni Grassio
Nino Pavese
D: Giorgio Ferroni

A quack doctor attempts to end the
feud between two frontier families.

Boy's Ranch (1946) MGM

Jackie "Butch" Jenkins
James Craig
Skippy Homeier
D: Roy Rowland

Branded (1951) Paramount

Alan Ladd
Mona Freeman
Charles Bickford
D: Rudolph Matè

*—[It's a] Great feelin' to know your own flesh
and blood's cometh around to take over what you
sweat to build. Greatest feelin' in the world.*
—Charles Bickford
Branded

A man poses as a cattle baron's long-lost son. Filmed in Arizona.

Au ★★

S ★★★◣

A ★★★

Branded Men (1931) Tiffany

Ken Maynard
June Clyde
Charles King
Irving Bacon
D: Phil Rosen

A lawman protects a boy from an outlaw.

The Brass Legend (1956) UA

Hugh O'Brian
Nancy Gates
Raymond Burr
Russell Simpson
D: Gerd Oswald

An outlaw escapes from a lawman.

The Bravados (1958) TCR ★★★◣

Gregory Peck
Joan Collins
Stephen Boyd
Lee Van Cleef
D: Henry King

A rancher relentlessly pursues outlaws accused
of murdering his wife. Filmed in Mexico.

Au ★★★◣

S ★★★◣

A ★★★★

—Now I know how you feel. Go after them, Jim, and catch them. Get them before…Kill them, kill them, kill them!

—Joan Collins
The Bravados

The Bravos (1972) ABC-TV ★★★

George Peppard
Pernell Roberts
Belinda Montgomery
L.Q. Jones
D: Ted Post

Indians kidnap a cavalry officer's son. Filmed in Sedona, AZ.

Au ★★★◣

S ★★★

A ★★★◣

Captive white boy, Santiago McKinn.
Taken by Chiricahua Apaches in 1885.

The Brazen Bell (1963) NBC-TV/Universal

James Drury

Lee J. Cobb
George C. Scott
Doug McClure
D: James Sheldon

A frightened school teacher must stand up in a gunfight.
An episode of "The Virginian" TV series released theatrically.

Breakheart Pass (1976) UA ★★★★

Charles Bronson
Ben Johnson
Richard Crenna
Jill Ireland
Eddie Little Sky
D: Tom Gries

A secret service agent investigates
a train carrying smuggled rifles.
Filmed at Lewiston, Idaho. #73 Best of the West.

Au ★★★★

S ★★★★

A ★★★★

Bret Maverick: The Lazy Ace (Maverick) (1981) NBC-TV ★★◀

James Garner
Ed Bruce
Stuart Margolin
D: Stuart Margolin

A gambler wins big and decides to settle down.
Pilot for the second "Maverick" TV series.
Filmed at Sable Ranch, California.

Au ★◀

S ★★★◀

A ★★★

—My ol' pappy used to say…
—James Garner
Bret Maverick: The Lazy Ace

The Bride Wasn't Willing see Frontier Gal

Bridger (1976) ABC-TV ★★

James Wainwright
Ben Murphy
Dirk Blocker
Sally Field
William Windom
D: David L. Rich

A mountainman is given forty days to blaze a trail through the Rockies.
Filmed in the Alabama Hills.

Au ★★◀

S ★★

A ★◀

Jim Bridger

122

Brigham Young (Brigham Young: Frontiersman)

(1940) 20th C. Fox

Tyrone Power
Linda Darnell
Dean Jagger
Brian Donlevy
John Carradine
Mary Astor
Chief Big Tree
D: Henry Hathaway

Brigham Young leads the Mormons to Utah.
Filmed in the Alabama Hills and Big Bear, CA.

Au ★★★★

S ★★★

A ★★★

Brigham Young circa 1853.

—We're going to establish Joseph's idea of the united order and build a mighty empire here based on labor and love and fellowship. And this time, dog gonnit, I mean to see that we stick to it!
—Dean Jagger (Brigham Young)
Brigham Young

—This is the right place, drive on.
—Brigham Young
July 24, 1847

Brighty of Grand Canyon (1967) FFCA

Joseph Cotten
Pat Conway
Jiggs (burro)
D: Norman Foster

When his master is murdered, a burro together with a boy and Teddy Roosevelt track the killer.

Brimstone (1949) Republic ★★

Rod Cameron
Adrian Booth
Walter Brennan
Forrest Tucker
Jim Davis
D: Joseph Kane

A lawman tracks a crooked cattleman and his sons.
Filmed in the Alabama Hills.

Au ★★

S ★⸙

A ★★

Teddy Roosevelt circa 1885.

—No use firing at a coyote until you really got a bead on him.
—Rod Cameron
Brimstone

Broken Arrow (1950) 20th C. Fox

James Stewart
Jeff Chandler
Debra Paget
Will Geer
Jay Silverheels
John War Eagle
Iron Eyes Cody
D: Delmer Daves

A frontiersman negotiates peace between hostile
Apaches and the United States. Based on a true
story and on Elliot Arnold's, *Blood Brothers*.
Oscar nominations for Jeff Chandler for best
supporting actor, cinematography: color, and
writing: screenplay. Filmed in Oak Creek Canyon
near Sedona, AZ, the Alabama Hills, and the
Iverson Movie Ranch. #53 Best of the West.

—I break the arrow. I will try the way of peace.
—Jeff Chandler
Broken Arrow

Au
S
A

Broken Lance (1954) 20th C. Fox

Spencer Tracy
Robert Wagner
Jean Peters
Richard Widmark
Katy Jurado
Hugh O'Brian
E.G. Marshall
D: Edward Dmytryk

A cattleman fights a mining company that is polluting his water supply.
Best supporting actress nomination for Jurado. Oscar for best
writing: original story. Filmed at the Iverson Movie Location Ranch.

Au
S
A

The Broken Land (1962) 20th C. Fox

Kent Taylor
Diana Darrin
Jody McCrea
Robert Sampson
Jack Nicholson
D: John Bushelman

A deputy stands up to his corrupt sheriff.

Au
S
A

Broken Sabre (1966) NBC-TV/Columbia

Chuck Connors
Kamala Devi

Peter Breck
Macdonald Carey
John Carradine
D: Bernard McEveety

A soldier is wrongly accused of cowardice. Comprised of several episodes of the "Branded" TV series and released theatrically.

The Broken Star (1956) Bel-Air/UA

Howard Duff
Lita Baron
Bill Williams
D: Lesley Selander

A lawman must track one of his own when a rancher is murdered. Filmed at Old Tucson.

Bronco Buster (1952) U-I

John Lund
Scott Brady
Joyce Holden
Chill Wills
D: Bud Boetticher

Two rodeo riders compete for the affection of the same woman.

Brotherhood of the Gun (1991) CBS-TV

Brian Bloom
David Carradine
Jamie Rose
D: Verne Gillum

An outlaw becomes sheriff of a town controlled by a crooked rancher. Filmed at Bonanza Creek Ranch, Eaves Movie Ranch, NM.

Au

S ★

A ★◗

—You and me, we're born to be enemies. Nothin' in the world will ever change that.
—David Carradine
Brotherhood of the Gun

Brother Outlaw (1971) FF—Ital.

Tony Kendall
James Rogers
D: Eward G. Muller (Edoardo Mulargia)

A falsely accused robber and his brother track down the true thieves.

Brothers Blue (1973) FF—Ital./Fr.

Jack Palance
Antonio Falsi
D: Marc Meyer (Luigi Bazzoni)

A bounty hunter chases an outlaw gang.

Buchanan Rides Alone (1958) Columbia ★★

Randolph Scott
Craig Stevens
Barry Kelly
Tol Avery
D: Bud Boetticher

A Texan risks his neck for a Mexican. Coscreenplay (uncredited) by Burt Kennedy and Charles Lang. Based on Jonas Ward's, *The Name's Buchanan.* Filmed at Old Tucson.

Au ★★

S ★★★

A ★★

—*I ain't much of a thinker, judge. I grew up chasin' cows.*
—Randolph Scott
Buchanan Rides Alone

Buck and the Preacher (1972) Columbia ★★◣

Sidney Poitier
Harry Belefonte
Ruby Dee
Cameron Mitchell
Denny Miller
D: Sidney Poitier

A black Union veteran and a preacher lead freed slaves to the West. Filmed in Kenya and Mexico.

Au ★★★

S ★★

A ★★★◣

Buckeye and Blue (1988) AJCP

Jeffrey Osterhage
Robyn Lively
Rick Gibbs
Will Hannah
D: J.C. Compton

Buckskin (1968) Paramount

Barry Sullivan
Joan Caulfield
Wendell Corey
Lon Chaney
John Russell
D: Michael Moore

The marshal of a frontier town leads its citizens in a water rights conflict against a cattle baron.

Harry Belafonte and Sidney Poitier in *Buck and the Preacher.*

—*That's right brother, I'm a preacher! And my text is fornication. He that committeth fornication sineth against his own body!*
—Harry Belafonte
Buck and the Preacher

125

126

Buckskin Frontier (1943) UA

Richard Dix
Jane Wyatt
Lee J. Cobb
George Reeves
D: Lesley Selander

A gunman opposes cattlemen attempting to stop the railroad.

The Buckskin Lady (1957) UA

Patricia Medina
Richard Denning
Gerald Mohr
D: Carl K. Hittleman

When a gambler falls for the new
doctor in town, her boyfriend objects.

Buffalo Bill (1944) 20th C. Fox

Joel McCrea
Maureen O'Hara
Linda Darnell
Edgar Buchanan
Anthony Quinn
Chief Thunder Cloud
Chief Many Treaties
D: William A. Wellman

The legendary frontiersman turns showman.
Technical advise by Joe De Yong.
Filmed in Kanab, UT.

Joel McCrea as Buffalo Bill.

Buffalo Bill and the Indians, or Sitting Bull's History Lesson (1976) UA ★★★★

Paul Newman
Burt Lancaster
Joel Grey
Kevin McCarthy
Harvey Keitel
John Considine
Denver Pyle
Will Sampson
Shelley Duvall
D: Robert Altman

Buffalo Bill becomes the greatest showman of his times.
Filmed in Alberta, Canada.

Au ★★★★⯪
S ★★★★
A ★★★★

Bufflao Bill, Hero of the Far West (1964) FF—Ital./Ger./Fr.

Gordon Scott
Mario Braga
D: John W. Fordson (Mario Costa)

Buffalo Bill Cody

Buffalo Bill is sent to stop Yellowhand from buying stolen guns.

Buffalo Bill in Tomahawk Territory (1952)

Clayton Moore
Slim Andrews
Rod Redwing
Chief Yowlachie
Chief Thundercloud
D: Bernard B. Ray

Buffalo Girls (1995) dPE/CFE/CBS-TV

Anjelica Huston
Melanie Griffith
Jack Palance
Sam Elliott
Reba McEntire
D: Rod Harty

Calamity Jane develops into a legend. Fictionalized account of her life based on Larry McMurtry's novel. Filmed in England and New Mexico. #31 Best of the West.

Au ★★★★
S ★★★★★
A ★★★★★

—But, never a day goes by that I don't miss my darlin' baby girl. I'll always be your mother.
Calamity Jane (Anjelica Huston)
Buffalo Girls

Buffalo Gun (1961) Globe

Webb Pierce
Marty Robbins
Carl Smith
D: Albert C. Gannaway

Three singing government agents investigate stolen shipments to Indians.

Buffalo Rider (1978) Starfire

Rick Guinn
John Freeman
Priscilla Laurie
George Sager
D: George Lauris

Buffalo Soldiers (1970) see The Red, White and Black

Buffalo Soldiers (1997) TNT ★★★★

Danny Glover
Mykelti Williamson
Glynn Turman
Michael Warren
D: Charles Haid

Danny Glover in *Buffalo Soldiers*.

128

A black cavalry troop tracks renegade Apaches. Filmed at the "Cochise Stronghold" located in the Coronado National Forest, AZ, and at Old Tucson (Mescal).

Au
S ★★★★
A ★★★★

Bugles in the Afternoon (1952) WB

Ray Milland
Helena Carter
Hugh Marlowe
Forrest Tucker
George Reeves
D: Roy Rowland

A cavalry officer is demoted by his superior who is jealous of a woman's affections. Story by Ernest Haycox.

UNCHARTED TERRITORY

Bullet for a Badman (1964) Universal ★★★

Audie Murphy
Darren Mcgavin
Ruta Lee
Alan Hale, Jr.
Ed Platt
D: R.G. Springsteen

A lawman searches for a bankrobber whose ex-wife he married. Based on Marvin Albert's novel, *Renegade Posse*. Filmed near St. George, Utah.

Au
S ★★★
A ★★★

Bullet for Sandoval (1969) FF—Ital./Sp.

Ernest Borgnine
George Hilton
D: Julio Buchs (Julio Garcia)

A confederate deserter avenges the death of his family.

UNCHARTED TERRITORY

A Bullet for the General (1966) FF—Ital.

Gian Maria Volontè
Lou Castel
Klaus Kinski
D: Damiano Damiani

A Mexican revolutionary is joined by a gringo. Django film.

UNCHARTED TERRITORY

A Bullet is Waiting (1953) Columbia

—Why do you murder my people for those who made you less than cattle?
—Harrison Lowe
Buffalo Soldiers

Audie Murphy in *Bullet for a Bad Man*.

Jean Simmons
Rory Calhoun
Stephen McNally
D: John Farrow

A lawman and his prisoner become stranded in the desert with an old man and his daughter.

Bullets and the Flesh (1965) FF—Ital./Fr./Sp.

Rod Cameron
Patricia Viterbo
D: Fred Wilson (Mariono Girolami)

A white girl falls in love with a Cherokee brave.

Bullets Don't Argue (Guns Don't Argue) (1964) FF—Ital./Ger./Sp.

Rod Cameron
Horst Frank
D: Mike Perkins (Mario Caiano)

A lawman tracks outlaws in Mexico.

The Bull of the West (1963) NBC-TV/Universal ★ ★

Lee J. Cobb
Brian Keith
Charles Bronson
Doug McClure
George Kennedy
Ben Johnson
James Drury
D: Paul Stanley and Jerry Hopper

A cowboy drifts into Wyoming and the ranch foreman attempts to help a neighbor. An episode of "The Virginian" TV series released theatrically.

Au ★ ★
S ★ ★
A ★ ★ ★

Bullwhip! (1958) AA

Guy Madison
Rhonda Fleming
James Griffith
John Beddoe
D: Harmon Jones

A man avoids hanging by marrying a half-breed.

The Burning Hills (1956) WB ★ ★ ★

Tab Hunter
Natalie Wood
Skip Homeier

Natalie Wood and Tab Hunter
in *The Burning Hills*.

Claude Akins
D: Stuart Heisler

A peon shepherd girl befriends a man targeted by the rancher
who murdered her father. Based on the Louie L'Amour story.
Filmed at Kernville, California.

Au ★★★
S ★★★
A ★★★

Bury Them Deep (To the Last Drop of Blood) (1968) FF—Ital.

Craig Hill
Ettore Manni
D: John Bird (Paolo Moffa)

A bounty hunter tracks an outlaw who robbed a payroll.

The Bushwackers (The Rebel) (1952) JBP

John Ireland
Wayne Morris
Lon Chaney, Jr.
Dorothy Malone
Jack Elam
D: Rod Amateau

A retired gunfighter must strap on his guns one more
time to avenge a newspaper editor's murder.

Butch and Sundance: The Early Days (1979) 20th C. Fox ★★

William Katt
Tom Berenger
Jill Eikenberry
Paul Plunkett
Brian Dennehy
Chris Lloyd
D: Richard Lester

Butch and Sundance team up and begin their legendary lives as outlaws.
Prequel to *Butch Cassidy and the Sundance Kid.* Oscar nomination for
costume design. Filmed at Eaves Movie Ranch, New Mexico.

Au ★★★
S ★
A ★★

Butch Cassidy and the Sundance Kid (1969) 20th C. Fox ★★★★★

Paul Newman
Robert Redford
Katherine Ross
Strother Martin
Sam Elliott
Cloris Leachman
D: George Roy Hill

Two outlaws rob trains and banks. Romanticized
account of the legendary badmen. Oscar nominations

—Who are those guys?
—Paul Newman
Butch Cassidy and
the Sundance Kid

Sundance (William Katt) and Butch (Tom Berenger)

The Faces of Butch and Sundance

With the Wild Bunch, the Sundance Kid (seated left) and Butch Cassidy (seated right).

Sundance (Robert Redford) and Butch (Paul Newman).

132

for best picture, direction, and sound. Oscars for
best writing: story and screenplay based on material
not previously published or produced, cinematography,
song, and original score. #24 Best of the West,
#50 AFI GM, #54 AFI MHPM, #7 IMDb.

Au ★★★
S ★★★★★
A ★★★★★

Paul Newman and Robert Redford in
Butch Cassidy and the Sundance Kid.

Cahill, United States Marshal (1973) WB ★★★

John Wayne
George Kennedy
Harry Carey, Jr.
Neville Brand
D: Andrew V. McLaglen

Lawman, J.D. Hill, tracks outlaws unaware
that his sons may be implicated in a robbery.
Filmed in Durango, Mexico.

Au ★★★★
S ★★★
A ★★★

*—I'm willin' to die tryin' to keep 'em. Question
is, are you willin' to die tryin' to take 'em?*
—John Wayne
Cahill, United States Marshal

Cain's Way (1970) (Cain's Cut-Throats) (1971) (Cane's Cutthroats) MDAAI ★★★

John Carradine
Scott Brady
Robert Dix
Don Epperson
D: Kent Osborne

A preacher turned bounty hunter helps
a man avenge the murder of his family.

Au ★★★★
S ★★★
A ★★★

Calamity Jane (1984) CBS-TV ★★★★

Jane Alexander
Frederick Forrest
Ken Kercheval
Walter Olkewicz
D: James Goldstone

Calamity Jane relates her story in a series
of letters written to her daughter. Base on
Jean Hicock McCormick's fraudulent diary.
Filmed at Old Tucson. #84 Best of the West.

Au ★★★
S ★★★★★
A ★★★★★

*—A woman goin' her own way, what she gets is
a hard trade every day of her life. And if she
ends up with some self-respect come sunset,
she's dam lucky. Cause if ya got that, little
darlin', can't nobody say ya didn't beat 'em all.*
—Jane Alexander
Calamity Jane

Calamity Jane and Sam Bass (1949) U-I

Yvonne De Carlo
Howard Duff
Dorothy Hart
William Parker
Lloyd Bridges
D: George Sherman

Calamity competes with another
woman for Sam Bass's affections.
Filmed at the Iverson Movie Ranch.

Au

S ⭐⭐⭐

A ⭐⭐⭐

Calibre .38 (1971) FF—Ital.

Scott Holden
Alberto Dell'Acqua
Keenan Wynn
D: Tony Secchi (Tony Dry)

A gunfighter helps his sister in her struggle against a land baron.

Sam Bass

California (1947) Paramount

Ray Milland
Barbara Stanwyck
Barry Fitzgerald
George Coulouris
Anthony Quinn
D: John Farrow

An Army deserter, a gambler and a miner prevent
a former slave-trader from building an empire.
Filmed in Sedona, AZ, and the Iverson Movie Ranch.

Au ⭐⭐⭐

S ⭐⭐⭐

A ⭐⭐⭐

California (1963) AI

Jock Mahoney
Faith Domergue
Michael Pate
D: Hamil Petroff

Californians revolt against Mexico in 1841.

California (1976) FF—Ital./Sp.

Giuliano Gemma
William Berger
D: Michele Lupo

134

A Missouri rancher faces off against outlaws.

California Conquest (1952) Columbia

Cornel Wilde
Teresa Wright
Alfonso Bedoya
D: Lew Landers

A Spanish adventurer and a gunsmith's daughter
oppose a Russian scheme to annex California.

Au ★

S ★

A ★

California Gold Rush (1981) NBC-TV/SSC

Robert Hayes
John Dehner
Henry Jones
Ken Curtis
D: Jack B. Hively

An aspiring young writer goes west to the rush.
TV movie made from two Bret Harte stories.

Hydraulic mining.

California Outpost see In Old Los Angeles

California Passage (1950) Republic ★ ❙

Forrest Tucker
Adele Mara
Estelita Rodriguez
Jim Davis
Iron Eyes Cody
D: Joseph Kane

A saloonkeeper frames his partner for gold robberies.
Filmed at the Iverson Movie Location Ranch.

Au ★★

S ★❙

A ★❙

—Nobody'll ever say you didn't have nerve, kid!
—Jim Davis
California Passage

California Trail (1933) Columbia

Buck Jones
Helen Mack
George Humbart
Luis Alberni
D: Lambert Hillyer

An American scout saves a Mexican
village from two ruthless brothers.

135

Call of the Klondike (1950) Mono.

Kirby Grant
Chinook (a dog)
D: Frank McDonald

A mountie tracks a killer wolf.

Call of the West (1930) Columbia

Dorothy Revier
Matt Moore
Tom O'Brien
Victor Potel
D: Albert Ray

A dancer marries a Texas rancher, but returns
to New York when he joins a posse.

Call of the Wild (1935) UA

Clark Gable
Loretta Young
Jack Oakie
D: William A. Wellman

Two miners prospect the Klondike with a dog
named Buck. From the Jack London novel.
Filmed at Mt. Baker, Washington.

Au ★★★
S ★★★◄
A ★★★★

Call of the Wild (La Selva Blanca) (1972) FF—W.Ger/Sp./Ital./Fr.

Charlton Heston
Michèle Mercier
Raimund Harmstorf
D: Ken Annakin

Remake of the Jack London classic.
Filmed in Norway.

Call of the Wild (1976) NBC-TV/CFP

John Beck
Bernard Fresson
John Mliam
D: Jerry Jameson

Remake of the Jack London classic.

Au ★★★★
S ★◄
A ★★◄

*—And the call that sounded in the
forest compelled him to turn his back
upon the comfort of the campfire.*
—Narrator
Call of the Wild (1976)

Call of the Wild (1993) CBS-TV

Rick Schroder
Gordon Tootoosie
Mia Sara
D: Alan Smithee

Remake of the Jack London classic.

Au ★★★★
S ★★★◀
A ★★★◀

Call of the Wild (1997) HHE

Rutger Hauer
Bronwên Booth
Charles Powell
Burke Lawrence
D: Peter Svatek

Remake of the Jack London classic.
Narrated by Richard Dreyfuss.

Au ★★★★★
S ★★★◀
A ★★★

Call of the Yukon (1938) Republic

Richard Arlen
Beverly Roberts
Lyle Talbot
Ray Mala
D: B. Reeves Eason

A trapper and a writer search for Yukon gold.
Based on James O. Curwood's, *Swift Lightning*.

Call to Glory (1965) NBC-TV/Columbia

Chuck Connors
Robert Lansing
David Brian
Kathy Browne
Noah Beery, Jr.
Lee Van Cleef

Edited from the "Branded" TV series.

Canaan's Way see Blind Justice

Camels West see Southwest Passage

Canadian Pacific (1949) 20ᵗʰ C. Fox

Randolph Scott
Jane Wyatt
J. Carrol Naish

Victor Jory
D: Edwin L. Marin

A surveyor encounters hostiles during the
construction of the Canadian Pacific Railroad.

The Canadians (1961) 20th C. Fox

Robert Ryan
John Dehner
Torin Thatcher
D: Burt Kennedy

A Mountie attempts to keep the
peace on the Canadian-U.S. border.
Kennedy's directorial debut.
Screenplay by Burt kennedy.
Filmed in Canada.

Canadian Wilderness (1969) FF—Sp./Ital.

George Martin
Diana Lorys
D: Armondo De Ossorio

Pioneers struggle against the Canadian wilds.

Cane's Cutthroats see Cain's Way

Cannon for Cordoba (1970) Mirisch

George Peppard
Giovanna Ralli
Raf Vallone
Peter Duel
D: Paul Wendkos

An Army officer must retrieve
cannons stolen by a bandido.

Canyon Pass see Raton Pass

Canyon Passage (1946) (reissued 1948) Universal

Dana Andrews
Susan Hayward
Brian Donlevy
Hoagy Camichael
Ward Bond
Andy Devine
Lloyd Bridges
Chief Yowlachie
D: Jacques Tourneur

A gambling banker and a freight
operator love the same woman.
Story by Ernest Haycox.

—*A man can choose his own gods,
Cornelius. What are your gods?*
—Dana Andrews
Canyon Passage

Filmed in Oregon.

Au

S ★★★

A ★★★

Canyon River (1956) AA

George Montgomery
Peter Graves
Marcia Henderson
Alan Hale (Jr.)
Jack Lambert
D: Harmon Jones

A rancher drives Herefords from Oregon to Wyoming in order to cross breed them to Texas Longhorns. Remake of *The Longhorns* (1951).

Au ★⟩

S ★★

A ★⟩

—Ya know, I still can't figure out why you all signed on as cowpunchers—forty dollars a month.

—Peter Graves
Canyon River

Captain Apache (1971) FF—Brit./Sp.

Lee Van Cleef
Carroll Baker
Stuart Whitman
D: Alexander Singer

Captain Apache tracks down the Indian commissioner's killer.

UNCHARTED TERRITORY

Captain Thunder (1930) WB⟩

Fay Wray
Victor Varconi
Charles Judels
Robert Elliott
D: Alan Crosland

When his fiancèe is forced to marry a rival, a gunman is helped by the bandido he is tracking.

Au ⟩

S ⟩

A ⟩

—No adios—hasta la vista!
—Fay Wray
Captain Thunder

Captive: The Longest Drive 2 see The Longest Drive 2

The Capture of Grizzly Adams (1981) NBC-TV ★⟩

Dan Haggerty
Kim Darby
Chuck Connors
Noah Berry, Jr.
Keenan Wynn

June Lockhart
D: Robert Michael Lewis

A mountainman leaves the hills to rescue his niece from an orphanage.
TV movie based on the series. Filmed in Utah.

Au

S

A

Carambola (1974) FF—Ital.

Paul Smith
Michael Coby
Horst Frank
D: Ferdinando Baldi

Two escaped convicts become gun runners.

The Caribou Trail (1950) 20th C. Fox

Randolph Scott
George Hayes
Bill Williams
Victor Jory
Jim Davis
Dale Robertson
D: Edwin L. Marin

A British Columbian prospector considers abandoning
his search for gold in favor of ranching.
Screenplay by Frank Gruber.

Carson City (1952) WB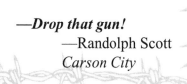

Randolph Scott
Lucille Norman
Raymond Massey
Pierce Lyden
D: Andrè de Toth

An engineeer attempts to build a railroad
from Carson City to Virginia City. Filmed
at Bell Ranch and Griffith Park, California.

Au

S

A

Caryl of the Mountains (1936) Rel./WS

Rin-Tin-Tin, Jr.
Francis X Bushman, Jr.
Lois Wild (Wilde)
D: Bernard B. Ray

A Mountie and his dog track an outlaw.
Based on a James O. Curwood story.

—*Drop that gun!*
—Randolph Scott
Carson City

Randolph Scott in *Carson City.*

Casey's Shadow (1978) Columbia

Walter Matthau
Alexis Smith
Robert Webber
Murray Hamilton
D: Martin Ritt

Cast a Long Shadow (1959) Mirisch/UA

Audie Murphy
Terry Moore
John Dehner
Rita Lynn
D: Thomas Carr

A drunken bastard develops self-respect when placed
in charge of a ranch. Filmed at Janns Ranch, California.

Audie Murphy and Rita Lynn in *Cast a Long Shadow.*

Catlow (1970) FF—ELP (MGM 1971) ★ ★

Yul Brynner
Richard Crenna
Leonard Nimroy
Jo Ann Pflung
D: Sam Wanamaker

A lawman must prevent a gold heist from occurring.
Based on the Louis L'Amour novel. Filmed in Spain.

Au ★★◀

S ★★★◀

A ★★★★◀

Cattle Annie and Little Britches

Bill Tilghman

Cattle Annie and Little Britches (1981) Universal ★ ★ ★

Scott Glenn
Redmond Gleesoni
William Russ
Ken Call
Burt Lancaster
Rod Steiger
D: Lamont Johnson

Two women go on the run with the Doolin-Dalton
gang. Filmed in Durango, Mexico.

Au ★★★◀

S ★★★◀

A ★★★◀

Cattle Drive (1951) U-I ★ ★★◀

Joel McCrea
Dean Stockwell
Chill Wills
Bob Steele

Bill Tilgham (Rod Steiger) and Bill Doolin (Burt Lancaster)

Harry Carey, Jr.
D: Kurt Neumann

When a spoiled kid is left in the desert by mistake, he must join a cattle drive. Filmed in Death Valley.

Au ★★◗

S ★★

A ★★

Cattle Empire (1958) 20th C. Fox ★ ★

Joel McCrea
Glorin Talbert
Don Haggerty
Phyllis Coates
D: Charles Marquis Warren

Upon his release from prison, a cattle boss hires hands from the town that convicted him. Filmed in the Alabama Hills.

Au ★★

S ★★

A ★★◗

—Ridin' with me means doin' your job.
—Joel McCrea
Cattle Empire

Cattle King (1963) MGM ★ ◖

Robert Taylor
Joan Caufield
Robert Loggia
William Windom
D: Tay Garnett

A wealthy rancher fights open grazing in Wyoming territory. Filmed in Kernville, CA

Au ★★

S ★

A ★

Cattle Queen (Queen of the West) (1951) ELC ◖

Maria Hart
Drake Smith
William Fawcett
Robert Gardette
D: Robert Tanscy

A rancher and her son receive help from paroled outlaws to protect their cattle.

Au ★

S ★

A ◗

—Whether prince or pauper, a man's only as good as the woman that stands behind him.
—Drake Smith
Cattle Queen

Cattle Queen of Montana (1954) RKO ★ ★ ◖

Barbara Stanwyck

Ronald Reagan
Gene Evans
D: Allan Dwan

A woman and an Army agent drive her father's cattle.
Story by Tom Blackburn. Filmed at the Iverson Ranch.

Au

S ★★★

A ★★★

Cattle Town (1952) WB ★★

Dennis Morgan
Philip Carey
Rita Moreno
Paul Picerni
Amanda Blake
Merv Griffin
D: Noel Smith

The governor of Texas sends a cowboy to make
peace between ranchers and a land baron.
Story by Tom Blackburn.

Au

S ★

A ★★

Caught (1931) Paramount

Richard Arlen
Frances Dee
Louise Dresser
D: Edward Sloman

An Army officer tracks Calamity Jane.

UNCHARTED TERRITORY

Cavalier of the West (1931) Artclass

Harry Carey
Carmen LaRoux
Kane Richmond
Paul Panzer
D: J.P. McCarthy

When town deputies turn against their sheriff,
an Army officer declares martial law.

UNCHARTED TERRITORY

Cavalry Charge (1964) FF—Sp.

Alan Scott
Frank Latimore
D: Ramon Torrado

Rare.

UNCHARTED TERRITORY

"Cavalry Officer in Campaign Dress."

Cavalry Scout (1951) Mono.

Rod Cameron
Audrey Long
Jim Davis
James Arness
Chief Yowlachie
D: Leslie Selander

A man prevents a gunrunner from
delivering Gatling guns to the Indians.
Story by Tom Blackburn.

Indians and scouts.

Cave of Outlaws (1951) U-I

Macdonald Carey
Alexis Smith
Edgar Buchanan
Hugh O'Brian
D: William Castle

An outlaw returns to the Carlsbad Caverns to retrieve his lost loot.

Cemetery Without Crosses (1968) FF—Ital./Fr.

Michèle Mercier
Robert Hossein
Sergio Leone
D: Robert Hossein

A gunfighter seeks revenge against a land baron.

Centennial (1978) NBC-TV/Universal ★ ★ ★

William Atherton and an all-star cast
D: Paul Krasney, Virgil W. Vogel, Harry Falk

Colorado pioneers and their heirs tame the frontier.
Twenty-six and a half hour mini-series
based on the James A. Michener novel.

Au ★ ★ ★ ⯪
S ★ ★ ★
A ★ ★ ★ ⯪

The Century Turns see Hec Ramsey: The Century Turns

The Challenge of Rin Tin Tin (1957) ABC-TV

Rin Tin Tin V
James Brown
Lee Aaker
D: Robert G. Walker

An orpaned boy and his dog are adopted as honorary troopers
by Fort Apache. Comprised of episodes of the TV series.

Challenge of the Mackennas (1969) FF—Ital./Sp.

Robert Woods
John Ireland
D: Leon Klimovsky

A drifter becomes entangled in a range war between ranchers.

Challenge to Be Free (Mad Trapper of the Yukon) (1976) PI

Mike Mazurki
Vic Christy
Jimmy Kane
D: Tay Garnett

A trapper is tracked through the Yukon for accidentally killing a trooper.

Champions of Justice (1956) WC

Clayton Moore
Jay Silverheels
Myron Healy
Dennis Moore
D: Earl Bellamy, Oscar Rudolph

Compilation of three episodes of "The Lone Ranger" TV series.

Little Bear, Cheyenne.

The Charge at Feather River (1953) WB ★★★◗

Guy Madison
Frank Lovejoy
Helen Wescott
Vera Miles
Neville Brand
D: Gordon Douglas

A troop of guardhouse cavalrymen rescue two captive women from Cheyenne Indians. Originally in 3-D. Filmed in Newhall and Vasquez Rocks, Agua Dulce, California.

Au ★★★◗
S ★★★★
A ★★★

—Better write this down, Johnson. This is the day the "Guardhouse Brigade" became an outfit.
—Guy Madison
The Charge at Feather River

Charge of the Seventh Cavalry (1964) FF—Ital./Sp./Fr.

Edmund Purdom
Paul Piaget
D: Herbert Martin (Alberto De Martino)

General Lee sends for Mexican army reinforcements.

Charlie One-Eye (1972) FF—Brit./Sp.

Richard Roundtree
Roy Thinnes
D: Don Chaffey

A Union deserter and a crippled
Indian defend their desert home.

Charro! (1969) NG

Elvis Presley
Ina Balin
Victor French
Barbara Werle
James Sikking
D: Charles Marquis Warren

A former outlaw is confronted by his old gang.
Filmed at Apacheland Movie Ranch, Apache Junction, AZ.

Au ★★

S ★★

A ★★

Chato's Land (1972) UA

Charles Bronson
Jack Palance
James Whitmore
Richard Basehart
D: Michael Winner

An Apache half-breed is hunted for shooting
the town sheriff. Filmed in Spain.

Au ★★★★

S ★★★

A ★★★★

Cheatin' Hearts see Paper Hearts

The Cherokee Kid (1996) HBO

Sinbad
James Coburn
Gregory Hines
Burt Reynolds
D: Paris Barclay

A farm boy avenges the murder of his family. Made for TV movie.

Cherokee Strip (1940) Paramount

Richard Dix
Florence Rice
Victor Jory
D: Leslie Selander

*—Just make a move! That's all I ask.
Just make a move!*

—Elvis
Charro!

Elvis in *Charro!*

*—Well, you don't see Apaches. You
don't hear 'em and you don't see
'em—like an act of God.*

—Jack Palance
Chato's Land

146

A town's new marshal fights its crooked banker and cronies.

Au

S

A

The Cherokee Trail (1981)

Cindy Pickett
Mary Larkin
Timothy Scott
Victor French
Buck Taylor
D: Keith Merrill

Made for TV movie.

UNCHARTED TERRITORY

Chetan, Indian Boy (1972) FF—Ger.

Marquard Bohm
Deschingis Bowakow
D: Mark Bohm

An old rancher and an Indian orphan take to one and other.

UNCHARTED TERRITORY

Cheyenne (The Wyoming Kid) (1947) Warner

Dennis Morgan
Bruce Bennett
Jane Wyman
Arthur Kennedy
Alan Hale
D: Raoul Walsh

An outlaw's wife falls for the man hired to kill him. Inspired the TV series. Based on a Paul I. Wellman story. Screenplay by Alan LeMay and T. Williamson. Filmed in Sedona, AZ.

Au

S

A

Jane Wyman and Dennis Morgan in *Cheyenne*.

Cheyenne (2002) BRI

Gary Hudson
Bobbie Phillips
Bo Svenson
(M.C.) Hammer
D: Dimitri Iogothetis

A bounty hunter falls for the woman he tracks. Filmed in 1996, but not released until 2002. Filmed in Moab, and Arches National Park, UT.

Au

—Woman, you got to be crazier than a dog humpin' on a rattlesnake!

—M.C. Hammer
Cheyenne

S ★✦

A ★

Cheyenne Autumn (1964) WB ★★★★

Jimmy Stewart
Richard Widmark
Carroll Baker
Ricardo Montalban
Karl Maulden
Sal Mineo
Gilbert Roland
Patrick Wayne
John Carradine
Ken Curtis
Edward G. Robinson
Harry Carey, Jr.
Ben Johnson
D: John Ford

Cheyenne Indians escape their Oklahoma reservation in order to return to Yellowstone. Ford's last epic Western. Based on a true story and on Willa Cather's novel, *Cheyenne Autumn*. Oscar nomination for cinematography. Filmed in Professor Valley, White's Ranch, Castle Valley, Colorado River, Fisher Canyon, Arches National Park, Monument Valley. #42 Best of the West.

Carroll Baker in *Cheyenne Autumn*.

Au ★★★★

S ★★★★

A ★★★★

—I'm a Pole…A Cossack is a man on a horse…Now, he kills Poles just because they're Poles, like we're tryin' to kill Indians just because they're Indians. I was proud to be an American soldier, but I ain't proud to be a Cossack!

—Mike Mazurki
Cheyenne Autumn

The Cheyenne Social Club (1970) NG ★★★

Jame Stewart
Henry Fonda
Shirley Jones
Sue Anne Langdon
Elaine Devry
D: Gene Kelly

An aging cowboy inherits his brother's Wyoming brothel. Filmed at the Eaves Movie Ranch, New Mexico.

Au ★★✦

S ★★★✦

A ★★★✦

—Yeah, thought I did once. [loved a woman] Come to find out it was indigestion.

—James Stewart
The Cheyenne Social Club

Cheyenne Warrior (1994) C-NHC ★★★★

Kelly Preston
Bo Hopkins
Dan Haggerty
Pato Hoffman

148

D: Mark Griffiths

A widow befriends an Indian who is wounded by the same
outlaws that murdered her husband. Made for TV movie.

Au  ★ ★ ★ ★ ✦

S ★ ★ ★ ★

A ★ ★ ★ ★

Chief Crazy Horse (Valley of Fury) (1955) U-I ✡ ✡ ✡

Victor Mature
Suzan Ball
John Lund
Dennis Weaver
D: George Sherman

Crazy Horse leads the Sioux. Filmed at Badlands National Park, SD.

Au ★ ★ ✦

S ★ ★ ★ ✦

A ★ ★ ★

Child Bride of Short Creek (1981) NBC-TV

Anthony Quinn
Dolores Del Rio
D: Hal Bartlett

UNCHARTED TERRITORY

Children of Sanchez (1978) CE

Anthony Quinn
Dolores Del Rio
D: Hal Bartlett

UNCHARTED TERRITORY

Children of the Dust (1995) CBS-TV ✡ ✡ ✡ ✦

Sidney Poitier
Michael Moriarty
Farrah Fawcett
D: David Greene

Saga of a black gunfighter. Filmed in Alberta, Canada.

Au ★ ★ ★ ★

S ★ ★ ★

A ★ ★ ★ ✦

China 9, Liberty 37 (1978) FF—Ital./Sp. ✡ ✡ ✡

Fabio Testi
Warren Oates
Jenny Agutter
Sam Peckinpah
Gianrico Tondinelli
D: Monte Hellman

A farmer's wife falls for a gunfighter
hired by the railroad to kill her husband.

Au ★★★
S ★★★
A ★★★◣

Chino (1973) FF—Ital./Sp./Fr. ★★★◣

Charles Bronson
Jill Ireland
Marcel Bozzuffi
Vincent Van Patten
D: John Sturges

A horse rancher becomes entangled in a dispute
over range land and the sister of a land baron.
Screenplay by Clair Huffaker and Dino Maiuri.

Au ★★★★
S ★★★★◣
A ★★★★◣

The Chisholms (1979) CBS-TV/ALP

Robert Preston
Rosemary Harris
Ben Murphy
D: Mel Stuart

A pioneer family treks from Virginia to Fort Laramie,
Wyoming. Four-part mini-series. Pilot for the series.

Chisum (1970) WB ★★★◣

John Wayne
Forrest Tucker
Christopher George
Ben Johnson
John Agar
John Mitchum
D: Andrew V. McLaglen

John Chisum builds a Texas cattle empire in the
summer of 1869. Filmed at the Eaves Movie Ranch, NM.

Au ★★◣
S ★★★★◣
A ★★★★◣

The Christmas Kid (1966) FF—Sp./Ital.

Jeffery Hunter
Louis Hayward
D: Sidney Pink

A gunfighter turned sheriff brings law and
order to an Arizona mining town.

John Chisum

> *—Well, what a man says and what a man does doesn't always end up to be the same thing.*
> —Charles Bronson
> *Chino*

John Wayne as Chisum.

> *—There's no law west of Dodge and no God west of the Pecos.*
> —Ben Johnson
> *Chisum*

Christmas Mountain (1980) Gold C.

Slim Pickens
Mark Miller
Barbara Stranger
Tina Minard
D: Pierre De Moro

An aging cowboy discovers the true meaning of Christmas when sheltering from a blizzard with a widow and her children.

Chrysanthemums for a Bunch of Swine (1968) FF—Ital.

Edmund Purdom
John Manera
D: Sergio Pastore

A sharpshooting monk rescues a kidnapped bride-to-be.

Chuck Moll (1970) FF—Ital.

Leonard Mann
Woody Strode
D: E.B. Clucher (Enzo Barboni)

A gunman unknowingly pursues his father.

Chuka (1967) Paramount

Rod Taylor
Ernest Borgnine
John Mills
Luciana Paluzi
James Whitmore
D: Gordon Douglas

A gunfighter warns an Army outpost about an impending Apache raid.

Au
S
A

Cimarron (1931) RKO-Radio ★★★

Richard Dix
Irene Dunne
Estelle Taylor
D: Wesley Ruggles

Homesteaders join the 1889 Oklahoma land rush and remain to build an empire. Nomination for best direction. Oscars for best picture, screenplay, art direction, and interior decoration.
Filmed at Jasmin Quinn Ranch, Bakersfield, CA.

Au

Richard Dix and Irene Dunne in *Cimarron*.

S ★★★⯪

A ★⯪

Cimarron (1960) MGM ★★★

Glenn Ford
Maria Schell
Anne Baxter
Arthur O'Connell
Vic Morrow
Edgar Buchanan
Henry Morgan
D: Anthony Mann

Remake of the 1931 version. From the Edna Ferber novel. Oscar nominations for art direction-set direction: color and sound. Filmed at Old Tucson.

Au ★★⯪

S ★★★★⯪

A ★★★★⯪

The Cimarron Kid (1952) U-I ★★

Audie Murphy
Yvette Dugay
Beverly Tyler
Noah Berry, Jr.
Hugh O'Brian
D: Bud Boetticher

Upon his parol from prison, Bill Doolin meets up with the Dalton gang. Filmed in Sonora, CA.

Au ★

S ★★★⯪

A ★★★⯪

Cisco (The Cisco Kid) (1966) FF—Ital.

William Berger
George Wang
D: Sergio Bergonzelli

A deputy and Mexican bandits plot to rob the town's bank.

The Cisco Kid (1994) TNT ★★⯪

Jimmy Smits
Cheech Marin
Bruce Payne
Sadie Frost
D: Luis Valdez

A Mexican adventurer and his sidekick defend Mexico from French imperialists. Lighthearted story based on the characters created by O'Henry.

—After all, what's the use of any of us bein' here if we're not chasin' some sort of a dream of some kind?
—Glenn Ford
Cimarron

—How many mistakes can a man make'n still hope to get away with it?
—Audie Murphy
The Cimarron Kid

Audie Murphy in *The Cimarron Kid.*

—Viva Benito Juarez!
—Cheech Marin
The Cisco Kid (1994)

Filmed in Mexico.

Au ★★★✦

S ★★

A ★★✦

The Cisco Kid and the Lady (1940) 20ᵗʰ C. Fox

Cesar Romero
Marjorie Weaver
Chris-Pin Martin
D: Herbert I. Leeds

The Cisco Kid confronts a claim jumper.
Filmed in the Alabama Hills.

UNCHARTED
TERRITORY

City of Badmen (1953) 20ᵗʰ C. Fox ✦ ✦

Jeanne Crain
Dale Robertson
Richard Boone
Lloyd Bridges
D: Harmon Jones

Carson City outlaws plan to steal the gate receipts
of the James Corbett vs. Bob Fitzsimmons title fight.
Filmed at Vasquez Rocks, Santa Clarita, California.

Au ★★

S ★★

A ★★

*—You'd hold onto a rattlesnake,
if it'd do you any good.*
—Dale Robertson
City of Badmen

Cjamango (1967) FF—Ital.

Sean Todd (Livio Lorenzon)
Mickey Haritay
D: Edward G. Muller (Edoardo Mulargia)

A bandit steals a gold treasure.

UNCHARTED
TERRITORY

The Claim (2000) UA/Pathe P./BBCF ✦ ✦ ✦

Wes Bentley
Milla Jovovich
Nastassja Kinski
Peter Mullen
Sarah Polley
D: Michael Winterbottom

Upon the death of his wife and his town, a wealthy
miner confronts his past. Inspired by Thomas Hardy's,
The Mayor of Casterbridge. Filmed in Alberta, Canada
and the Durango-Silverton Railway, Colorado.

Au ★★★★★

S ★★

A ★★★★

Milla Jovovich in *The Claim*.

*—A man loses heart. Even if he makes
a strike, he loses heart.*
—Tom McCamus
The Claim

Claws (1977) AP

Myron Healey
Leon Ames
Jason Evers
D: Richard Bansbach, R.E. Pierson

Hunters track a killer grizzly.

Clint the Stranger (1968) FF—Ital./Sp./Ger.

George Martin
Marianne Koch
D: Alfonso Balcazar

A rancher returns home from prison
only to find his family has disappeared.

Coffin for a Stranger (1965) FF—Ital./Sp.

Anthony Steffen
Eduardo Fajardo
D: Williams Hawkins (Mario Caiano)

A town's sheriff and most respectable businessman face off.

Cole Younger, Gunfighter (1958) AA

Frank Lovejoy
James Best
Abby Dalton
John Mitchum
D: R.G. Springsteen

Cole Younger rescues his friend by holding up a courtroom.
Filmed at the Iverson Movie Location Ranch.

Au ★

S ★◗

A ★◗

—Well your Honor, I'm only going to stay long enough to get on my horse.
—Frank Lovejoy
Cole Younger, Gunfighter

Colorado Charlie (1965) FF—Ital./Sp.

Jack Berthier
Charlie Lawrence
D: Robert Johnson (Roberto Mauri)

A retired sheriff returns to protect the town from a bandit and his gang.

Colorado Territory (1949) WB

Joel McCrea
Virginia Mayo
Dorothy Malone
James Mitchell
D: Raoul Walsh

An outlaw plans one final job before retirement.

Adapted from W.R. Burnett's novel, *High Sierra*.

Colt Concert see Massacre Time

Colt .45 (Thundercloud) (1950) WB ★★★

Randolph Scott
Zachary Scott
Ruth Roman
Lloyd Bridges
Alan Hale
Chief Thunder Cloud
D: Edwin L. Marin

Bank robbers steal two prized revolvers.
Based on a Tom Blackburn story.
Filmed at Vasquez Rocks, California.

Au ★★★
S ★★★
A ★★★

Colt 45, Five Dollars, and a Bandit (1967) FF—Ital.

William Cliff
D: Richard Chardon

Rare.

Colt in the Hand of the Devil (1967) FF—Ital.

Bob Henry
Marisa Solinas
D: Sergio Bergonzelli

Mexican bandits enslave a work force for their Mojave sulphur mine.

Colt in the Hand of the Devil (1972) FF—Ital.

Robert Woods
William Berger
D: Frank G. Carrol (Gianfranco Baldanello)

A Texas Ranger tracks down outlaws.

Colt Is the Law (1965) FF—Ital./Sp.

Anthony Clark
Lucy Gilly
D: Al Bradly

Two undercover lawmen investigate missing railroad funds.

Column South (1953) U-I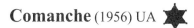

Audie Murphy
Joan Evans
Robert Sterling
Dennis Weaver
Jack Kelly
D: Frederick de Cordova

A cavalry officer defends Navajos despite
the inexperience of his commander.
Filmed in Apple Valley, California.

Au

S

A

Comanche (1956) UA

Dana Andrews
Kent Smith
Nestor Paiva
D: George Sherman

A scout makes peace with the Comanches. Filmed in Durango, Mexico.

Au

S

A

Audie Murphy and Joan Evans in *Column South.*

Comanche Crossing (1968)

Caruth C. Byrd
Cynthia Hull
Tony Huston
D: Larry Buchanan

—I always figured to die. Question is, when.
—John Wayne
The Comancheros

The Comancheros (1961) 20th C. Fox

John Wayne
Stuart Whitman
Ina Balin
Nehemiah Persoff
Lee Marvin
Michael Ansara
Patrick Wayne
Jack Elam
Edgar Buchanan
D: Michael Curtiz

A Texas Ranger pursues gun runners.
Based on Paul Wellman's, *The Comancheros.*
Screenplay by Clair Huffaker. Filmed in Professor
Valley, Dead Horse Point St. Park, King's Bottom,
La Sal Mountains, Fisher Valley and Onion Creek, UT.

Au

S

A

John Wayne, Ina Balin and Stuart Whitman in *The Comancheros.*

Comanche Station (1960) Columbia

Randolph Scott
Nancy Gates
Claude Akins
Skip Homeier
D: Budd Boetticher

A gunman escorts home a woman kidnapped by Indians.
Screenplay by Burt Kennedy. Filmed in the Alabama Hills.

Comanche Territory (1950) U-I ★ ★ ★

Maureen O'Hara
Macdonald Carey
Will Geer
Iron Eyes Cody
D: George Sherman

Jim Bowie attempts to preserve a treaty with the Indians.
Filmed in Sedona, AZ.

Au ★ ◄
S ★ ★ ★ ◄
A ★ ★ ★ ◄

—You call me a lady once more and I'll fill you full of lead!

—Maureen O'Hara
Comanche Territory

Come and Get It (1935) UA

Edward Arnold
Joel McCrea
Frances Farmer
Walter Brennan
D: Howard Hawks, William Wyler

The Comeback Trail (1982) Rearguard Prod.

Buster Crabbe
Chuck McCann
Robert Staats
Ina Balin
Hugh Hefner
D: Harry Hurwitz

Curly, Crow scout, 1883.

Comin' at Ya (1981) FF—Ital.

Tony Anthony
Victoria Abril
Gene Quintano
D: Ferdinando Baldi

An outlaw searches for his kidnapped wife.
Filmed in 3-D.

—Get 'em ready! Get plenty of ammunition!

—Guy Madison
The Command

The Command (1953) WB

Guy Madison

Joan Weldon
James Whitmore
Iron Eyes Cody
D: David Butler

A doctor finds himself in command of escorting a wagon train through hostile country. Filmed at Warner Ranch, Calabasas, CA.

Au ★

S ★★

A ★★★◄

Compañeros (1970) FF—Ital./Sp./Ger.

Franco Nero
Tomas Milian
Jack Palance
Fernando Rey
D: Sergio Corbucci

Sequel to *A Professional Gun*.

UNCHARTED
TERRITORY

Conagher (1991) THE ★ ★ ★ ◄

Sam Elliott
Katherine Ross
Barry Corbin
D: Reynaldo Villalobos

A cowboy falls for a widow and her children. Story by Louie L'Amour. Filmed at Canon City, CO.

Au ★★★★

S ★★★◄

A ★★★◄

El Condor (1970) NG ★ ★

Jim Brown
Lee Van Cleef
Patrick O'Neal
Mariana Hill
Iron Eyes Cody
D: John Gullermin

Two adventurers raid a Mexican fort full of gold.

Au ★★

S ★★

A ★◄

The Conquering Horde (1931) Paramount

Richard Arlen
Fay Wray
George Mendoza
Chief Standing Bear
D: Edward Sloman

A Civil War veteran returns to confront carpetbaggers

—You don't know music until you hear the wind in the cedars.

—Katherine Ross
Conagher

Sam Elliott and Katherine Ross.

—Yeah, I'm a bastard too…Yeah, ain't it great? Most of the best people are.

—Lee Van Cleef
El Condor

158

in Texas. Story by Emerson Hough.

The Conquerors (1932) RKO Radio ◗

Richard Dix
Ann Harding
Edna May Oliver
Guy Kibbee
Jason Robards
D: William A. Wellman

Newlyweds begin to build a banking empire in 1870s Nebraska.

Au ◗

S ◗

A ◗

Conquest of Cochise (1953) Columbia ★ ◗

John Hodiak
Robert Stack
Joy Page
Rico Alaniz
D: William Castle

Following the Gadsen Purchase, a cavalry officer joins Cochise against Comanches. Filmed at Vasquez Rocks, California.

Au ★ ★

S ★

A ★ ◗

—*Indians are vindictive if they think they're right. They can be cruel. They have torches! They hang a man to a tree by the skin of his stomach! Cut patterns with knives! Mutilate beyond recognition!*
—Robert Stack
Conquest of Cochise

Convict Stage (1965) 20th C. Fox

Harry Lauter
Donald (Red) Barry
Jodi Mitchell
D: Lesley Selander

Copper Canyon (1950) Paramount ★ ★ ◗

Ray Milland
Hedy Lamarr
Macdonald Carey
Harry Carey, Jr.
D: John Farrrow

A fugitive rebel helps miners with their gold shipments. Filmed in Sedona, AZ.

Au ★ ★ ★

S ★ ★ ◗

A ★ ★ ★ ◗

Hedy Lamarr in *Copper Canyon.*

Copper Sky (1957) RF/20ᵗʰ C. Fox

Jeff Morrow
Coleen Gray
Paul Brinegar
Strother Martin
D: Charles Marquis Warren

When an outlaw and a school teacher survive an Indian massacre, they must escape through hostile territory. Filmed at Johnson Canyon, Kanab, Utah.

Au ⭐

S 🎖

A 🎖

Coroner Creek (1948) Columbia ⭐ ⭐

Randolph Scott
Marguerite Chapman
George Macready
Sally Eilers
Edgar Buchanan
Forrest Tucker
D: Ray Enright

When a gunman's fiancè kills herself during an Indian raid, he sets out to avenge her death. Based on the Luke Short novel. Filmed in Sedona, AZ.

Au ⭐⭐🎖

S ⭐⭐

A ⭐⭐

—I've waited eighteen months for this!
—Randolph Scott
Coroner Creek

Randolph Scott and Sally Eilers in *Coroner Creek*.

Cost of Dying (1968) FF—Ital./Fr.

Andrea Giordana
John Ireland
D: Sergio Merolle

Rustlers take refuge in a Colorado town.

UNCHARTED TERRITORY

The Country Beyond (1936) Fox

Paul Kelly
Rochelle Hudson
Robert Kent
Alan Hale
D: Eugene Ford

A girl and her dog help Mounties capture a murderer. Based on a James O. Curwood story.

UNCHARTED TERRITORY

Count the Clues (1956) WC

Clayton Moore
Jay Silverheels
Rand Brooks
Claire Carleton
Slim Pickens
D: Earl Bellamy, Oscar Rudolph

Compilation of three episodes of "The Lone Ranger" TV series.

Count Three and Pray (1955) Columbia

Van Heflin
Joanne Woodward
Phil Carey
Raymond Burr
D: George Sherman

Following the Civil War, a man with a past becomes the preacher in a frontier town. Woodward's screen debut.

Au

S

A

"Indian Scouts Watching Custer's Advance."

The Courage of Kavil, The Wolf Dog (1980) NBC-TV

John Ireland
Ronny Cox
Linda Sorenson
D: Peter Carter

Taken from his family, a sled dog makes the 2000 mile journey home.

The Court-Martial of George Armstrong Custer (1977) NBC-TV/NRP/WB

James Olson
Blythe Danner
D: Glenn Jordon

Fictionalized account of what might have occurred had Custer survived the Little Big Horn. Made for TV movie.

Cowards Don't Pray (1968) FF—Ital./Sp.

John Garko
Sean Todd
D: Marlon Sirko (Marcio Siciliano)

Three old friends meet again, but on opposite sides of the law.

Cowboy (1958) Columbia

Glenn Ford
Jack Lemmon
Anna Kashfi
Brian Donlevy
Dick York
D: Delmer Daves

A greenhorn hotel clerk joins up with a cattle drive to Mexico. Oscar nomination for film editing. Filmed at Bonanza Creek Ranch, New Mexico.

Cowboy.

Au

S ★★★★

A ★★★★

The Cowboys (1972) WB ★★★★

John Wayne
Roscoe Lee Browne
Bruce Dern
A. Martinez
Alfred Barker, Jr.
Nicolas Beauvy
Slim Pickens
Dick Farnsworth
D: Mark Rydell

When a gold strike creates a shortage of trail hands, a rancher resorts to hiring boys for his cattle drive. Based on William D. Jennings', *The Cowboys*. Filmed in San Juan Valley, Pegosa Springs, Colorado. #54 Best of the West, #50 IMDb.

John Wayne and Sean Kelley in *The Cowboys.*

—Every man wants his children to be better than he was. You are.

—John Wayne
The Cowboys

Au

S ★★★★

A ★★★★

Cow Country (1953) AA ★

Edmond O'Brien
Helen Wescott
Bob Lowry
D: Lesley Selander

A Texas cowboy saves indebted cattlemen. Filmed at the Iverson Movie Location Ranch.

Au

S ★

A ★

Coyote (1964) FF—Sp./Ital.

Abel Salazar
Gloria Marin
D: Joaquin L. Marchent (Joaquin Romero Hernandez)

A gunfighter turns freedom fighter.

Crazy Horse (1996) TNT ★★★★

Michael Greyeyes
Irene Bedard
Lorne Cardinal
Ned Beatty
Peter Horton
D: John Irvin

Crazy Horse defends his people's way of life. Filmed in the Black Hills, South Dakota.

—It's a good day to fight! It's a good day to die! Bravehearts, stronghearts to the front!

—Michael Greyeyes
Crazy Horse

#77 Best of the West.

Au ★★★★★

S ★★★⯪

A ★★★★

A Criminal Story of the Far West see Sonny and Jed

Cripple Creek (1952) Resolute/Columbia ✪

George Montgomery
Karin Booth
Jerome Courtland
D: Ray Nazarro

A gold smuggling operation is infiltrated by federal agents.
Filmed at the Iverson Movie Location Ranch.

Au ★⯪

S ★⯪

A ★⯪

Crossfire Trail (Louie L'Amours's Crossfire Trail) (2001) TNT ★★★⯪

Tom Selleck
Virginia Madsen
Wilford Brimley
Ken Pogue
Mark Harmon
D: Simon Wincer

A drifter fulfills his promise to a dying friend
in 1880 Wyoming. Filmed in Alberta, Canada.

Au ★★★★⯪

S ★★⯪

A ★★★★

Tom Selleck in *Crossfire Trail.*

Cry Blood, Apache (1970) G.Eag.

Jody McCrea
Dan Kemp
Jack Starrett
Don Henley
Joel McCrea
D: Jack Starrett

Prospectors murder a band of Apaches in order
to discover the location of a gold mine.

Cry for Me Billy see Face to the Wind

Cry for Revenge (1968) FF—Ital./Sp.

Mark Damon
Anthony Steffen
D: Rafael Romero Marchent

*—He's tougher than the back wall
of a shootin' gallery…*
—Wilford Brimley
Crossfire Trail

Two bounty hunters help a widow avenge her husband's murder.

A Cry in the Wilderness (1974) ABC-TV

George Kennedy
Joanna Pettet
Lee H. Montgomery
D: Gordon Hessler

When a farmer is bitten by a rabid skunk and chains himself to his barn, a flood approaches.

The Cry of the Black Wolves (1972) FF—Ger.

Ron Ely
Raimund Harmsdorf
D: Harold Reini

Based on Jack London's, *The Son of the Wolf.*

Cry to the Wind (1979) Sebastian Int.

Sheldon Woods
Cameron Garnick
D: Robert W. Davison

A young man survives in the wilderness.

La Cucaracha see The Soldiers of Pancho Villa

Cuchillo (1978) FF—Mex.

Andrés Garcia
Monica Prado
Armando Silvestre
D: Rodolfo de Anda

An Apache defends his land from the cavalry.

The Culpepper Cattle Company (1972) 20th C. Fox ★★★★⯪

Gary Grimes
Billy "Green" Bush
Luke Askew
Bo Hopkins
Geoffrey Lewis
D: Dick Richards

A young boy works a cattle drive to Ft. Lewis, Colorado.

—Nobody calls me a son-of-a-bitch, nobody!
—Geoffrey Lewis
The Culpepper Cattle Company

Filmed at Eaves Movie Ranch, NM. #26 Best of the West.

Au

S ★★★★

A ★★★★◗

Custer of the West (A Good Day for Fighting) (1968) FF—CRC/Sp. ★★◗

Robert Shaw
Mary Ure
Jeffrey Hunter
Robert Ryan
D: Robert Siodmak

General Custer leads the 7th Cavalry to infamy. Filmed in Spain.

Au ★◗

S ★◗

A ★◗

—*...I'm not the best of all men—I'm a soldier.*
—Robert Shaw (Custer)
Custer of the West

Custer's Last Stand (1936) S&S

Rex Lease
Jack Mulhall
Ruth Mix
D: Elmer Clifton

A Custer scout protects settlers from Indians. Feature version of the 15 chapter serial.

Cutter's Trail (1970) CBS-TV

John Gavin
Manual Padilla, Jr.
Marisa Pavin
D: Vincent McEveety

The Santa Fe marshal returns to find the town raided by outlaws.

7th Cavalrymen.

Cut-Throats Nine (1973) FF—Sp./Ital.

Robert Hundar
Emma Cohen
D: Joaquin Romero Marchent

A Union Army escort of criminals over the Rockies becomes a survival ordeal.

Robert Shaw in *Custer of the West.*

George Armstrong Custer

**The Faces
of
Custer**

Richard Mulligan in *Little Big Man.*

Errol Flynn in *They Died With Their Boots On.*

Dakota (1945) Republic

John Wayne
Vera Ralston
Walter Brennan
Ward Bond
Yakima Canutt
D: Joseph Kane

A young couple discover a land grabbing scheme.

Au ★★

S ★★

A ★★★

Dakota Incident (1956) Republic

Linda Darnell
Dale Robertson
John Lund
Ward Bond
Skip Homeier
D: Lewis R. Foster

Stagecoach passengers are trapped in a drywash by hostiles. Filmed at Red Rock Canyon, Cantil, California.

Au ★★◖

S ★★★

A ★★★

Dakota Lil (1950) 20ᵗʰ C. Fox

George Montgomery
Marie Windsor
Rod Cameron
D: Leslie Selander

A saloon dancer falls for an undercover agent investigating counterfeiters. Screenplay by M. Selander and Frank Gruber.

UNCHARTED
TERRITORY

Dallas (1950) WB

Gary Cooper
Ruth Roman
Steve Cochran
Raymond Massey
D: Stuart Heisler

A Confederate renegade brings law and order to post-Civil War Dallas. Filmed at Warner Ranch, CA.

Au ★★★

S ★★★

A ★★★★

Dallas (1972) FF—Sp./Ital.

Anthony Steffen
Frank Baña

John Wayne and Vera Ralston in *Dakota*.

—You're nothin' but a no good woman, that's all. And when a woman two-times a man, there's only one thing to do. And that's—put on the pressure!
—Walter Brennan
Dakota

—Forget about me, I'm a wanted criminal.
—Gary Cooper
Dallas

D: Juan Bosch

A gunfighter attempts to retire in Dallas.

The Dalton Girls (1957) Bel-Air/UA

Merry Anders
Lisa Davis
Penny Edwards
John Russell
D: Reginald Le Borg

Four girls turn outlaw when their father is killed.

Gratton Dalton

Bob Dalton

The Coffeyville Fiasco

Emmett Dalton served
fifteen years.

Bob and Gratton Dalton dying or dead.

168

The Daltons Ride Again (1945) Universal

Alan Curtis
Kent Taylor
Lon Chaney
Noah Berry, Jr.
D: Ray Taylor

The famous outlaws attempt to go straight.
Filmed at the Iverson Movie Location Ranch.

Au

S

A

> —...the country is everything I dreamed it would be. There can be no place like this on earth.
> —Kevin Costner
> *Dances With Wolves*

The Dalton's Women (1950) Western Adventure/Howco

Lash LaRue
Al St. John
Jack Holt
D: Thomas Carr

Lawmen hunt an outlaw gang terrorizing a small town.

The Dalton That Got Away (1960) DFC

Michael Connors
Elsie Cardenas (Elsa Cardenas)
Carlos Rivas
D: Jimmy Salvador

Dalva (1996)

Carroll Baker
Powers Boothe
Farrah Fawcett
Rod Steiger
D: Ken Cameron

Made for TV movie.

Damned Pistols of Dallas (1964) FF—Sp./Ital./Fr.

Fred Bier
Evi Marandi
D: Joseph Trader (Josè Maria Zabalza)

The Dallas sheriff organizes the townspeople
to defend themselves against the Mexican army.

Dan Candy's Law see Alien Thunder

Dances With Wolves (1990) G/TP ★★★★★

Kevin Costner
Mary McDonnell
Graham Greene
Rodney A. Grant
Floyd Red Crow
Wes Studi
D: Kevin Costner

A soldier in Dakota Territory becomes a member of the Sioux. Oscar nominations for best actor (Costner), supporting actor (Greene), supporting actress (McDonnell), art direction-set decoration, costume design, and film editing, Oscars for best picture, director, writing: based on material from another medium, cinematography, sound, and scoring: original music. Filmed at Badlands National Park, Belle Fourche River, Spearfish Canyon in the Black Hills, South Dakota. #2 Best of the West, #75 AFI GM, #24 IMDb, #7 LPFF.

Kevin Costner holding Mary McDonnell in *Dances With Wolves.*

Au ★★★★✦
S ★★★★★
A ★★★★★

The Dangerous Days of Kiowa Jones (1966) ABC-TV/MGM

Robert Horton
Diane Baker
Sal Mineo
D: Alex March

A dying lawman asks a man to transport two outlaws to jail. Unsuccessful pilot.

Dark Command (1940) Republic ★★★✦

Claire Trevor
John Wayne
Walter Pidgeon
Roy Rogers
George "Gabby" Hayes
D: Raoul Walsh

A Texas cowboy turned lawman protects a Kansas town from Confederate raiders. Based on W.R. Burnett's, *The Dark Command.* Oscar nominations for art direction: B&W and original score. Filmed at Pacerita Ranch, Newhall, CA.

Roy Rogers, John Wayne and Gabby Hayes in *Dark Command.*

Au ★★★✦
S ★★★✦
A ★★★✦

Daughter of the West (1949) Film Classics

Martha Vickers
Philip Reed
Donald Woods
D: Harold Daniels

A Navajo Indian and a woman discover a

—Ever hear what William Shakespeare said? All's well that ends well.
—Roy Rogers
Dark Command

170

scheme to steal mineral rights from Indians.

The Daughters of Joshua Cabe (1972) ABC-TV/SGP

Buddy Ebsen
Karen Valentine
Lesley (Ann) Warren
Sandra Dee
Jack Elam
D: Philip Leacock

In order to meet homestead law, a trapper recruits three "daughters." First pilot for the series.

The Daughters of Joshua Cabe Return (1975) ABC-TV/SGP

Dan Daily
Dub Taylor
Ronne Troup
Arthur Hunnicutt
D: David Lowell Rich

An old rancher hires three shady ladies as his daughters. Made for TV sequel to *The Daughters of Joshua Cabe.* Second pilot for the series.

Jim Baker, trapper and guide.

Davy Crockett and the River Pirates (1956) BV ★ ★ ◖

Fess Parker
Buddy Ebsen
Jeff York
D: Norman Foster

Davy Crockett competes with Mike Fink in a riverboat race. Lighthearted Disney adventure.

Au ★ ★ ◖

S ★ ★ ★

A ★ ★ ◖

> —*Well, you're better than a king, Mike [Fink]. You're a first class friend. In fact, you're the finest fightin' man I know.*
> —Fess Parker
> *Davy Crockett and the River Pirates*

Davy Crockett, Indian Scout (Indian Scout) (1950) UA ★ ◖

George Montgomery
Ellen Drew
Philip Reed
Noah Berry, Jr.
Chief Thunder Cloud
John Hamiton
D: Lew Landers

Davy Crockett's nephew protects a wagon train. Filmed in part in Monument Valley.

Au ★ ◖

S ★ ◖

A ★ ★

Davy Crockett, King of the Wild Frontier (1955) BV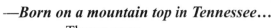

Fess Parker
Buddy Ebsen
Basil Ruysdael
Hans Conried
D: Norman Foster

Davy Crockett becomes a frontier legend.
Compilation of three Disney TV episodes.
Screenplay by Tom Blackburn. Filmed at
Great Smoky Mts. National Park, TN, Janss
Conejo Ranch, Thousand Oaks, California.

Au ★★
S ★★★★
A ★★★◗

♪
—Born on a mountain top in Tennessee…
—Theme song
Davy Crockett, King of the Wild Frontier

Davy Crockett: Rainbow in the Thunder (1988) GCP/Disney

Tim Dunigan
Johnny Cash
Cheryl L. Arutt
Samantha Eggar
D: David Hemmings

Made for TV movie.

Dawn at Socorro (1954) Columbia ★★◗

Rory Calhoun
Piper Laurie
David Brian
Edgar Buchanan
Skip Homeier
Lee Van Cleef
D: George Sherman

A retired gunfighter and a saloon owner play a high stakes card game.
Filmed in Victorville, California.

Au ★★★
S ★★◗
A ★★★

Dawn on the Great Divide (1942) Mono.

Buck Jones
Raymond Hatton
Mona Barrie
D: Howard Bretherton

Three friends lead a wagon train full of munitions for the railroad.
Based on a James O. Curwood's "Wheels of Fate."

Day of Anger (1967) FF—Ital./Ger.

Lee Van Cleef
Giuliano Gemma
D: Tonino Valerii

172

A gunfighter and his pupil face off.

UNCHARTED TERRITORY

A Day of Fury (1956) U-I ★★

Dale Robertson
Mara Corday
Jock Mahoney
D: Harmon Jones

A lawman is reluctant to arrest an
outlaw to whom he owes his life.

Au ★★

S ★★

A ★★

*—I turned over a rotten log. I didn't create
what came crawling out from under it.*
—Dale Robertson
A Day of Fury

Day of the Badman (1958) U-I ★★★

Fred MacMurray
Joan Weldon
John Ericson
Edgar Buchanan
Lee Van Cleef
D: Harry Keller

A judge stands between four outlaws and
a condemned killer they wish to free.
Story by John M. Cunningham.

Au ★★★

S ★★★

A ★★★

Badman George "Big Nose" Parrott.
Lynched and reportedly partially skinned to
make a bag and pair of shoes.

Day of the Evil Gun (1968) MGM ★★★

Glenn Ford
Arthur Kennedy
Dean Jagger
John Anderson
D: Jerry Thorpe

A gunfighter helps a neighbor search
for his family kidnapped by Apaches.
Filmed in Durango, Mexico.

Au ★★

S ★★★

A ★★★

*—Ther's more to marriage than signing a
piece of paper.*
—Glenn Ford
Day of the Evil Gun

The Day of the Outlaw (1959) UA ★★★★

Robert Ryan
Burl Ives
Tina Louise
David Nelson
D: Andrè de Toth

Outlaws terrorize a small town.

Au
S
A

Days of Heaven (1978) Paramount

Richard Gere
Brooke Adams
Sam Sheppard
Linda Manz
D: Terrence Malick

Days of Violence (1967) FF—Ital.

Peter Lee Lawrence
Rosalba Neri
D: Al Bradly (Alfonso Brescia)

Confederate rebels rob stagecoaches in Missouri.

The Day They Hanged Kid Curry see Alias Smith and Jones

Dead Are Countless (1969) FF—Ital./Sp.

Anthony Steffen
Peter Lee Lawrence
D: Rafael Romero Marchent

A serial killer stalks Army officers.

Dead for a Dollar (1968) FF—Ital.

George Hilton
John Ireland
D: Osvaldo Civirani

Three outlaws rob a bank.

Deadlock (1970) FF—Ger.

Mario Adorf
Anthony Dawson
Marquard Bohm
D: Roland Klick

Two outlaws meet in a deserted mining town to divide their loot.

The Deadly Companions (1961) P-A

Maureen O'Hara
Brian Keith
Steve Cochran
Chill Wills
Strother Martin
D: Sam Peckinpah

174

A woman sets out to bury her son in a ghost town in Apache territory. Filmed at Old Tucson.

Deadly Peacemaker see Man With a Gun

Deadly Trackers (1972) FF—Ital.

Richard Harrison
Anita Ekberg
D: Amergo Anton (Tanio Boccia)

A wagon train is guided through Wyoming.

The Deadly Trackers (1973) WB ★★★★

Richard Harris
Rod Taylor
Al Lettieri
Neville Brand
D: Barry Shear

A small town sheriff avenges the murder of his wife and child. Filmed in Mexico. #63 Best of the West.

Au ★★★★
S ★★★★
A ★★★★

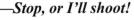

—Stop, or I'll shoot!
—Al Lettieri
The Deadly Trackers

Dead Man (1996) T-GP ★★★★

Johnny Depp
Gary Farmer
Lance Henriksen
Michael Wincott
John Hurt
Robert Mitchum
Gabriel Byrne
Alfred Molina
Iggy Pop
D: Jim Jarmusch

A greenhorn accountant goes west and finds himself on the run with a mystical Indian. Music by Neil Young. The most bizarre Western I've ever seen. Filmed at Sedona, Grants Pass, OR, California, Virginia City, NV, and New York. #35 IMDb.

Au ★★★★
S ★★★
A ★★★★

Johnny Depp in *Dead Man*

Dead Man's Gun (1997) FF—Can.

John Ritter
John Glover
Frank Whaley
D: Neill Fearnley, Joseph L. Scanlan and Brad Turner

A dead man's gun curses three

—Hell, ain't we more fu••ed than a whore at closin' time!
—Michael Wincott
Dead Man

different men. Made for TV movie.

Dead Man's Revenge (1994) USAN ⭐⭐⭐

Bruce Dern
Randy Travis
Michael Ironside
D: Alan J. Levi

A wronged homesteader joins in
the sting of a ruthless railroad baron.

Au ⭐⭐⭐⭒

S ⭐⭐

A ⭐⭐⭒

Dead Man's Walk (1996) ABC-TV ⭐⭐⭐

Jonny Lee Miller
David Arquette
Keith Carradine
Brian Dennehey
Edward James Olmos
D: Yves Simoneau

Two young Texas Rangers develop a lifelong
friendship. Prequel to *Lonesome Dove.*
97 Best of the West.

Au ⭐⭐⭐⭐⭐

S ⭐⭐⭒

A ⭐⭐⭒

Dead Men Ride (1970) FF—Ital./Sp.

Fabio Testi
Eduardo Fajardo
D: Aldo Florio

An ex-convict protects Mexican farmers.

Dead or Alive (1967) see A Minute to Pray, a Second to Die

Dead or Alive (The Tracker) (1988) LHP/ITCEG ⭐⭐⭐

Kris Kristofferson
Scott Wilson
Mark Moses
David Huddleston
D: John Guillermin

A legendary tracker reluctantly allows his son to accompany
him as he hunts down killer, "Red Jack." Theatrically released
as *Dead or Alive,* but re-released later that year on HBO as

Captain Peak, Texas Ranger.
Tracked Sam Bass.

Jonny Lee Miller, David Arquette and Keith Carradine (foreground).

Au ★★★★

S ★★★✦

A ★★★★

Deadwood '76 (1965) Ember/Fairway

Arch Hall, Jr.
Jack Lester
Melissa Morgan
D: James Landis

A young man is mistaken for Billy the Kid in Deadwood. U.S.
production, but only released in England six years after it was made.

Deaf Smith and Johnny Ears (1972) FF—Ital. ✦ ✦

Franco Nero
Anthony Quinn
Pamela Tiffin
D: Paolo Cavara

Two men help Sam Houston pursue
his dream of statehood for Texas.

Au ★★★

S ★★

A ★✦

> *—You can ask me to do anything!*
> *Anything! But, don't take away my*
> *pleasure in women! Don't even try!*
> —Franco Nero
> *Deaf Smith and Johnny Ears*

Death at Owell Rock (1967) FF—Ital.

Mark Damon
Stephen Forsyte
D: George Lincoln (Riccardo Freda)

A gunfighter seeks revenge for his father's murder.

Death Dance at Banner see Stranger on the Run

Death Dance Dance at Madella (1970) ✦ ✦

Don Murray
Anne Francis
Edward O'Brien
D: ?

When a gunfighter becomes marshal, he lacks the
nerve to face Jesse James and the Younger brothers.

Au ★✦

S ★

A ★★

Ben Thompson, gunfighter turned
Austin City marshal

Death Is Sweet from the Soldier of God (Django…Adios!) (1972) FF—Ital.

Brad Harris

Josè Torres
D: Robert Johnson (Roberto Mauri)

A mysterious vigilante tracks an outlaw.

Death Knows No Time (1968) FF—Sp./Ital.

William Bogart
Pedro Sanchez
D: Leon Klimovsky

A bounty hunter settles in a Texas border town.

Death of a Gunfighter (1969) Universal

Richard Widmark
Lena Horne
Carroll O'Connor
David Opatoshu
Harry Carey, Jr.
D: Allen Smithee (Combined pseudonym for Robert Totten and Don Siegel)

Set in his old ways, a marshal is confronted by his town
anxious to modernize. Based on Lewis Patten's,
Death of a Gunfighter. Filmed at Old Tucson.

Death on High Mountain (1969) FF—Ital./Sp.

Peter Lee Lawrence
Luis Dàvila (Luis Dawson)
D: Fred Ringoold (Fernando Cerchio)

Two bystanders foil a bank robbery then keep the loot.

Death on the Oregon Trail (1977) GTHV

Rod Taylor
Charles Napier
Stella Stevens
D: Richard Benedict

A captain leads a rag-tag wagon train across the
desert southwest. Compilation of episodes from
"The Oregon Trail" TV series for video release.

Death Played the Flute (1972) FF—Ital./Sp.

Michael Forrest
Steven Tedd
D: Elo Panaccio

178

The story of a flute playing bounty hunter.

Death Rides a Horse (1969) FF—Ital.

Lee Van Cleef
John Philip Law
D: Giulio Petroni

A boy grows up to avenge the death of his parents.

Au ★★★★

S ★★★

A ★★★

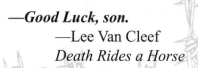

—Good Luck, son.
—Lee Van Cleef
Death Rides a Horse

Death Rides Alone (1968) FF—Ital./Sp.

Mike Marshall
Robert Hundar
D: Joseph Warren (Giuseppe Vari)

A gunfighter searches for the men who killed his mother and sister.

Death Sentence (1967) FF—Ital.

Robin Clark
Richard Conte
D: Mario Lanfranchi

A gunfighter tracks down the four men responsible for his brother's death.

Death Valley (1946)

Robert Lowery
Nat Pendleton
Helen Gilbert
Barbara Reed
D: Lew Landers

A murderer and thief flees into Death Valley.

Death Walks in Laredo (1966) FF—Ital./Sp.

Thomas Hunter
James Shigeta
Nadir Moretti
D: Enzo Peri (Elio Petri)

Three half brothers inherit a gold mine.

"The Fall of the Cowboy."

Decision at Sundown (1957) Columbia

Randolph Scott
John Carroll
Karen Steele
Noah Berry, Jr.
Bob Steele
D: Bud Boetticher

A gunfighter confronts the man he
blames for stealing his wife.

Au ★★

S ★★

A ★★

James Westerfield, Noah Berry, Jr. and Randolph Scott in *Decision at Sundown.*

Deguello (Degueyo) (1966) FF—Ital.

Giacomo Rossi Stuart (Jack Stuart)
Dan Vadis
D: Joseph Warren (Giuseppi Vari)

An outlaw attempts to discover the location of a hidden fortune.

Denver and Rio Grande (1952) Paramount

Edmond O'Brian
Sterling Hayden
Dean Jagger
D: Byron Haskin

Railroads compete to first cross the Rockies.
Story by Frank Gruber. Filmed near Durango, CO.

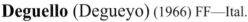

*—Doc, if you'd been tendin' bar as long
as I have, you wouldn't expect so much
out of the human race.*
—James Westerfield
Decision at Sundown

The Deputies see Law of the Land

Deputy Marshal (1949) Lippert

Frances Langford
Jon Hall
Dick Foran
D: William Berke

A lawman tracks brothers with a map belonging to the railroad.

Deserter (The Devil's Backbone) (1970) FF—U.S./Ital./Yug.

Bekim Fehmiu
Richard Crenna
Chuck Connors
Ricardo Montalban
Brandon De Wilde
Slim Pickens
Woody Strode
John Huston
D: Niska Fulgizzi and Burt Kennedy

A secret cavalry unit fights Indians along the Mexican border.

Bekim Fehmiu in *Deserter.*

Filmed at Alicante, Almeria, and El Torcal, Spain.

Desert Guns (1936) Beaumont

Conway Tearle
Margaret Morris
Charles K. French
Slim Whitaker
D: Charles Hutchison

A lawman saves a girl's inheritance.

Desert Pursuit (1952) Mono.

Wayne Morris
Virginia Grey
Anthony Caruso
D: George Blair

A prospector and a girl are hunted by outlaws.

Desert Shooter see The Shooter

The Desperado (1954) Silvermine/AA

Wayne Morris
James J. Lydon
Beverly Garland
Lee Van Cleef
D: Thomas Carr

A gunfighter saves a framed man.

Desperado (1974) FF—Sp./Ital.

Michael Forest
Fred Harrison
D: Al Bagrain (Alfonso Balcazar)

A gunfighter defends terrorized farmers.

Desperado (1978)

Jim Beaver
Judy Echols
Geraldine Edgin
James Edgin
Richard "Trooper" Harris
D: James Edgin

A young gunfighter's attempt to go straight is challenged

by his old partners. Made for TV movie

Desperado (1987) Universal-TV

Alex McArthur
Lise Cutter
David Warner
Pernell Roberts
Robert Vaughn
D: Virgil W. Vogel

NBC-TV pilot. Filmed at Old Tucson.

Desperado: Avalanche at Devil's Ridge (1988) Mirisch/CESJP/Universal-TV

Alex McArthur
Rod Steiger
Lise Cutter
Hoyt Axton
D: Richard Compton

Desperado: Badlands Justice (1989) Mirisch/Universal-TV

Alex McArthur
John Rhys-Davies
James B. Sikking
D: E.W. Swackhamer

The Desperadoes (1943) Columbia

Randolph Scott
Glenn Ford
Claire Trevor
Edgar Buchanan
Guinn "Big Boy" Williams
D: Charles Vidor

An outlaw helps a lawman expose bank robbers.
Based on a Max Brand (Frederick Faust) story.
Filmed in Kanab, Utah.

Au
S
A

The Desperadoes (1969) Columbia

Vince Edwards
Jack Palance
George Maharis
Neville Brand
D: Henry Levin

A Confederate and his sons become

Guinn Williams, Glenn Ford and Randolph Scott in *The Desperadoes*.

*—If you're not gone by mornin',
Cheyenne, I'll be comin' for ya!*
—Randolph Scott
The Desperadoes (1943)

—Burn it! Burn the town!
—Jack Palance
The Desperadoes

postwar outlaws in Texas.

Au ★★

S ★◖

A ★★

The Desperadoes Are in Town (1956) Regal/20th C. Fox ★

Robert Arthur
Kathy Nolan
Rhys Williams
D: Kurt Neumann

Outlaws attempt to force a Texan to rob a bank.

Au ★

S ★

A ★

Desperado: The Outlaw Wars (1989) Mirisch/Universal-TV ★★◖

Alex McArthur
Richard Farnsworth
James Remar
Lise Cutter
D: E.W. Swachmer

A marshal gives an outlaw a chance at
amnesty when he comes home to his lover.
Filmed at Mescal, Arizona.

Au ★★★

S ★★

A ★★◖

The Desperate Mission (Joaquin Murrieta) (1971) ABC-TV/20th C. Fox ★★◖

Ricardo Montalban
Slim Pickens
Jim McMullan
Rosey Grier
D: Earl Bellamy

Joaquin Murrieta fights for
justice in old California.
Filmed at Durango, Mexico.

*—Shoot, there ain't enough in one of
these [drinks] to drown a buffalo gnat.*
—Slim Pickens
The Desperate Mission

Au ★★

S ★★◖

A ★★◖

Desperate Siege see Rawhide

The Desperate Trail (1994) THE ★★★✦

Sam Elliott
Linda Florentino
Craig Sheffer
D: P.J. Pesce

A lawman tracks the escaped murderess of his son. Filmed at Bonanza Creek Ranch, NM.

Au ★★★★★
S ★★★
A ★★★

—Yes, mam, we're gonna wrap a necklace, a good Kentucky hemp around that little neck a yours. D'ever heard the sound a broken neck bone makes? Like a carrot.
—Sam Elliott
The Desperate Trail

Desperate Women (1978) Lorimar Prod. ★★✦

Susan Saint James
Dan Haggerty
Ronee Blakley
Ann Dusenberry
John Crawford
D: Jack Sowards

Three convicts become stranded in the desert en route to Tucson. Made for TV movie.

Au ★★✦
S ★✦
A ★★★

—I read something once that said a man's pride under trust was better than a written contract.
—Audie Murphy
Destry

Destry (1955) U-I ★★★

Audie Murphy
Mari Blanchard
Lyle Bettger
Edgar Buchanan
Wallace Ford
Alan Hale, Jr.
D: George Marshall

Remake of *Destry Rides Again.*

Au ★★
S ★★★✦
A ★★★

Audie Murphy and Mari Blanchard in *Destry.*

Destry Rides Again (1939) Universal ★★★

Marlene Dietrich
James Stewart
Charles Winninger
Mischa Auer
Brian Donlevy
Bill Cody, Jr.
Chief Big Tree
D: George Marshall

A crooked gambler's girl falls for an unconventional

—I had a friend once...
—James Stewart
Destry Rides Again

lawman. Remake of the 1932 Tom Mix version. Based on the Max Brand novel. #26 IMDb.

Au

S ★★★★✦

A ★★★★✦

The Devil's Backbone see Deserter

Devil's Canyon (1953) RKO ★★✦

Virginia Mayo
Dale Robertson
Stephen McNally
Arthur Hunnicutt
D: Alfred Werker

A killer seeks revenge on a fellow inmate in an Arizona prison. Filmed in Sedona, Arizona.

Au ★★✦

S ★★✦

A ★★✦

Devil's Children (1962)

Charles Aidman
Charles Bickford
Burt Brinckerhoff
James Drury
Doug McClure
D: James Sheldon

UNCHARTED TERRITORY

Devil's Doorway (1950) MGM

Robert Taylor
Louis Calhern
Paula Raymond
James Mitchell
Edgar Buchanan
Chief Big Tree
D: Anthony Mann

An educated Indian and a decorated Union Army veteran utilize military tactics to reclaim Indian land.

UNCHARTED TERRITORY

El Diablo (1990) HBO ★★

Anthony Edwards
Louis Gossett, Jr.
John Glover
Joe Pantoliano
D: Peter Markle

A tenderfoot and a gunman travel to Mexico in search of a kidnapper named El Diablo.

Jimmy Stewart breaks up a fight between Una Merkel and Marlene Dietrich.

—*She was slicker than a greased pig.*
—Arthur Hunnicutt
Devil's Canyon

Loa-Kum-Ar-Nuk, Warm Springs Tribe. Army scout during the Modoc War, 1873.

Filmed at Old Tucson, AZ, Indian Dunes, CA.

Au

S ★◢

A ★★◢

El Diablo, El Sainto Y El Tonto (1987) FF—Mex.

Vincente Fernandez
Sasha Montenegro
Pedro Weber
D: Rafael Villasensor Kuri

UNCHARTED
TERRITORY

Dig Your Grave, Friend…Sabata's Coming (1970) FF—Ital./Sp./Fr.

Richard Harrison
Fernando Sancho
D: John Wood

A bandit joins a gunman to avenge a murder.

UNCHARTED
TERRITORY

Dirty Little Billy (1972) Columbia

Michael J. Pollard
Lee Purcell
Richard Evans
Charles Aidman
Dick Van Patten
Gary Busey
D: Stan Dragoti

Billy the Kid becomes a psychopathic killer.
Filmed at Old Tucson and Lincoln County, NM.

—They say the boy's crazy. You know, he's always gamblin' and drinkin' and foolin' with women.
—Gary Busey
Dirty Little Billy

Au ★★

S ★★

A ★★◢

A Distant Trumphet (1964) WB

Troy Donahue
Suzanne Pleshette
Diane McBain
James Gregory
William Reynolds
Claude Akins
Richard X
Russell Johnson
D: Raoul Walsh

The cavalry pursues Apaches in the southwest.
Filmed at Painted Desert, AZ, Red Rock Canyon, NM.

Au ★

S ★◢

A ★◢

Django (1966) FF—Ital./Sp.

Franco Nero
Loredana Nusciak
Eduardo Fajardo
D: Sergio Corbucci

A gunman faces a sadistic outlaw. First of twenty
Django films, excluding more than ten additional
films that were retitled for French distribution.

Django, A Bullet for You (1966) FF—Sp./Ital.

James Philbrook
Aldo Berti
D: Leon Klimovsky

A gunfighter protects farmers from a land baron. Intended as a sequel to *Django*.

Django...Adios! see Death Is Sweet from the Soldier of God

Django Always Draws Second see Hero Called Allegria

Django and Sartana Are Coming...It's the End (1970) FF—Sp./Ital.

Hunt Powers
Gorden Mitchell
D: Dick Spitfire (Demofilo Fidani)

Two gunfighters track kidnappers into Mexico.

Django Challenges Sartana (1970) FF—Ital.

Tony Kendall
George Ardisson
D: William Redford (Pasquale Squittieri)

Two bounty hunters track a gang of outlaws.

Django Does Not Forgive (1967) FF—Ital./Sp.

John Clark
Hugo Blanco
Frank Braña
Julio Buchs (Julio Garcia)

A bounty hunter tracks the man that raped and murdered his sister.

Django, Kill...If You Live, Shoot! (Django Kill) (1967) FF—Ital./Sp.

Tomàs Milian
Ray Lovelock
Roberto Camardiel
D: Giulio Questi

A bounty hunter pursues a sadistic
gay bandit. Excessive violence.

Django Kills Softly (1968) FF—Ital.

George Eastman
Edwin G. Ross
D: Max Hunter (Massimo Pupillo)

A bounty hunter defends a town against its boss and his brother.

Django, Last Killer (1967) FF—Ital.

George Eastman
Anthony Ghidra
D: Joseph Warren (Giuseppe Vari)

A bounty hunter teaches a farmer to shoot after his parents are murdered.

Django Shoots First (1966) FF—Ital.

Glenn Saxon
Fernando Sancho
D: Alberto De Martino

A bounty hunter tracks the man who murdered his father.

Django's Cut Price Corpses see Even Django Has His Price

Django Strikes Again (1987) FF—Ital./Sp./Ger.

Franco Nero
Donald Pleasence
Christopher Connelly
D: Ted Archer (Nello Rossati)

After retreating to a monastery for ten years, a bounty hunter
tracks his daughter's kidnapper. The only true sequel to *Django*.

Django the Bastard (1969) FF—Ital./Sp.

Anthony Steffen
Lu Kamenke
D: Sergio Garrone

A bounty hunter hunts down Confederate traitors.

Django the Condemned see Outlaw of Red River

Django the Honorable Killer see Outlaw of Red River

Riders resting.

Djurado (1966) FF—Ital./Sp.

Montgomery Clark
Scilla Gabel
D: Gianni Narzisi

A gambler protects a saloon and its owner from an outlaw.

Doc (1971) UA ★★★★

Stacy Keach
Harris Yulin
Faye Dunaway
D: Frank Perry

Doc Holiday pursues a life of self-destruction.

Au ★★★★
S ★★★★
A ★★★★

Stacy Keach in *Doc.*

Val Kilmer in *Tombstone.*

The Faces of Doc Holliday

Jason Robards (right) as Holliday
in *Hour of the Gun.*

Doc Holliday

Dodge City (1939) WB

Errol Flynn
Olivia De Havilland
Ann Sheridan
Bruce Cabot
Alan Hale
Ward Bond
D: Michael Curtiz

A lawman delivers law and order to Dodge City. Loosely based on Wyatt Earp. Filmed at Modesto, San Francisco, Warner Ranch, CA.

Au

S

A

A Dollar a Head see Navajoe Joe

Dollar for the Dead (1998) FF—Sp./U.S.

Emilio Estevez
William Forsythe
Joaquim de Almeida
Howie Long
D: Gene Quintano

When a gunman is tracked by a rancher for killing his son, he becomes involved in a search for hidden gold. Made for TV movie.

UNCHARTED
TERRITORY

Dollar of Fire (1967) FF—Ital./Sp.

Michael Riva
Diana Garson
D: Nick Nostro

A new sheriff fights corruption in a frontier town.

UNCHARTED
TERRITORY

Dollars for a Fast Gun (1968) FF—Sp./Ital.

Robert Hundar
Peter Martell
Pamela Tudor
D: Joaquin Romero Marchent

A widowed rancher hires a gunfighter to ward off a dishonest land baron.

UNCHARTED
TERRITORY

Domino Kid (1957) Rorvic/Columbia

Rory Calhoun
Kristine Miller
Andrew Duggan
Ray Corrigan
D: Ray Nazarro

Ann Sheridan in *Dodge City.*

—*There's gonna be no mob rule around this town as long as I'm sheriff!*
—Errol Flynn
Dodge City

Dodge City circa 1882.

—*Mistakes can get a man killed.*
—Rory Calhoun
Domino Kid

190

A Civil War veteran avenges the death of his father.

Au

S

A

Donner Pass: The Road to Survival (1978) NBC-TV/SSC

Robert Fuller
Andrew Prine
Michael Callan
D: James L. Conway

A pioneer struggles to help a wagon
train survive in the Sierra Nevadas.

Do Not Touch the White Woman (1974) FF—Ital.

Marcello Mastroianni
Catherine Denevue
D: Marco Ferreri

General Custer battles hostiles from contemporary
high-rise developers to the Old West.

"Tidings of the Relief Column—
Listening to Officer's Call."

Don Ricardo Returns (1946)

Fred Colby
Lita Baron (Isabelita)
Martin Garralaga
D: Terry Morse

A swashbuckler contests his cousin for
the family fortune in old California.

Au

S

A

*—You say you live to fight?…
Come, amigo, for you life has begun.*
—Fred Colby
Don Ricardo Returns

Don't Wait, Django…Shoot! (1969) FF—Ital.

Sean Todd
Pedro Sanchez
D: Edward G. Muller (Edoardo Mulargia)

A gunfighter is hired to avenge the death of an old cattle rancher.

FREDERIC REMINGTON

The Doolins of Oklahoma (The Great Manhunt) (1949) Columbia ★ ★

Randolph Scott
George Macready
Louise Albritton
John Ireland
Noah Beery, Jr.
Jock O'Mahoney (Jock Mahoney)
D: Gordon Douglas

The Doolins avenge the massacre of the Daltons.
Filmed in the Alabama Hills.

Au ★ ★

S ★ ★

A ★ ★

John Ireland, Randolph Scott and Jock Mahoney.

—No…no, eh, I must have had too much education. Got too much imagination. I like excitement of the wilderness.
—Noah Berry, Jr.
The Doolins of Oklahoma

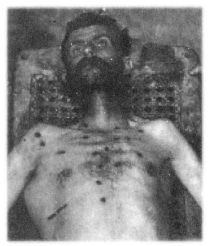

The bullet ridden corpse of Bill Doolin.

El Dorado (1967) Laurel/Paramount ★ ★ ★ ★

John Wayne
Robert Mitchum
James Caan
Charlene Holt
Ed Asner
Jim Davis
Johnny Crawford
Arthur Hunnicutt
Olaf Weighorst
D: Howard Hawks

A hired gun becomes entangled in a water rights dispute between two ranchers. Technical advice by Joe De Yong. Title paintings by Olaf "Swede" Weighorst. Filmed at Old Tucson. #64 Best of the West, #32 IMDb.

Au ★ ★ ✦

S ★ ★ ★ ✦

A ★ ★ ★ ★

James Caan (left), John Wayne, and Arthur Hunnicutt in *El Dorado*.

—I'll be a suck-egg mule!
—Arthur Hunnicutt
El Dorado

Down the Long Hills (1986) Disney-TV

Bruce Boxleitner
Bo Hopkins

Michael Wren
Jack Elam
D: Burt Kennedy

Story by Louie L'Amour.

Dragoon Wells Massacre (1957) AA ★★⬨

Barry Sullivan
Dennis O'Keefe
Mona Freeman
Jack Elam
Sebastian Cabot
John War Eagle
D: Harold Schuster

A cavalry captain leads an Indian trader, convict wagon and stagecoach passengers through hostile Apache territory.

Au ★★
S ★★⬨
A ★★⬨

—…among the Indians, as amoungst our people, the good in heart outnumber the bad. And they will offer their lives to prove it.
—Alan Ladd
Drum Beat

Draw! (1984) HBO/PF ★★

Kirk Douglas
James Coburn
Alexandra Bastedo
Graham Jarvis
D: Steven H. Stern

An outlaw prepares for a showdown with an ex-lawman. Filmed at Fort Edmonton, Canada.

Au ★★
S ★★
A ★★

—Well, there's two things in this world that you got to be careful of, son. That's where you put your trust and who you choose as your friends.
—Kirk Douglas
Draw!

Dream West (1986) SC/CBS-TV ★★★★⬨

Richard Chamberlain
Alice Krige
F. Murray Abraham
Ben Johnson
Rip Torn
Claude Akins
D: Dick Lowry

John C. Fremont establishes himself as America's premier explorer of the West. Three part mini-series. Filmed at Old Tucson. #28 Best of the West.

Au ★★★★★
S ★★★★
A ★★★★⬨

—The future's in the West, Jessie. That's where the dream is.
—Richard Chamberlain
Dream West

Dr. Quinn, Medicine Woman: The Movie (1999) CBS-TV ★★ ◗

Jane Seymour
Joe Lando
D: James Keach

A frontier doctor and her husband search for their kidnapped daughter. Made for TV series based on the series.

Au ★★

S ★◗

A ★◗

Jane Seymour and Joe Lando.

Drum Beat (1954) WB ★★

Alan Ladd
Audrey Dalton
Marisa Pavan
Charles Bronson
D: Delmer Daves

An Indian fighter negotiates peace between the Modocs and settlers. Filmed in Sedona, Arizona, and the Iverson Movie Location Ranch.

Au ★★

S ★★

A ★★

—…take comfort in the truth, that God never gives us more than we can handle.
—Geoffrey Lower
Dr. Quinn Medicine Woman: The Movie

Drummer of Vengeance (1971) FF—Brit./Ital.

Ty Hardin
Craig Hill
Gorden Mitchell
D: Robert Paget (Mario Gariazzo)

A "stranger" tracks his wife's murderers.

UNCHARTED TERRITORY

—Now look, you don't have to see a skunk to know he's around.
—Walter Brennan
Drums Across the River

Drums Across the River (1954) U-I ★★

Audie Murphy
Lisa Gaye
Lyle Bettger
Walter Brennan
Hugh O'Brian
Jay Silverheels
Chief Yowlachie
D: Nathan Juran

A miner and his father attempt to prevent a Ute uprising. Filmed in Kernville, California.

Au ★◗

S ★★

A ★★

Audie Murphy and Hugh O'Brian in *Drums Across the River.*

194

Duck, You Sucker (Fistful of Dynamite) (1971) FF—Ital. ⭐

James Coburn
Rod Steiger
Maria Monti
D: Sergio Leone

A mercenary and a peon become freedom fighters
during the Mexican Revolution. #38 IMDb.

Au ⭐⭐⭑

S ⭐

A ⭑

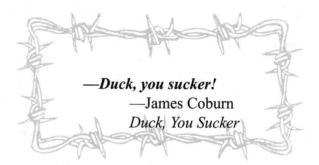

—Duck, you sucker!
—James Coburn
Duck, You Sucker

Duel at Apache Wells (1957) Republic ⭑

Anna Marie Alberghetti
Ben Cooper
Jim Davis
D: Joseph Kane

Ranchers face off over a water hole.

Au ⭐

S ⭑

A ⭑

"The Fight for the Waterhole."

Duel at Diablo (1966) UA ⭐ ⭐

James Garner
Sidney Portier
Bibi Anderson
Dennis Weaver
Richard Farnsworth
D: Ralph Nelson

A scout avenges his Comanche wife's murder. Based on Marvin
Albert's, "Apache Rising." Filmed at Kanab Movie Ranch, UT.

Au ⭐⭑

S ⭐⭐

A ⭐⭐⭑

The Duel at Silver Creek (1952) U-I ⭐ ⭐

Audie Murphy
Faith Domergue
Stephen McNally
Lee Marvin
D: Don Siegel

A marshal deputizes the Silver Kid to track claim jumpers.
Filmed at the Iverson Movie Location Ranch.

Au ⭐⭑

S ⭐⭐

A ⭐⭐

Duel at Sundown (1967) FF—Fr./Ger.

Peter Van Eyck
Carole Gray
D: Leopoldo Lahola

Two brothers face off over a land-grabbing scheme.

Duel in Durango see Gun Duel in Durango

Duel in the Eclipse (1967) FF—Sp.

Lang Jeffries
Femi Benussi
Fernando Sancho
D: Eugenio Martin, Josè Luis Merino

A gunfighter infiltrates an outlaw gang to avenge his brother's murder.

Duel in the Sun (1948) SRO

Jennifer Jones
Joseph Cotton
Gregory Peck
Lionel Barrymore
Walter Huston
Harry Carey
D: King Vidor

Two brothers fight over a woman and their crippled father. Nicknamed *Lust in the Dust* by critics. Oscar nomination for Jennifer Jones for best actress. Filmed at Corriganville, CA, Tucson and Yuma, Arizona.

Au ★★★
S ★★★★
A ★★★★

Gregory Peck and Jennifer Jones in *Duel in the Sun.*

Durango Is Coming, Pay or Die (1972) FF—Ital./Sp.

Brad Harris
Josè Torres
D: Luis Monter (Roberto Montero)

A gunfighter searches for a killer. Rare.

Dust in the Sun (1973) FF—Fr.

Bob Cunningham
Maria Schell
D: Richard Balducci

Rare.

Dynamite Jim (1966) FF—Sp./Ital.

Luis Dàvila
Fernando Sancho

196

Rosalba Neri
D: Alfonso Balcazar, Josè A. De La Loma

A Union spy attempts to smuggle gold from Mexico to Iowa.

Dynamite Joe (1966) FF—Ital./Sp.

Rick Van Nutter (Clyde Rogers)
Halina Zalewska
D: Anthony Dawson

A government agent investigates stagecoach robberies.

The Eagle and the Hawk (1950) Paramount

Pearl Hart, the last stage robber.

John Payne
Rhonda Fleming
Dennis O'Keefe
D: Lewis R. Foster

Two Americans are sent to Mexico to prevent an invasion of Texas.
Filmed in Sedona, AZ.

Au ★★

S ★★◀

A ★★◀

—He was a patriot.
Are there any [men] greater?
—John Payne
The Eagle and the Hawk

Eagle's Wing (1980) FF—Brit./Sp.

Martin Sheen
Sam Waterston
Harvey Keitel
D: Anthony Harvey

A trapper becomes obsessed with capturing a legendary white stallion.

Au ★★★★

S ★★◀

A ★★★★

Ebenezer (1997) FF—Can.

Jack Palance
Rick Schroder
Amy Locane
Joshua Silberg
D: Ken Jubenvill

Western adaptation of Dicken's, *A Christmas Carol.*
Made for TV movie.

The Emporer of California (1936) FF—Ger.

Luis Trenker
Viktoria von Ballasko
Else Aulinger

D: Luis Trenker

Sutter's dreams of an empire are shattered by the imperialist forty-niners.

End of the Trail (1936) Columbia

Jack Holt
Louise Henry
Douglas Dumbrille
D: Erle C. Kenton

Upon discharge from the Spanish-American War,
a veteran turns to rustling. Story by Zane Grey.

Escape from Fort Bravo (1953) MGM

William Holden
Eleanor Parker
John Forsyth
William Demerest
D: John Sturges

While tracking escaped Confederates in the Arizona desert,
a Union officer is trapped in a dry wash by Apaches.
Filmed in Death Valley.

Au ★★◗

S ★★◗

A ★★★

—Well, he [my father] was something. He taught me how to ride and how to shoot and how to see and how to hear. He was big…A man is bigger than any thing he does, or should be. It's like a bible that's bigger than any religion. I guess he was my bible.
—William Holden
Escape from Fort Bravo

Escape from Red Rock (1958) RF/TCF

Brian Donlevy
Elaine Janssen
Gary Murray
D: Edward Bernds

A rancher escapes to Mexico after being
forced to help an outlaw in a holdup.

Au ★★

S ★

A ★

Escape From the Dark see The Littlest Horse Thieves

La Escondida see The Hidden One

Escort West (1959) Romina/UA ★★

Victor Mature
Elaine Stewart
Faith Domergue
Noah Berry, Jr.
Harry Carey, Jr.
Slim Pickens

William Ching
D: Francis D. Lyon

An ex-Confederate officer must escort survivors of
an Indian raid to safety. Filmed at Corriganville, CA.

Au

S

A

Eukaliptus (2002) FF—Pol.

Leszek Zdybal
Dorota Stalinska
D: Michal Krzysztalowicz

UNCHARTED
TERRITORY

Even Django Has His Price (Django's Cut Price Corpses) (1971) FF—Ital./Sp.

Jeff Cameron
John Desmont
D: Paolo Solvay (Luigi Batzella)

A bounty hunter tracks bounty hunters.

UNCHARTED
TERRITORY

Execution (1968) FF—Ital./Fr.

John Richardson
Mimmo Palmara (Dick Palmer)
D: Domenico Paolella, Fernando Franchi

Upon his release from prison, a robber hunts his double-crossing ex-partner.

UNCHARTED
TERRITORY

An Eye for an Eye (Talion) (1966) Embassy

Robert Lansing
Pat Wayne
Slim Pickens
Gloria Talbot
Strother Martin
D: Michael Moore

A retired bounty hunter avenges his family's murder.
Filmed in the Alabama Hills.

Au

S ★

A ★

*—I'll guarantee ya, ya ain't gonna leave
this town alive!*

—Slim Pickens
An Eye for an Eye

Eye for an Eye (1972) FF—Ital./Sp./Mex.

Cameron Mitchell
Isela Vega
Helena Rojo
D: Albert Marshall (Alberto Mariscal)

An incestuous mother hires a gunfighter to teach her

son the skills necessary to avenge her husband's murder.

The Fabulous Texan (1947) Republic

William Elliott
John Carroll
Catherine McLeod
Andy Devine
D: Edward Ludwig

Two Confederate officers return to postwar Texas.
Filmed in Sedona, AZ.

Catherine McLeod and Bill Elliott in *The Fabulous Texan.*

Face of a Fugitive (1959) Columbia

Fred MacMurray
Lin McCarthy
Dorothy Green
D: Paul Wendkos

A fugitive assumes a new identity in a new town.

Au ★★

S ★✦

A ★★

—I had me to take care of. That's all anybody's got.
—Fred MacMurray
Face of a Fugitive

Face to Face (1967) FF—Ital.

Tomàs Milan
Gian Maria Volantè
D: Sergio Sollima

A history professor and a half-breed outlaw team up.

Face to the Wind (Naked Revenge) (Cry for Me Billy) (1972) WB

Cliff Potts
Xochitl
Harry Dean Stanton
D: William A. Graham

A gunfighter avenges the rape of an Indian girl by cavalrymen.

Fair Warning (1931) Fox

George O'Brien
Louise Huntington
Mitchell Harris
George Brent
D: Alfred Werker

A cowboy proves that two gunmen are robbers.
Based on the Max Brand (Frederick Faust) novel, *The Untamed.*

The Far Country (1955) U-I ★★★★

Jimmy Stewart
Ruth Roman
Corinne Calvet
Walter Brennan
Henry Morgan
Jack Elam
D: Anthony Mann

Two cowboys parlay their cattle profits into
a Klondike fortune in gold. Story by Borden Chase.
Filmed in Alberta, Canada. #47 Best of the West.

Au ★★★★

S ★★★★

A ★★★★★

Ruth Roman, Eddy C. Waller and Jimmy Stewart
in *The Far Country.*

The Far Horizons (1955) Paramount ★★★★

Fred MacMurray
Charlton Heston
Donna Reed
William Demarest
D: Rudolph Matè

Lewis and Clark explore the West. Filmed at Grand Teton Natl. Pk.

Au ★★★

S ★★★

A ★★★★

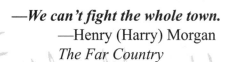

—We can't fight the whole town.
—Henry (Harry) Morgan
The Far Country

The Far Out West (1967) CBS-TV/Universal

Ann Sheridan
Ruth McDevitt
Douglas Fowley
Lon Chaney, Jr.
Jay Silverheels
D: Joe Connelly

Compilation of episodes of the "Pistols 'n Petticoats" TV series.

The Fastest Guitar Alive (1967) MGM

Roy Orbison
Sammy Jackson
Maggie Pierce
Joan Freeman
Iron Eyes Cody
D: Michael Moore

A guitar-toting Confederate spy hijacks a San
Francisco shipment of gold intended for the Union.

Meriwether Lewis

The Fastest Gun Alive (1956) MGM ★★★

Glenn Ford
Joanne Crain

William Clark

Broderick Crawford
Noah Berry, Jr.
D: Russell Rouse

A storekeeper must cope with his father's reputation
as a gunfighter. Filmed at Red Rock Canyon, Cantil, CA.

Au

S

A

Fasthand (1972) FF—Ital./Sp.

Alan Steel (John Wyler)
William Berger
D: Frank Bronston

Ex-Confederates terrorize a cavalry fort.

Father Kino, The Padre on Horseback (1977) KI

Richard Egan
Ricardo Montalban
John Ireland
Cesar Romero
Joe Campanella
Stephen McNally
Rory Calhoun
Keenan Wynn
Michael Ansara
Victor Jory
D: Ken Kennedy

The Feud (1977)

Jeff Goldin
Gary Kasper
A.J. Marik
D: Jeff Goldin

Few Dollars for Django (1966) FF—Ital./Sp.

Anthony Steffen
Gloria Osuna
Frank Wolff
D: Leon Klimovsky

A bounty hunter and an outlaw defend peasant farmers from a town boss.

The Fiend Who Walked the West (1958) TCF

Hugh O'Brian
Robert Evans
Doloras Michaels
Linda Cristal
D: Gordon Douglas

Upon his release from prison, an outlaw kills his
former cellmate's partner and kidnaps his wife.

Fifteen Scaffolds for the Killer (1968) FF—Ital./Sp.

Craig Hill
Susy Anderson
D: Stelvio Massi

A man and his friends are falsely accused of murder.

The Fighter (1952) UA

Richard Conte
Vanessa Brown
Lee J. Cobb
D: Herbert Kline

A young man boxes to earn money for guns for
Mexican revolutionaries. Story by Jack London.

The Fighter (1994) FMEI

Oliver Gruner
Ian Ziering
Ashley Laurence
Michael Palance
James Brolin
D: Isaac Florentine

A French kickboxer fights a town boss and his gang.
Filmed at the Veluzat Ranch, Santa Clarita, CA.

Au ★

S ★

A ★

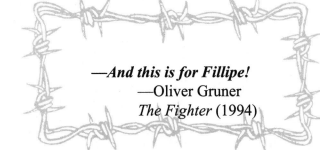

—And this is for Fillipe!
—Oliver Gruner
The Fighter (1994)

Fighters from Ave Maria (1970) FF—Ital./Ger.

Tony Kendall
Peter Thorris
Alberto Dell'Acqua
D: Al Albert

Traveling circus performers team with a revolutionary to fight a town boss.

Fighting Caravans (Blazing Arrows) (1931) Paramount

Gary Cooper
Lita Damita
Iron Eyes Cody
D: Otto Brower, David Burton

A wagon train scout marries a woman to avoid prison.
Loosely adapted from the Zane Grey novel.

Filmed at Sonora, California.

Au ★★★★
S ★★★
A ★★★

Fighting Fists of Shanghai Joe (1973) FF—Ital.

Klaus Kinski
Chen Lee
Robert Hundar
D: Mario Caiano

A man educated in a Buddhist monastery discovers the West.

—I've always been free and I don't know's that I'd like a woman to tell me this here and that there. I ain't never been tied down to nothin'!
—Gary Cooper
Fighting Caravans

The Fighting Lawman (1953) AA ★

Wayne Morris
Virginia Grey
John Kellogg
D: Thomas Carr

A lawman tracks bank robbers. Filmed at Corriganville.

Au ★
S ★
A ★

—Whoever's in there, come out with your hands up!
—Wayne Morris
The Fighting Lawman

Fighting Man of the Plains (1949) 20th C. Fox

Randolph Scott
Bill Williams
Victor Jory
D: Edwin L. Marin

A former Quantrill's Raider and Jesse James clean up the town of Lanyard. Story by Frank Gruber.

The Fighting Seventh see Little Big Horn

The Final Hour (1963) NBC-TV/Universal

Lee J. Cobb
James Drury
Doug McClure
D: Robert Douglas

Ranchers and Polish miners clash over a girl. An episode of "The Virginian" released theatrically.

Find a Place to Die (1968) FF—Ital.

Jeffrey Hunter
Pascale Petit
D: Anthony Ascott

A gunfighter helps a woman
recover stolen gold. Django film.

Finders Killers (1969) FF—Ital.

Donald O'Brien
Gordon Mitchell
D: Gianni Crea

A man avenges his brother's death.

Finger on the Trigger (1965) FF—Sp./Ital./U.S.

Rory Calhoun
Aldo Sambrell
D: Sidney Pink

Union veterans encounter rebels in New Mexico.

Firecreek (1968) WB-7 Arts ★★★★

James Stewart
Henry Fonda
Gary Lockwood
Ed Begley
Jack Elam
Inger Stevens
D: Vincent McEveety

A sodbuster stands up to outlaws. Filmed
in Sedona, AZ. #66 Best of the West.

Au ★★★★

S ★★★★

A ★★★★⯪

The First Texan (1956 AA ★★

Joel McCrea
Felicia Farr
Jeff Morrow
Wallace Ford
D: Byron Haskin

Sam Huston avoids fighting to free Texas from
Mexico until President Jackson orders him to act.

Au ★★

S ★★

A ★★

Fistful of Death (1971) FF—Ital.

Hunt Powers
Klaus Kinski
Gordon Mitchell

—...the day a man decides not to face the world is the day he'd better step out of it. Now, give me the gun!!
—James Stewart
Firecreek

Jimmy Stewart in *Firecreek*.

—Good luck—and remember the Alamo.
—Sam Houston (Joel McCrea)
The First Texan

D: Miles Deem (Demofilo Fidani)

The sole survivor of an ambush by the Wild Bunch infiltrates the gang.

Clint Eastwood in *A Fistful of Dollars*.

A Fistful of Dollars (1964/U.S. 1967) FF—Ital./Ger./Sp.

Clint Eastwood
Marianne Koch
Gian Maria Volontè
D: Sergio Leone (Bob Robertson)

In a Mexican border town, a drifter plays two smuggling gangs against each other. First of the Leone trilogy. Originally titled, *The Magnificent Stranger*. Adapted from Kurosawa's, *Yojimbo* (1961). #21 IMDb.

Au ★★★

S ★★

A ★★★

Fistful of Dynamite see Duck, You Sucker

A Fistful of Rawhide (1970)

?
D: W.G. Beggs

—Ya see, my mule don't like people laughin'! He gets the crazy idea you're laughin' at him. Now if you apologize, like I know you're going to, I might convince him that you really didn't mean it.
—Clint Eastwood
A Fistful of Dollars

Five Bad Men (1935) Sunset

Noah Beery, Jr.
Buffalo Bill, Jr.
Sally Darling
D: Clifford Smith

Five Bloody Graves (1970) I-I

Robert Dix
Scott Brady
Jim Davis
John Carradine
D: Al Adamson

A gunfighter pursues outlaws running guns to Indians.

Five Bold Women (1960) Citation

Jeff Morrow
Merry Anders
Jim Ross
Guinn "Big Boy" Williams
D: Jorge Lopez-Portillo

Female convicts escape their prison transport.

5 Card Stud (1968) Paramount

Dean Martin
Robert Mitchum
Inger Stevens
Roddy McDowell
D: Henry Hathaway

A preacher methodically eliminates those
responsible for hanging his brother.

Au

S

A

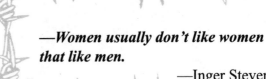

*—Women usually don't like women
that like men.*

—Inger Stevens
5 Card Stud

Five Dollars for Ringo (1968) FF—Ital./Sp.

Anthony P. Taber (Julio P. Tabernero)
Frank Wolff
D: Ignacio Iquino

A gunfighter is hired to protect peons from Mexican bandidos.

Five Giants from Texas (1966) FF—Ital./Sp.

Guy Madison
Monica Randall
D: Aldo Florio

Five men avenge the death of their friend.

Five Guns to Tombstone (1961) UA

James Brown
John Wilder
Walter Coy
D: Edward L. Cahn

A gunfighter is lured out of retirement to become a government agent.

Five Guns West (1955) ARC

John Lund
Dorothy Malone
Touch (Mike) Connors
D: Roger Corman

Five Confederate gunmen pursue a
stagecoach carrying a deserter and gold.
Filmed at Chatsworth and Jack Ingram Ranch, CA

Au

S

A

Five Man Army (1969) FF—Ital.

Peter Graves
Bud Spencer
James Daly
D: Don Taylor with Italo Zingarelli (and Dario Argento)

Mercenaries are hired to rescue a Mexican revolutionary.

Five Savage Men see The Animals

Five Thousand Dollars on One Ace (1965) FF—Sp./Ital.

Robert Woods
Fernando Sancho
D: Alfonso Balcazar

A gambler wins part ownership in a ranch.

Flame of the Barbary Coast (1945) Republic

John Wayne
Ann Dvorak
Joseph Schildkraut
William Frawley
D: Joseph Kane

A cowboy turns professional gambler. Screenplay by
Borden Chase. Oscar nomination for scoring: drama/comedy.

John Wayne and Ann Dvork in *Flame of the Barbary Coast.*

Flaming Feather (1952) Paramount

Sterling Hayden
Forrest Tucker
Arleen Whelan
Edgar Buchanan
D: Ray Enright

A posse pursues a woman captured by hostiles.
Screenplay by G.D. Adams and Frank Gruber.
Filmed in Sedona, AZ. and at the Iverson Ranch.

Flaming Frontier (1958) RF/20ᵗʰ C.Fox

Bruce Bennett
Don Garrard
Jim Davis
D: Sam Newfield

A half-breed cavalry officer attempts to settle Indian hostilities.

Flaming Frontier (Old Surehand) (1965) FF—Ger./Yug.

Stewart Granger
Pierre Brice
Paddy Fox
Terence Hill

Sterling Hayden in *Flaming Feather.*

D: Alfred Vohrer

An outlaw stirs up trouble with the Comanches.
Last in the series of "Winnetou" films.

Flaming Star (1960) 20ᵗʰ C. Fox

Elvis Presley
Barbara Eden
Steve Forrest
John McIntire
D: Don Siegel

A Kiowa half-breed raised in a "white" world become trapped
between two cultures. Story by Clair Huffaker. Filmed at
Janss Conejo Ranch, Thousand Oaks, CA and Utah.

Flesh and the Spur (1956) A-I

John Agar
Marla English
Touch (Mike) Connors
D: Edward L. Cahn

A young man tracks his twin brother's murderer.

Barbara Eden and Elvis in *Flaming Star*.

*—When I was fighting off the Kiowas
I saw the flaming star of death.*
—Elvis
Flaming Star

Floating Outfit: Trigger Fast see Trigger Fast

For a Few Dollars More (1965/U.S. 1967) FF—Ital./Sp./Ger. ★ ★ ★

Clint Eastwood
Lee Van Cleef
Gian Maria Volontè
Rosemary Dexter
D: Sergio Leone

Two bounty hunters throw in together to track an outlaw. Sequel
to *A Fistful of Dollars* and second of the Leone trilogy. #15 IMDb.

Au ★ ★ ★ ⯪
S ★ ★
A ★ ★ ★

For Better, for Worse see Zandy's Bride

For One Hundred Thousand Dollars Per Killing (1967) FF—Ital.

John Garko (Gary Hudson)
Carlo Gaddi
D: Sidney Lean (Giovanni Fago)

A bounty hunter teams with a sheriff against an outlaw gang.

For One Thousand Dollars Per Day (1966) FF—Ital./Sp.

Dick Palmer
Zachary Hatcher
Josè Calvo
D: Silvio Amadio

A crippled gunfighter teaches a young man how to shoot in order that he may avenge his parents' murder.

Forewarned, Half-Killed…the Word of the Holy Ghost (1971) FF—Ital./Sp.

John Garko
Paolo Gizlino
Victor Israel
D: Anthony Scott (Guiliano Carmineo)

A mysterious gunfighter and a preacher raid a fort in search of gold.

Forgotten Pistolero (1970) FF—Ital./Sp.

Leonard Mann
Luciana Paluzzi
Alberto De Mendoza
D: Ferdinando Baldi

A gunfighter tracks his father's murderer.

John Wayne, Grant Withers and Henry Fonda in *Fort Apache.*

Fort Apache (1948) RKO-Radio

John Wayne
Henry Fonda
Shirley Temple
John Agar
Pedro Armendariz
Ward Bond
Victor McLaglen
Ben Johnson
Harry Carey
D: John Ford

A demoted general is stationed in Apache territory. Based on James Bellah's short story, "Massacre." Filmed in Monument Valley, San Juan River at Mexican Hat, UT. #16 Best of the West, #22 IMDb, # 9 LPFF.

Au ★★★★✦
S ★★★★★
A ★★★★★

—Their pay is thirteen dollars a month. Their diet beans and hay. Maybe horse meat before the campaign is over. They'll fight over cards or rotgut whiskey, but share the last drop in their canteens. The faces may change, the names, but they're there. They're the regiment, the regular Army—now and fifty years from now.

—John Wayne
Fort Apache

210

Fort Bowie (1958) UA

Ben Johnson
Jan Harrison
Kent Taylor
Jana Davi
D: Howard W, Koch

When Apaches capture their fort, the cavalry must retake it.

Fort Courageous (1965) 20th C. Fox

Fred Beir
Donald "Red" Barry
Hanna Landy
Harry Lauter
D: Lesley Selander

A court-martialed sergeant assumes command
of a fort prone to Indian attacks.

Fort Defiance (1951) UA/Ventura Pict.

Dane Clark
Ben Johnson
Peter Graves
Iron Eyes Cody
D: John Rawlins

A man seeks revenge against a Civil War deserter
who caused an entire company to be wiped out.
Filmed in Arizona.

Au ★★
S ★★
A ★★

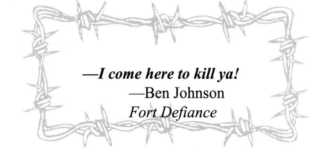

—I come here to kill ya!
—Ben Johnson
Fort Defiance

Fort Dobbs (1958) WB ★★⊁

Clint Walker
Virginia Mayo
Brian Keith
D: Gordon Doughly

A fugitive escorts a mother and her child to
Fort Dobbs during a Comanche uprising.
Screenplay by Burt Kennedy. Filmed at CO River,
Matt Martin Wash, and Professor Valley, UT.

Au ★★⊁
S ★★⊁
A ★★★

*—Cause I got me a rule. I never fight a man
over a woman. Figure it ain't worth it.*
—Brian Keith
Fort Dobbs

For the Love of Mike (1960) 20th C. Fox

Richard Basehart
Stu Erwin
Arthur Shields
Rex Allen
D: George Sherman

An Indian boy trains a horse to race in order to build a new church.

Fort Laramie see Rails Into Laramie

Fort Massacre (1958) MC/UA

Joel McCrea
Forrest Tucker
Susan Cabot
John Russell
D: Joseph M. Newman

After an Indian attack, a cavalry sergeant leads the survivors of his troop back to their fort.

Fort Osage (1952) Mono.

Rod Cameron
Jane Nigh
Morris Ankrum
Iron Eyes Cody
D: Lesley Selander

A scout leads a wagon train west.

Running Antelope, Hunkpapa Dakota, 1872.

Fort Utah (1967) Paramount ★★

John Ireland
Virginia Mayo
Scott Brady
John Russell
Jim Davis
D: Lesley Selander

Tom Horn and an Indian agent take refuge from renegade cavalrymen in an abandoned fort. Filmed at Vasquez Rocks, CA.

Au ★

S ★★

A ★★

Fort Vengeance (1953) AA ★★

James Craig
Rita Moreno
Keith Larsen
D: Lesley Selander

Two brothers enter Canada and join the Mounties. Filmed at Corriganville Ranch, CA.

Au ★★

S ★★

A ★★

—I wanted to take you back alive, kid. But, I don't have to!

—James Craig
Fort Vengeance

Fort Worth (1951) WB

Randolph Scott
David Brian
Phyllis Thaxter
Bob Steele
D: Edward L. Marin

A gunfighter turned newspaper editor must
take up his guns when threatened by outlaws.
Filmed at the Iverson Movie Location Ranch.

Au

S

A

Randolph Scott in *Fort Worth*.

*—I still believe the printed word is
stronger than guns.*
—Randolph Scott
Fort Worth

Forty Guns (1957) GE/20th C. Fox

Barbara Stanwyck
Barry Sullivan
Dean Jagger
D: Samuel Fuller

A gunman is forced to kill again
to avenge his brother's death.

UNCHARTED
TERRITORY

40 Guns to Apache Pass (1967) Admiral Films/Columbia

Audie Murphy
Michael Burns
Kenneth Toby
Laraine Stephens
D: William Witney

A cavalry officer fights Indians and retrieves
repeating rifles. Murphy's last staring Western.
Filmed near Lancaster, California, at Lovejoy Buttes.

Au

S

A

The Forty-Niners (1954) Westwood/AA

Bill Elliott
Virginia Grey
Henry Morgan
D: Thomas Carr

A gunman tracks three killers during the rush.

UNCHARTED
TERRITORY

Fort Yuma (1955) Bel-Air/UA

Peter Graves
Jean Vohs
Joan Taylor
D: Lesley Selander

Trouble develops when a settler kills an Apache chief.

Fort Yuma Gold (1966) FF—Ital./Fr./Sp.

Giulliano Gemma
Dan Vadis
Sophie Daumier
D: Calvin J. Padget (Giorgio Ferroni)

A Confederate rebel plans to raid Fort Yuma.

Four Came to Kill Sartana (1969) (Beyond the Frontiers of Hate) (reissued 1972) FF—Ital.

Jeff Cameron
Anthony G. Staton
Daniela Giordano
D: Miles Deem (Demofilo Fidani, Alessandro Santini)

A gunfighter leads vigilantes against an outlaw gang.

Four Dollars for Vengeance (1965) FF—Sp./Ital.

Robert Woods
Ghia Arlen
Angelo Infanti
D: Alfonso Balcazar

A gunfighter helps a settler track her parents' murderers.

Four Eyes and Six Guns (1965) FF—Sp./Ital. ★★★★

Judge Reinhold
Fred Ward
Patricia Clarkson
Don Hedaya
D: Piers Haggard

Lightedhearted story of a New York optometrist
who ventures west to Tombstone.

Au ★★★★
S ★★★★
A ★★★★

Four Faces West (They Passed This Way) (1948) ★★

Joel McCrea
Charles Bickford
Frances Dee
D: Alfred E. Green

A cowboy turns outlaw in order to
save his father's ranch. Based on a
Eugene M. Rhodes story. Filmed at
El Morro National Monument, New Mexico

and Red Rock Canyon, California.

Au ★★★⯪

S ★

A ★★

Four Fast Guns (1960) U-I

James Craig
Martha Vickers
Edgar Buchanan
D: William J. Hole, Jr.

A gunfighter is forced into a showdown with his brother.

UNCHARTED
TERRITORY

—Back home it all sounded so exciting—nurse for the railroad, new frontiers, the romantic West. Romantic West—look at it…all you've got here is, is miles of rocks and desert, hills with no trees—rattlesnakes!

Frances Dee
Four Faces West

4 for Texas (1964) WB ★

Frank Sinatra
Dean Martin
Anita Ekberg
Ursula Andress
Charles Bronson
The Three Stooges
Bob Steele
D: Richard Aldrich

Two gunmen and their girlfriends fight over $100,000. intended to finance a Texas casino.

Au ★

S ★

A ★

Four Gunmen of the Apocalypse (1975) FF—Ital.

Fabio Testi
Tomàs Milian
Lynn Frederick
D: Lucio Fulci

Four escaped convicts are terrorized by a sadistic outlaw.

UNCHARTED
TERRITORY

Four Gunmen of the Holy Trinity (1971) FF—Ital.

Peter Lee Lawrence
Evelyn Stewart
D: Giorgio Cristallini

A lawman helps a woman fight claim jumpers.

UNCHARTED
TERRITORY

Four Guns to the Border (1954) U-I ★ ★

Rory Calhoun
Coleen Miller
George Nader
Walter Brennan
Jay Silverheels

D: Richard Carlson

Escaping outlaws stop to help an old man and
his daughter. Based on the Louie L'Amour novel.
Filmed at Apple Valley and Bell Ranch, CA.

Au
S
A

Four Rode Out (1969) Hercules/U.A. Films (FF—Ital./Sp./U.S.)

Pernell Roberts
Leslie Nielson
Sue Lyon
D: John Peyser

A Mexican who is falsely accused of murder flees
south pursued by a lawman and a Pinkerton agent.

Frank and Jesse (1995) Trimark Pict.

Rob Lowe
Bill Paxton
Randy Travis
D: Robert Boris

A detective named Pinkerton tracks the legendary brothers.
Filmed at Van Buren, Arkansas.

Au
S
A

Freckles (1960) 20ᵗʰ C. Fox

Martin West
Carol Christiansen
Jack Lambert
Steven Peck
Ken Curtis
D: Andrew V. McLaglen

Frenchie (1951) U-I

Joel McCrea
Shelley Winters
Paul Kelly
D: Louis King

A woman opens a saloon and avenges the murder of her father.

Frenchie King (1971) FF—Fr./Ital./Sp./Brit.

Brigitte Bardot
Claudia Cardinale
Michael J. Pollard
D: Christian-Jaque

Two women gunfighters and their gangs tangle.

Frisco Kid (1935) WB

James Cagney
Margaret Lindsey
Ricardo Cortez
Lily Damita
D: Lloyd Bacon

A sailor opposes gambling on the Barbary Coast.

Frisco Sal (1945) Universal

Susanna Foster
Turhan Bey
Alan Curtis
Andy Devine
D: George Waggner

A New England singer searches for her
brother's murderer on the Barbary Coast.

From Hell to Texas (Manhunt) (1958) 20th C. Fox

Don Murray
Diane Varsi
Chill Wills
Dennis Hopper
Harry Carey, Jr.
D: Henry Hathaway

An innocent man runs from the family of his alleged victim.
Filmed in the Alabama Hills.

From Noon Till Three (1976) UA ★★★⯪

Charles Bronson
Jill Ireland
Douglas V. Fowley
Don "Red" Barry
D: Frank D. Gilroy

A gunfighter is immortalized in a dime novel
after an afternoon affair with a rich widow.

Au ★★★★
S ★★★★
A ★★★⯪

Frontier Badmen (1943) Universal ★★★

Pobert Paige
Diana Barrymore
Leo Carrillo

Andy Devine
Tex Ritter
Anne Gwynne
Noah Berry, Jr.
Lon Chaney, Jr.
D: Willaim McGann, Ford Beebe

Two Texas cowboys confront a Kansas cattle monopoly.

Au ★★★
S ★★◗
A ★★★◗

Frontier Gal (The Bride Wasn't Willing) (1945) Universal

Yvonne De Carlo
Rod Cameron
Andy Devine
Sheldon Leonard
D: Charles Lamont

An outlaw and a saloon girl marry at gunpoint.

Frontier Gambler (1956) AFRC

John Bromfield
Coleen Gray
Jim Davis
D: Sam Newfield

A lawman investigates the murder of a female town boss.

Frontier Gun (1958) RF/20th C. Fox

John Agar
Joyce Meadows
Barton MacLane
D: Paul Landres

An unwilling lawman must clean up a town.

Frontier Marshal (1934) Fox

George O'Brien
Irene Bentley
Ward Bond
D: Lewis Seiler

Frontier Marshal (1939) 20th C. Fox

Randolph Scott
Nancy Kelly
Cesar Romero
Binnie Barnes
John Carradine
Ward Bond
Lon Chaney, Jr.
D: Allan Dwan

Randolph Scott in *Frontier Marshal.*

A marshal delivers law and order to a frontier town.
Inspired by Wyatt Earp. Remake of the 1934 version.

Frontier Uprising (1961) UA

Jim Davis
Nancy Hadley
Ken Mayer
D: Edward L. Cahn

A wagon train heads west in the 1840s
as war breaks out with Mexico.

The Furies (1950) Paramount

Barbara Stanwyck
Walter Huston
Wendell Corey
Gilbert Roland
D: Anthony Mann

A cattle baron's daughter and a gambler must repossess a ranch.

Fury at Furnace Creek (1948) 20th C. Fox

Victor Mature
Coleen Gray
Glenn Langan
Reginald Gardner
Jay Silverheels
D: Bruce Humberstone

Two brothers attempt to clear their father's name.

Fury at Gunsight Pass (1956) Columbia

David Brian
Neville Brand
Richard Long
D: Fred F. Sears

An undertaker helps outlaws rob the town bank.

Fury at Showdown (1957) GP/UA

John Derek
John Smith
Carolyn Craig
Nick Adams
D: Gerd Oswald

A gunfighter attempts to go straight.

Fury in Paradise (1955) Filmmakers

Peter Thompson
Rea Iturbi
Edward Norlega
D: George Bruce

An American tourist becomes involved in a Mexican revolutionary plot.

Fury of Johnny Kid (1967) FF—Sp./Ital.

Peter Lee Lawrence
Paul Naschy
D: Gianni Puccini

A gunman tracks his parents' murderers.

Fury of the Apaches (1966) FF—Sp./Ital.

Frank Latimore
Nuria Torray
D: Joe Lacy (Josè M. Elorrieta)

Indians attack a wagon train. Remake of *Massacre at Fort Grant*.

The Gallant Legion (1948) Republic

William Elliott
Adrian Booth
Joseph Schildkraut
Bruce Cabot
Andy Devine
Iron Eyes Cody
D: Joseph Kane

A Texas Ranger and a newswoman defend
the Rangers from crooked politicians.
Filmed at Vasquez Rocks, California.

—Reckon you ain't gonna be treated like a man much longer, Faulkner. Hee, hee, hee.
—Andy Devine
The Gallant Legion

Au ★★

S ★

A ★

The Gal Who Took the West (1949) U-I

Yvonne De Carlo
Charles Coburn
Scott Brady
John Russell
D: Frederick de Corva

Three cousins feud over a New York singer.
Filmed at Clarence Brown Ranch, Calabasas, CA.

Au ★★★

S ★★⯪

A ★★★

The Gambler (Kenny Rogers as "The Gambler") (1980) K&C/CBS-TV ★★◖

Kenny Rogers
Bruce Boxleitner
Lee Purcell
Christine Belford
D: Dick Lowry

A gambler portrays the story made famous in the
popular song of the same name. Filmed at Old Tucson.

Au ★★★★

S   ★★

A   ★★◖

The Gambler II (The Adventure Continues) (Kenny Rogers as "The Gambler"—The Adventure Continues) (1983) Lion S.P./CBS-TV ★★★

Kenny Rogers
Linda Evans
Bruce Boxleitner
Cameron Mitchell
Johnny Crawford
D: Dick Lowry

A gambler hunts down the man holding his son.
Two-part mini-series sequel to *The Gamber*.

Au ★★★

S   ★★★

A   ★★★

A misdeal.

Gamber III: The Legend Continues (1987) WHPI/CBS-TV

Kenny Rogers
Bruce Boxleitner
Linda Gray
George Kennedy
D: Dick Lowry

Three-part mini-series. Second sequel to *The Gambler*.

The Gambler Returns: Luck of the Draw (1991) NBC-TV ★★

Kenny Rogers and an all-star cast of genre favorites.
D: Dick Lowry

A gambler goes west. Two-part mini-series. Third sequel to *The Gambler*.
Filmed at Big Sky Ranch and Newhall, California.

Au ★★

S   ★★

A   ★★★

Gambler V: Playing for Keeps (1994) CBS-TV

Kenny Rogers
Bruce Boxleitner
Dixie Carter

Loni Anderson
Kris Kamm
D: Jack Bender

A gambler searches for his son who has joined
the Wild Bunch. Fourth sequel to *The Gambler.*

The Gambler Wore a Gun (1961) UA

Jim Davis
Mark Allen
Addison Richards
D: Edward L. Cahn

A gambler buys a ranch only to discover that it is a refuge for stolen cattle.

Garden of Evil (1954) 20th C. Fox

Gary Cooper
Susan Hayward
Richard Widmark
Cameron Mitchell
Rita Moreno
D: Henry Hathaway

A woman hires three mercenaries to find her husband in Mexico.
Filmed in Mexico.

Au ★★◣

S ★★★

A ★★★◣

—I'm gonna make you kill a man to his face!

—Gary Cooper
Garden of Evil

Garter Colt (1967) FF—Ital./Sp./Ger.

Nicoletta Machiavelli
Claudio Camaso Volentè
D: Gian Andrea Rocco

Revolutionary Benito Juarez enlists a female spy to overthrow Maximilian.

The Gatling Gun (1972) EE ★◣

Guy Stockwell
Woody Strode
Barbara Luna
Robert Fuller
Patrick Wayne
Pat Buttram
John Carradine
D: Robert Gordon

A cavalry patrol prevents a Gatling gun from being
captured by Apaches. Filmed at Eaves Movie Ranch, NM.

Au ★◣

S ★◣

A ★◣

Gavilan (The Ballad of Gavilan) (1968)

George DeVries
Christopher George
D: William J. Jugo

The Gay Cavalier (1946) Mono.

Gilbert Roland
Martin Garralaga
Nacho Galindo
D: William Nigh

The Cisco Kid investigates a stagecoach
robbery. Based on O'Henry's character.

A Genius (Nobody's the Greatest) (1975) FF—Fr./Ger./Ital.

Terence Hill
Miou Miou
Patrick McGoohan
Klaus Kinski
D: Damiano Damiani

Outlaws attempt to con an Army officer.
Filmed in part in Monument Valley.

Gentle Annie (1944) MGM

James Craig
Donna Reed
Marjorie Main
Henry Morgan
D: Andrew Martin

A waitress, two outlaws and their mother are
befriended by a U.S. Marshal in 1901 Oklahoma.

Au ★★

S ★

A ★

Gentleman Killer (1969) FF—Sp./Ital.

Anthony Steffen
Eduardo Fajardo
D: George Finley (Giorgio Stegani)

Outlaws take over a border town.

Geronimo (1940) Paramount

Preston Foster
Ellen Drew
Andy Devine
William Henry
Chief Thunder Cloud

General Nelson A. Miles

D: Paul H. Sloane

A cavalryman attempts to stop an Indian war.
Filmed in the area of El Paso, TX. and the
Iverson Movie Location Ranch.
Technical advise by Joe De Yong.

Au

S

A

Geronimo (1962) UA

Chuck Connors
Kamala Devi
Ross Martin
Pat Conway
Adam West
D: Arnold Laven

The Apache leader fights to preserve his dignity.
Filmed in Durango, Mexico.

Au

S

A

—I want respect for what I am, not for what they want me to be.
—Chuck Connors
Geronimo (1962)

Geronimo (1993) TNT

Joseph Runningfox
August Schellenberg
Jimmy Herman
Andrew Mora
Ryan Black
D: Roger Young

The legendary Apache reflects on his life. Filmed in Professor
Valley and George White Ranch, Utah, and at Old Tucson.

Au

S

A

Geronimo (far right) and three warriors during
an 1886 conference with General Crook.

Geronimo: An American Legend (1993) Columbia

Jason Patric
Robert Duvall
Gene Hackman
Wes Studi
D: Walter Hill

An Army officer is ordered to capture the Apache renegade.
Oscar nomination for best sound. Filmed in Professor Valley,
Potash Trail, Potash Plant, Bate's Ranch, Lawson Ranch, Onion Creek, UT.

Get the Coffin Ready (1968) FF—Ital.

Terence Hill
Horst Frank
D: Ferdinando Baldi

224

Django avenges his wife's murder.

Ghost Dancing (1983) ABC-TV

Dorothy McGuire
Bruce Davison
Bill Erwin
Richard Farnsworth
D: David Greene

Ghost of Zorro (1959) Republic

Clayton Moore
Pamela Blake
Roy Barcroft
D: Fred C. Brannon

A descendent of Don Diego protects a telegraph line.
Feature length version of the 1949 serial.

Ghost Town (1956) Bel-Air/UA

Kent Taylor
John Smith
Marian Carr
D: Allen Miner

When attacked by Indians, a stagecoach takes refuge in a ghost town.

Ghoul's Gold see Uninvited

Girl Crazy (1932) RKO Radio

Bert Wheeler
Robert Woolsey
Eddie Quillan
Mitzi Green
D: William Seiter

The Girl From Alaska (1942) Republic

Ray Middleton
Jean Parker
Jerome Cowan
D: Nick Grinde

A man becomes involved with outlaws who
attempt to cheat a girl from her Alaskan claim.

A Girl Is a Gun (1970) FF—Fr.

Jean-Pierre Lèaud

"Going to the Sundance."

Rachel Keserber
D: Luc Moullet

Billy the Kid falls in love with the girlfriend of a man that he murdered.

The Girl of the Golden West (1930) FN

Ann Harding
James Rennie
Harry Bannister
Ben Hendricks, Jr.
Chief Yowlachie
D: John Francis Dillon

A gold rush sheriff competes with an outlaw for the love of a saloon keeper.

The Girl of the Golden West (1938) MGM

Jeanette MacDonald
Nelson Eddy
Walter Pidgeon
Leo Carrillo
Buddy Ebsen
Noah Berry, Sr.
Bill Cody, Jr.
D: Robert Z. Leonard

Remake of the 1930 version.
Filmed at Buffalo Flats, Malibu, CA.

—You can't hate a man for lovin' ya like I love you.
—Walter Pidgeon
The Girl of the Golden West (1938)

Au ★★★
S ★
A ★✦

Girl of the Golden West (Signora dell 'Ovest) (1942) FF—Ital.

Michel Simon
Rossano Brazzi
Valentina Cortese
D: Carlo Koch (Carl Koch)

An ex-music hall artiste and her lover join forces with a cattle baron
in a mining venture. The first feature-length spaghetti Western.

Girl of the Rio (1932) RKO Radio

Dolores Del Rio
Leo Carrillo
Norman Foster
Stanley Fields
D: Herbert Brenon

A Mexican dancer must gamble with an outlaw for the one she loves.

The Glory Guys (1965) UA

Tom Tyron
Harvey Presnell
Michael Anderson, Jr.
James Caan
Slim Pickens
D: Arnold Laven

An officer sacrifices his men for his own personal glory.
Filmed in Durango, Mexico.

Au
S ★
A ★◖

—*Martin, you scare me like that again and
I'll kick your brains in!*
—James Caan
The Glory Guys

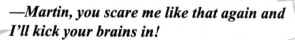

The Glory Trail (1936) Crescent

Tom Keene
Joan Barclay
James Bush
D: Lynn Shores

Following the war, Confederates establish
a town on the Bozeman Trail.

Go Away! Trinity Has Arrived in El Dorado (1972) FF—Ital.

Stan Cooper
Gorden Mitchell
D: Dick Spitfire (Demofilo Fidani)

Two conmen scam their way through the West.

The God Child (1974) ABC-TV/MGM

Jack Palance
Jack Warden
Keith Carradine
D: John Badham

Made for TV remake of *Three Godfathers*.

God Does Not Pay on Saturday (1968) FF—Ital.

Robert Mark
Larry Ward
D: Amerigo Anton (Tanio Boccia)

A retired gunfighter and a woman defend themselves against outlaws.

God Forgives, I Don't (1966) FF—Ital./Sp.

Terence Hill
Bud Spencer
Frank Wolff
D: Giuseppe Colizzi

Three gunmen vie for possession of stolen gold.

God in Heaven…Arizona on Earth (1972) FF—Sp./Ital.

Peter Lee Lawrence
Roberto Camardiel
Maria Pia Conte
Frank Braña
D: John Wood

A bounty hunter avenges his father's death.

God is My Colt .45 (1972) FF—Ital.

Jeff Cameron
Donald O'Brien
Krista Nell
D: Dean Jones (Luigi Batzella)

An Army captain goes undercover to resolve a town's corruption.

God Made Them…I Kill Them (1968) FF—Ital.

Dean Reed
Peter Martell
D: Paolo Bianchi (Paolo Bianchini)

A border town hires a gunfighter to protect their gold shipments.

God's Country and the Woman (1937) WB

George Brent
Beverly Roberts
Barton McLane
Robert Barrat
Alane Hale
D: William Keighly

The new manager of a timber company locks horns with the female owner of the rival camp. Based on a James O. Curwood story.

God's Gun (1976) FF—Ital./Isr.

Lee Van Cleef
Jack Palance
Leif Garrett
Richard Boone
D: Frank Kramer (Gianfranco Parolini)

A gunfighter avenges the

—Johnny, time to spread God's word.
—Lee Van Cleef
God's Gun

228

death of his twin brother.

Au

S

A

God Will Forgive My Pistol (1969) FF—Ital.

Wayde Preston
Loredana Nusciak
D: Mario Gariazzo with Leopoldo Savona

A Texas Ranger investigates a murder.

Goin' South (1978) Paramount

Jack Nicholson
Mary Steenburgen
Christopher Lloyd
John Belushi
Danny DeVito
Ed Begley, Jr.
D: Jack Nicholson

A horse thief avoids hanging by marrying a
woman who intends that he work her gold mine.
Filmed in Durango, Mexico. #57 Best of the West.

Au

S

A

*—I'll never forget you, Hermine. You's
the first woman I didn't have to pay for.*
—Jack Nicholson
Goin' South

Go Kill and Come Back (1968) FF—Ital.

Ed Byrnes
George Hilton
Gilbert Roland
D: Enzo G. Castillari (Enzo Girolami)

Gunmen search for hidden gold.

Golden Girl (1951) 20ᵗʰ C. Fox

Mitzi Gaynor
Dale Robertson
Dennis Day
James Barton
D: Lloyd Bacon

Gold rush actress Lotta Crabtree falls
in love with a Confederate spy.

The Golden West (1932) Fox

George O'Brien
Janet Chandler
Marion Burns
Onslow Stevens

California placer miners circa 1850.

South Dakota placer miners circa 1877.

The Many Faces of Gold Mining

Placer mining in *Wells Fargo.*

Mexican-American miners circa 1890.

California placer miners circa 1850.

230

Chief Big Tree
John War Eagle
D: David Howard

After his father is killed by Indians,
a boy is raised by the tribe and leads
an attack on settlers. Based on
Zane Grey's, *The Last Trail*.

Gold, Glory and Custer (1962) WB

Clint Walker
Julie Adams
D: George Waggner

Compilation of several episodes of the "Cheyenne" TV series.

Gold Is Where You Find It (1938) WB

George Brent
Olivia de Haviland (Olivia de Havilland)
Claude Rains
George ("Gabby") Hayes
D: Michael Curtiz

Hydraulic mining creates hostilities
between California miners and farmers.
Filmed at Warner Ranch and Weaverville, CA.
#83 Best of the West.

Au ★★★★★
S ★★★★
A ★★★★

*—Perhaps. But, gold is where
you find it, Serena.*
—George Brent
Gold Is Where You Find It

Gold of the Heroes (1971) FF—Ital./Fr.

George Ardisson
Linda Veras
D: Don Reynolds (Renato Savino)

A fortune in gold is discovered
in an abandoned fortress.

Gold of the Seven Saints (1961) WB

Clint Walker
Roger Moore
Leticia Roman
Chill Wills
D: Gordon Douglas

Two gold-rich trappers evade thieves as they return from their diggin's.
Filmed at Fisher Towers, CO River, White's Ranch, Arches National Park,
Dead Horse Point St. Park, Seven Mile Wash, Klondike Flats

Au ★★★
S ★★★
A ★★★★

Gone With the West (Little Moon And Jud McGraw) (1976) Cougar Prod.

James Caan
Stefanie Powers
Aldo Ray
Sammy Davis, Jr.
Peter Fonda
D: Bernard Girard

When a reporter and his girlfriend visit a ghost
town, they are told a story of the town's past.

Good Day for a Hanging (1959) Columbia

Fred MacMurray
Maggie Hayes
Robert Vaughn
Joan Blackman
James Drury
D: Nathan Juran

A town is coerced into reducing
the sentence of a murderer.

Au ★★☆
S ★★☆
A ★★★

*—Since when is a young rattlesnake
any less poisonous than an old one?*
—Fred MacMurray
Good Day for a Hanging

A Good Day for Fighting see Custer of the West

Clint Walker (left), Chill Wills and Roger Moore as prospectors in *Gold of the Seven Saints.*

The Good Guys and the Bad Guys (1969) WB ★★

Robert Mitchum
George Kenned
David Carradine
Tina Louise
John Carradine
Martin Balsam
Buddy Hackett
D: Burt Kennedy

Two gunmen attempt to prevent a train robbery.
Filmed at Chama, NM.

Au ★★

S ★✦

A ★★

—What I need is the warmth of my constituents.
—Martin Balsam
The Good Guys and the Bad Guys

The Good Old Boys (1995) TNT ★★★★★

Tommy Lee Jones
Sam Shephard
Sissy Spacek
Wilford Brimley
D: Tommy Lee Jones

An aging cowboy returns home to circa 1906 Texas only
to confront a changing world and the end of an era.
Filmed at Alamo Village, Brackettville, TX. #8 Best of the West.

Au ★★★★★

S ★★★★★

A ★★★★★

*—Well, we could say that ol' Rasmussen was a feller in mossy horns who crossed
does crossing on the Red River when most of us was followin' our mothers aroun'
the kitchen. We could say that it 'as him, his kind, that beat out the trails an' shot
the Yankees an' whooped the Indians off so we could have the easy life we're living
here today. Some say an ol' drifter like this mighta used up his welcome. But, how
many times has a feller just like this come up on a downed fence an' rode into
somebody's headquarters to tell about it? Or rode upon a calf stuck out in the mud,
dropped a loop on it an' pulled it out an' rode off without a thought ta ever gettin'
paid? Even when we turned our back on him, he never turned it on us, so, here he is
an' we all better take a look at him before he rides on off 'cause they ain't a makin'
any more like him.*

—Tommy Lee Jones
The Good Old Boys

The Good, the Bad, and the Ugly (1966/U.S. 1968) FF—Ital.

Clint Eastwood
Lee Van Cleef
Eli Wallach
Aldo Giuffre
Frank Braña
Rada Rassimov
D: Sergio Leone

Three men search for $200,000. in gold.
The third of Sergio Leone's "Dollars" trilogy.
Originally known as "The Magnificent Rogues."
#44 Best of the West, #1 IMDb.

Au ★★★★★
S ★★★★
A ★★★★

Eli Wallach and Clint Eastwood.

Gore Vidal's Billy the Kid see Billy the Kid

Go West, Young Girl (1978) ABC-TV/B-KP/Columbia

Karen Valentine
Sandra Will
Stuart Whitman
D: Alan J. Levi

A cavalry widow and a New England writer
search for Billy the Kid. Filmed at Old Tucson.

Au ★★
S ★★
A ★★

—Drop that gun or I'll shoot you—everybody!
—Karen Valentine
Go West, Young Girl

Go With God, Gringo (1966) FF—Ital./Sp.

Glenn Saxon
Lucretia Love
D: Edward G. Muller (Edoardo Mulargia)

An innocent cowboy escapes from
prison with a gang of outlaws.

The Grand Duel see The Big Showdown

Grayeagle (1977) AI ★

Ben Johnson
Alex Cord
Lana Wood
Iron Eyes Cody
Jack Elam
D: Charles B. Pierce

A mountainman searches for his daughter
who was kidnapped by a Cheyenne.

*—He never had much, Lord, exceptin' his old
dog. And somehow that just don't seem right.*
—Ben Johnson
Grayeagle

234

Filmed in Helena National Forest, Montana.

Au

S

A

The Great Barrier (Silent Barriers) (1937) FF—Guamont-Brit.

Richard Arlen
Antoinette Cellier
Barry Mackay
Lilli Palmer
D: Milton Rosmer, Geoffrey Barkas

A gambler becomes a railroad builder in Canada.

UNCHARTED TERRITORY

Great Day in the Morning (1956) RKO ★ ★

Virginia Mayo
Robert Stack
Ruth Roman
Raymond Burr
D: Jacques Tourneur

A North vs. South rivalry develops among Denver prospectors.

Au ★ ★

S ★ ★

A ★ ★

—All men aren't alike, Phil. It's always hard to be different.
—Robert Stack
Great Day in the Morning

The Great Divide (1929) First National

Dorothy Mackaill
Ian Keith
Myrna Loy
D: Reginald Barker

When an arrogant eastern woman visits the West, she is abducted by a miner.

Au

S ★

A

Greatest Robbery in the West (1968) FF—Ital.

George Hilton
Walter Barnes
D: Maurizio Lucidi

An outlaw disguised as a friar robs a bank.

UNCHARTED TERRITORY

The Great Gundown (The Savage) (Savage Red, Outlaw White) (1976) SP

Robert Padilla
Malia St. Duval
Richard Rust
Steven Oliver

D: Paul Hunt

A gunman recruits a band of mercenaries
to face a legendary outlaw.

The Great Jesse James Raid (1953) Lippert

Willard Parker
Barbara Payton
Tom Neal
D: Reginald Le Borg

Jesse joins Bob Ford to steal
gold hidden in a mine.

The Great Manhunt see The Doolins of Oklahoma

The Great Man's Lady (1942) Paramount

Barbara Stanwyck
Joel McCrea
Brian Donlevy
D: William A. Wellman

An old woman reflects on her life in the
Old West with a senator and a gambler.

Au ★★◄
S ★★
A ★★★◄

Barbara Stanwyck and Joel McCrea.

The Great Missouri Raid (1951) Paramount

Wendell Corey
Macdonald Carey
Ellen Drew
Edgar Buchanan
D: Gordon Douglas

Frank and Jesse James become outlaws
when they mistakenly kill a Union soldier.
Story by Frank Gruber.

"On Outpost Duty."

The Great Northfield, Minnesota Raid (1972) Universal

Cliff Robertson
Robert Duvall
Luke Askew
R.G. Armstrong
D: Philip Kaufman

The Youngers and James brothers stage an ill-fated
bank robbery. Filmed at Jacksonville, Oregon.

Au ★★★★★
S ★★★
A ★★★★

Cliff Robertson's Cole Younger (left) leads
gang members into Northfield, Minnesota.

Great Silence (The Big Silence) (1968) FF—Ital./Fr.

Jean-Louis Trintignant
Klaus Kinski
Frank Wolff
D: Sergio Corbucci

Sadistic bounty hunters ambush hill people
who are forced into a life of crime to survive.

UNCHARTED
TERRITORY

The Great Sioux Massacre (1965) Columbia ★

Joseph Cotten
Darren McGavin
Philip Carey
Iron Eyes Cody
D: Sidney Salko

Two of Custer's officers give their account
of the Little Big Horn. Filmed at Old Tucson.

Au ★
S ★
A ★★

*—Whatever his mistakes, George
Armstrong Custer died a brave man.*
—Darren McGavin
The Great Sioux Massacre

The Great Sioux Uprising (1953) U-I ★★

Jeff Chandler
Faith Domergue
Lyle Bettger
John War Eagle
D: Lloyd Bacon

An ex-Union surgeon must prevent Confederates and
rustlers from turning the Sioux against Union soldiers.
Filmed at Pendleton, Oregon.

Au ★★
S ★★
A ★★

7th Cavalry, "On the March—the Advance Guard."

Great Treasure Hunt (1967) FF—Ital./Sp.

Mark Damon
Stan Cooper

Rosalba Neri
D: Tonino Ricci

A fortune in gold is stolen from a bandit.

The Grey Fox (1983) UAC ★★★★★

Richard Farnsworth
Jackie Burroughs
Wayne Robson
Ken Pogue
Timothy Webber
D: Philip Borsos

Upon his release from prison, stagecoach robber, Bill
Miner, seeks a new line of work. Filmed in British
Columbia, Canada and Washington. # 6 Best of the West.

Au ★★★★★
S ★★★★★
A ★★★★★

—A professional always specializes.
—Richard Farnsworth
The Grey Fox

Bill Miner

Dick Farnsworth as Bill Miner.

Gringo see Gunfight at Red Sands

Guardian of the Wilderness (1976) SC

Denver Pyle
John Dehner
Ken Berry
Cheryl Miller
D: David O'Malley

A man prevents loggers from
cutting the sequoias in Yosemite.

The Gun and the Pulpit (1974) ABC-TV/DTP ★★

Marjoe Gortner
Slim Pickens
David Huddleston
D: Daniel Petrie

A gunfighter poses as a preacher. Made
for TV movie. Filmed at Old Tucson.

Au ★★★

S ★★

A ★★★

Gun Battle at Monterey (1957) AA ★★

Sterling Hayden
Pamela Duncan
Ted de Corsia
Lee Van Cleef
D: Carl K. Hittleman, Sidney A. Franklin, Jr.

An outlaw tracks his partner who double-crossed him. Filmed at Red Rock Canyon, CA.

Au ★★

S ★★

A ★★

Gun Belt (1953) Globel/UA

George Montgomery
Tab Hunter
Helen Wescott
Jack Elam
D: Ray Nazarro

A gunfighter discovers the difficulty
in retiring from his profession.

Gun Brothers (1956) UA

Buster Crabbe
Ann Robinson
Neville Brand
Michael Ansara
Slim Pickens
D: Sidney Salko

A man returns home only to discover
his brother has turned outlaw.

UNCHARTED
TERRITORY

Gun Duel in Durango (Duel in Durango) (1957) Peerless/UA ★

George Montgomery
Ann Robinson
Steve Brodie
Bobby Clark
D: Sidney Salko

When the leader of an outlaw gang quits to
marry a rancher, his replacement frames him.

Au ★

S ★

A

Gun Fever (1958) UA

Mark Stevens
John Lupton
Larry Storch
Iron Eyes Cody
D: Mark Stevens

A gunfighter avenges his father's murder.

Gun Fight (1961) UA

James Brown
Joan Staley
Gregg Palmer
D: Edward L. Cahn

When a veteran heads west, he
discovers his brother is an outlaw.

A Gunfight (1971) Paramount

Kirk Douglas
Johnny Cash
Jane Alexander
Raf Vallone
Karen Black
Keith Carradine
D: Lamont Johnson

Two gunfighters stage a professional shootout.

Au

S

A

*—Well now, we could kill 'em both, but there's
no sense in bein' wasteful because we're
gonna be needin' one of 'em.*
—DeForest Kelley
Gunfight at Comanche Creek

Gunfight at Comanche Creek (1963) AA

Audie Murphy
Ben Cooper
Colleen Miller
De Forrest Kelly
D: Frank McDonald

An agency detective baits a jailbreak.
Second remake of *Star of Texas*.
Filmed at Chatsworth, California.

Au

S

A

Audie Murphy in *Gunfight at Comanche Creek.*

The Gunfight at Dodge City (1959) Mirisch/UA

Joel McCrea
Julie Adams
John McIntire

Nancy Gates
D: Joseph M. Newman

Bat Masterson is hired to clean up a town.

Gunfight at High Noon (1963) FF—Sp./Ital.

Richard Harrison
Fernando Sancho
D: Joaquin Romero Marchent

Three brothers tangle over
their father's murderer.

—*If I was doin' you a favor, I'd let 'em hang you right now and get it all over with. But, I don't want you to get off that light…You'll see what I mean. Just waaait.*

—Gregory Peck
The Gunfighter

Gunfight At Red Sands see Gringo

Gunfight at the O.K. Corral (1957) Paramount ★★★⯪

Burt Lancaster
Kirk Douglas
Rhonda Fleming
Jo Van Fleet
John Ireland
Dennis Hopper
Martin Milner
Lee Van Cleef
Jack Elam
D: John Sturges

The Earps and Clantons face off in the famous Tombstone gunfight. (Note: The producers originally had Humphrey Bogart in mind to play Wyatt, but Douglas insisted on Lancaster.) Oscar nomination for sound recording and film editing. Filmed at the Paramount Ranch, Tombstone and Old Tucson. #46 IMDb.

—*Here's my chance to start a new life in a new country. Someday to have a few head of cattle, your own corral. Drawing water from your well instead of guns from your holster.*

—Randolph Scott
The Gunfighters

Au ★★
S ★★★★⯪
A ★★★★⯪

Gunfighter (1997) PCP

Chris Lybert
Lou Schwiebert
Will Hutchins
Robert Carradine
Martin Sheen
D: Christopher Coppala

A mysterious cowboy relates the story of Hopalong Cassidy to a struggling musician. Filmed in Alberta, Canada.

♪
—*Hopalong, where have ya gone? Will you be comin' back this way?*

—Robert Carradine
Gunfighter

Au ★★★⯪
S ★★⯪
A ⯪

The Gunfighter (1950) 20ᵗʰ C. Fox

Gregory Peck
Helen Westcott
Millard Mitchell
Karl Malden
Skip Homeier
Alan Hale, Jr.
D: Henry King

An aging gunfighter attempts to reconcile
with his abandoned wife and son.
Oscar nomination for writing: original
story. Filmed in the Alabama Hills. #34 Best
of the West, #28 IMDb.

Au ★★★

S ★★★★

A ★★★★

Gregory Peck and Skip Homeier in *The Gunfighter.*

Gunfighters (The Assassin) (1947) Columbia

Randolph Scott
Barbara Britton
Dorothy Hart
Forrest Tucker
D: George Waggner

A retired gunfighter avenges his friend's
murder. From Zane Grey's, *Twin Somberos.*
Screenplay by Alan Lemay. Filmed in Sedona, AZ.

Au ★★

S ★★

A ★★

Randolph Scott in *Gunfighters.*

The Gunfighters (1990) TEC/FF—Canada

Art Hindle
Reiner Schone
Tony Addabbo
George Kennedy
D: Clay Borris

Three ranchers protect their interests from a local tyrant.
Pilot for the Canadian TV series. Filmed in part in Fort
Edmonton Park, Canada.

Au ★★★

S ★★

A ★★

*—Someday, he might just get to be as famous
as Billy the Kid…eh, eh, eh, eh, eh, eh.*
—George Kennedy
The Gunfighters (1990)

Gunfighter's Moon (1995) ★★★

Lance Henriksen
Kay Lentz
David Mcllwrath
D: Larry Ferguson

A gunfighter discovers an unknown daughter in a Wyoming town. Filmed in British Columbia.

Au ★★★◗

S ★★★

A ★★★

—And all I really wanted was to go back and start again.
—Lance Henriksen
Gunfighter's Moon

Gunfighters of Abilene (1960) UA ◗

Buster Crabbe
Barton MacLane
Judith Ames
D: Edward L. Cahn

A gunfighter avenges his brother's murder. Filmed at Melody Ranch, California.

Au ★

S ◗

A ◗

Gunfighters of Casa Grande (1965) FF—Sp./U.S.

Alex Nicols
Jorge Mistral
Steve Roland
D: Roy Rowland

Mexican bandits raid an American owned hacienda. Story by Borden and Patricia Chase.

Gunfight in Abilene (1967) Universal ★ ★

Bobby Darin
Emily Banks
Leslie Nielsen
Donnelly Rhodes
D: William Hale

A gunshy Confederate reluctantly becomes sheriff.

Au ★★

S ★★

A ★★◗

—If you stay out in the West, Mr. Warren, you're gonna find you can't negotiate with a Bowie knife or a six-shooter.
—Phil Carey
Gun Fury

Gunfight in Black Horse Canyon (1961) CBS-TV ★ ◗

Dale Robertson
Ellen Burstyn
George Kennedy
William Demarest
Claude Akins
D: R.G. Springsteen

An outlaw seeks revenge against the Wells Fargo agent that sent him to prison. From the "Tales of Wells Fargo" TV series.

Au

S ★

A ★

Gunfire at Indian Gap (1957) Republic

Vera Ralston
Anthony George
George Macready
D: Joseph Kane

Gunmen pursue a shipment of gold and a half-breed girl.

Gun for a Coward (1957) U-I

Fred MacMurray
Jeffrey Hunter
Janice Rule
Chill Wills
Iron Eyes Cody
Bob Steele
D: Abner Biberman

A rancher attempts to raise his younger brothers.
Filmed at Vasquez Rocks, California.

Au ★★

S ★

A ★★

—It's right to live life as it comes…You're lost to wait 'til everything's perfect—I'm not waitin' anymore!

—Fred MacMurray
Gun For a Coward

Gun Fury (1953) Columbia

Rock Hudson
Donna Reed
Phil Carey
D: Raoul Walsh

A pacifist tracks the outlaw who abducted his fiancèe.
Filmed in Sedona, AZ.

Au ★★

S ★★

A ★★★

Rock Hudson in *Gun Fury.*

Gun Glory (1957) MGM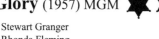

Stewart Granger
Rhonda Fleming
Chill Wills
D: Roy Rowland

An unwanted gunfighter is a town's

♪
—You'll always remember sweet Betsy from Pike. Who crossed the high mountains with her lover Ike.

—Chill Wills
Gun Glory

only solution to a crooked rancher.

Au

S ★ ★

A ★ ★

The Gun Hawk (1963) AA

Rory Calhoun
Rod Cameron
Ruta Lee
Rod Lauren
D: Edward Ludwig

A dying gunfighter reforms a young gunman. Filmed in Griffith Park, California.

Au ★ ✦

S ★

A ★

—A man doesn't like to be reminded of his failures.

—Rory Calhoun
The Gun Hawk

Gunman of One Hundred Crosses (1971) FF—Ger./Ital.

Tony Kendall
Marina Mulligan
D: Lucky Moore (Carlo Croccolo)

A widowed rancher seeks revenge for her husband's murder.

UNCHARTED TERRITORY

Gunman's Walk (1958) Columbia

Van Heflin
Tab Hunter
Kathryn Grant
James Darren
Chief Blue Eagle
D: Phil Karlson

A gunfighter becomes his own law.

Au ★ ★

S ★ ★

A ★ ★

—But what, what's wrong with a man wanting his son to be like him. To live like him. To ride like him…

—Van Heflin
Gunman's Walk

Gunmen and the Holy Ghost (1973) FF—Ital.

Vassili Karis
Dick Palmer
D: Roberto Mauri

Two gunfighters recruit an army of gunmen to defend a border town.

UNCHARTED TERRITORY

Gunmen From Laredo (1959) Columbia

Robert Knapp
Jana Davi
Walter Coy

D: Wallace McDonald

A rancher is framed for the murder of his wife.
Filmed at the Iverson Movie Location Ranch.

Au

S

A

Gunmen of Rio Grande (1964) FF—Ital./Sp./Fr.

Guy Madison
Fernando Sancho
Madeleine Lebeau
D: Tullio Demichelli

Wyatt Earp changes his name to "Laramie" in order to cross the border and defend a Mexican mining town.

Gunpoint (1966) Universal

Audie Murphy
Joan Staley
Warren Stevens
Edgar Buchanan
D: Earl Bellamy

A lawman and his posse pursue train robbers.
Filmed in St. George, Utah.

Au

S

A

The Gun Riders (1969) I-I

Robert Dix
Jim Davis
Scott Brady
John Carradine
D: Al Adamson

Lawmen pursue a gunrunner supplying weapons to Yaqui Indians.

Guns Don't Argue (1957) VD

Myron Healey
Jim Davis
Lyle Talbot
Jean Harvey
Lash LaRue
D: Bill Karn, Richard C. Kahn

Guns Don't Argue (1963) see The Two From Rio Bravo

Guns Don't Argue (1964) see Bullets Don't Argue

246

Gunsight Ridge (1957) UA

Joel McCrea
Mark Stevens
Joan Weldon
Slim Pickens
D: Francis D. Lyon

An undercover agent investigates a crooked mine operator. Filmed at Old Tucson, Bell Ranch, Janss Conejo Ranch, California.

Au ★★

S ★

A ★

—Yaaah! Yaah! Yaahoo! Git on there boy! Yaah! Yaaahoo! Yaaahoooyaahaa!
—Slim Pickens
Gunsight Ridge

Guns in the Afternoon see Ride the High Country

Gunslinger (1956) ARC

John Ireland
Beverly Garland
Allison Hayes
D: Roger Corman

When the marshal is killed, his wife assumes his duties.

Gun Smoke (1931) Paramount

Richard Arlen
Mary Brian
Eugene Pallette
Louise Fazenda
D: Edward Sloman

—You're pretty tough with that gun strapped around your waist. I wonder how tough you'd be without it?
—Jack Kelly
Gunsmoke

Gunsmoke (1953) U-I ★ ★

Audie Murphy
Susan Cabot
Paul Kelly
Jack Kelly
D: Nathan Juran

A gunfighter shows interest in a Montana cattleman's ranch and his daughter. Based on Norman Fox's, *Roughshod*. Filmed in Big Bear, California.

Au ★½

S ★★

A ★★

Audie Murphy in *Gunsmoke*.

Gunsmoke in Tuscon (1958) AA ★

Mark Stevens
Forrest Tucker
Gale Robbins
D: Thomas Carr

A lawman suspects his outlaw brother of murder.

Au ★

S ★

A ★

Gunsmoke: One Man's Justice (1994) CBS-TV ★ ★ ◀

James Arness
Bruce Boxleitner
Kelly Morgan
Amy Stock-Poynton
D: Jerry Jameson

Matt Dillon helps a boy track the murderers of his mother.
Filmed in Arizona.

Au ★ ★ ★

S ★ ★ ◀

A ★ ★ ◀

*—God may have created man,
but Sam Colt made 'em equal.*
—Bruce Boxleitner
Gunsmoke: One Man's Justice

Gunsmoke: Return to Dodge (1987) CBS-TV ★ ★

James Arness
Amanda Blake
Buck Taylor
Fran Ryan
D: Vincent McVeety

Retired Marshal Dillon returns to Dodge to rescue Miss Kitty.
TV movie based on the series. Filmed in the U.S. and Edmonton,
Canmore, Calgary and Kananaskis County, Alberta, Canada.

Au ★ ★ ◀

S ★ ★

A ★ ★

*—Drop the gun! Now, that hideout
gun that's holdin' up your backbone!*
—James Arness
Gunsmoke: Return to Dodge

Gunsmoke: The Last Apache (1990) CBS-TV ★ ★ ◀

James Arness
Richard Kiley
Michael Learned
Hugh O'Brian
D: Charles Correl

Matt Dillon must rescue his kidnapped daughter
from Geronimo. Based on the TV series. Filmed
at Big Bend Ranch State Natural Area, Alamo Village,
Brackettville, TX, Bill Moody's Rancho, Rio Grande.

Au ★ ★ ◀

S ★ ★ ★

A ★ ★ ◀

*—If the Lord asked me what kind of daughter
I wanted, I'd sure know what to tell 'em. I'm
real proud of you.*
—James Arness
Gunsmoke: The Last Apache

248

Gunsmoke: The Long Ride (The Long Ride) (1993) CBS-TV ★★★

James Arness
James Brolin
Amy Stock-Poynton
D: Jerry Jameson

Retired lawman, Matt Dillon, searches for a look-alike
who murdered a miner. Filmed at Old Tucson.

Au ★★★

S ★★★

A ★★★

*—Ya know eh, a man spends too much time
a lookin' for the perfect woman he might
wind up being single.*
—James Arness
Gunsmoke: The Long Ride

Gunsmoke: To the Last Man (1991) CBS-TV ★★★

James Arness
Pat Hingle
Amy Stock-Poynton
Matt Mulhern
D: Jerry Jameson

Retired marshal, Matt Dillon, and his daughter become entagled
in a feud between rustlers and vigilantes. Filmed at Old Tucson.

Au ★★★

S ★★★

A ★★★

"Mysterious Dave Mather,"
Dodge City marshal circa 1870.

Guns of a Stranger (1973) Universal ★

Marty Robbins
Chill Wills
Dovie Beams
Steve Tackett
D: Robert Hinkle

A singing drifter saves a family from outlaws.

Au ★

S ★

A ★

The Guns of Diablo (1965) MGM

Charles Bronson
Susan Oliver
Kurt Russell
Jan Merlin
D: Boris Sagal

Edited from "The Travels of Jamie McPheeters" TV series.

Audie Murphy and Dorothy Crider in *The Guns of Fort Petticoat.*

The Guns of Fort Petticoat (1957) UI ★★

Audie Murphy
Kathryn Grant
Hope Emerson

Jeff Donnell
Dorothy Crider
D: George Marshall

An officer and a group of women hold off an Indian attack.
Filmed at Old Tucson and at the Iverson Movie Ranch.

Au

S ★★

A ★★

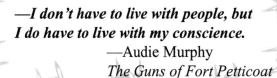

*—I don't have to live with people, but
I do have to live with my conscience.*
—Audie Murphy
The Guns of Fort Petticoat

Guns of Honor (1994) Vidmark

Martin Sheen
Jurgen Prochnow
Christopher Atkins
D: Peter Edwards

A father and son ex-Confederates help peons
fight the French in Mexico. Made for TV movie.

Au ★★◗

S ★◗

A ★

Guns of the Magnificent Seven (1969) FF—Sp.

George Kennedy
James Whitmore
Monte Markham
Bernie Casey
D: Paul Wendkos

Mercenaries rescue a revolutionary in Mexico.
Second sequel to *The Magnificent Seven.*

UNCHARTED
TERRITORY

—Sorry partner.
—Gilbert Roland
Guns of the Timberland

Guns of the Timberland (Stampede) (1960) WB

Alan Ladd
Jeanne Crain
Gilbert Roland
Frankie Avalon
Lyle Bettger
Noah Beery, Jr.
D: Robert D. Webb

When opposed by local ranchers and townspeople, two loggers with a government
contract disagree. Based on the Louie L'Amour novel. Filmed in Williams, AZ.

Au ★★

S ★★

A ★★◗

Guns of Violence see Ten Thousand Dollars Blood Money

Gun Street (1961) UA

James Brown
Jean Willes
John Clarke

D: Edward L. Cahn

A lawman must prevent a convict from murdering the
man that sent him to prison and married his wife.

The Gun That Won the West (1955) Columbia

Dennis Morgan
Paula Raymond
Richard Denning
D: William Castle

An improved model of the Springfield rifle
helps the cavalry establish forts in Wyoming.

Au ★★

S ★⌐

A ★⌐

Gun the Man Down (1956) UA

James Arness
Angie Dickinson
Robert Wilke
Harry Carey, Jr.
D: Andrew V. McLaglen

A bank robber seeks revenge upon his former partners.
McLaglen's directorial debut.
Based on a story by Sam C. Freedle.

The Half-Breed (1952) RKO

Robert Young
Janis Carter
Jack Buetel
Chief Yowlachie
Chief Thunder Cloud
D: Stuart Gilmore

A gambler and a half-breed prevent an Apache uprising.
Filmed in Sedona, AZ.

Au ★⌐

S ★⌐

A ★⌐

*—And in my book lying is cheap
device of a cheap...*
—Robert Young
The Half-Breed

Half Breed (1966) FF—Ger./Yug./Ital.

Lex Barker
Pierre Brice
D: Harold Phillipp

Chief Winnetou and his friend restore peace when whites
attempt to claim jump an Apache mine. Sixth in the
series of Lex Barker/Pierre Brice "Winnetou" films.

Half-breed bit.

Half Way to Hell (1961) VAP

Lyle Felice
Carroll Montour
Sergio Virell
D: Denver Dixon (Victor Adamson)

A girl falls in love with one of Pancho Villa's men.

Halleluja to Vera Cruz (1973) FF—Ital.

Lionel Stander
Ricardo Salvino
D: Newman Rostel (Stelvio Massi)

Two outlaws disguised as priests join revolutionaries to steal a fortune in gold.

The Hallelujah Trail (1965) UA ★ ★ ★

Burt Lancaster
Lee Remick
Jim Hutton
Pamela Tiffin
Donald Pleasence
Brian Keith
Martin Landau
D: John Sturges

An Army officer leads a wagon train of whiskey to Denver.
From the Bill Gulick novel. Filmed in the Alabama Hills and NM.

Au ★ ★ ◗

S ★ ★ ★

A ★ ★ ★

Ute camp near Denver, 1874.

The Halliday Brand (1957) UA ★ ★ ◗

Joseph Cotten
Viveca Lindfors
Betsy Blake
Ward Bond
D: Joseph H. Lewis

The son of a sheriff rebels against his father's injustice. Filmed at the Iverson Movie Ranch.

Au ★ ★

S ★ ★ ★ ◗

A ★ ★ ◗

—Ya know Dan'l, you got a soft spot in your heart just like your mother. She could always see some good in people, no matter what they'd done. But, outside of that you got the Halliday brand.
—Ward Bond
The Halliday Brand

Hands of a Gunman (1965) FF—Ital./Sp.

Craig Hill
Gloria Milland
D: Rafael Romero Marchent

Bounty hunters force an outlaw out of retirement.

The Hanged Man (1974) ABC-TV/Fenedy A./BCP

Steve Forrest
Cameron Mitchell
Sharon Acker
Will Geer
D: Michael Caffey

An ex-gunfighter who survives hanging becomes
an avenger for justice in the Old West. ABC-TV
Movie of the Week. Filmed at Old Tucson.

James B. Daniels lynched in 1866.

Hang 'Em High (1968) UA

Clint Eastwood
Inger Stevens
Ed Begley
Ben Johnson
Bruce Dern
Dennis Hopper
Allen Hale, Jr.
Bob Steele
D: Ted Post (Sergio Leone)

An ex-lawman saved from hanging accepts a marshal's
badge in order to track the men who hanged him. Eastwood's
first film love scene. Filmed in the Chihuahuan desert and
at White Sands National Monument, NM.

Au ★ ★ ★ ✦

S ★ ★ ★

A ★ ★ ★ ★

*—When you hang a man,
you better look at him!*
—Clint Eastwood
Hang 'Em High

The Hanging Tree (1959) WB

Gary Cooper
Maria Schell
Karl Malden
George C. Scott
D: Delmer Daves

A gunfighting doctor assists a temporarily blinded woman.
George C. Scott's film debut. Oscar nomination for best song.

The Hangman (1959) Paramount

Robert Taylor
Fess Parker
Tina Louise
Jack Lord
D: Michael Curtiz

A marshal is confronted with a wanted
outlaw who has reformed himself.

Randolph Scott, Lee Marvin and Donna Reed in *Hangman's Knot*.

Hangman's Knot (1952) S-B/Columbia

Randolph Scott
Donna Reed
Claude Jarman, Jr.

Lee Marvin
D: Roy Huggins

A Confederate officer highjacks a Union gold
shipment prior to discovering the war is over.
Filmed in the Alabama Hills.

Au ★★★◗

S ★★◗

A ★★★★

Hannah Lee (Outlaw Territory) (1953) Broder/Realart ★★★

Joanne Dru
Macdonald Carey
John Ireland
Stuart Randall
D: John Ireland, Lee Garmes

Cattlemen hire a regulator to "evict" squatters. Filmed in Chatsworth, CA.

Au ★★★

S ★★★

A ★★★

Hannie Caulder (1971) FF—Brit./Sp./Fr. ★★◗

Raquel Welch
Robert Culp
Ernest Borgnine
Christopher Lee
Jack Elam
Strother Martin
D: Burt Kennedy

A woman avenges her own rape and the murder of her
husband. Coscreenplay by Burt Kennedy and David Raft
under the combined pseudonym "Z.X. Jones."
Filmed in Spain.

Au ★★◗

S ★★◗

A ★★◗

Hard Bounty (1995)

Matt McCoy
Kelly LeBrock
Kimberly Kelley
Rochelle Swanson
D: Jim Wynorski

A bounty hunter and three whores seek revenge for
the murder of a whore. Filmed in Old Tucson.

Hardcase (1972) ABC-TV/H-BP

Clint Walker
Stephanie Powers
Pedro Armendariz, Jr.

Alex Karris
D: John Lewellyn

A drifter returns home only to find his ranch sold
and his wife with a Mexican revolutionary.

The Hard Man (1957) Romson/Columbia

Guy Madison
Valerie French
Lorne Greene
D: George Sherman

When a Texas Ranger becomes sheriff,
a woman wants him to kill her husband.

Au ★

S ★

A ★

Hard on the Trail (Hard Trail) (1971) Brentwood I.

Lash LaRue
Donna Bradley
Bruce Kemp
D: Greg Corarito

A Hard Road to Vengeance see Hec Ramsey: A Hard Road to Vengeance

Harry Tracy—Desperado (1982) IMC-I/Silverstein Int.

Bruce Dern
Helen Shaver
Michael C. Gwynne
Gordon Lightfoot
D: William A. Graham

Outlaw, Harry Tracy, robs his way across the
northwest at the turn of the century.
Filmed in Alberta, Canada. #35 Best of the West.

Au ★★★★

S ★★★★★

A ★★★★★

Harry Tracy dead at the Eddy Ranch.

Hate for Hate (1969) FF—Ital.

Antonio Sabàto
John Ireland
D: Domenico Paolella

An outlaw attempts to return stolen money to a rancher.

*—I dreamed of bein' an outlaw. Yes sir,
I dreamed of bein' an outlaw.*
—Bruce Dern
Harry Tracy—Desperado

Hate Thy Neighbor (1969) FF—Ital.

George Eastman
Clyde Gardner
Horst Frank
D: Ferdinando Baldi

An outlaw avenges the death of his brother.

Hatred of God (1967) FF—Ital./Ger.

Tony Kendall
Carlo Giordana
D: Claudio Gora

A rancher avenges the murder of his wife.

Have a Good Funeral, My Friend…Sartana Will Pay (1971) FF—Ital.

Gianni Garko
Daniela Giordano
D: Anthony Ascott

A vigilante gunfighter seeks justice for a dishonest banker and his niece.

Hawken's Breed (1987) MLGP

Peter Fonda
Serene Hedin
Jack Elam
Bill Thurman
D: Charles B. Pierce

Hawmps! (1976) Mulberry Sq.

James Hampton
Christopher Connelly
Slim Pickens
Denver Pyle
Jack Elam
D: Joe Camp

A remote outpost becomes the training center for utilizing camels in the cavalry. Filmed at Old Tucson.

Heads or Tails (1969) FF—Ital./Sp

John Ericson
Franco Lantieri
D: Peter E. Stanley (Piero Pierotti)

A bounty hunter tracks a gambler.

Camels at the Nevada silver mines.

Heads You Die...Tails I Kill You (1971) FF—Ital.

George Hilton
Charles Southwood
D: Anthony Ascott (Giuliano Carmineo)

A gunfighter is hired by Mexican revolutionaries to steal Maximilian's jewels.

Heartland (1979) Filmhaus

Rip Torn
Conchata Ferrell
Barry Primus
D: Richard Pearce

A widow agrees to a marriage of convenience with a Wyoming rancher in 1910. Based on letters written by Elinore Randall Stewart. Filmed in Wheatland, Fergus and Meagher counties, Montana.

Au ★★★★★

S ★★★

A ★★★★

—I never did care much for 'em [marriages] myself. They're a sight better than funerals.
—Concheta Ferrell
Heartland

Heaven Only Knows (Montana Mike) (1947) UA

Robert Cummings
Brian Donlevy
Marjorie Reynolds
D: Albert S. Rogell

An angel is sent to earth to save the souls of a saloon owner and a gambler. Story by Ernest Haycox.

Heaven's Gate (1980) UA ★★★★

Kris Kristofferson
Christopher Walken
John Hurt
Sam Waterston
Jeff Bridges
D: Michael Cimino

A marshal finds himself caught between the cattle industry and homesteaders during the Johnson County Wars. Filmed at Glacier National Park, MT. #70 Best of the West.

Au ★★★★★

S ★★★★

A ★★★★

"A Dispute Over a Brand."

Heaven With A Gun (1969) MGM

Glenn Ford
Carolyn Jones
Barbara Hershey
John Anderson
David Carradine
Noah Beery, Jr.

—It's your choice—gunman or preacher. Heaven or hell. But, don't be half and half of anything. That can really be hell.
—Carolyn Jones
Heaven With a Gun

D: Lee H. Katzin

A gunfighter turned preacher searches for a nonviolent
solution to a range war. Filmed at Old Tucson.

Au ★

S ★◖

A ★★

Hec Ramsey (Hec Ramsey: The Century Turns) (The Century Turns) (1972) NBC-TV

Richard Boone
Rick Lentz
Sharon Acker
Harry Morgan
D: George Marshall and Daniel Petrie

At the turn of the century in Oklahoma territory, an aging lawman
accepts a deputy job with a young college-educated lawman. Pilot
for the TV series within the "NBC Sunday Mystery Movie."

Au ★★★

S ★★◖

A ★★★

Hec Ramsey: A Hard Road to Vengeance (A Hard Road to Vengeance) (1973) NBC-TV

Richard Boone
Rick Lentz
D: Alex March

In order to clear his name, a former marshal returns to a
town where a young boy that he killed is to be honored.

Au ★★★

S ★★

A ★★★

Hec Ramsey: Only Birds and Fools (Only Birds and Fools) (1974) NBC-TV/Universal

Richard Boone
Robert Foxworth
Cliff Potts
Harry Morgan
D: ?

An aging lawman investigates a murder at the turn of the century.
From the final episode of "Hec Ramsey."

UNCHARTED
TERRITORY

Hec Ramsey: The Mystery of Chalk Hill (The Mystery of Chalk Hill) (1973)

NBC-TV/Universal

Richard Boone
Sharon Acker
Bruce Davidson
D: ?

An aging gunfighter turned detective investigates a murder.

Hec Ramsey: The Mystery of the Green Feather (The Mystery of the Green Feather)
(1972) NBC-TV/Universal
Richard Boone
Rory Calhoun
Marie Windsor
D: ?

Hec Ramsey questions the guilt of Indians accused of a massacre.

Hec Ramsey: The Mystery of the Yellow Rose (The Mystery of the Yellow Rose) (1972)
NBC-TV

Richard Boone
Rory Calhoun
Marie Windsor
D: Douglas Benton

Hec Ramsey questions the guilt of Indians accused of a massacre.

Au ★★★
S ★★★
A ★★★

Hell Bent for Leather (1960) U-I ★★★

Audie Murphy
Felicia Farr
Stephen McNally
Bob Steele
D: George Sherman

A horse trader is framed for murder.
Filmed in the Alabama Hills.

Au ★★★
S ★★★
A ★★★

Hell Canyon Outlaws (1957) Zukor/Republic

Dale Robertson
Brian Keith
Rossana Rory
D: Paul Landres

A lawman must confront outlaws controlling a small town.

Heller in Pink Tights (1960) Paramount

Sophia Loren
Anthony Quinn
Margaret O'Brien
Steve Forrest
D: George Cukor

A travelling actress and her troupe entertain frontier towns. Loosely based on the life of Adah Isaacs Menken. From Louie L'Amour's, *Heller With a Gun*.

Au ★★★

S ★★★

A ★★★★

From Menken's theatrical poster.

—We are alike, the two of us. All we care about is what we want.
—Sophia Loren
Heller in Pink Tights

Hellfire (1949) Republic

William Elliot
Marie Windsor
Forrest Tucker
Jim Davis
D: R.G. Springsteen

A preacher attempts to convince an outlaw to surrender in order that he can build a church with her reward money.

Au ★★

S ★★

A ★★

—I like him because he's so good and he likes me because I'm so bad.
—Marie Windsor
Hellfire

Hellgate (1952) Lippert

Sterling Hayden
Joan Leslie
Ward Bond
James Arness
D: Charles Marquis Warren

A man is falsely imprisoned in New Mexico's Hellgate Prison.

Hell's Crossroads (1957) Republic

Stephen McNally
Peggie Castle
Robert Vaughn
D: Franklin Adreon

Bob Ford and Vic Rodel (Dick Liddil??) seek pardons for eliminating Jesse James. Filmed at the Iverson Movie Location Ranch.

Au ★

S ★

A ★

—I'll give you Jesse James for a Christmas present.
—Bob Ford (Robert Vaughn)
Hell's Crossroads

260

Hell's Outpost (1954) Republic

Rod Cameron
Joan Leslie
John Russell
Chill Wills
Jim Davis
D: Joseph Kane

When a veteran returns to work his claim, he must confront a crooked banker.
Based on Luke Short's, *Silver Rock*.

Here We Go Again, Eh Providence? (1973) FF—Ital./Fr./Sp.

Tomàs Milian
Gregg Hunter
D: Alberto De Martino

A bounty hunter discovers himself obsolete. Sequel to
Sometimes Life Is Hard, Right Providence.

He Rides Tall (1964) Universal

Tony Young
Dan Duryea
Jo Morrow
D: R.G. Springsteen

A lawman shoots it out with an outlaw and his gang.

Au

S

A

> *—Mr. McCloud, you let a rattlesnake crawl under your house. But, don't worry. Right now we've got him defanged.*
> —Dan Duryea
> *He Rides Tall*

Heritage of the Desert (1939) Paramount

Donald Woods
Evelyn Venable
Russell Hayden
Robert Barrat
D: Lesley Selander

When an Eastern lawyer inspects his frontier mining investment, he discovers
he has been cheated. Story by Zane Grey. Remake of the 1932 version.

Hero Called Allegria (Django Always Draws Second) (1971) FF—Ital.

Peter Martell
Gordon Mitchell
D: Dennis Ford, Slim Alone (Demofilo Fidani)

Two outlaws are robbed of their loot by a bandit.
Last of the original Django films.

Heroes of the Alamo (1937) Sunset (re-released by Columbia in 1938)

Rex Lease
Lane Chandler
Roger Williams
D: Harry Fraser

Western legends defend the Alamo.

Heroes of the West (1964) FF—Sp./Ital.

Walter Chiari
Raimondo
D: Steno (Stefano Vanzina)

Two outlaws find themselves in the midst of a feud between families.

He Was Called the Holy Ghost (1972) FF—Ital.

Vassili Karis
Dick Palmer
D: Robert Johnson (Roberto Mauri)

A gunfighter protects settlers from a foreclosure scheme.

Hey Amigo! A Toast to Your Death! (1971) FF—Ital.

Wayde Preston
Rik Battaglia
D: Paul Maxwell (Paolo Bianchini)

An aging bounty hunter tracks his man into Mexico.

Hidden Guns (1956) Republic

Richard Arlen
Bruce Bennett
John Carradine
Angie Dickinson
D: Al Gannaway

An outlaw hires a gunman to eliminate the sheriff and a witness.

The Hidden One (La Escondida) (1956) FF—Mex.

Carlos Agosti
Pedro Armendàriz
D: Roberto Gavaldòn

High Country Pursuit (1981) DC

Stuart Whitman
Ben Johnson
Will Sampson
Slim Pickens

262

D: ?

Two frontiersmen and an Indian warrior join to track the men who stole their women.

High Hell (1958) Paramount

John Derek
Elaine Stewart
Patrick Allen
Jerold Wells
D: Burt Balaban

A miner, his wife and his partner become snowed in for the winter.

High Lonesome (1950) ELC

John Barrymore, Jr.
Chill Wills
Lois Butler
Jack Elam
D: Alan LeMay

Two brothers set out to destroy their enemies.
Story and screenplay by Alan Le May.

High Noon (1952) UA ★★★★

Gary Cooper
Thomas Mitchell
Lloyd Bridges
Katy Jurado
Grace Kelly
Otto Kruger
Lon Chaney, Jr.
Henry Morgan
Jack Elam
Lee Van Cleef
D: Fred Zinnemann

A retiring marshal discovers the true character of his town when
he chooses to face a killer rather than compromise his standards.
Story by John M. Cunnigham. Oscar nominations for best picture, director,
and writing: screenplay. Oscars for best actor (Cooper), scoring: drama/comedy,
song, and editing. Filmed at Columbia State Park, California.
#38 Best of the West, #33 AFI GM, #20 AFI MHPM, #3 IMDb, #10 IMDb.

Gary Cooper and Grace Kelly.

Au ★★★
S ★★★★
A ★★★★

High Noon (2000) TBS-TV ★★★

Tom Skerritt
Susanna Thompson
Maria Conchita Alonso
Dennis Weaver
D: Ron Hardy

Tom Skerritt in *High Noon* (2000).

Remake of the 1952 version.
Filmed in Alberta, Canada.

Au ★★★┥

S ★★★

A ★★★

—Amy, I only have an hour. He's comin' on the noon train.
—Tom Skerritt
High Noon (2000)

High Noon Part II: The Return of Will Kane (1980) CBS-TV ★★┥

Lee Majors
David Carradine
Pernell Roberts
J.A. Preston
D: Jerry Jameson

The retired sheriff returns to Hadleyville to face the man who replaced him. Sequel to *High Noon.* Filmed at Old Tucson.

Au ★★┥

S ★★

A ★★┥

High Plains Drifter (1973) Universal ★★★★

Clint Eastwood
Verna Bloom
Mariana Hill
Mitchell Ryan
Geoffrey Lewis
Billy Curtis
D: Clint Eastwood

When a gunfighter mysteriously returns to protect the town of Lago from outlaws, its vigilantes are unaware that he is their former marshal who they whipped to death. Eastwood's Western film directorial debut. Filmed entirely at Mono Lake, California. #55 Best of the West. #39 IMDb.

Au ★★★★

S ★★★★

A ★★★★

Clint Eastwood in *High Plains Drifter.*

—Well, it's what people know about themselves inside that makes them afraid.
—Clint Eastwood
High Plains Drifter

High Venture see Passage West

High Vermilion see Silver City

The Highwayman Rides see Billy the Kid

The Hills Run Red (1966) FF—Ital. ★

Thomas Hunter
Henry Silva
D: Lee W. Beaver (Carlo Lizzani)

"One of the Boys."

An ex-Confederate seeks revenge
against his former comrade.

Au

S ⬥

A ⬥

The Hired Gun (1957) Rorvic/MGM ★ ★

Rory Calhoun
Anne Francis
Vince Edwards
Chuck Connors
D: Ray Nazarro

A wealthy Texan hires a gunman to
return an escaped woman for hanging.

Au

S ★ ★

A ★ ★

The Hired Hand (1971) Universal ★ ★ ★ ★

Peter Fonda
Warren Oates
Verna Bloom
Robert Pratt
D: Peter Fonda

A drifter returns to his family after seven years.
Filmed at Cabezon and Chama, NM. #99 Best of the West.

Au

S ★ ★ ★ ★

A ★ ★ ★ ★

His Name Was Holy Ghost (1970) FF—Ital./Sp.

Gianni Garko
Victor Israel
D: Anthony Scott

A mysterious gunfighter rescues a border town from
bandits in an attempt to reinstate the governor.

His Name Was King (1971) FF—Ital.

Richard Harrison
Klaus Kinski
D: Don Reynolds (Renato Savino)

A gunman avenges his brother's murder and his sister's rape.

His Name Was Madron see Madron

His Name Was Sam Walbash, But They Called Him Amen (1971) FF—Ital.

Robert Woods
Dean Stratford
D: Miles Deem (Denofilo Fidani)

The sole survivor of an outlaw gang's murderous rampage seeks revenge.

Hitched (1971) NBC-TV

Sally Field
Tim Matheson
Neville Brand
Slim Pickens
D: Boris Sagal

Teenage newlyweds encounter outlaws.

Au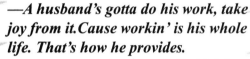

—*A husband's gotta do his work, take joy from it.Cause workin' is his whole life. That's how he provides.*

—Sally Field
Hitched

Au ★ ▌

S ★ ▌

A ★ ▌

Hi-Yo Silver (1940) Republic

Lee Powell
Herman Brix (Bruce Bennett)
Chief Thunder Cloud
Lynne Roberts
D: William Whitney and John English

Edited from the 1938 serial "The Lone Ranger."

Hole in the Forehead (1968) FF—Ital./Sp.

Robert Hundar
Anthony Ghidra
D: Joseph Warren (Giuseppe Vari)

A bounty hunter and a bandit search for lost treasure.

Holy Water Joe (1971) FF—Ital.

Ty Hardin
Richard Harrison
D: Mario Gariazzo

A bounty hunter sets out to recover his own savings lost in a bank robbery.

Hombre (1967) 20th C. Fox

Paul Newman
Fredrick March
Richard Boone
Diane Cilento
Cameron Mitchell
Martin Balsam
D: Martin Ritt

A white man raised by
Apaches returns to live
in a "white" world.
Based on Elmore Leonard's
Hombre. Filmed at
Old Tucson. #47 IMDb.

Au ★★★

S ★★★★

A ★★★★

Paul Newman in *Hombre*.

—We all die. It's just a question of when.
—Paul Newman
Hombre

Hondo (1953) WB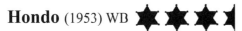

John Wayne
Geraldine Page
Ward Bond
James Arness
D: John Farrow

Apaches take a homesteader
and her son captive. From the
Louie L'Amour novel. Best
supporting actress Oscar
nomination for Page.
Filmed at Camargo, Mexico.

Au ★★★★

S ★★★★

A ★★★★

John Wayne in *Hondo*.

Hondo and the Apaches (1967) Batjac/Fenady/MGM

Ralph Taeger
Michael Rennie
John Smith
Gary Clark
Noah Beery, Jr.
Jim Davis
D: Lee H. Katzin

Based on Louie L'Amour's "The Gift of Cochise."

Honeychile (1951) Republic

Judy Canova
Eddie Foy, Jr.
Alan Hale
D: R.G. Springsteen

A song publisher believes a song from a hick girl was written by a famous composer.

Honky Tonk (1941) MGM

Clark Gable
Lana Turner
Frank Morgan
Claire Trevor
Chill Wills
D: Jack Conway

Law and order come at a high price
for the town of Yellowcreek.

Au ★★★◣
S ★★★★
A ★★★★

Honky Tonk (1974) MGM

Richard Crenna
Stella Stevens
Will Geer
Margot Kidder
D: Don Taylor

Made for TV remake of the 1941 version.

Horizons West (1952) U-I

Robert Ryan
Julia Adams
Rock Hudson
Raymond Burr
James Arness
Dennis Weaver
D: Budd Boetticher

Two brothers return to Texas following the Civil War.
Filmed at Jauregui Ranch, California.

Au ★★★
S ★★★
A ★★★

*—Honey, guess we're gonna have
to wait a while to build our empire.*
—Robert Ryan
Horizons West

A Horse Called Comanche see Tonka

Hostile Guns (1967) Paramount

George Montgomery
Yvonne De Carlo
Tab Hunter
Brian Donlevy
John Russell
D: R.G. Springsteen

Two lawmen take a prison wagon across hostile country.

Hot Spur (1968)

268

John Alderman
James Arena
Wes Bishop
Angel Carter
D: Lee Frost

A deranged stable hand avenges the rape of his sister.

Hour of Death (1968) FF—Sp./Ital.

Paul Piaget
Gloria Milland
D: Paul Marchenti (Joaquin Romero Marchent)

A wagon train crosses the plains.

—The whole thing's hypocrisy. The rules they tack on say unless you're wearin' that badge or a soldier's uniform, you can't kill. But, they're the only rules there are.
—Doc Holliday (Jason Robards)
Hour of the Gun

Hour of the Gun (1967) UA ★★★

James Garner
Jason Robards, Jr.
Robert Ryan
Jon Voight
William Windom
D: John Sturges

The Earps pursue Ike Clanton in the aftermath of the gunfight at the OK Corral. Sequel to *Gunfight at the OK Corral*. Filmed at Durango, Mexico.

Au ★★

S ★★★★

A ★★★★

Robert Ryan in *Hour of the Gun.*

Mike Witney as Ike in *Doc.*

The Faces of Ike Clanton

Ike Clanton

Houston: The Legend of Texas (1986) CBS-TV/JDGP/TEG

Sam Elliott
Davon Ericson
Michael Beck
Bo Hopkins
Katharine Ross
D: Peter Levin

Frontier legend, Sam Houston, contributes
to the development of Texas.

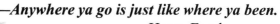

—Anywhere ya go is just like where ya been.
—Henry Fonda
How the West Was Won

How the West Was Won (1963) MGM

George Peppard and an all star cast
D: John Ford, Henry Hathaway and George Marshall

Three generations of a family's migration west tells
the story of westward expansion from 1830 to 1890.
Filmed in Cinerama. Narrated by Spencer Tracy. Oscar
nominations for best picture, cinematography: color,
art direction-set direction: color, costume design: color
and scoring: substantially original. Oscars for original
writing: original screenplay, sound, and film editing.
Filmed in and around Prescott, Arizona, Durango, Colorado,
Corriganville, and Monument Valley. #21 Best of the West.

Au ★★★★

S ★★★★★

A ★★★★

John Wayne in *How the West Was Won.*

How the West Was Won (1976) MGM/ABC-TV

Jim Arness
Eva Marie Saint
Bruce Boxleitner
Anthony Zerbe
Don Murray
Jack Elam
John Dehner
D: Burt Kennedy and Daniel Mann

Three-part mini-series based on the 1963 version and the
telefeature, *The Macahans*. The mini-series served as the pilot
for the 1978-79 series by the same name. Filmed in Kanub, Utah.

The Hunting Party (1971) FF—Brit./Ital./Sp.

Oliver Reed
Gene Hackman
Candice Bergen
Ron Howard
D: Don Medford

A cattle baron leads his hunting party against kidnappers.

Au ★★

S ★★

A ★★

Hunt to Kill see The White Buffalo

I Am Sartana, Trade Your Guns for a Coffin (1972) FF—Ital.

> George Hilton
> Charles Southwood
> D: Anthony Ascott

> Two gunfighters face off against a crooked banker
> and a bandit. Last in the "Sartana" series.

I Am Sartana, Your Angel of Death (1969) FF   Ital./Fr.

> John Garko
> Frank Wolff
> Klaus Kinski
> Gordon Mitchell
> D: Anthony Ascott (Giuliano Carmino)

> A mysterious vigilante investigates a bank robbery in which
> he has been falsely accused. Second in the "Sartana" series.

I Do Not Forgive...I Kill! see Ballad of a Bounty Hunter

If One Is Born a Swine (1972) FF—Ital./Sp.

> Richard Wyler
> Fernando Sancho
> D: Al Bradley (Alfonso Bescia)

> A gunfighter defends a gold miner and his claim.

If One Is Born a Swine...Kill Him! (1968) FF—Ital.

> Glenn Saxon
> Gordon Mitchell
> D: Al Bradly (Alfonso Bescia)

> A lawman poses as a gunfighter to stop cattlemen from defrauding local farmers.

If You Live, Shoot! see Django, Kill...If You Live, Shoot!

If You Shoot...You Live! (1974) FF—Sp.

> James Philbrook
> Frank Braña
> D: Joe Lacy (Josè Maria Elorrieta)

> A land baron terrorizes settlers in order to obtain their land.
> Taken from the script of *If You Want to Live...Shoot!*.

If You Want to Live...Shoot! (1967) FF—Ital./Sp.

> Sean Todd
> Ken Wood

D: Willy S. Regan (Sergio Garrone)

A land baron terrorizes settlers in order to obtain their land.

I Killed Wild Bill Hickok (1956) WCP

John Forbes (John Carpenter)
Helen Wescott
Tom Brown
D: Richard Talmadge

A man avenges the death of his daughter by killing Wild Bill Hickok.

I'll Sell My Skin Dearly (1968) FF—Ital.

Mike Marshall
Michele Girardon
D: Ettore Fizarotti

A rancher avenges the murder of his family.

I Married Wyatt Earp (1983) NBC-TV

Marie Osmond
Bruce Boxleitner
John Bennett
Ross Martin
D: Michael O'Herlihy

Josephine Marcus chronicles her adventures in the West.
Working title, *The Wife of Wyatt Earp*. Filmed at Old Tucson.

In a Colt's Shadow (1965) FF—Ital./Sp.

Stephen Forsyte
Conrado Sanmartin
D: Giovanni Grimaldi

A bounty hunter elopes with his partner's daughter.

Incident at Phantom Hill (1966) Universal

Robert Fuller
Jocelyn Lane
Dan Duryea
Claude Akins
Noah Beery, Jr.
D: Earl Bellamy

A prisoner is offered a pardon for leading soldiers to
retrieve gold bullion stolen by Confederates.

The Incredible Rocky Mountain Race (1977) NBC-TV

Christopher Connelly
Forrest Tucker
Larry Storch
D: James L. Conway

Mark Twain and Mike Fink enter into a grudge race from
Missouri to California. Lighthearted made for TV movie.

UNCHARTED
TERRITORY

Independence (1987) SC

John Bennett Perry
Isabella Hofmann
Anthony Zerbe
Sandy McPeak
D: John Patterson

A lawman avenges his family's murder.

Au ★★

S ★

A ★

*—You look like you got the world by
the tail on a down-hill drag.*
—John Bennett Perry
Independence

The Indian Fighter (1955) Bryna/UA

Kirk Douglas
Elsa Martinelli
Walter Abel
Walter Matthau
Lon Chaney, Jr.
Alan Hale, Jr.
D: Andrè de Toth

A scout attempts to negotiate a treaty with the Sioux
to allow a wagon train to pass through Indian lands.

Au ★★◣

S ★★★

A ★★★◣

*—To me the West is like a beautiful woman.
My woman. I like her just the way she is—I
don't want her changed. I'm jealous. I don't
want to share her with anybody.*
—Kirk Douglas
The Indian Fighter

Indian Paint (1965) TP/EAF/CIP

Johnny Crawford
Jay Silverheels
Pat Hogan
D: Norman Foster

An Indian boy tames a wild horse.

UNCHARTED
TERRITORY

Indian Scout see Davy Crockett: Indian Scout

Indian Uprising (1952) Columbia ★★

George Montgomery
Audrey Long
Carl Benton
Robert Shayne
D: Ray Nazarro

"A Friendly Scout Signaling the Main Column."

Already facing a court-martial, an officer confronts Geronimo. Filmed in Sedona, AZ.

Au

S

A

Warner Baxter in *In Old Arizona*.

—They'll be no treaty! Geronimo's chiefs are going to prison in Florida!
—Robert Shayne
Indian Uprising

In Old Arizona (1929) Fox

Warner Baxter
Edmond Lowe
Dorothy Burgess
J. Farrell MacDonald
D: Raoul Walsh and Irving Cummings

A lawman pursuedes a woman to disarm the Cisco Kid. Considered by some to be the first sound Western film and the first sound picture filmed outdoors. Walsh lost an eye in a traffic accident and was replaced with Cummings. Academy nomination for best picture, direction, and cinematography. Best actor for Warner Baxter. Based on O'Henry's "The Cabellero's Way."

In Old California (1942) Republic

John Wayne
Binnie Barnes
Albert Dekker
D: William McGann

A Boston druggist and a gambler compete for the affection of a gold rush saloon singer. Filmed at Kernville, CA.

Au

S

A

John Wayne and Binnie Barnes in *In Old California*.

In Old Los Angeles (California Outpost) (1948) Republic

William Elliot
John Carroll
Catherine McLeod
Andy Devine
D: Joseph Kane

A lawman seeks revenge in L.A.

Au

S

A

In Old Sacramento (Flame of Sacramento) (1946) Republic

William Elliot
Constance Moore
Hank Daniels
D: Joseph Kane

A masked bandit romances a singer. Screenplay
by Frances Lyland and Frank Gruber.

Au

S ★★

A ★◗

In the Name of the Father (1968) FF—Ital.

Paolo Villaggio
D: Ruggero Deodato

Rare.

UNCHARTED
TERRITORY

In the Name of the Father, the Son and the Colt (1972) FF—Fr./Ital.

Craig Hill
Nuccia Cardinali
D: Frank Bronston (Mario Bianchi)

A sheriff investigates stagecoach robbers disguised as prostitutes.

UNCHARTED
TERRITORY

Into the Badlands (1991) Ogiens/Kane P.

Bruce Dern
Mariel Hemingway
Helen Hunt
Dylan McDermott
D: Sam Pillsbury

A bounty hunter tracks badman, Red Roundtree.
Made for TV movie.

UNCHARTED
TERRITORY

The Intruders (1970) Universal

Don Murray
Anne Francis
Edmond O'Brien
John Saxon
Harrison Ford
D: William A. Graham

A gunfighter turned marshal is afraid to face Jesse James
and the Younger brothers. Made for TV movie.

Au ★◗

S ★

A ★◗

Invasion of Johnson County (1976) RHP/Universal

Bill Bixby
Bo Hopkins
John Millerman
Billy Green Bush

D: Jerry Jameson

A newspaper reporter opposes the Wyoming
Stock Growers Association's part in the
Johnson County War. Made for TV movie.

Au
S
A

Invitation to a Gunfight see A Gunfight

Invitation to a Gunfighter (1964) UA

Yul Brynner
Janice Rule
Brad Dexter
Alfred Ryder
George Segal
Strother Martin
D: Richard Wilson

A southern town boss hires a
gunfighter to silence an outcast.

Au
S
A

The Iron Sheriff (1957) GrP/UA

Sterling Hayden
Constance Ford
John Dehner
D: Sidney Salko

A sheriff must prove his son's innocence.

Ishi: The Last of His Tribe (1978) NBC-TV/EMLP

Dennis Weaver
Eloy Phil Casados
Devon Ericson
D: Robert Ellis Miler

The last Yahi Indian is discovered in Northern California
by an anthropologist. Made for TV movie.

Big Foot dead in the snow at the Wounded Knee Massacre, 1891.

276

I Shot Jesse James (1949) Lippert/Screen Guild

John Ireland
Preston Foster
Barbara Britton
D: Samuel Fuller

Bob Ford shoots Jesse James in order to marry his childhood
sweetheart. Filmed at the Iverson Movie Location Ranch.

I Take This Woman (1931) Paramount

Gary Cooper
Carole Lombard
Helen Ware
Lester Vail
D: Marion Gering

I Will Fight No More Forever (1975) DWP

James Whitmore
Ned Romero
Sam Elliott
D: Richard T. Heffron

Chief Joseph leads the Nez Perce
to Canada. Made for TV movie.

Jackass Mail (1942) MGM

Wallace Berry
Marjorie Main
J. Carrol Naish
D: Norman Z. McLeod

Escaping from hanging, an outlaw
foils a robbery and becomes a hero.

The Jack Bull (1999) HBO ★★★★

John Cusack
John Goodman
L.Q. Jones
Miranda Otto
D: John Badham

An honest horse trader's obsession with justice leads to
his confrontation with law and order in Wyoming Territory.
Inspired by a true story. Made for TV movie. Filmed in
Alberta, Canada. #72 Best of the West.

John Ireland as Bob Ford
in *I Shot Jesse James.*

Bob Ford

*—You're haulin' shit up a mountain,
Rayborn. Careful it doesn't spill on you.*
—Ken Pogue
The Jack Bull

Jack McCall, Desperado (1953) Columbia ★★◣

George Montgomery
Angela Stevens
Douglas Kennedy
Jay Silverheels
D: Sidney Salkow

Tried for murder, Jack McCall relates his own
account of the shooting of Wild Bill Hickok.

Au ★

S ★◣

A ★◣

—I have the answer in one bullet.
—George Montgomery
Jack McCall, Desperado

Jack Slade (1953) AA ★★ ★◣

Mark Stevens
Dorothy Malone
Barton MacLane
Lee Van Cleef
D: Harold Schuster

A lawman goes bad.

Au ★★

S ★★★◣

A ★★

*—I guess we're all alone, really. Nobody knows
what's inside of us or what makes us the way we are.*
—Mark Stevens
Jack Slade

Jaguar (1964) FF—Sp.

Josè Suarez
Silvia Sorente
D: Jess Franco

The Venezuelan civil war is fought in the U.S.??

James A. Michener's Texas see Texas

The Jayhawkers (1959) Paramount ★★★

Jeff Chandler
Fess Parker
Nichol Maurey
Henry Silva
D: Melvin Frank

A man escapes from prison only to discover
that his wife was murdered by Jayhawkers.
Filmed at Bronson Canyon, Griffith Park, CA.

Au ★★★◣

S ★★

A ★★★◣

278

Jeremiah Johnson (1972) WB

Robert Redford
Will Geer
Stefan Gierasch
Allyn Ann McLerie
D: Sidney Pollack

A mountainman becomes a living legend
while learning to survive in the wilderness.
Based on the life of "Liver Eating Johnson"
and Vardis Fisher's, *Mountain Man*.
Filmed at Uinta National Forest and Sundance
Resort, Utah. #5 Best of the West, #43 IMBd.

Robert Redford and Will Geer in *Jeremiah Johnson*.

Au
S
A

Jericho (2001)

Mark Valley
Leon Coffee
R. Lee Ermey
Buck Taylor
D: Merlin Miller

UNCHARTED
TERRITORY

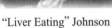

"Liver Eating" Johnson

Jesse James (1939) 20ᵗʰ C. Fox

Tyrone Power
Henry Fonda
Nancy Kelly
Randolph Scott
Brian Donlevy
John Carradine
Lon Chaney, Jr.
John Russell
Henry Hull
D: Henry King

The legendary badman fights the railroad.
Filmed at Pineville, MO.#15 Best of the West.

*—If we are ever to have law and order in the
West, first thing we gotta do is take out all the
lawyers and shoot'em down like dogs.*
—Major Rufas Cobb
Jesse James

Au ★★★
S ★★★★★
A ★★★★★

Tyrone Power and Henry Fonda as Jesse and Frank James.

Frank and Jesse James

Jesse James' Kid (1966) FF—Sp./Ital.

Robert Hundar
Mercedes Alonso
D: Antonio Del Amo (Adrian Hoven)

Jesse's son avenges his murder.

Jesse James vs. the Daltons (1954) Columbia

Brett King
Barbara Lawrence
James Griffith
D: William Castle

A gunman joins the Dalton gang in order to determine if Jesse James is his father and if the ten year old reports of his murder are accurate.

Au ★ɪ

S ★ɪ

A ★ɪ

Jessi's Girls (Wanted Women) (1975) M Prod.

Sondra Currie
Geoffrey Land
Ben Frank
Regina Carroll
Rod Cameron
D: Al Adamson

Three female prisoners assist a woman in avenging her own rape and the murder of her husband.

Joaquin Murrieta see Desperate Mission

Joe Dakota (1957) U-I

Jock Mahoney
Luana Patten
Charles McGraw
Claude Akins
Lee Van Cleef
D: Richard Bartlett

A cavalry officer discovers his old Indian scout was hanged by a land grabber. Filmed at Conejo Valley, California.

Au ★ɪ

S ★

A ★

—As I understand it, possession is nine points of the law. And as you can see, I'm in possession of this place.
—Jock Mahoney
Joe Dakota

Joe Dexter (1965) FF—Sp./Ital.

George Martin
Audrey Amber
D: Ignacio Iquino

Two women fall for the same gunfighter.

Joe Kidd (1972) Universal

Clint Eastwood
Robert Duvall
John Saxon
Don Stroud
Dick Van Patten
D: John Sturges

A wealthy New Mexican rancher hires a gunfighter to guide him on a manhunt. Originally known as "Sinola." Filmed at Old Tucson and Alabama Hills.

Au
S
A

> —*Next time I'll knock your damned head off!*
> —Clint Eastwood
> *Joe Kidd*

Johnny Colt (1966) FF—Ital.

Robert Woods
Elga Andersen
D: Giovanni Grimaldi

A gunfighter pursues a crooked banker.

Johnny Concho (1956) UA

Frank Sinatra
Keenan Wynn
William Conrad
Wallace Ford
Claude Akins
D: Don McGuire

When his brother is killed, a coward must stand on his own.

> —*How many men have you forgotten?*
> —Sterling Hayden
>
> —*As many women as you've remembered.*
> —Joan Crawford
> *Johnny Guitar*

Johnny Guitar (1954) Republic

Joan Crawford
Sterling Hayden
Scott Brady
Mercedes McCambridge
Ward Bond
John Carradine
Ernest Borgnine
D: Nicholas Ray

A guitar-playing gunfighter is hired by a saloon keeper to help defend her. Filmed in Sedona, Arizona. #29 IMDb.

Au
S
A

Joan Crawford in *Johnny Guitar.*

Johnny Hamlet (1968) FF—Ital.

Chip Gorman (Andrea Giordana)
Gilbert Roland
D: Enzo Castellari (Enzo Girolami)

A soldier returns from the Civil War to discover his father dead and his
mother remarried to a crook. A Western version of Shakespeare's "Hamlet."

Johnny Reno (1966) Paramount

Dana Andrews
Jane Russell
Lon Chaney, Jr.
John Agar
D: R.G. Springsteen

A marshal delivers law and order
to a town ruled by lynch law.

Frank Reno of the Reno gang.

Tom Beringer (center) as Nate Champion with Adam Storke and Luke Perry.

Johnny Yuma (1966) FF—Ital.

Mark Damon
Lawrence Dobkin
Rosalba Neri
D: Romolo Guerrieri

A gunman fights for his inheritance.

Johnson County War (2002) Hallmark E. ★★★★

Tom Beringer
Luke Perry
Rachel Ward
Burt Reynolds
Adam Storke
Ken Pogue
D: David S. Cass, Sr.

Three homesteader brothers
stand up to Wyoming cattle
barons. Fictionalized account
of Nate Champion's part in the
Johnson County War. Based on
Frederick Manfred's, *Riders of
Judgement*. Teleplay by Larry
McMurtry and Diana Osana.
Filmed in Alberta.
#100 Best of the West.

Nate Champion (left).

Au ★★★★★
S ★★★★
A ★★★★

John the Bastard (1967) FF—Ital.

John Richardson
Claudio Camaso
D: Armando Crispino

—The way to kill a snake is to cut off his head!
—Burt Reynolds
Johnson County War

A "Casanova" gunfighter journeys to Mexico to visit his father.

Jory (1972) AE

John Marley
B.J. Thomas
Bobby Benson
Brad Dexter
D: Jorge Fons

A boy chooses between life as a gunfighter or as a rancher.

Joshua (1977) LSP

Fred Williamson
Isela Vega
Calvin Bartlett
Brenda Venus
D: Larry Spangler

A black gunman faces the last of an outlaw gang in a cave.

The Journeyman (2001)

Brad Hunt
Daniel Lapaine
Barry Corbin
Willie Nelson
D: James Crowley

Journey to Shiloh (1968) Universal

James Caan
Michael Sarrazin
Brenda Scott
(Jan) Michael Vincent
Noah Berry, Jr.
Harrison Ford
D: William Hale

Texans join the Confederate army only
to become disillusioned with their cause.
Story by Will Henry.

Au ★

S ★

A ★

Jubal (1956) Columbia

Glenn Ford
Ernest Borgnine
Rod Steiger
Valerie French

Noah Beery, Jr.
Charles Bronson
Jack Elam
D: Delmer Daves

A new ranch foreman dodges the advances of the boss's wife.
Based on Paul Wellman's, *Jubal Troop*. Filmed at Jackson Hole, WY.

Au ★ ★ ★ ⯪

S ★ ★ ⯪

A ★ ★ ★ ★

Jubilee Trail (1954) Republic

Vera Ralston
Joan Leslie
Forrest Tucker
John Russell
Pat O'Brien
Jim Davis
Jack Elam
D: Joseph Inman Kane

A New York saloon singer befriends a pioneer widow.
Filmed at Red Rock Canyon, California.

Au ★ ★ ⯪

S ★ ★

A ★ ⯪

—I'm not one that, ah, anybody should figure on settlin' down.
—Forrest Tucker
Jubilee Trail

Lilly Langtry

Judge Roy Bean (1970) FF—Fr.

Robert Hossein
Silva Monti
D: Richard Owens

Legendary hanging judge, Roy Bean, operates in Sacramento.

UNCHARTED TERRITORY

Justice of the West (1956) WC

Clayton Moore
Jay Silverheels
Allen Pinson
Mickey Simpson
Denver Pyle
D: Earl Bellamy and Oscar Rudolph

Compilation of three episodes of "The Lone Ranger" TV series.

UNCHARTED TERRITORY

The Kansan (1943) UA

Richard Dix
Jane Wyatt
Victor Jory
D: George Archainbaud

A drifter must clean up the town in which he wishes to settle.
Story by Frank Gruber. Oscar nomination for scoring: drama/comedy.

UNCHARTED TERRITORY

284

Kansas Pacific (1953) AA

Sterling Hayden
Eve Miller
Randolph Scott
Clayton Moore
D: Ray Nazarro

An Army engineer contends with southern
sympathizers while building a railroad.

Au ★★

S ★★

A ★◗

—Sunshine and pretty girls go together.
—Sterling Hayden
Kansas Pacific

Kansas Raiders (1950) U-I ★◗

Audie Murphy
Brian Donlevy
Marguerite Chapman
Tony Curtis
D: Ray Enright

Jesse James becomes disenchanted with Quantrill.
Filmed in Idyllwild, California.

Au ★

S ★◗

A ★★

*—To hear the Yankees tell it, Quantrill's
got two horns, two hoofs and a long tail.*
—Tony Curtis
Kansas Raiders

Kenny Rogers as "The Gambler" see The Gambler

Kenny Rogers as "The Gambler"—The Adventure Continues see The Gambler II

Kentucky Rifle (1956) Howco Prod.

Chill Wills
Lance Fuller
Cathy Downs
D: Carl K. Hittleman

Upon abandoning a wagon train in Comanche territory,
settlers protect their cargo of rifles.

Keoma (1975) FF—Ital./Sp.

Franco Nero
Woody Strode
William Berger
D: Enzo Castellari (Enzo Girolami)

Two brothers encounter a corrupt town boss.

The Kid and the Gunfighter (Born to Fight) (1985) SFI

Chuck Biller
Cole McKay
Paul Jones
Connie Angeles

D: Romy Suzara

The Kid and the Killers (1979) CS

Jon Cypher
Gerry Ross
Elida Alicia
John Garces
D: Ralph Bluemke

When his partner rapes and murders a girl, an
outlaw joins the girl's brother to seek justice.

Kid Blue (1973) 20ᵗʰ C. Fox

Dennis Hopper
Warren Oates
Peter Boyle
Ben Johnson
D: James Frawley

Peculiar tale of a train robber who attempts
to go straight. Filmed in Mexico.

Au ★★

S ★◗

A ★◗

The Kid From Texas (1950) U-I

Audie Murphy
Gale Storm
Albert Dekker
Will Geer
D: Kurt Newmann

Billy the Kid avenges his friend's murder
during the Lincoln County War. Murphy's
first Western. Filmed in Idyllwild, California.

Au ★◗

S ★★

A ★★

*—You don't judge a rattlesnake by his
age. He's a rattler, whether he's got one
rattle or a dozen.*

—Bing Russell
The Kid From Texas

Kid Rodelo (1966) FF—U.S./Sp.

Don Murray
Janet Leigh
Broderick Crawford
Richard Carlson
D: Richard Carlson

Upon their release from prison, three outlaws set out to
retrieve their stolen gold. Based on the Louie L'Amour novel.

Kid Vengeance (1976) FF—Ital./U.S./Isr.

Lee Van Cleef
Jim Brown
Leif Garrett
D: Joe Manduke

A gunfighter avenges the murder of his family.

Kill Django…Kill First (1971) FF—Ital.

Giacomo Rossi Stuart (Jack Start)
George Wang
D: Willy S. Regan (Sergio Garrone)

A gunfighter tracks a Mexican bandit in Texas.

Killer Caliber .32 (1967) FF—Ital.

Peter Lee Lawrence
Agnes Spaak
D: Al Bradly

A gunfighter is hired to stop stagecoach robberies.

Killer Goodbye (1969) FF—Ital./Sp.

Peter Lee Lawrence
Marisa Solinas
Eduardo Fajardo
D: Primo Zeglio

A sheriff and his deputy attempt to restore law and order to Fulton City.

Killer Kid (1967) FF—Ital.

Anthony Steffen
Liz Barret
D: Leopoldo Savona

A government agent disguised as gun runner becomes
involved with Mexican freedom fighters.

Killer on a Horse see Welcome to Hard Times

Kill Johnny Ringo (1966) FF—Ital.

Brett Halsey
Greta Polyn
D: Frank G. Carrol (Gianfranco Baldanello)

A Texas Ranger investigates counterfeiters.

Kill or Die (1966) FF—Ital.

Robert Mark
Elina De Witt
D: Amerigo Anton (Tanio Boccia)

A mysterious gunfighter encounters feuding families.

Kill the Poker Player (1972) FF—Ital./Sp.

Robert Woods
Ivano Staccioli
Frank Braña
D: Frank Bronston (Mario Bianchi)

A gambler accuses a town boss of cheating.

The King and Four Queens (1956) RFC

Clark Gable
Eleanor Parker
Jo Van Fleet
D: Raoul Walsh

A conman must convince the widows of four outlaws that he was their partner in order to obtain a share of their loot. Filmed at St. George, Utah.

Au ★❙
S ★
A ★❙

King of Texas (2002) TNT/Hallmark P. ★ ★ ★

Patrick Stewart
Marcia Gay Harden
Lauren Holly
Julie Cox
Roy Scheider
D: Uli Edel

Western adaptation of Shakespeare's, *King Lear*.

Au ★★★★
S ★★★
A ★★★

Roy Scheider and Patrick Stewart in *King of Texas*.

—There ain't no better feelin' in the world is there, Mister, than to know ya done right by your children.

—Patrick Stewart
King of Texas

King of the Bandits (1947) Mono.

Gilbert Roland
Angela Greene
Chris-Pin Martin
D: Christy Cabanne

The Cisco Kid tracks his own impersonator in Arizona.

King of the Grizzlies (1970) BV

John Yesno
Chris Wiggins
Hugh Webster
Jack Van Evera
D: Ron Kelly

A Cree Indian boy raises a bear cub.

King of the Wild Horses (1947) Columbia

Preston Foster
Gail Patrick
Bill Sheffield
D: George Archainbaud

A boy tames a wild stallion.

"His First Lesson."

King of the Wild Stallions (1959) AA ★★✦

George Montgomery
Diane Brewster
Edgar Buchanan
D: R.G. Springsteen

A ranch foreman must capture a prize stallion in order to protect
a widow from a cattle baron. Filmed at Vasquez Rocks, California.

Au ★★✦

S ★

A ★★✦

The Kissing Bandit (1949) MGM ★

Frank Sinatra
Kathryn Grayson
J. Carrol Naish
Mildred Natwick
Ricardo Montalban
D: Laslo Benedek

A woman reforms a highwayman in old California.

Au ★

S ✦

A ✦

Kit Carson (1940) UA ★★★✦

Jon Hall
Lynn Bari
Dana Andrews
Harold Huber
Ward Bond
Clayton Moore
Iron Eyes Cody
D: George B. Seitz

Kit Carson and John C. Frèmont

The legendary scout guides Frèmont's expedition to California.
Technical advise by Joe De Yong. Filmed in Monument Valley and
at the Iverson Movie Location Ranch.

Kit Carson and the Moutain Men (1977)

Christopher Connelly
Robert Reed
Gary Lockwood
Dub Taylor
D: ?

Made for TV movie.

Kitosch, the Man Who Came from the North (1967) FF—Ital./Sp.

George Hilton
Krista Nell
D: Joseph Marvin (Josè Merino)

A Canadian Mounted Policeman smuggles gold through hostile territory.

Klondike Annie (1936) Paramount

Mae West
Victor McLaglen
Philip Reed
Helen Jerome Eddy
D: Raoul Walsh

After killing a man in self-defense, a woman heads to the Klondike.

Klondike Fever (1980) CFL

Rod Steiger
Angie Dickinson
Lorne Greene
Barry Morse
D: Peter Carter

Jack London experiences the Klondike.

Klondike Kate (1943) Columbia

George Martin
Audrey Amber
D: Ignacio Iquino

A woman inherits a Klondike saloon from her father.

290

Knights of the Range (1940) Paramount

Russell Hayden
Victor Jory
Jean Parker
Britt Wood
D: Lesley Selander

A young man is lured into rustling. Story by Zane Grey.

Kung Fu Brothers in the Wild West (1973) FF—Ital./HK

Jason Pai-Pico
William Berger
D: Yeo Ban Yee

Two Chinese brothers reunite in America's West.

Kung Fu (1972) ABC-TV/WB ★★◀

David Carradine
Barry Sullivan
Albert Salmi
Wayne Maunder
D: Jerry Thorpe

A Chinese American Shaolin monk defends Chinese railroad laborers. Pilot for the TV series. Filmed at Vasquez Rocks, California.

Au ★★

S ★★★

A ★★◀

Kung Fu: The Movie (1986) CBS-TV ★★★

David Carradine
Kerrie Keane
Mako
Brandon Lee
Martin Landau
D: Richard Lang

A Chinese American Shaolin monk is
tracked by a Chinese warlord's assassin.

Au ★★★◀

S ★★★

A ★★★

—A man must move through life as his destiny wills.

—David Carradine
Kung Fu: The Movie

Lacy and the Mississippi Queen (1978) NBC-TV

Kathleen Lloyd
Debra Feuer
Edward Andrews
Jack Elam
D: Robert Butler

A tomboy and a beautiful woman avenge their father's murder. Unsuccessful pilot.

The Lady From Cheyenne (1941) Universal

Lorreta Young
Robert Preston
Edward Arnold
Frank Craven
D: Frank Lloyd

A Wyoming schoolmarm fights a crooked
land baron by lobbying for the women's vote.

Au ★

S ★★★

A ★★★

The Lady from Texas (1951) U-I

Howard Duff
Mona Freeman
Josephine Hull
D: Joseph Pevney

Two ranch hands save a widow from a land-grabber.
Filmed at the Jauregui Ranch and Walker Ranch, CA.

Au ★★★

S ★★★★

A ★★★★

Lakota Moon (1992)

Richard Tyson
Rodney A. Grant
Barbara Carrera
D: Christopher Cain

An Indian must convince the father of the woman he
loves that he is worthy of her. Made for TV movie.

Long Feather, Dakota.

Land Raiders (1969) FF—U.S./Sp.

Telly Savalas
George Maharis
Arlene Dahl
D: Nathan Juran

An Apache-hating land baron and his
brother feud during an Indian attack.

Au ★

S ★

A ★

*—Alright, you fought with Colonel Chivington,
Major. Remember what he told his men at
Sands Creek, "Kill them all, big and little."*

—Telly Savalas
Land Raiders

Lariats and Sixshooters (1931) Cosmos

Jack Perrin
Ann Lee
George Chesebro
D: Alvin J. Neitz

Larry McMurtry's Streets of Laredo see Streets of Laredo

The Lash (Adios) (1930) FN

Richard Barthelmess
Mary Astor
Fred Kohler
Marion Nixon
D: Frank Lloyd

A young man returns from school to old California to discover lawlessness. Filmed at Russell Ranch, Thousand Oaks, CA.

Au

S

A

—Tell them El Puma is not coming back.
—Richard Barthelmess
The Lash

Lassie's Adventure in the Gold Rush see The Painted Hills

The Last Bandit (1949) Republic

William Elliott
Andy Devine
Jack Holt
Forrest Tucker
D: Joseph Kane

An outlaw robs the train that his brother is guarding.

The Last Challenge (Pistolero of Red River) (1967) MGM

Glenn Ford
Angie Dickinson
Chad Everett
Gary Merrill
Jack Elam
D: Richard Thorpe

A gunfighter turned marshal finds it difficult to hang up his guns. Filmed at Old Tucson.

Au

S

A

Last Command (1955) Republic

Sterling Hayden
Anna Maria Alberghetti
Richard Carlson
Ernest Borgnine

Jim Davis
Slim Pickens
D: Frank Lloyd

Jim Bowie takes on his last command—the Alamo.
Filmed at Brackettville, Texas.

Au ★ ★ ★

S ★ ★ ★ ★

A ★ ★ ★ ★

> *—I say to you now, that the only course left*
> *open to us is to show the military authorities*
> *that we will not passively submit to injustice!*
> —Richard Carlson
> *The Last Command*

The Last Day (1975) NBC-TV ★ ★ ★ ★

Richard Widmark
Christopher Connelly
Robert Conrad
D: Vincent McEveety

The Dalton gang forces a
gunfighter out of retirement.

Au ★ ★ ★ ★

S ★ ★ ★ ★

A ★ ★ ★ ★

The Last Days of Frank and Jesse James (1988) NBC-TV/JCP ★ ★ ★

Johnny Cash
Kris Kristofferson
Ed Bruce
Willie Nelson
D: William A. Graham

The career of the legendary brothers draws to a close. Filmed in Tennessee.

Au ★ ★ ★ ★ ★

S ★ ★ ★

A ★ ★ ★

The Last Frontier see Savage Wilderness

Last Gun (1964) FF—Ital.

Cameron Mitchell
Carl Mohner
Ketty Carver
D: Sergio Bergonzelli

A retired gunfighter must defend his town.

UNCHARTED
TERRITORY

The Last Hard Men (1976) 20ᵗʰ C. Fox ★ ★ ★ ★

Charlton Heston
James Coburn
Barbara Hershey
Chris Mitchum
D: Andrew V. McLaglen

A sheriff's daughter is kidnapped by

294

an escaped outlaw in 1909 Arizona.
Filmed at Old Tucson. #80 Best of the West.

Au ★★★★
S ★★★★
A ★★★★

—Comes to a showdown, he'll hesitate.
...and that's when I'll get him.
—Charlton Heston
The Last Hard Men

The Last Hunt (1956) MGM

Robert Taylor
Stewart Granger
Lloyd Nolan
D: Richard Brooks

An Indian hater is intent on eliminating the buffalo from the plains.

Last of the Badmen (1957) AA ★★★

George Montgomery
Keith Larsen
James Best
Douglas Kennedy
D: Paul Landres

A Chicago detective investigates stagecoach robberies.
Remake of *Star of Texas*. Filmed at the Iverson Ranch.

Au ★★
S ★★
A ★★

Last of the Badmen (1967) see Time of Vultures

The Last of the Comanches (The Sabre and the Arrow) (1953) Columbia ★★★

Broderick Crawford
Barbara Hale
Johnny Stewart
Lloyd Bridges
John War Eagle
Jay Silverheels
D: Andrè de Toth

Cavalrymen surviving an Indian massacre lead a Comanche and civilians
across the desert. Filmed at Buttercup Dunes, Imperial County, California.

Au ★★★
S ★★★
A ★★★

Last of the Desperados (1955) Assoc. ★

James Craig
Jim Davis
Barton McLane
Margia Dean
Bob Steele
D: Sam Newfield

Billy the Kid's gang pursues Pat

Garrett to avenge Billy's murder.

Au
S
A

The Last of the Fast Guns (1958) U-I

Jock Mahoney
Gilbert Roland
Linda Cristal
Lorne Greene
Edward C. Platt
D: George Sherman

A tycoon hires a gunfighter to find his
brother in Mexico. Filmed in Mexico.

Au
S
A

*—The money you make with a gun you gotta
spend fast before it starts to stare back at you.*
—Jack Mahoney
The Last of the Fast Guns

Last of the Wild Horses (1948) Lippert/Screen Guild

James Ellison
Mary Beth Hughes
Jane Frazee
Douglass Dumbrille
D: Robert L. Lippert

An outlaw frames a man for murder.

The Last Outlaw (1993) HBO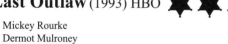

Mickey Rourke
Dermot Mulroney
Ted Levine
John C. McGinley
D: Geoff Murphy

A bank robber seeks revenge. Filmed in New Mexico.

Au
S
A

The Last Outpost (1951) Paramount

Ronald Reagan
Rhonda Fleming
Bruce Bennett
Noah Beery, Jr.
John War Eagle
Iron Eyes Cody
Chief Yowlachie
D: Lewis R. Foster

Two brothers on opposite sides of the Civil War compete

*—I brought you for your shootin' iron,
not for your brain.*
—Ronald Reagan
The Last Outpost

for Arizona gold shipments. Filmed at Old Tucson.

Au ★ ★

S ★ ★

A ★ ★

The Last Posse (1953) Columbia ★

Broderick Crawford
John Derek
Charles Bickford
Wanda Hendrix
Skip Homeier
D: Alfred Werker

A posse must account for missing loot.

Au ★ ⌐

S ⌐

A ★

—Respect, the only men I ever respected were those I fought.
—Broderick Crawford
The Last Posse

The Last Rebel (1961) FF—Mex.

Carlos Thompson
Adriadne Welter
Rudolph Acosta
Charles Fawcett
D: Miguel Contreras Torres

Joaquin Murrieta turns bandido when his wife is murdered.

UNCHARTED TERRITORY

The Last Rebel (1971) FF—Ital./U.S./Sp. ★

Joe Namath
Jack Elam
Woody Strode
D: Denys McCoy

Three conmen operate a pool hustling scheme.

Au ★

S ★

A ★ ★

—Just another poker hand, kid.
—Jack Elam
The Last Rebel

The Last Ride of the Dalton Gang (1979) NBC-TV ★ ★

Cliff Potts
Randy Quaid
Larry Wilcox
Sharon Farrell
Jack Palance
Dale Robertson
D: Dan Curtis

The Daltons' dime-novel career draws to an end.
Filmed at Griffith Park and Columbia, California.

Au ★ ★ ⌐

—Whata ya'll waitin' for? Shoot! Shoot, damned you! Shoot!
—Jack Palance
The Last Ride of the Dalton Gang

S ★★
A ★★★◗

Last Ride to Santa Cruz (1969) FF—Ger./Fr.

Edmund Purdom
Mario Adorf
D: Rolf Olsen

A crooked lawman convicts an innocent man.

The Last Round-Up (1934) Paramount

Randolph Scott
Barbara Fritchie
Barton McLane
Fuzzy Knight
D: Henry Hathaway

Based on Zane Grey's, *The Border Legion*.

The Last Stagecoach West (1957) Ventura/Republic

Jim Davis
Mary Castle
Victor Jory
Lee Van Cleef
D: Joe Kane

A railroad detective poses as a "snake oil" salesman to investigate train sabotage.
Filmed at Towsley Canyon, Newhall, California.

Au ★◗
S ◗
A ★

Last Stand at Sabre River (1997) TNT ★★★★

Tom Selleck
Suzy Amis
Rachel Duncan
David Dukes
David Carradine
D: Dick Lowry

A Confederate soldier returns to Arizona to discover
Union sympathizers have claimed his homestead.
From an Elmore Leonard novel. Filmed at Las Vegas,
New Mexico. #76 Best of the West.

Au ★★★★★
S ★★★◗
A ★★★★

Tom Selleck in *Last Stand at Sabre River.*

The Last Sunset (1961) U-I ★★★✦

Rock Hudson
Kirk Douglas
Joseph Cotton
Dorothy Malone
Neville Brand
Jack Elam
D: Robert Aldrich

While pursuing his trail boss's wife and daughter, an outlaw is shadowed by a Texas lawman. Filmed in Mexico.

Au ★★★✦

S ★★★★

A ★★★✦

—*That sister of yours was just a free drink on the house and nobody went home thirsty. I mean nobody!*
—Kirk Douglas
The Last Sunset

Last Train from Gun Hill (1959) Paramount ★★★★

Kirk Douglas
Anthony Quinn
Carolyn Jones
D: John Sturges

A marshal avenges his wife's murder. Filmed at Old Tucson. #74 Best of the West.

Au ★★★★

S ★★★★

A ★★★★

—*The human race stinks. I'm practically an authority on that subject.*
—Carolyn Jones
Last Train from Gun Hill

The Last Wagon (1956) 20ᵗʰ C. Fox ★★★

Richard Widmark
Felicia Farr
Susan Kohner
Nick Adams
James Drury
D: Delmer Daves

A wagon train is massacred by Indians and the survivors with one wagon must escape the hostile Apaches. Filmed in Sedona, Arizona.

Au ★★★

S ★★★

A ★★★✦

Richard Widmark in *The Last Wagon*.

The Law and Jake Wade (1958) MGM ★★★

Robert Taylor
Richard Widmark
Patricia Owens
Robert Middleton
D: John Sturges

A lawman is forced by his former outlaw partner to recover their buried loot. Based on Marvin Albert's, *Renegade Posse*. Filmed in the Alabama Hills.

Au ★★★

—*No matter how pleasant they are to have around, a woman does slow a man up.*
—Richard Widmark
The Law and Jake Wade

S ★★★
A ★★★◗

Law and Order (Guns A'Blazing) (1932) Universal ★◗

Walter Huston
Harry Carey
Raymond Hatton
Andy Devine
Walter Brennan
D: Edward Cahn

The Earps establish law and order in Tombstone.
Fictionalized account of their exploits. Based on
the W.R. Burnett (James Updyke) novel, *Saint Johnson*.
Filmed at Vasquez Rocks, California.

—Nope, if the West wants law and order, they'll have to get it without me.
—Walter Huston
Law and Order (1932)

Au ★★
S ★◗
A ★◗

Law and Order (1953) U-I ★◗

Ronald Reagan
Dorothy Malone
Preston Foster
Alex Nicol
Dennis Weaver
Russell Johnson
Jack Kelly
D: Nathan Juran

When the marshal of Tombstone retires, another town
requires his services. Remake of the 1932 version.
Filmed at Red Rock Canyon, California.

Au ★◗
S ★◗
A ★★

Alex Nichol and Ronald Reagan in *Law and Order.*

The Lawless (1956) WC

Clayton Moore
Jay Silverheels
Myron Healey
Trevor Bardette
D: Earl Bellamy, Oscar Rudolph

Compilation of three episodes of "The Lone Ranger" TV series.

The Lawless Breed (1953) U-I ★★

Rock Hudson
Julia Adams
Mary Castle
John McIntire
Hugh O'Brian
Dennis Weaver
Lee Van Cleef
D: Raoul Walsh

John Wesley Hardin, the most notorious gunfighter of
the West. He fled Abiline when Wild Bill Hickok
pursued him for shooting a man dead for snoring.

John Wesley Hardin recalls his criminal past.
Filmed at Jauregui Ranch and Vasquez Rocks, CA.

Au ★★

S ★◗

A ★★

—I know that if you wanna win you gotta take a chance. You gotta add something to the pot.
—Rock Hudson
The Lawless Breed

The Lawless Eighties (1958) Ventura/Republic ◗

Buster Crabbe
John Smith
Marilyn Saris
Ted de Corsia
D: Joseph Kane

A gunfighter helps a circuit preacher wounded by outlaws.

Au ◗

S ◗

A ◗

—A man's stomach has more sense in it than either his heart or his head.
—Randolph Scott
A Lawless Street

A Lawless Street (1955) S-B/Columbia ★◗

Randolph Scott
Angela Lansbury
Warner Anderson
Wallace Ford
D: Joseph H. Lewis

A marshal is compelled to clean up
one more town before resigning.

Au ★★

S ★◗

A ★◗

Angela Landsbury and Randolph Scott in *The Lawless Eighties*.

Law Man see Star in the Dust

Lawman (1971) UA ★★★◗

Burt Lancaster
Robert Ryan
Lee J. Cobb
Sheree North
Joseph Wiseman
Robert Duvall
D: Michael Winner

A lawman is committed to punishing the drunken
saddle tramps responsible for shooting up his town
and killing an old man. Filmed in Mexico.

Au ★★★◗

S ★★★

A ★★★★

—You can't change what you are. And if you try, somethin' always calls you back.
—Burt Lancaster
Lawman

Law of the Land (The Deputies) (1976) NBC-TV/QMP

Jim Davis
Don Johnson

Cal Bellini
D: Virgil W. Vogel

A lawman tracks a psychopath.

Law of the Lawless (1964) Paramount

Dale Robertson
Yvonne de Carlo
William Bendix
Bruce Cabot
Barton Maclane
John Agar
Lon Chaney, Jr.
D: William F. Claxton

A gunfighter turned judge is reluctant to rely on his guns for justice.

Law of Violence (1969) FF—Sp./Ital.

George Greenwood
Conrad Steve
D: Gianni Crea

A border town sheriff confronts Mexican bandits.

The Law vs. Billy the Kid (1954) Columbia

Scott Brady
Betta St. John
James Griffith
Alan Hale, Jr.
D: William Castle

William Bonney is forced into a life of crime.
Filmed at Melody Ranch and Walker Ranch, CA.

Au ★

S ★

A ★

> —You know, Billy's a good listener these days. And Betsy here can hardly wait for her chance to speak. Ha, ha, ha.
>
> —Jack Hale, Jr.
> *The Law vs. Billy the Kid*

The Law West of Tombstone (1938) RKO

Harry Carey
Tim Holt
Evelyn Brent
Ward Bond
D: Glenn Tyron

A gunfighter falls in love with the daughter of a crooked judge.

The Lazarus Man (1996) TNT ★★★½

Robert Urich
John Christian Graas
D: John E. Jensen

In post-Civil War Texas, a man returns from the grave with only the memory of an unknown enemy. Pilot for the TV series.

Au

S

A

The Left Handed Gun (1958) WB

Paul Newman
Lita Milan
John Dehner
Hurd Hatfield
D: Arthur Penn

Billy the Kid becomes a victim of circumstances.
Adapted from Gore Vidal's play.
Filmed in Santa Fé, New Mexico.

Au

S

A

Paul Newman and Lita Milan.

Left Handed Johnny West (1965) FF—Sp./Ital.

Dick Palmer (Mimmo Palmara)
Mike Anthony
D: Frank Kramer (Gianfranco Parolini)

A lawman exposes a land baron's killer.

[UNCHARTED TERRITORY]

The Legend of Alfred Packer (1980) ANE

Patrick Day
Ron Haines
Jim Dratfield
D: Jim Roberson

Prospectors take on a severe Colorado Rockies winter.

[UNCHARTED TERRITORY]

—Don't move, Billy. I don't wanna kill ya!
—John Dehner (Pat Garrett)
The Left Handed Gun

Legend of Death Valley (1977) ANE

Robert Dawson
D: Kent Durden

A young man tracks his great grandfather's prospecting trips in Death Valley.

[UNCHARTED TERRITORY]

The Legend of Frank Woods (1977) FF—Ital./U.S.

Brad Stewart
Troy Donahue
Kitty Vallacher
D: Deno Paoli (Hagen Smith)

[UNCHARTED TERRITORY]

The Legend of Jake Kincaid (2002)

Alan Autry
Kimberlee Autry
Lauren Autry
D: Alan Autry

Made for TV movie.

The Legend of Jesse James (1965) ABC-TV

Christopher Jones
Allen Case
Robert J. Wilke
D: Don Siegel

Pilot for the TV series.

The Legend of Jud Starr (1967)

Stuart Whitman
Darren McGavin
Beau Bridges
D: Vincent McEveety

Made for TV movie.

The Legend of Nigger Charley (The Legend of Black Charley) (1972) Paramount

Fred Williamson
D'Urville Martin
Don Pedro Coley
Gertrude Jeanette
D: Martin Goldman

A former slave heads West.
Filmed at Old Tucson.

The Legend of the Golden Gun (1979) NBC-TV ★ ★

Jeff Osterhage
Carl Franklin
Hal Holbrook
D: Alan J. Levi

A young farmer trains with a master gunsmith to
avenge the deaths of his family and horse. Pilot.

Au ★ ★

S ★ ★

A ★ ★

> *—Evil has it's way of tipping the odds in it's favor,
> sometimes…That seventh bullet is for evil.*
> —Hall Holbrook
> *The Legend of the Golden Gun*

The Legend of the Lone Ranger (1949) Apex

Clayton Moore
Jay Silverheels
Glenn Strange

Jack Clifford
D: George B. Seitz, Jr.

The sole survivor of ambushed Texas Rangers is nursed back to
health by an Indian and they fight for law and order. Compilation
of the first three episodes of the TV series.

Au ★

S ★★

A ★★

The Legend of the Lone Ranger (1981) Universal

Klinton Spilsbury
Michael Horse
Christopher Lloyd
Matt Clark
Jason Robards
Richard Farnsworth
Tom Laughlin
D: William A. Fraker

The legendary gunman becomes childhood blood brothers
with Tonto, grows up and avenges his brother's murder.
Filmed at Bonanza Creek Ranch, NM and in Monument Valley,
Marble Arch, Utah.

Au ★★★

S ★★

A ★

"The Trapper"

Legend of the Wild (1981) JF

Don Haggerty
Denver Pyle
Don Shanks
Ken Curtis
D: Charles E. Sellier, Jr.

The further adventures of Grizzly Adams.

The Legend of Tom Dooley (1959) Columbia

Michael Landon
Jo Morrow
Jack Hogan
D: Ted Post

A Confederate soldier attacks a Union stage unaware
that the war is over. Based on the popular song.
Filmed at Chatsworth, California.

Au ★★★

S ★★★

A ★★★

The Legend of Walks Far Woman (1982) NBC-TV ★★

Raquel Welch
Bradford Dillman

George Clutesi
Nick Mancuso
D: Mel Damski

During her 102 years of life, a Blackfoot
woman experiences the end of plains
Indian life. Filmed in Montana.

Au ★★★

S ★★

A ★

*—I don't understand why you plant things to
grow when everywhere around you there is
plenty to pick and eat.*
—Raquel Welch
The Legend of Walks Far Woman

Lemonade Joe (1966) FF—Czech.

Karel Fiala
Milos Kopecky
D: Oldrich Lipsky

An Arizona cowboy gets his strength from drinking lemonade.

Let Freedom Ring (1939) MGM

Nelson Eddy
Virginia Bruce
Victor McLaglen
Lionel Barrymore
D: Jack Conway

A lawyer cleans up his frontier town.

Let Them Rest (1967) FF—Ital./Ger.

Lou Castel
Mark Damon
D: Carlo Lizzani

A psychedelic story of a gay outlaw.

Let's Go and Kill Sartana (1972) FF—Ital./Sp.

Gordon Mitchell
George Martin
D: Mario Pinzauti

An ex-convict who has settled down must face his
former partner who unknowingly raided his ranch.

The Life and Legend of Buffalo Jones (1976) Starfire

Rick Guinn
John Freeman
George Sagar
Rich Scheeland
D: ?

306

The Life and Times of Grizzly Adams (1975) SC

Dan Haggerty
Don Shanks
Marjorie Harper
Lisa Jones
D: Richard Friedenberg

A fugitive trapper finds refuge
in the mountain wilderness.

*—Some say he never did return. Like the
historians, they call it a romantic fabrication.
Hell, what do they know?*
—Ned Beatty
The Life and Times of Judge Roy Bean

The Life and Times of Judge Roy Bean (1972) NG ★★★★

Paul Newman
Jacqueline Bisset
Tab Hunter
John Huston
Ava Gardner
Stacy Keach
Roddy McDowall
Anthony Perkins
Victoria Principal
Ned Beatty
Dick Farnsworth
D: John Huston

The legendary hanging judge maintains law
and order in the town of Langtry. Filmed
at Old Tucson, AZ. #46 Best of the West.

Au ★★★
S ★★★★
A ★★★★⯪

Paul Newman in *The Life and
Times of Judge Roy Bean.*

The Faces of Judge Roy Bean

Judge Roy Bean

Walter Brennan in *The Westerner.*

The Light in the Forest (1965) Disney

Fess Parker
Wendell Corey
Joanne Dru
Jessica Tandy
John McIntire
D: Hershel Daugherty

A young white man raised by Indians returns to his biological family.

The Light of the Western Stars (1930) Paramount

Richard Arlen
Mary Brian
Regis Toomey
D: Otto Brower

A cowboy falls in love with the sister of
his murdered friend. Story by Zane Grey.

The Light of Western Stars (1940) Paramount

Russell Hayden
Victor Jory
Jo Ann Sayers
Noah Beery, Jr.
Alan Ladd
D: Lesley Selander

Remake of the 1930 version.

Lightning Jack (1994) FF—Austr.

Paul Hogan
Cuba Gooding, Jr.
Beverly D'Angelo
Kamila Dawson
D: Simon Wincer

A black mute tags along with an Australian
outlaw. Filmed at Old Tucson and Australia.

Au

S

A

Light the Fuse...Sartana Is Coming (1971) FF—Ital./Fr.

John Garko
Susan Scott
D: Anthony Scott

A mysterious gunfighter vigilante breaks gunman
out of prison. Fifth in the "Sartana" series.

308

Linda and Abilene (1969)

Sharon Matt
Roxanne Jones
Kip Marsh
D: Herschell G. Lewis (Lewis H. Gordon)

Two sibling orphans become attracted to each other.

The Lion and the Horse (1952) WB

Steve Cochran
Ray Teal
Bob Steele
D: Louis King

A cowboy protects his stallion from an uncaring new owner.

Little Big Horn (The Fighting Seventh) (1951) Lippert

Lloyd Bridges
Marie Windsor
John Ireland
Jim Davis
Hugh O'Brian
D: Charles Marquis Warren

A cavalry patrol attempts to warn Custer.
Filmed at the Iverson Movie Location Ranch.

Richard Mulligan as Custer in *Little Big Man.*

Little Big Man (1971) NG ★★★⬩

Dustin Hoffman
Faye Dunaway
Martin Balsam
Richard Mulligan
Chief Dan George
D: Arthur Penn

An old man recounts his life in a satirical look at the Old West. Supporting actor Oscar nomination for George. Filmed in Alberta. #19 IMDb.

Au ★★★
S ★★★⬩
A ★★★⬩

—[Your white wife], Does she cook and does she work hard? [She does?] That surprises me. Does she show pleasant enthusiasm when you mount her? [She does?] That surprises me even more! I tried one of them once, but she didn't show any enthusiasm at all.

—Chief Dan George
Little Big Man

Little House: Bless All the Dear Children (1984) NBC-TV

Melissa Gilbert
Dean Butler
Richard Bull
Victor French
D: Victor French

The Wilder family becomes involved in several children's

lives. Made for TV movie based on the series.

Little House: Look Back to Yesterday (1983) NBC-TV

Michael Landon
Melissa Gilbert
Victor French
Dean Butler
Matthew Laborteaux
D: Victor French

Charles Ingalls stops in Walnut Grove to see the Wilders.
TV movie based on the series "Little House on the Prairie."

Au ★★

S ★

A ★

Little House on the Prairie (1974) NBC-TV

Michael Landon
Karen Grassle
Melissa Gilbert
Melissa Sue Anderson
Lindsay Green Bush
Sidney Green Bush
Victor French
D: Michael Landon

A pioneer family begins a new life on the Kansas frontier.
Pilot for the TV series. Filmed at Big Sky Ranch, California.

Au ★★◗

S ★★

A ★★◗

Little House: The Last Farewell (1984) NBC-TV

Michael Landon
Karen Grassle
Melissa Gilbert
Victor French
D: Michael Landon

Upon their return to Walnut Grove, the Ingalls lead the opposition to
a land grabber. TV movie based on the series. Filmed at Simi Valley, CA.

Au ★★★

S ★◗

A ★★

Little Moon And Jud McGraw see Gone With the West

The Llano Kid (1939) Paramount

Tito Guizar
Gale Sondergaard
Alan Mowbray
Jane Clayton

D: Edward Venturini

A gunman poses as the legendary kissing bandit. Remake of *The Texan* (1930).

Lock, Stock and Barrel (1971) NBC-TV

Tim Matheson
Belinda Montgomery
Claude Akins
Neville Brand
Burgess Meredith
D: Jerry Thorpe

A young frontier couple elope.

The Lone Gun (1954) Superior/UA

George Montgomery
Dorothy Malone
Frank Faylen
Neville Brand
Skip Homeier
D: Ray Nazarro

A disillusioned lawman investigates rustlers.

Au

S ★★★◣

A ★★

—Some men get their kicks out of women, others whiskey. Me…I like cards.
—Frank Faylen
The Lone Gun

The Lone Hand (1953) U-I

Joel McCrea
Barbara Hale
Alex Nicol
James Arness
D: George Sherman

A Pinkerton detective goes undercover without informing his family. Filmed at Durango, CO.

Au ★◣

S ★◣

A ★◣

—There's always the chance I might not come back. So, I wanted you to know so you wouldn't spend the rest of your life hating me.
—Joel McCrea
The Lone Hand

Lone Justice see Ned Blessing: The True Story of My Life

Lone Justice 2 (1995)

Donzaleigh Abernathy
Luis Avalos
Brenda Bakke
Wes Studi
D: Jack Bender

The Lonely Man (1957) Paramount

Jack Palance
Anthony Perkins
Elaine Aiken
Neville Brand
Lee Van Cleef
D: Henry Levin

A reformed outlaw returns to his son who hates him for leaving his mother. Filmed in the Alabama Hills and the Iverson Ranch.

Au ★★★★

S ★★★★

A ★★★★

The Lone Ranger (1956) Wrather/WB

Clayton Moore
Jay Silverheels
Lyle Bettger
D: Stuart Heisler

A dime-novel hero and his Indian sidekick prevent a greedy land baron from breaking an Indian treaty. Filmed at Bronson Canyon and Warner Ranch, CA.

Au ★

S ★★

A ★★

Tonto (Jay Silverheels) and the Lone Ranger (Clayton Moore)

The Lone Ranger and the Lost City of Gold (1958) UA

Clayton Moore
Jay Silverheels
Douglas Kennedy
Charles Watts
D: Lesley Selander

The legendary duo investigate hooded outlaws. Filmed at Old Tucson.

Au ★★

S ★★

A ★★

—Hi-yo Silver! Away!
—Clayton Moore
*The Lone Ranger and
the Lost City of Gold*

Lonesome Dove (1989) QEI ★★★★★

Robert Duvall
Tommy Lee Jones
Danny Glover
Diane Lane
Robert Urich
Ricky Schroder
Anjelica Huston
D: Simon Wincer

Two former Texas Rangers lead an epic cattle drive. TV mini-series based on Larry McMurtry's novel. Filmed primarily at several locations in New Mexico including: Cook Ranch, Bonanza Creek Ranch, Santo Domingo Pueblo,

Robert Duvall in *Lonesome Dove.*

312

and San Ildefonso Pueblo. Some filming in southwestern TX.
#7 Best of the West, #8 LPFF.

Au

S

A

—It's been quite a party!
—Robert Duvall
Lonesome Dove

The Lonesome Trail (1930) Syndicate

Charles Delaney
Virginia Brown Faire
Yakima Canutt
Ben Corbett
D: Bruce M. Mitchell

Two women fall for the same gunfighter.

The Lonesome Trail (1955) Lippert

Wayne Morris
John Agar
Margia Dean
Edgar Buchanan
D: Richard Bartlett

When land-grabber attempt to steal his land,
the owner retaliates with a bow and arrow.

Lone Star (1952) MGM

Clark Gable
Ava Gardner
Broderick Crawford
Lionel Barrymore
William Farnum
D: Vincent Sherman

A Texas cattleman prevents an attempt
to secede Texas from the Union. Story by
Borden Chase. Filmed in Colorado.

Au ★★★

S ★★★★

A ★★★★

Lone Texan (1959) 20ᵗʰ C. Fox

Willard Parker
Grant Williams
Audrey Dalton
D: Paul Landres

A Civil War veteran returns home to find his brother a corrupt lawman.

Longarm (1988) MCA-TV

Daphne Ashbrook
Rene Auberjonois
Lee de Broux
John T. Terlesky
D: Virgil W. Vogel

Long Day of the Massacre (1968) FF—Ital.

Peter Martell
Glenn Saxon
D: Albert Cardiff (Alberto Cardone)

Rare.

Long Days of Vengeance (1967) FF—Ital./Sp.

Giuliano Gemma
Francisco Rabal
D: Stan Vance (Florestano Vancini)

An escapee seeks revenge against the man responsible for his imprisonment.

The Longest Drive (The Quest: The Longest Drive) (1976) CP-TV

Kurt Russell
Tim Matheson
Dan O'Herlihy
Keenan Wynn
Woody Strode
Erik Estrada
D: Bernard E. McEveety

Two brothers and a gang of misfits drive cattle to market.
Pilot for "The Quest" TV series. Filmed at Old Tucson.

Au ★ ✦
S ★
A ★ ✦

—*Well, if that ain't the bull's behind!*
—Keenan Wynn
The Longest Drive

The Longest Drive 2 (Captive: The Longest Drive 2) (1976) CP-TV

Kurt Russell
Tim Matheson
Susan Day
D: Lee H. Katzin

Sequel to *The Longest Drive.*

The Longest Hunt (Shoot, Gringo..Shoot!) (1968) FF—Ital./Fr.

Brian Kelly
Fabrizio Moroni
Keenan Wynn

314

D: Frank B. Corlish (Bruno Corbucci)

A land baron hires a gunfighter to
return his son from an outlaw gang.

Au

S ★

A ★◖

The Longhorn (1951) Mono.

Wild Bill Elliott
Myron Healey
Phyllis Coates
John Hart
D: Lewis Collins

Two cowboys drive Herefords to
crossbreed with Texas longhorns.

UNCHARTED
TERRITORY

The Long Ride see Gunsmoke: The Long Ride

Long Ride from Hell (1968) FF—Ital.

Steve Reeves
Wayde Preston
D: Alex Burkes

A gunman seeks revenge against a land baron.

UNCHARTED
TERRITORY

The Long Ride Home see A Time for Killing

The Long Riders (1980) UA ★★★◖

David Carradine
Keith Carradine
Robert Carradine
James Keach
Stacy Keach
Dennis Quaid
Randy Quaid
Harry Carey, Jr.
D: Walter Hill

Legendary outlaws make the Northfield,
Minnesota raid. Filmed at Parrott, Georgia.
#48 IMDb.

Au ★★★★

S ★★★◖

A ★★★

Los Locos (1997)

Mario Van Peebles
Rene Auberjonois
Tom Dorfmeister
D: Jean-Marc Vallée

Frank and Jesse James (seated) Cole and Bob Younger (standing)

Robert Carradine (Bob Younger), Randy Quaid (Clell Miller),
Stacy Keach (Frank James) and James Keach (Jessie James).

*—We's all in the war. Robbin' the first Yankee bank cause
we didn't know no better. An' it seemed like a good idea at
the time. After that we's just in the habit. So, I guess we'll
just keep on goin' till they lock us up or hang us.*
—Clell Miller (Randy Quaid)
The Long Riders

Filmed at Old Tucson.

Louis L'Amour's Crossfire Trail see Crossfire Trail

Louis L'Amour's "Down the Long Hills" (1986) Disney-TV

Bruce Boxleitner
Bo Hopkins
Michael Wren
Jack Elam
D: Burt Kennedy

Upon escaping a massacre, a boy and girl lead their stallion through the Utah wilderness.

Louis L'Amour's "The Sacketts" see The Sacketts

Louis L'Amour's "The Shadow Riders" see The Shadow Riders

Louis L'Amour's Shaughnessy see Shaughnessy

Love Me Tender (1956) 20ᵗʰ C. Fox

Richard Egan
Debra Paget
Elvis Presley
Neville Brand
D: Robert D. Webb

A singing Texan marries his brother's girlfriend unaware that his brother is still alive.

Elvis and Debra Paget in *Love Me Tender.*

Lovin' Molly (The Wild and the Sweet) (1974) Columbia

Anthony Perkins
Beau Bridges
Blythe Danner
Edward Binns
D: Sidney Lumet

A Texas woman must choose between a well established man and a drifter. Based on a Larry McMurtry novel.

Lucky Cisco Kid (1940) 20ᵗʰ C. Fox

Cesar Romero
Mary Beth Hughes
Dana Andrews
D: H. Bruce Humberstone

An outlaw poses as the Cisco Kid. Based on O'Henry's character.

316

Lucky Johnny: Born in America (1973) FF—Ital./Mex.

Glen Lee
Virgil Frye
D: Josè Antonio Balanos

A gunfighter falls for the wife of an outlaw.

Lust for Gold (1949) Columbia

Ida Lupino
Glenn Ford
Gig Young
Edgar Buchanan
D: Sylvan Simon

A gunman competes with a couple for control
of the legendary Lost Dutchman Goldmine.

Au ✦

S ✦

A ✦

—They tricked us! Them shaft-bellied horn swagglers!
—Edgar Buchanan
Lust for Gold

Macahans (1976) ABC-TV/ASRP/MGM

James Arness
Eva Marie Saint
Richard Kiley
John Crawford
Bruce Boxleitner
D: Bernard McEveety

A frontiersman moves his family west in 1860.
Based on *How the West Was Won* (1963).
Launched the mini-series, *How the West Was Won* (1977).

Machine Gun Killers (1968) FF—Ital./Sp.

Robert Woods
John Ireland
D: Paolo Bianchini (Paolo Bianchi)

When Richard Gatlin (Gatling) introduces his new gun
to the Union Army, he is kidnapped by a Mexican bandit.

James Arness in *Macahans*.

Machismo—40 Graves For 40 Guns (1971) (The Revenge of the Wild Bunch) (1976) BI

Robert Padilla
Stanley Adams
Rita Rogers
Sue Bernard
D: Paul Hunt

A bandito is offered a pardon to capture an outlaw gang.

Macho Callahan (1970) AE

David Janssen
Jean Seberg
Lee J. Cobb
James Booth
David Carradine
D: Bernard Kowalski

Upon escaping from prison, a Union soldier seeks revenge.

Macho Killers (1977) FF—Ital.

Carlos Monson
George Hilton
D: Mark Andrew

A gambler infiltrates an outlaw gang in order to recover stolen gold.

MacKenna's Gold (1969) Columbia

Gregory Peck
Omar Shariff
Telly Savalas
Camilla Sparv
Keenan Wynn
Lee J. Cobb
Burgess Meredith
Edward G. Robinson
Eli Wallach
D: J. Lee Thompson

A sheriff holds the map to a legendary valley of Apache gold. Story by Will Henry. Filmed in Glen Canyon National Recreation Area and in Monument Valley.

Au ★★★◗

S ★★★◗

A ★★★★

—I never understand the gringo—never!
—Omar Sharif
MacKenna's Gold

Mackintosh and T.J. (1976) PP

Roy Rogers
Clay O'Brien
Billy Green
Andrew Robinson
D: Marvin Chomsky

A hard-working, religious Texas cowboy contends with his drifting teenage son.

Madron (His Name Was Madron) (1970) FF—Isr.

Richard Boone
Leslie Caron
Paul Smith
Mosko Alkalai
D: Jerry Hopper

A nun who survived an Indian massacre is cared for by an old gunfighter.

Mad Trapper of the Yukon see Challenge to Be Free

The Magnificent Seven (1960) UA ★ ★ ★ ★

Yul Brynner
Eli Wallach
Steve McQueen
Horst Buchholz
Charles Bronson
Robert Vaughn
Brad Dexter
James Coburn
Vladimir Sokoloff
Rosenda Monterosa
Jorge Martinez de Hoyos
D: John Sturges

A Mexican village hires seven
mercenaries to defend them
from bandits. Oscar nomination
for scoring: drama/comedy.
Filmed at Cuernavaca, Morelos, Mexico.
#43 Best of the West,
#79 AFI MHPM, #17 IMDb.

Steve McQueen, James Coburn, Horst Buchholz, Yul Brynner, Brad Dexter,
Robert Vaughn and Charles Bronson in *The Magnificent Seven.*

Au ★ ★ ★

S ★ ★ ★ ★

A ★ ★ ★ ★ ★

Magnificent Seven (1963) FF—Sp./Ital.

Geoffrey Horne
Robert Hundar
D: Joaquin R. Marchent (Joaquin Luis Romero Hernandez

Three gunmen unite settlers in order to
defend themselves against Mexican bandits.

*—The graveyards are full of boys who were
young and very proud.*

—Yul Brynner
The Magnificent Seven

The Magnificent Seven (1998) CBS-TV ★ ★

Michael Biehn
Eric Close
Andrew Kavovit
Dale Midkiff
D: Geoff Murphy

Seven mercenaries protect an Indian village from
ex-Confederates. Adapted from the 1960 version.
Pilot for the series. Filmed at Old Tucson.

Au ★ ★ ★ ★

S ★ ★

A ★ ★

The Magnificent Seven Ride! (1972) UA

Lee Van Cleef

Stefanie Powers
Mariette Hartley
Michael Callan
D: George McGowan

A lawman returns to again protect a village from bandidos.
Third sequel to *The Magnificent Seven.*

Magnificent Texan (1967) FF—Ital./Sp.

Glenn Saxon
Benny Deus
D: Lewis King (Luigi Capuano)

A gunfighter defends Mexican peons from a land baron.

Magnificent West (1972) FF—Ital.

Vassili Karis
Lorenzo Fineschi
D: Gianni Crea

A gunman searches for the gold stolen by his former partner.

Mail Order Bride (West of Montana) (1964) MGM

Buddy Ebsen
Keir Dullea
Lois Nettleton
Warren Oates
D: Burt Kennedy

An old lawman orders a bride
for a hell-raising young man.

Au ★★

S ★★

A ★★★

—Me, Take a bride? Not on your life, he said. I'm too frolicsome. I'm wild and wooly and full of fleas and never been combed below the knees. The very thought of a wife gives me the chills in the grooves.

—Buddy Ebsen
Mail Order Bride

Major Dundee (1965) Columbia

Charlton Heston
Richard Harris
Jim Hutton
James Coburn
Warren Oates
Ben Johnson
Slim Pickens
D: Sam Peckinpah

A Union officer leads rebels and outlaws on a raid against Apaches in Mexico.
Screenplay by Burt Kennedy. Filmed at Durango, Mexico. #61 Best of the West.

Au ★★★★

S ★★★★

A ★★★★★

Charlton Heston in *Major Dundee.*

320

Mallory Must Die (1971) FF—Ital.

Robert Woods
Gabriella Giorgelli
D: Mario Moroni

A bounty hunter tracks an escaped killer.

A Man Alone (1955) Republic

Ray Milland
Mary Murphy
Ward Bond
Raymond Burr
Lee Van Cleef
Alan Hale, Jr.
D: Ray Milland

An innocent man hides from a corrupt sheriff and businessmen who robbed their own bank.

Au ★ ◗

S ★ ★

A ★ ◗

Man and a Colt (1967) FF—Sp./Ital.

Robert Hundar
Fernando Sancho
D: Tullio Demichelli

A gunfighter confronts a town boss and Mexican bandido.

Man And Boy (1971) L-P ★ ★

Bill Cosby
Gloria Foster
Leif Erickson
George Spell
D: E.W. Swackhamer

A black cowboy and his son search for stolen horses.

Au ★ ★ ★

S ★ ◗

A ★ ★

The Man Behind the Gun (1953) WB ★ ★ ★

Randolph Scott
Patrice Wymore
Dick Wesson
Alan Hale, Jr.
James Brown (II)
D: Felix Feist

Ward Bond and Mary Murphy in *A Man Alone.*

—*Back east they all talk about how wonderful the West is. How a man can get rich overnight. Just throw out a handful of seed or pick up some gold from a stream bed. Folks that tell ya that have never seen the West.*

—Ward Bond
A Man Alone

—*That's right. Get us a horse just like the one I had when I was a mustangin' cowboy. Did I ever tell ya 'bout that?*

—Bill Cosby
Man And Boy

A gunman works undercover
at a southwest military post.
Filmed at Bell Ranch, California.

Au

S

A

Man Called Amen (1972) FF—Ital.

Luc Merenda
Sydne Rome
D: Alfio Caltabiano

A gunfighter discovers his former
partner is a crooked reverend.

Man Called Blade (Mannaja) (1977) FF—Ital.

Maurizio Merli
John Steiner
D: Sergio Martino

A bounty hunter tracks the man who left him for dead.

Man Called Django (1971) FF—Ital.

Anthony Steffen
Stelio Candelli
D: Edward G. Muller (Edoardo Mulargia)

A gunfighter avenges the death of his lover.

A Man Called Gannon (1969) Universal

Tony Franciosa
Michael Sarrazin
Judi West
Susan Oliver
D: James Goldstone

Remake of *Man Without a Star.*

Man Called Gringo (1964) FF—Ger./Sp.

Gotz George
Sieghardt Rupp
D: Roy Rowland

A lawyer seeks revenge against a rancher by hiring a
gunfighter to kill him unaware that the man is his father.

James Brown, Alan Hale, Jr. and Randolph Scott in
The Man Behind the Gun.

*—When I put out my neck,
I want it in friendly hands.*
—Randolph Scott
The Man Behind the Gun

A Man Called Horse (1970) NG

Richard Harris
Dame Judith Anderson
Jean Gascon
Manu Tupou
Edward Little Sky
Iron Eyes Cody
Richard Fools Bull
D: Elliott Silverstein

An English nobleman earns the respect of his Sioux captors by becoming a warrior. Filmed at Custer State Park, SD and Durango, Mexico. #17 Best of the West.

Au ★★★★★
S ★★★★
A ★★★★★

Richard Harris in *A Man Called Horse*.

Man Called Invincible (1973) FF—Ital.

George Hilton
Cris Huerta
D: Anthony Ascott (Giuliano Carmineo)

A gambler is hired to transport gold to Dallas.

UNCHARTED TERRITORY

Man Called Noon (1974) FF—Brit./Sp./Ital.

Richard Crenna
Rosanna Schiaffino
Stephen Boyd
D: Peter Collinson

A gunfighter suffering from amnesia seeks to avenge his family's murder. Based on the Louie L'Amour novel.

Au ★★★
S ★★
A ★★

—Let the dead past bury its dead.
—Richard Crenna
Man Called Noon

Man Called Sledge (1970) FF—Ital./U.S. ★★★

James Garner
Laura Antonelli
Dennis Weaver
Claude Akins
D: Vic Morrow, Giorgio Gentili

An outlaw gang steals gold then fights among themselves over their loot. Filmed in southern Spain.

Au ★★★
S ★★★
A ★★★

—You try to take that gold you're committin' suicide!
—Dennis Weaver
Man Called Sledge

A Man for Hanging (1973)

Peter Breck
Paul Carr
Brooke Bundy
D: Joseph Mazzuca

A psychopath rapes and kills while searching for
his partners in a bank robbery. Made for TV movie.

The Man from Bitter Ridge (1955) U-I

Lex Barker
Mara Corday
Stephen McNally
D: Jack Arnold

An investigator must determine who is responsible for a series
of stagecoach robberies. Based on a William MacLeod story.

Man from Canyon City (1965) FF—Sp./Ital.

Robert Woods
Fernando Sancho
D: Alfonso Balcazar

A gambler and a bandido escape from prison chained together.
Sequel to *Five Thousand Dollars on One Ace*.

The Man from Colorado (1948) Columbia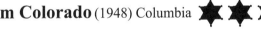

Glenn Ford
William Holden
Ellen Drew
Edgar Buchanan
D: Henry Levin

Following the Civil War, a marshal confronts
his friend who has become a corrupt federal judge.
Story by Borden Chase. Filmed at the Iverson Ranch.

Au ★★★
S ★★★
A ★★★

Ellen Drew and Glenn Ford in
The Man From Colorado.

Man From Del Rio (1956) UA

Anthony Quinn
Katy Jurado
Peter Whitney
D: Harry Horner

A Mexican sheriff is socially shunned
by the "good" men he is protecting.

*—Time. That's what men need when they get
back from a war. Time and people standing by
that really care about them and believe in them.*

—Edgar Buchanan
The Man from Colorado

Man From God's Country (1958) AA ★★▌

George Montgomery
Randy Stuart
James Griffith
D: Paul Landres

Two Civil War veterans face a corrupt town boss.
Filmed at the Iverson Movie Location Ranch.

Au ★★▌

S ★★▌

A ★★▌

*—No boy's ashamed of his father.
Maybe disappointed and hurt, but not
ashamed of him!*
—George Montgomery
Man From God's Country

The Man from Laramie (1955) Columbia ★★★★

James Stewart
Arthur Kennedy
Donald Crisp
Jack Elam
John War Eagle
D: Anthony Mann

A man searches for the gunrunner responsible
for his brother's death. Filmed at Bonanza
Creek Ranch, New Mexico. #96 Best of the West.

Au ★★★

S ★★★★

A ★★★★

—Why, you scum!
—James Stewart
The Man from Laramie

Man from Oklahoma (1965) FF—Ital./Sp./Ger.

Rick Horn
Josè Calvo
D: Robert M. White (Jaime J. Balcazar with Roberto Montero)

A sheriff faces off against the town boss and his gang of outlaws.

The Man From Texas (1947) EL

James Craig
Jynn Bari
Johnny Johnston
Sara Allgood
D: Leigh Jason

The El Paso Kid attempts to settle down.

The Man From the Alamo (1953) U-I ★★★▌

Glenn Ford
Julia Adams
Chill Wills
Hugh O'Brian
Guy Williams
Dennis Weaver
Neville Brand

Glenn Ford in *The Man From the Alamo.*

D: Budd Boetticher

The sole survivor of the Alamo returns home
only to discover his family murdered.

Au
S
A

Man: His Pride and His Vengeance (1967) FF—Ital./Ger.

Franco Nero
Klaus Kinski
D: Luigi Bazzoni

A Mexican officer and his lover join a gang of smugglers.

Manhunt see From Hell to Texas

The Manhunt (1985) Fulvia/SGC

John Ethan Wayne
Ernest Borgnine
Bo Svenson
Raidmund Harmstorf
D: Larry Ludman (Fabrio De Angelis)

Man in the Saddle (1951) S-B/Columbia

Randolph Scott
Joan Leslie
Ellen Drew
Cameron Mitchell
Tennessee Ernie Ford
Alfonso Bedoya
D: Andrè de Toth

A cowboy is run off the range by the man who marries
his former fiancèe. Story by Ernest Haycox.

Alfonso Bedoya and Randolph Scott in *Man in The Saddle.*

Man in the Wilderness (1971) WB ★ ★ ★ ★

Richard Harris
John Huston
Henry Wilcoxon
Percy Herbert
D: Richard C. Sarafian

Left for dead after being mauled by a grizzly,
a Northwest Territory scout seeks revenge.

Au ★ ★ ★ ★ ⯪
S ★ ★ ★ ★
A ★ ★ ★ ★

—I never much agreed with God's will.
—Richard Harris
Man in the Wilderness

Mannaja see Man Called Blade

Man of Conquest (1939) Republic

Richard Dix
Gail Patrick
Joan Fontaine
Edward Ellis
George Hayes
D: George Nichols, Jr.

Sam Houston leads the Texas rebellion. Oscar nominations for art direction, scoring: original music, and sound recording. Filmed at the Iverson Movie Ranch.

Au

S ★★

A ★◀

> *—I'm goin' to Texas. There's an empire to be built down there.*
>
> —Richard Dix
> *Man of Conquest*

Man of the Cursed Valley (1964) FF—Ital./Sp.

Ty Hardin
Iran Eory
D: Omar Hopkins (Primo Zeglio)

A white girl's marriage to an Indian creates turmoil.

Man of the East (1973) FF—Ital./Fr.

Terence Hill
Gregory Walcott
Harry Carey, Jr.
D: E.B. Clucher (Enzo Barboni)

An aristocrat learns the ways of the West.

Man of the West (1958) UA

Gary Cooper
Julie London
Lee J. Cobb
Arthur O'Connell
Jack Lord
D: Anthony Mann

After playing it straight for years, a gunman reunites with his fellow outlaws. Filmed at Melody Ranch and Red Rock Canyon, CA.

Au ★★★★

S ★★★

A ★★★★

Jack Lord, Gary Cooper and Julie London in
Man of the West.

Man or Gun (1958) Republic

Macdonald Carey
Audrey Totter
James Craig
D: Albert C. Gannaway

A drifter faces off with a ruthless family.

Au

S

A

Man Who Cried for Revenge (1969) FF—Ital./Sp.

Anthony Steffen
William Berger
D: William Hawkins (Mario Caiano)

A gunfighter avenges his wife's murder.

Man Who Killed Billy the Kid (1967) FF—Ital.

Peter Lee Lawrence
Fausto Tozzi
D: Julio Buchs

Pat Garrett and the Kid's friend, Mark Liston, track Billy.

The Man Who Loved Cat Dancing (1973) MGM

Burt Reynolds
Sarah Miles
Lee J. Cobb
Jack Warden
George Hamilton
Jay Silverheels
D: Richard C. Sarafian

An outlaw on the run for killing the man who raped his Indian wife and a woman running from her husband find each other. Filmed at Old Tucson.

The Man Who Shot Liberty Valance (1962) Paramount

John Wayne
James Stewart
Vera Miles
Lee Marvin
Edmond O'Brien
Andy Devine
Woody Strode
Lee Van Cleef
Strother Martin
John Carradine
D: John Ford

A tenderfoot lawyer attempts to rid a town of a punk outlaw. Oscar nomination for costume design. Filmed at Janss Conejo Ranch, Thousand Oaks, CA. #40 Best of the West, #8 IMDb.

Au

S

A

Lee Marvin, Jimmy Stewart and John Wayne in
The Man Who Shot Liberty Valance.

Man Without a Star (1955) U-A ★ ★ ⅃

Kirk Douglas
Jeanne Craine
Claire Trevor
Richard Boone
Jack Elam
D: King Vidor

A drifter is seduced into helping a woman with her cattle ranch.
Screenplay by Borden Chase. Filmed at Conejo Valley, California.

Au ★ ★

S ★ ★ ⅃

A ★ ★ ★ ⅃

Man With the Golden Pistol (1966) FF—Sp./Ital.

Carl Mohner
Luis Dàvila
D: Alfonso Balcazar

A drifter assumes the identity of a dead gunfighter and is hired as temporary sheriff.

UNCHARTED
TERRITORY

Man With the Gun (Deadly Peacemaker) (1955) UA

Robert Mitchum
Jan Sterling
Karen Sharpe
Angie Dickinson
D: Richard Wilson

A gunfighter cleans ups a town in order to win back his estranged wife.

UNCHARTED
TERRITORY

The Marauders (1955) MGM ★

Dan Duryea
Jeff Richards
Keenan Wynn
D: Gerald Mayer

A homesteader protects his well and land
from marauders. Filmed at Mecca, California.

Au ★ ⅃

S ★

A ★

Dan Duryea and Keenan Wynn in *The Marauders*.

Marie Ann (1978) FF—Can.

Andrée Pelletier
John Juliani
Tantoo Cardinal
D: Martin Walters

A kidnapped married woman becomes attached to an Indian.

UNCHARTED
TERRITORY

Mark of the Gun (1969) Emerson

Ross Hagan
Brad Thomas
Chris Carter
Wallace J. Campodanio
D: ?

Jack Slade and his gang raid the West.

Mark of the Renegade (1951) U-I

Ricardo Montalban
Cyd Charisse
J. Carroll Naish
Gilbert Roland
D: Hugo Fregonese

A Mexican agent attempts to protect his country's interests in Southern California. Based on a story by Johnston McCulley.

The Mark of Zorro (1940) 20ᵗʰ C. Fox

Tyrone Power
Linda Darnell
Basil Rathbone
Gale Sondergaard
D: Rouben Mamoulian

A masked swordsman opposes Spanish oppression in old California. Based on Johnston McCulley's, *The Curse of Capistrano*. Oscar nomination for original score.

Au ★★★★
S ★★★★
A ★★★★

> —*We're gonna follow the customs of California…Well, we're going to marry and raise fat children and watch our vinyards grow.*
>
> —Tyrone Power
> *The Mark of Zorro* (1940)

Mark of Zorro (1963) FF—Ital.

Sean Flynn
Mario Petri
Daniete de Metz
Gaby Andre
D: Mario Caiano

The Mark of Zorro (1974) 20ᵗʰ C. Fox ★★

Frank Langella
Ricardo Montalban
Gilbert Roland
Yvonne De Carlo
D: Don McDougall

Made for TV remake of the 1940

330

version. Filmed at Old Tucson.

Au

S ★ ★

A ★ ★

The Marshal's Daughter (1953) UA

Hoot Gibson
Laurie Anders
Harry Lauter
Preston Foster
Johnny Mack Brown
D: William A. Berke

A marshal's daughter disguised as "El Coyote" fights outlaws.

The Mask of Zorro (1998) Amblin E. ★ ★ ★ ★

Antonio Banderas
Anthony Hopkins
Catherine Zeta-Jones
D: Martin Campbell

Lighthearted story of an aging Zorro
who trains his successor in order to
avenge the murder of his wife and
the abduction of his daughter. Oscar
nominations for best sound, sound
editing, and sound effects editing.
Filmed in Mexico. #85 Best of the West.

Au ★ ★ ★ ★

S ★ ★ ★ ★

A ★ ★ ★ ★

Catherine Zeta-Jones in *The Mask of Zorro*.

Masquerade (1956) WC

Clayton Moore
Jay Silverheels
Allen Pinson
Wayne Burson
D: Earl Bellamy

Compilation of three episodes of "The Lone Ranger" TV series.

Massacre (1934) First National

Richard Barthelmess
Ann Dvork
Dudley Diggs
D: Alan Crosland

An educated chief opposes crooked Indian agents.

Massacre (1956) Lippert/20ᵗʰ C. Fox

Dane Clark
James Craig
Marta Roth
D: Louis King

A government agent tracks gunrunners.

Massacre at Fort Grant (1972) see A Reason to Live, a Reason to Die

Massacre at Fort Holman see Massacre at Fort Perdition

Massacre at Fort Perdition (Massacre at Fort Grant) (1963) FF—Sp.

Jerry Cobb
Mariano Vidal
D: J. Douglas (Josè M. Elorrieta)

Indians attack a wagon train.

Massacre at Grand Canyon (1963) FF—Ital.

James Mitchum
Jill Powers
D: Stanley Corbett (Albert Band and Sergio Corbucci)

A gunman avenges his father's murder.

Massacre at Marble City (1964) FF—Ger./Ital./Fr.

Mario Adorf
Brad Harris
Horst Frank
D: Franz J. Gottlieb

Gold is discovered in Indian territory.

Massacre at Sand Creek (1956) CBS-TV

John Derek
Everette Sloane
Gene Evans
D: Arthur Hiller

Poorly armed Cheyenne are attacked by the cavalry.

Massacre Canyon (1954) Columbia

Phil Carey
Audrey Totter
Douglas Kennedy
Jeff Donnell
D: Fred F. Sears

An Army sergeant delivers rifles to the incompetent

Colonel John M. Chivington, responsible for the Sand Creek Massacre.

commander of a frontier outpost. Originally titled
Massacre at Moccasin Pass, but changed prior to release.

Au

S ⭐

A ⭐

Massacre River (1949) Windsor Prod./AA ⭐⭐⚝

Guy Madison
Rory Calhoun
Johnny Sands
Carole Mathews
Iron Eyes Cody
D: John Rawlins

Two Army officers battle hostiles while falling for
the same woman. Filmed at the Iverson Movie Ranch.

Au ⭐⭐⚝

S ⭐⭐⚝

A ⭐⭐⚝

Massacre Time (Colt Concert) (1966) FF—Ital./Sp./Ger.

Franco Nero
George Hilton
D: Lucio Fulci

A New Mexican land baron turns over his operations to his sadistic son.

UNCHARTED
TERRITORY

The Master Gunfighter (1975) T-LP ⭐

Tom Laughlin
Ron O'Neal
Lincoln Kilpatrick
Geo Anne Sosa
D: Frank Laughlin

A philosophical gunfighter pursues justice with both
his six gun and Samurai sword. Filmed at Monterey, CA.

Au ⭐⚝

S ⚝

A ⭐

Masterson of Kansas (1955) Columbia ⭐

George Montgomery
Nancy Gates
James Jean Willes
Jay Silverheels
D: William Castle

Bat Masterson and his legendary colleagues prevent
an Indian war. Filmed at Corriganville, California.

Au ⭐

Bat Masterson

S
A

Matalo! (1971) FF—Ital./Sp.

Lou Castel
Corrado Pani
D: Cesare Canavari

Wells Fargo hires a bounty hunter to recover stolen gold.

The Maverick (1952) Silvermine/AA

Bill Elliott
Phyllis Coates
Myron Healey
D: Thomas Carr

A cavalry officer escorts two women home while attempting
to see that two outlaws are brought to justice.

Maverick (1994) WB

Mel Gibson
Jodie Foster
James Garner
James Coburn
Clint Black
D: Richard Donner

Bret Maverick joins a "best of the West" poker championship.
Lighthearted story based on the television series. Oscar
nomination for best costume design. Filmed in Glen Canyon
National Recreation Area, Alabama Hills and Yosemite.

Au ★★★
S ★★★
A ★★★★

The Maverick Queen (1956) Republic

Barbara Stanwyck
Barry Sullivan
Scott Brady
Wallace Ford
Jim Davis
D: Joe Kane

A Pinkerton agent poses as an outlaw to break up the Wild Bunch.
Based on the Zane Gray novel. Filmed at Durango, Colorado.

Au ★★★
S ★★★
A ★★★

May God Forgive You…But I Won't (1968) FF—Ital.

Georges Ardisson
Anthony Ghidra

—*Bat Masterson laid down his guns and rode east to become a famous newspaper man. But, out west they'll always remember him as Masterson of Kansas.*
—Narrator
Masterson of Kansas

—*I'll drop you like a poisonous snake!*
—Barbara Stanwyck
The Maverick Queen

334

D: Glenn Vincent Davis (Vincenzo Musolino)
A gunman avenges the murder of his family.

McCabe and Mrs. Miller (1971) WB

Warren Beatty
Julie Christie
Rene Auberjonois
Hugh Naughton
Shelley Duvall
Keith Carradine
D: Robert Altman

A gambler and a whore become partners in a mining
town. Based on Edmond Naughton's, *McCabe*. Best actress
Oscar nomination for Christie. Filmed in British
Columbia, Canada. #18 Best of the West, #30 IMDb.

Au ★★★★★
S ★★★★
A ★★★★★

John Wayne in *McLintock!*

McLintock! (1963) Batjac/UA

John Wayne
Maureen O'Hara
Yvonne De Carlo
Patrick Wayne
Stefanie Powers
Chill Wills
Jerry Van Dyke
Edgar Buchanan
Strother Martin
Bob Steele
D: Andrew V. McLaglen

A wealthy cattleman attempts to tame his strong-willed
wife while confronting settlers and Indians.
Filmed in Old Tucson and near Tombstone. #45 IMDb.

Au ★★★
S ★★★
A ★★★★

*—But, Pilgrim, you caused alot of trouble this
morning. Might of got somebody killed. And
somebody otta belt you in the mouth. But, I
won't, I won't…The hell I won't!*

—John Wayne
McLintock!

The Meanest Men in the West (1967/re-released 1982) MCA-TV

Charles Bronson
Lee Marvin
James Drury
Lee J. Cobb
D: Sam Fuller and Charles Dubin

Outlaws kidnap a judge. Compilation of two unrelated episodes of
"The Virginian" TV series. Terrible editing makes this one of the
strangest Westerns I've ever seen. Filmed at Vasquez Rocks, CA.

Au ★★
S ★
A ★★★

Meanwhile, Back at the Ranch (1997)

Eilene Janssen
D: Richard Patterson

An outlaw gang terrorizes the people of Peaceful Valley.

Medecine Stallion see Peter Lundy and the Medecine Hat Stallion

Men of Texas (Men of Destiny) (1942) Universal

Robert Stack
Broderick Crawford
Jackie Cooper
D: Ray Enright

Two newspaper men travel West to report on postwar Texas.

Mercenary (1968) FF—Ital./Sp.

Franco Nero
Jack Palance
Eduardo Fajardo
D: Sergio Corbucci

A bounty hunter is hired to escort silver shipments to Mexico City.

Mexican Spitfire Out West (1940) RKO

Lupe Velaz
Leon Errol
Donald Woods
Elizabeth Risdon
D: Leslie Goodwins

When the "Mexican Spitfire" heads west for a divorce, her uncle attempts to stop her.

The Michigan Kid (1947) Universal

Jon Hall
Rita Johnson
Victor McLaglen
Andy Devine
William Ching
Milburn Stone
D: Ray Taylor

Four plains Indian war veterans reunite in Arizona when one of them needs help. Based on the Rex Beach story. Filmed at Kernville, California.

Minnesota Clay (1964) FF—Ital./Sp./Fr.

Cameron Mitchell
Fernando Sancho
D: Sergio Corbucci

A sheriff who is going blind is determined to clean up his town before it's too late.

A Minute to Pray, a Second to Die (Dead or Alive) (1967) FF—Ital. ★★✴

Robert Ryan
Alex Cord
Arthur Kennedy
D: Franco Giraldi

The governor of New Mexico protects an outlaw to whom he has granted amnesty.

Au ★★★

S ★

A ★✴

> *—That's it! Easy as pie.*
> —Robert Ryan
> *A Minute to Pray, a Second to Die*

Miracle in the Sand see Three Godfathers

Miracle in the Wilderness (1991) TNT ★★★

Kris Kristofferson
Kim Cattrall
Sheldon Peters Wolfchild
D: Kevin James Dobson

A trapper and his wife translate the birth of Christ into an Indian fable for the Blackfeet who kidnapped their son.

Au ★★★★✴

S ★★

A ★★★

The Miracle of the Hills (1959) 20th C. Fox

Rex Reason
Theona Bryant
Jay North
D: Paul Landres

A minister reforms a mining town.

Miss Dynamite (1972) FF—Ital./Fr.

Antonio Sabàto
Fernando Sancho
D: Sergio Grieco

Rare.

The Missouri Breaks (1976) UA ★★★★★

Marlon Brando
Jack Nicholson
Randy Quaid
Kathleen Lloyd
Frederic Forrest
Harry Dean Stanton
D: Arthur Penn

A psychopathic regulator stalks horse rustlers.
Filmed at Nevada City, Virginia City, MT and
High Plains, New Mexico. #12 Best of the West.

Au ★★★★★

S ★★★★½

A ★★★★★

Marlon Brando pays his respects in *The Missouri Breaks.*

Molly And Lawless John (1973) PDC

Vera Miles
Sam Elliott
Clu Gulager
John Anderson
D: Gary Nelson

After running off with her husband's prisoner,
a sheriff's wife claims she was kidnapped.

The Moment to Kill (1968) FF—Ital./Ger.

George Hilton
Walter Barnes
Horst Frank
D: Anthony Ascott (Guiliano Carmineo)

Two gunfighters search for Confederate gold

—Ya know what woke ya up?
Lee, you just had your throat cut.
—Jack Nicholson
The Missouri Breaks

Money, Women And Guns (1959) U-I ★

Jock Mahoney
Kim Hunter
Tim Hovey
Lon Chaney, Jr.
D: Richard Bartlett

A frontier detective investigates the murder
of a prospector. Filmed at Lone Pine, California.

Au ★

S ★

A ★

Montana (1950) WB

Errol Flynn
Alexis Smith
S.Z. "Cuddles" Sakall
D: Ray Enright

A sheepman invades Montana cattle country. Story by

338

Ernest Haycox. Screenplay by J.R. Webb and Borden Chase.

Montana Belle (1952) RKO

Jane Russell
George Brent
Scott Brady
Forrest Tucker
Andy Devine
Iron Eyes Cody
D: Allan Dwan

Belle Starr romances a saloon keeper as
part of a scheme to obtain his fortune.

Au ★

S ★★

A ★★

Montana Mike see Heaven Only Knows

Montana Territory (1952) Columbia ★★

Lon McCallister
Wanda Hendrix
Preston Foster
Clayton Moore
Jack Elam
D: Ray Nazarro

A deputy discovers that his sheriff is an outlaw. Filmed at Chatsworth, CA.

Au ★★

S ★★

A ★★★

Jane Russell as Belle Starr.

Belle Starr

Monte Walsh (1970) NG ★★★★★

Lee Marvin
Jeanne Moreau
Jack Palance
Mitch Ryan
Jim Davis
Dick Farnsworth
D: William A. Fraker

A bronc buster faces the end of the Wild West and his
life-style. Filmed in Alberta, Canada, and at the Mescal
location of Old Tucson which was built for this film.
#27 Best of the West.

Au ★★★★★

S ★★★★★

A ★★★★

Montana Winchester see Winchester '73

Montezuma's Lost Gold (1978) GKE

Miles Hinshaw
Tom Hinshaw
Michael Carr
William Lewis
D: John Burrud, Miles Hinshaw

A drifter searches for Aztec gold.

UNCHARTED TERRITORY

The Moonlighter (1953) WB ★ ★

Barbara Stanwyck
Fred MacMurray
Ward Bond
Jack Elam
D: Roy Rowland

After escaping from a lynching, a rustler surrenders to his ex-girlfriend. Originally in 3-D.

Au ★ ★

S ★ ★

A ★ ★ ◄

More Dead Than Alive (1969) UA ★ ★

Clint Walker
Vincent Price
Anne Francis
Paul Hampton
D: Robert Sparr

Upon his release from prison, a gunfighter finds work as a Wild West show sharpshooter.

Au ★ ★

S ★ ★ ◄

A ★ ★

—Does an outhouse stink?
—Vincent Price
More Dead Than Alive

More Dollars for the MacGregors (1970) FF—Ital./Sp.

Peter Lee Lawrence
George Forsyte
Stan Cooper
D: J.L. Merino (Josè Luis Merino)

A bounty hunter and a mysterious stranger hunt down bandidos.

UNCHARTED TERRITORY

More Than Magic (1956) WC

Clayton Moore
Jay Silverheels
Allen Pinson
Wayne Burson
D: Earl Bellamy, Oscar Rudolph

Compilation of three episodes of "The Lone Ranger" TV series.

More Wild Wild West (1980) CBS-TV

Robert Conrad
Ross Martin
Jonathan Winters
Harry Morgan
Jack LaLanne
Joyce Brothers
D: Burt Kennedy

Two secret service agents investigate a megalomaniac. Second pilot for an intended revival of the TV series which never happened due in part to Ross Martin's untimely death in 1981. Filmed at Old Tucson.

Au ★

S ★★

A ★★

—For starters, I intend to dominate the entire world!

—Jonathan Winters
More Wild Wild West

The Mountain Men (1980) Columbia

Charlton Heston
Brian Keith
Victoria Racimo
Stephen Macht
D: Richard Lang

A die-hard trapper and his friend protect an Indian from her avenging husband. Filmed in Wyoming.

Au ★★★★

S ★★★★

A ★★★★

—Yeah, Henry. Yeah, it's up there. A whole valley full of prime beaver. A man could live easy the rest of his days.

—Charlton Heston
The Mountain Men

Mr. Horn (1979) Lorimar Prod.

David Carradine
Richard Widmark
Karen Black
Richard Masur
D: Jack Starrett

Tom Horn tracks Geronimo, works as a detective and is tried for murder. Two-part TV movie. Filmed in Mexico.

Au ★★★

S ★★★

A ★★★★

—You [Geronimo] can die out here in the mountains, or you can live in peace in your reservation. I give you my word. Surrender, and you can stay here in Arizona.

—Tom Horn (David Carradine)
Mr. Horn

John C. Coble

Glendolene M. Kimmell

Horn the Pinkerton with
Harry Heeber circa 1892.

**The Faces
of the
Tom Horn
Story**

Tom Horn weaving a horse
hair lariat in Laramie County
Jail. He allegedly completed
the job on November 20,
1903, the day he was hung.

Joe Lefors

Al Sieber crippled for life during the Apache Kid affair.

Mrs. Mike (1949) N-H

Dick Powell
Evelyn Keyes
J.M. Kerrigan
Chief Yowlachie
D: Louis King

A city girl marries a Mountie and moves to the frontier.

Mrs. Sundance (1974) ABC-TV/20th C. Fox

Elizabeth Montgomery
Robert Foxworth
L.Q. Jones
Arthur Hunnicutt
D: Marvin Chomsky

Etta Place discovers that the Sundance Kid did not die in Bolivia.
Made for TV sequel to *Butch Cassidy and the Sundance Kid.*
Filmed at Bronson Canyon, Griffith Park, California.

Au ★★

S　★★

A　★★

Mrs. Sundance Rides Again (Wanted: The Sundance Woman) (1976) ABC-TV/20th C. Fox

Katharine Ross
Steve Forrest
Stella Stevens
Michael Constantine
D: Lee Phillips

The Sundance Kid's girlfriend, Etta Place,
runs guns to Pancho Villa. Working title,
The Most Wanted Woman. Filmed at Old Tucson.

Au ★★

S　★★★

A　★★★

Mulefeathers (The West Is Still Wild) (1977) BAMP

Rory Calhoun
Richard Webb
Angela Richardson
Doodles Weaver
D: Don Von Mizener

Murieta (1963) FF—Sp./U.S.

Jeffrey Hunter
Arthur Kennedy
D: George Sherman

California gold rush bandido, Joaquin Murrieta, avenges the murder of his wife.

Mutiny at Fort Sharp (1966) FF—Ital./Sp.

Broderick Crawford
Elisa Montes
D: Fernando Cerchio

French soldiers join rebel forces in Texas to defend a fort from hostiles.

My Brother the Outlaw see My Outlaw Brother

My Colt, Not Yours (1972) FF—Sp./Fr./Ital.

Robert Woods
Olga Omar
D: Steve McCohy (Ignacio F. Iquino)

A sheriff faces off with the town boss.

—We'll be waitin' for ya, Marshal,
at the O.K. Corral!
—Walter Brennan
My Darling Clementine

My Darling Clementine (1946) 20ᵗʰ C. Fox

Henry Fonda
Victor Mature
Linda Darnell
Walter Brennan
Ward Bond
D: John Ford

The Earps establish law and order in Tombstone.
Rare example of a Western without a musical score.
Based on Stuart Lake's, *Wyatt Earp, Frontier Marshal*.
Filmed in Monument Valley and Shipwreck, NM.
#36 Best of the West, #9 IMDb.

Henry Fonda and Victor Mature.

My Horse, My Gun, Your Widow (1972) FF—Ital./Sp.

Craig Hill
Claudia Lange
D: John Wood (Ignacio Iquino)

A bank robber searches for his double-crossing partner.

My Name Is Legend (1975) Film Ctr.

Duke Kelly
Tom Kirk
Stan Foster
Kerry Smith
D: Duke Kelly

Burt Lancaster (left) as Earp in *Gunfight at the O.K. Corral.*

Harris Yulin (right) as Earp in *Doc.*

Henry Fonda (right) as a lawman based on Earp in *Warlock.*

The Hollywood Legend
of
Wyatt Earp

James Garner (right) as Earp in *Hour of the Gun.*

George O'Brien as a lawman based
on Earp in *Frontier Marshal* (1934).

James Stewart (center) in *Cheyenne Autumn.*

Henry Fonda (center) as Earp in *My Darling Clementine.*

Robert Mitchum (left) in *Young, Billy Young.*

Randolph Scott as a lawman inspired
by Earp in *Frontier Marshal* (1939).

My Name is Nobody (1973) FF—Ital. ★★★◀

Terence Hill
Henry Fonda
D: Tonino Valerii and Sergio Leone

An aging gunfighter teams up with a young gunman in 1899.
Filmed primarily in Europe and in part in Monument Valley.

Au ★★★◀

S ★★★◀

A ★★★◀

My Name is Pecos (1966) FF—Ital.

Robert Woods
Lucia Modugno
D: Maurice A. Bright

A Mexican gunman avenges his parent's murder.

UNCHARTED
TERRITORY

My Outlaw Brother (My Brother the Outlaw) (1951) ELC

Mickey Rooney
Wanda Hendrix
Robert Preston
Robert Stack
D: Elliott Nugent

A young man joins a ranger in pursuit of his outlaw brother.

UNCHARTED
TERRITORY

My Son Alone see American Empire

The Mysterious Rider (Mark of the Avenger) (1938) Paramount

Douglass Dumbrille
Sidney Toler
Russell Hayden
Stanley Andrews
D: Lesley Selander

Homesteaders are swindled out of their land. Remake of the 1933 version.

UNCHARTED
TERRITORY

The Mystery of Chalk Hill see Hec Ramsey: The Mystery of Chalk Hill

The Mystery of the Green Feather see Hec Ramsey: The Mystery of Green Feather

The Mystery of the Yellow Rose see Hec Ramsey: The Mystery of the Yellow Rose

The Mystic Warrior (1984) ABC-TV ★◀

Robert Beltran
Nick Ramos
Victoria Racimo
D: Richard T. Heffron

An Indian calls on the spirits of his ancestors

—I am a peaceman. I wear the shirt of a peaceman. I ask peace among enemies.

—Robert Beltran
The Mystic Warrior

to save his people. Made for TV movie.

Au ★★★
S ★
A ★

The Naked Gun (1956) AFRC

Willard Parker
Mara Corday
Barton MacLane
Billy House
D: Edward Dew

An insurance agent encounters outlaws after Aztec treasure.

Cheyenne painted for a sundance.

The Naked Hills (1956) AA ★ ◗

David Wayne
Keenan Wynn
James Barton
Jim Backus
D: Josef Shaftel

A Missourian travels overland to the California gold rush.

Au ★★
S ★◗
A ★◗

Naked Revenge see Face to the Wind

The Naked Spur (1953) MGM ★★★

James Stewart
Janet Leigh
Ralph Meeker
Robert Ryan
D: Anthony Mann

A bounty hunter tracks a killer and an outlaw's daughter. Oscar nomination for writing: story and screenplay. Filmed in Durango, Colorado.

Au ★★◗
S ★★★
A ★★★

—*Why? Tell me why! I'm takin' him back, I swear it! I'm gonna sell him for money!*
—James Stewart
The Naked Spur

Navajo Joe (A Dollar a Head) (1966) FF—Ital./Sp. ★

Burt Reynolds
Aldo Sanbrell
Fernando Rey
D: Sergio Corbucci

The sole survivor of a massacre tracks down bandits.

348

Reynolds' only Spaghetti Western.

Au

S ★

A ◗

Navajo Run (1964) AI

Johnny Seven
Warren Kemmerling
Virginia Vincent
D: Johnny Seven

A half-breed is hunted by his brother.

—You're gonna pay for her life!
—Burt Reynolds
Navajo Joe

The Nebraskan (1953) Columbia

Phil Carey
Robert Haynes
Wallace Ford
Lee Van Cleef
Jay Silverheels
D: Fred F. Sears

An Indian scout is falsely accused of killing an Indian chief. Originally in 3-D. Filmed at Corriganville, California.

—My son dies like a brave warrior!
—Jay Silverheels
The Nebraskan

Au ★◗

S ★

A ★◗

Ned Blessing: The Story of My Life and Times (1993) CBS-TV

Brad Johnson
Wes Studi
Luis Avalos
Tim Scott
D: Jack Bender

A gunman investigates the disappearance of his lawman father. Mini-series.

Ned Blessing: The True Story of My Life (Lone Justice) (1992) CBS-TV

Daniel Baldwin
Luis Avalos
Chris Cooper
D: Peter Werner

An old man chronicles his adventures in the Old West.

Au ★★★◗

S ★★★★

A ★★★◗

The Nevadan (1950) Columbia

Randolph Scott
Dorothy Malone
Forrest Tucker
D: Gordon Douglas

An undercover marshal searches for stolen gold.
Filmed at the Iverson Movie Location Ranch.

Au ★★◗

S ★★★

A ★★★

Randolph Scott in *The Nevadan*.

Nevada Smith (1966) Paramount ★★★◗

Steve McQueen
Karl Malden
Brian Keith
Arthur Kennedy
Suzanne Pleshette
Martin Landau
Strother Martin
Iron Eyes Cody
D: Henry Hathaway

A half-breed avenges the murder of his parents.
"Prequel" to Harold Robbins' *The Carpetbaggers*.
Filmed in the Alabama Hills and Bishop, CA.

Au ★★★

S ★★★★◗

A ★★★★

Nevada Smith (1975) NBC-TV/R-HP/MGM ★★

Cliff Potts
Lorne Greene
Adam West
D: Gordon Douglas

A half-breed gunfighter and his mentor guide an explosives
shipment. Remake of the 1966 version. Unsuccessful pilot.

Au ★★

S ★◗

A ★★◗

The Newcomers see The Wild Country

The New Daughters of Joshua Cabe (1976) ABC-TV/SGP

Liberty Williams
Renne Jarrett
Lezlie Dalton
John Dehner
D: Bruce Bilson

Cabe's "daughters" break him out of prison.

Second sequel to *The Daughters of Joshua Cabe.*

The New Land (1972) FF—Swed. ★★★★⯪

Max von Sydow
Liv Ullman
Eddie Axberg
Hans Alfredson
D: Jan Troell

Swedish immigrants face hardships in
frontier Minnesota. #30 Best of the West.

Au ★★★★★

S ★★★★

A ★★★★⯪

—As my old pappy used to say…
—James Garner
The New Maverick

The New Maverick (1978) ABC-TV/Cherokee P./WB ★★

James Garner
Charles Frank
Jack Kelly
Susan Blanchard
D: Hy Averback

Cousin Beau's son joins Bret and Bart in their
adventures. Pilot for the "Young Maverick"
series. Filmed at Old Tucson.

Au ★★

S ★★

A ★★⯪

New Mexico (1951) UA

Lew Ayres
Marilyn Maxwell
Andy Devine
Raymond Burr
D: Irving Reiss

A cavalry captain must prevent an Indian uprising.
Filmed at the Iverson Movie Location Ranch.

James Garner as Brett Maverick.

The Night of the Grizzly (1966) Paramount ★★⯪

Clint Walker
Martha Hyer
Keenan Wynn
Nancy Culp
Jack Elam
D: Joseph Pevney

Homesteaders are terrorized by a grizzly.
Filmed at Big Bear, California.

Au ★★

—Ain't a man alive that hasn't got trouble.
How he handles that trouble is what counts.
—Clint Walker
The Night of the Grizzly

S
A

Night of the Serpent (1969) FF—Ital.

Luke Askew
Luigi Pistilli
D: Giulo Petroni

Bank robbers become trapped in the town's saloon.

Night Passage (1957) U-I

James Stewart
Audie Murphy
Dan Duryea
Dianne Foster
Jack Elam
D: James Neilson

A railroad employee must clear his name after his younger
brother robs the payroll. Screenplay by Borden Chase.
Filmed in Durango and Silverton, Colorado.

*—A man likes to know his woman'll back
him when he's down and you didn't.*
—James Stewart
Night Passage

Au
S
A

The Night Rider (1932) Artclass

Harry Carey
Eleanor Fair
George Hayes
D: Fred Newmeyer

A gunman impersonates a hooded outlaw in order to catch him.

The Night Rider (1979) ABC-TV/SJCP/Universal

David Selby
Percy Rodrigues
Kim Canttrall
Pernell Roberts
D: Hy Averback

A New Orleans gentleman avenges the murder of his family.

Night Riders (Los Diablos de los Terror) (1958) FF—Mex.

Gaston Santos
Alma Rosa Aguirre
Pedro D'Aguillon
D: Fernando Menez

A government agent investigates masked night
riders terrorizing a small town. Filmed in Mexico.

Nikki, Wild Dog of the North (1961) BV

Jean Coutu
Emile Genest
Uriel Luft
Nikki (a dog)
D: Jack Couffer

A young wolf and a bear cub separated from their master must survive in the wild. Based on James O. Curwood's, *Nomads of the North*. Filmed in Alberta, Canada.

Nobody's the Greatest see A Genius

No Graves on Boot Hill (1968) FF—Ital.

Craig Hill
Ken Wood
D: Willy S. Regan (Sergio Garrone)

A priest recruits three convicts to save an innocent boy from hanging.

No Man's Land (1984) NBC-TV

Stella Stevens
Terri Garber
Melissa Michaelsen
D: Rod Holcomb

A gunwoman earns a sheriff's badge by foiling a New Mexican madman's plot to sink the Royal Navy with a submarine. Pilot.

Au ★🡒
S ★
A ★

No Name on the Bullet (1959) U-I ★ ★ ★

Audie Murphy
Charles Drake
Joan Evans
D: Jack Arnold

When a gunfighter comes to town, the people guess who will be his target. Filmed near Los Angeles, California.

Au ★ ★ ★
S ★ ★ ★ 🡒
A ★ ★ ★ 🡒

Audie Murphy in *No Name on the Bullet.*

None of the Three Were Called Trinity (1974) FF—Sp.

Danny Martin
Fanny Grey
D: Pedro L. Ramirez (Ignacia Iquino)

A man is wrongly accused of robbing a bank.

Noose For a Gunman (1960) UA

Jim Davis
Lyn Thomas
Ted de Corsia
Harry Carey, Jr.
D: Edward L. Cahn

A gunfighter faces the hired gun of a land baron.

No Room to Die (1969) FF—Ital.

Anthony Steffen
William Berger
D: Willy S. Regan (Sergio Garrone)

Two bounty hunters track slave traders. Django film.

Northern Passage see Baree

—The wilderness is callin' north of the Great Divide.

—Roy Rogers
North of the Great Divide

North of the Great Divide (1950) Republic

Roy Rogers
Penny Edwards
Gordon Jones
Jack Lambert
D: William Witney

An Indian agent assists a tribe who is being cheated by a salmon cannery. Filmed at Big Bear, California.

Au ★

S ★

A ✦

Salmon canning factory on the Columbia River.

North Star (Tashunga) (1995) FF—Fr./Ital./Nor./Brit.

James Caan
Christopher Lambert
Catherine McCormack
D: Nils Gaup

A half-breed hunter seeks revenge against claim jumpers during the Alaskan gold rush.

North to Alaska (1960) 20ᵗʰ C. Fox ★★⧸

John Wayne
Stewart Granger
Ernie Kovaks
Fabian
Capucine
Mickey Shaughnessy
D: Henry Hathaway

Two miners discover gold and
the same woman. Filmed in the
Alabama Hills and Big Bear, CA.

Au ★★⧸

S ★★⧸

A ★★★

John Wayne and Capucine in *North to Alaska.*

Klondike actresses fording the Dyea River.

*—Well, what I can't stand is when people look
down on others who aren't doin' them any harm.*
—John Wayne
North to Alaska

Northwest Mounted Police (1940) Paramount ★★★

Gary Cooper
Madeleine Carroll
Paulette Goddard
Preston Foster
Lon Chaney, Jr.
Robert Ryan
Chief Thundercloud
D: Cecil B. DeMille

A Texas Ranger tracks a murderer to Canada.
Technical advise by Joe De Yong. Screenplay
by Alan LeMay, J. Laskey, Jr., and C.G. Sullivan.
Oscar nominations for cinematography: color,
sound recording, art direction, and original score.
Oscar for film editing. Filmed at Big Bear, California.

Au ★★⧸

S ★★★

A ★★★

*—And I'll say the Mounted Police are the
greatest outfit I ever tangled with—and
the luckiest.*
—Gary Cooper
Northwest Mounted Police

Not Above Suspicion (1956) WC

Clayton Moore
Jay Silverheels
Dennis Moore
D: Earl Bellamy, Oscar Rudolph

Compilation of three episodes of "The Lone Ranger" TV series.

Not Exactly Gentlemen see Three Rogues

Oath of Zorro see Behind the Mask of Zorro

Oh! Susanna (1951) Republic

Rod Cameron
Adrian Booth
Forrest Tucker
Chill Wills
Jim Davis
D: Joseph Kane

A West Point graduate must prevent his commanding officer from breaking an Indian treaty in the Black Hills.

Au ★

S ★

A ★

The Oklahoma Kid (1939) WB

James Cagney
Humphrey Bogart
Rosemary Lane
Donald Crisp
Ward Bond
D: Lloyd Bacon

A settler avenges the murder of his father by a crooked land grabber. Filmed at the Iverson Movie Location Ranch.

The Oklahoman (1957) AA

Joel McCrea
Barbara Hale
Brad Dexter
D: Francis D. Lyon

A doctor establishes his practice in Oklahoma. Filmed at the Iverson Movie Location Ranch.

Oklahoma Territory (1960) UA

Bill Williams
Gloria Talbott
Ted de Corsia
D: Edward L. Cahn

A district attorney protects an Indian chief wrongly accused of murder.

—You can't expect the Sioux to know anything about prize ring rules!
—Rod Cameron
Oh! Susanna

James Cagney in *The Oklahoma Kid.*

The Oklahoma Woman (1956) Sunset/ARC

Richard Denning
Peggie Castle
Cathy Downs
Touch (Mike) Connors
D: Roger Corman

A woman secures her lover's freedom.

Old Gringo (1989) Fonda F./Columbia ★★★★★

Jane Fonda
Gregory Peck
Jimmy Smits
Patricio Contreras
D: Luis Puenzo

Writer Ambrose Bierce, an American schoolmarm, and a general in Villa's army experience the last of the frontier during the Mexican Revolution. #23 Best of the West.

Au ★★★★★

S ★★★★

A ★★★★★

Old Shatterhand see Apache's Last battle

Old Surehand see Flaming Frontier (1965)

Old Yeller (1958) BV ★★★★

Fess Parker
Dorothy McGuire
Tommy Kirk
Kevin Corcoran
Jeff York
Chuck Connors
D: Robert Stevenson

A stray yellow dog helps a family operate their Texas homestead in the absence of their father. Based on Fred Gipson's novel.

Au ★★★★

S ★★★★★

A ★★★★

Ole Rex (1961) U-I

"Rex"
Billy Hughs
William Foster
D: Robert Hinkle

A young boy nurses a shaggy white dog back to health. Filmed in the Texas oil fields.

—*...The young general who wanted to change the world. The old writer who wanted to bid it farewell. I am the one who will live to remember them both.*
—Jane Fonda
Old Gringo

Teen and dog.

Tommy Kirk in *Old Yeller*.

♪
—*Here Yeller, come back Yeller! Best doggone dog in the West.*
—Theme song
Old Yeller

Once Upon a Texas Train (Texas Guns) (1988) CBS-TV ★ ★ ★

Willie Nelson
Richard Widmark
Shawn Cassidy
Jack Elam
Chuck Connors
Ken Curtis
Dub Taylor
Angie Dickinson
Harry Carey, Jr.
D: Burt Kennedy

A former Texas Ranger leads an over the hill posse
after an ex–con and his band of over the hill outlaws.
Filmed in Ely, Nevada, and at Old Tucson.

Au ★ ★ ★
S ★ ★
A ★ ★ ★ ★

Once Upon a Time in the West (1968) FF—Ital. ★ ★ ★ ★

Henry Fonda
Claudia Cardinale
Charles Bronson
Jason Robards
Jack Elam
Woody Strode
Keenan Wynn
D: Sergio Leone

An outlaw protects a widow's land
from the railroad. Based on an outline
written by Leone, Bertolucci and
Dario Argento. Screenplay by Leone
and Sergio Donati. Sound score by
Ennio Morricone. The films opens
with the infamous Elam fly scene.
The U.S. released version is heavily
edited and is reviewed here. The
European version is considered to be
much better. Critics differ on this film
perhaps more so than any other. Some
consider it the finest Spaghetti Western
ever made. Others consider it one of the
worst Westerns ever made. Filmed
primarily in Guadix, Spain, and in part
in Monument Valley. #2 IMDb.

Jack Elam's infamous fly scene.

Au ★ ★ ★ ★
S ★ ★ ★
A ★ ★ ★ ★

One After Another (1968) FF—Sp./Ital.

Richard Harrison
Pamela Tudor
D: Nick Howard (Nick Nostro)

A mysterious gunfighter avenges the death of his friend.

Henry Fonda in *Once Upon a Time in the West*.

One Against One...No Mercy (1968) FF—Sp./Ital.

Peter Lee Lawrence
William Bogart
D: Rafael Romero Marchent

A gunman is double-crossed by his partner.

One Damned Day at Dawn...Django Meets Sartana (1971) FF—Ital.

Hunt Powers
Fabio Testi
D: Miles Deem (Demofilo Fidani)

A sheriff confronts gun runners.

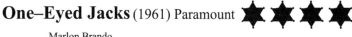

—You're a one-eyed jack around here, Ned.
I seen the other side of your face.
—Marlon Brando
One-Eyed Jacks

One–Eyed Jacks (1961) Paramount ★★★★

Marlon Brando
Karl Malden
Pina Pellicer
Ben Johnson
Slim Pickens
D: Marlon Brando

A bandit locates his ex-partner who
betrayed him. The only film Brando ever
directed. Oscar nomination for cinematography:color.
Filmed at Monterey and Big Sur, CA.
#39 Best of the West.

Au ★★★★⸴

S ★★★⸴

A ★★★★★

Marlon Brando and Pina Pellicer.

One Foot in Hell (1960) 20ᵗʰ C. Fox ★★

Alan Ladd
Don Murray
Dan O'Herlihy
Dolores Michaels
D: James B. Clark

When his pregnant wife dies for lack of medicine, an Arizona
sheriff seeks revenge. Filmed at the Iverson Movie Ranch.

Au ★★

S ★★

A ★★

100 Rifles (1969) FF—Sp. ★★

Jim Brown
Raquel Welch
Burt Reynolds
Fernando Lamas
D: Tom Gries

A sheriff, bank robber and Yaqui woman

359

fight a corrupt Mexican general.

Au ★★⯪
S ★★
A ★⯪

One Hundred Thousand Dollars for Ringo (1966) FF—Ital./Sp.

Richard Harrison
Fernando Sancho
D: Alberto De Martino

A Texas Ranger attempts to restore law and order to a border town.

One Little Indian (1973) BV

James Garner
Vera Miles
Pat Hingle
Morgan Woodward
Jay Silverheels
Boyd "Red" Morgan
Jim Davis
D: Bernard McEveety

A soldier befriends an Indian boy. Disney. Filmed at Kanab, UT.

Au ★★★
S ★★★⯪
A ★★★

One Man's Hero (1999) Orion

Tom Berenger
Joaquim de Almeida
Daniela Romo
D: Lance Hool

Based on the true story of John Riley and "The St. Patrick's Brigade" who desert to Mexico from the U.S. Army.

Au ★★★★
S ★★★
A ★★★

One Mask Too Many (1956) WC

Clayton Moore
Jay Silverheels
Roy Barcroft
D: Earl Bellamy, Oscar Rudolph

Compilation of three episodes of "The Lone Ranger" TV series.

One More Train to Rob (1971) Universal

George Peppard
Diana Muldaur

360

John Vernon
France Nuyen
Merlin Olsen
Harry Carey, Jr.
D: Andrew V. McLaglen

A train robber gets even with a former
partner who sent him to prison.

Au ★★★

S ★★

A ★★★

One Thousand Dollars on the Black see Blood at Sundown

Only Birds and Fools see Hec Ramsey: Only Birds and Fools

Only the Valiant (1951) WB

Gregory Peck
Barbara Payton
Gig Young
Ward Bond
Lon Chaney, Jr.
Neville Brand
D: Gordon Douglas

A cavalry officer struggles to gain the respect of his misfit troops.
Filmed at Gallup, New Mexico.

Au ★★★★

S ★★★★

A ★★★★

On the Third Day Arrived the Crow (1972) FF—Ital./Sp.

Lincoln Tate
William Berger
D: Gianni Crea

A woman and her brothers investigate a mining company's missing bullion.

O Pioneers! (1992) WB/CAP

Jessica Lang
David Strathairn
Tom Aldredge
D: Glenn Jordan

The daughter of Swedish emigrants enjoys her
Nebraska farm. From the Willa Cather novel.

Au ★★★★

S ★★

A ★★★

*—We come and go, but the land is always here.
And the people who love it and understand it are
the people who own it—for a little while.*
—Jessica Lang
O Pioneers!

Oregon Passage (1958) AA

John Ericson
Lola Albright
Toni Gerry
Edward Platt
D: Paul Landres

A cavalry officer rescues an Indian girl from a tribal ceremony.

The Oregon Trail (1959) 20ᵗʰ C. Fox

Fred MacMurray
William Bishop
Nina Shipman
John Carradine
Iron Eyes Cody
D: Gene Fowler, Jr.

A reporter is sent to Oregon to investigate Indian attacks.

Bannock Indian family, Idaho 1871.

The Oregon Trail (1976) NBC-TV/Universal

Rod Taylor
Blair Brown
David Huddleston
Douglas V. Fowley
D: Boris Segal

A family leaves Illinois in 1842 to join a
wagon train west. Pilot for the TV series.

O'Rourke of the Royal Mounted see Saskatchewan

The Other Side of the Law (1995) Gaumont-TV

Jurgen Prochnow
Yves Renier
Xavier Deluc
Marc de Jonge
D: Gilles Carle

Upon avenging his wife's murder, a man and his son
begin a new life. Based on a James O. Curwood story.

The Outcast (1954) Republic

John Derek
Joan Evans
Jim Davis
Slim Pickens
Harry Carey, Jr.
D: William Witney

A cowboy fights with his uncle over his father's ranch.

Au ★ ⸸

S ★ ⸸

A ★

The Outcasts of Poker Flats (1937) RKO ★ ★

Preston Foster
Jean Muir
Van Heflin
Virginia Weidler
D: Christy Cabanne

Outcasts from a gold rush town become snowbound in a mountain cabin. Story by Bret Harte. Remake of John Ford's 1919 silent version.

Au ★★★

S ★★

A ★★

> —He didn't have to trust in the turn of the cards. He was strong—the strongest and yet, the weakest of them all.
> —Van Heflin
> *The Outcasts of Poker Flats*

The Outcasts of Poker Flats (1952) 20ᵗʰ C. Fox

Anne Baxter
Dale Robertson
Miriam Hopkins
Cameron Mitchell
D: Joseph M. Newman

Remake of the 1937 version.

UNCHARTED TERRITORY

The Outing see Scream

The Outlaw (1943) (reissued 1946) HHP ★ ★

Jack Beutel
Jane Russell
Thomas Mitchell
Walter Huston
D: Howard Hawks and Howard Hughes

Pat Garrett attempts to rid Lincoln, New Mexico of Billy the Kid and Doc Holliday who are quarrelling over a horse and a woman. Based on a legend related to Hawks in New Mexico. Technical advise by Joe De Yong. Filmed at Red Rock Canyon, California.

Au ★ ⸸

S ★★

A ★★

Jane Russell in *The Outlaw.*

Outlawed Guns (1935) Universal

Buck Jones
Ruth Channing
Frank McGlenn, Sr.
Charles King
D: Ray Taylor

A gunman prevents his younger brother's further involvement in an outlaw gang.

The Outlaw Josey Wales (1976) WB ★★★★★

Clint Eastwood
Chief Dan George
Sondra Locke
Bill McKinney
John Vernon
Sam Bottoms
Richard Farnsworth
D: Clint Eastwwod (and Philip Kaufman)

After his wife is murdered by Union renegades, a Confederate soldier refuses to give up the war. Original director Kaufman was fired by Eastwood early in the shooting. Based on Forrest (Asa "Ace") Carter's novel, *The Rebel Outlaw: Josey Wales* (aka *Gone to Texas*). Oscar nomination for best scoring: original music. Filmed at the Old Pariah film set near Page, Utah, and at Old Tucson. #10 Best of the West, #27 IMDb.

Au ★★★★✦
S ★★★★★
A ★★★★★

Clint Eastwood as Josey Wales.

Outlaw of Red River (Django the Condemned) (1966) (Django the Honorable Killer) (re-released title, 1968) FF—Sp.

George Montgomery
Elisa Montes
D: Maury Dexter

A Texan is falsely accused of shooting his wife.

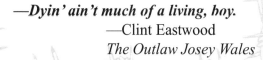

—Dyin' ain't much of a living, boy.
—Clint Eastwood
The Outlaw Josey Wales

Outlaw Queen (1957) GRC

Andrea King
Harry James
Robert Clarke
D: Herbert Greene

The Outlaw's Daughter (1954) RF

Jim Davis
Kelly Ryan
Bill Williams
D: Wesley Barry

A young girl is implicated in a stagecoach robbery. Filmed in Sedona, Arizona.

Jim Davis in *The Outlaw's Daughter.*

Outlaw's Son (1957) Bel-Air/UA

Dane Clark
Ben Cooper
Lori Nelson
Ellen Drew
D: Lesley Selander

An outlaw's son turns outlaw.

Au 🔪

S ★

A 🔪

Outlaws: The Legend of O.B. Taggart (1994)

Ned Beatty
Ernest Borgnine
Larry Gatlin
Ben Johnson
Randy Travis
D: Rupert Hitzig

UNCHARTED TERRITORY

Outlaw Territory see Hannah Lee

Outlaw Women (Boot Hill Mamas) (1952) Howco Prod.

Marie Windsor
Richard Rober
Allen Nixon
Jackie Coogan
D: Samuel Newfield, Ron Ormond

Dancehall girls control a frontier town.

UNCHARTED TERRITORY

The Outrage (1964) MGM

Paul Newman
Laurence Harvey
Claire Bloom
Edward G. Robinson
William Shatner
D: Martin Ritt

Three participants give their own account of a rape and murder.
Screenplay by Akira Kurosawa. Filmed at Old Tucson.

UNCHARTED TERRITORY

The Outriders (1950) MGM ★ ★ 🔪

Joel McCrea
Arlene Dahl
Barry Sullivan
James Whitmore
D: Roy Rowland

Three escaped Confederates lead a wagon

—I'd never let a woman come between me and the cause.

—Barry Sullivan
The Outriders

train full of Union gold into an ambush.

Au

S

A

The Outsider (2002) Hallmark E./Showtime

Timothy Daly
Naomi Watts
Keith Carradine
David Carradine
D: Randa Haines

A pacifist woman nurses a wounded gunfighter back
to health and is tempted to turn him against the men
who murdered her husband. Made for TV movie.

UNCHARTED
TERRITORY

Overland Pacific (1954) Reliance/UA

Jack (Jock) Mahoney
Peggy Castle
Adele Jergens
D: Fred F. Sears

A railroad agent investigates Indian raids.

Au

S

A

*—We're gonna push those tracks right
through that mountain pass and no man,
red or white, is gonna stop us!*
—Jock Mahoney
Overland Pacific

The Ox-Bow Incident (Strange Incident) (1943) 20ᵗʰ C. Fox

Henry Fonda
Dana Andrews
Mary Beth Hughes
Anthony Quinn
Henry Morgan
Francis Ford
D: William Wellman

Three men are wrongly lynched for rustling.
Oscar nomination for best picture. Based on
Walter Van Tillburg Clark's novel. #11 IMDb.

Au

S

A

Henry Fonda (left) in *Ox-Bow Incident*.

Paid in Blood (1972) FF—Ital.

Jeff Cameron
Donald O'Brien
D: Paolo Solvay

A gunman avenges his brother's murder.

UNCHARTED
TERRITORY

*—There's always some fool who'll lose his
head and start hangin' everybody in sight.*
—Henry Fonda
The Ox-Bow Incident

The Painted Desert (1931) RKO-Pathe

William Boyd
Helen Twelvetrees
Clark Gable
William Farnum
D: Howard Higgin

A miner falls in love with the daughter of his father's rival.
Filmed in Arizona.

Au ⯪

S ⯪

A ⯪

The Painted Hills (Shep of the Hills) (1951) (Lassie's Adventures in the Gold Rush)

(re-released 1973) MGM ★★

Lassie
Paul Kelly
Gary Cowling
Gary Gray
Chief Yowlachie
D: Harold F. Kress

A collie named Shep avenges the
murder of his gold-miner master.

Au ★★

S ★★

A ★★

Gary Gray and Lassie.

Pale Rider (1985) WB ★★★★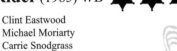

Clint Eastwood
Michael Moriarty
Carrie Snodgrass
Christopher Penn
D: Clint Eastwood

A nameless gunman protects a
mining camp from a corporate
takeover. Filmed in the Sawtooth
Range, Idaho. #86 Best of the West.

Au ★★★★

S ★★★⯪

A ★★★★

*—...and I looked and beheld a
pale horse: and his name that
sat on him was Death, and Hell
followed with him.*
—Sydney Penny
Pale Rider
(Revelation 6:8)

Clint Eastwood in *Pale Rider.*

Pancho Villa (1972) FF—Sp./Brit.

Telly Savalas
Clint Walker
Chuck Connors
Anne Francis
D: Eugenio Martin

The legendary Mexican revolutionary-bandido invades the U.S.

Pancho Villa Returns (1950) HCF

Leo Carrillo
Esther Fernandez
Rodolfo Acosta
D: Miguel Contreras Torres

The bandit general leads peons in revolution.

Panhandle (1948) AA

Rod Cameron
Cathy Downs
Reed Hadley
D: Lesley Selander

A retired gunfighter avenges his brother's murder.

Paper Hearts (Cheatin' Hearts) (1993)

Paula Baz
James Brolin
Mickey Cottrell
Kris Kristofferson
D: Rod McCall

An abandoned girl's father returns on
her wedding day with a new girlfriend.

The Paradise Trail (1981) Mark IV P.

Burt Douglas
Robert Somers
Teri Hernandez
Gene Otis
D: Donald W. Thompson

A gunfighter and a blind preacher join and discover religious salvation.
"Bible belt" production shown exclusively to churches.

The Parson and the Outlaw (1957) Columbia

Anthony Dexter
Sonny Tufts
Marie Windsor
Bob Steele
D: Oliver Drake

Billy the Kid resumes gunfighting when his friend is murdered.

The Parson of Panamint (1941) Paramount

Charlie Ruggles
Ellen Drew
Phillip Terry

Joseph Schildkraut
D: William McGann

A reverend attempts to reform a rough-and-tumble mining town.

El Paso (1949) Paramount ★ ★

John Payne
Gail Russell
Sterling Hayden
George F. Hayes
Chief Yowlachie
D: Lewis R. Foster

A Southern lawyer turns gunfighter in post-Civil War Texas. Filmed at the Iverson Movie Ranch.

Au ★ ★

S ★ ★

A ★ ★

—Mob rule's no good no matter how we try to justify it!
—John Payne
El Paso

Passage West (High Venture) (1951) Paramount

John Payne
Dennis O'Keefe
Arlene Whelan
D: Lewis R. Foster

Outlaws join a wagon train to avoid capture.

Passion (1954) RKO

Cornel Wilde
Yvonne De Carlo
Raymond Burr
Lon Chaney, Jr.
Stuart Whitman
D: Allan Dwan

A California vaquero avenges the murder of his parents.

Pat Garrett and Billy the Kid (1973) MGM ★ ★ ★ ★ ◗

James Coburn
Kris Kristofferson
Richard Jaeckel
Katy Jurado
Chill Wills
Jason Robards
Bob Dylan
Rita Cooledge
Jack Elam
Emilio Fernandez
Slim Pickens
D: Sam Peckinpah

Pat Garrett and Billy the Kid represent

—You're crazier than a mule humpin' a goat!
—Chill Wills
Pat Garrett and Billy the Kid

opposing camps during the Lincoln
County War. Music by Bob Dylan. Filmed
at Durango, Mexico. #19 Best of the West.

Au

S ★★★★

A ★★★★★

Pawnee (1957) Republic

George Montgomery
Bill Williams
Lola Albright
Francis McDonald
D: George Waggner

The adopted son of a Pawnee chief is
hired to scout a wagon train to Oregon.

Au

S ★✦

A ★✦

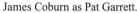

James Coburn as Pat Garrett.

Pat Garrett

Payment in Blood see Blake's Marauders

Peace for a Gunfighter (1965) CIP

Burt Berger
JoAnne Meredith
Everette King
D: Raymond Boley

A gunfighter finds it difficult to retire in a small town.

UNCHARTED
TERRITORY

The Peacemaker (1956) UA

James Mitchell
Rosemarie Bowe
Jan Merlin
D: Ted Post

A gunslinger turned parson settles a
dispute between ranchers and farmers.

Au

S ★

A ★

Pecos Cleans Up (1967) FF—Ital.

Robert Woods
Luciana Gilli
D: Maurizio Lucidi

A Mexican peon searches for lost treasure.

UNCHARTED
TERRITORY

—I know very little of your manners and traditions. Yet, I've heard of a delightful custom that does away with many words at a time like this.

—Lola Albright
Pawnee

—Indifference condones violence, excuses crime, pardons dishonesty. A community neutral toward hate cannot prosper. A nation that does not take sides with God cannot exist.

—James Mitchell
The Peacemaker

A Perilous Journey (1956) Republic

Vera Ralston
David Brian
Scott Brady
D: R.G. Springsteen

Searching for her husband, a woman travels to
California via Panama with mail order brides.

The Persuader (1957) W-W/AA

William Talman
James Craig
Kristine Miller
D: Dick Ross

A preacher discovers his brother has been murdered.

Peter Lundy and the Medicine Hat Stallion (Medecine Hat Stallion) (1977) NBC-TV/EFP

Leif Garrett
Milo O'Shea
Bibi Besch
D: Michael O'Herlihy

A youngster rides for the Pony Express in Nebraska territory.

Pony Express saddle.

Phantom of Santa Fe (1937) B-TP

Norman Kerry
Nena Quartero
Frank Mayo
D: Jacques Jaccard

Disguised as a coward, the "Hawk"
pursues a gang of outlaws.

The Phantom Stagecoach (1957) Columbia

William Bishop
Kathleen Crowley
Richard Web
D: Ray Nazarro

Two stageline operators fight over a right of way.
Filmed at the Iverson Movie Location Ranch.

Pillars of the Sky (1956) U-I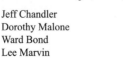

Jeff Chandler
Dorothy Malone
Ward Bond
Lee Marvin
D: George Marshall

An Army sergeant fights off Indians with men he dislikes, but

*—The pillars of the sky, Doc, they
were sacred to the tribe long before
you came with the word of God.*
—Jeff Chandler
Pillars of the Sky

learns to respect. Story by Will Henry (Henry W. Allen). Filmed in Oregon.

Au

S

A

Piluk, the Timid One (1968) FF—Ital.

Edmund Purdom
Peter Holden
D: Guido Celano

An old man avenges the death of his son.

Pioneer Woman (1973) ABC-TV

Joanna Pettet
William Shatner
David Janssen
Lance Le Gault
D: Buzz Kulik

A woman faces the hardships of homesteading 1860s Wyoming.
Filmed at Waterton Park, Longview, Heritage Park, Alberta, Canada.

Au

S

A

Pirates of Monterey (1947) U-I

Maria Montez
Rod Cameron
Mikhail Rasumny
D: Alfred Werker

A woman meets a soldier of fortune in old California
who wishes to overthrow the Spanish.

Pirates of the Mississippi (1963) FF—Ger./Ital./Fr.

Brad Harris
Horst Frank
D: Jurgen Roland

Pioneers and Indians join forces to fight river pirates.

Pistole (1975)

Barry Fincham
Barbara M. Benson
Corey Brandon
D: Bernard Bossick

Pistolero of Red River see The Last Chance

Pistol for a Hundred Coffins (1968) FF—Ital./Sp.

Peter Lee Lawrence
John Ireland
D: Umberto Lenzi

Upon his release from prison, a gunman
searches for his double-crossing partner.

A Pistol for Ringo (1965) FF—Ital./Sp.

Montgomery Wood
Fernando Sancho
Giuliano Gemma
D: Duccio Tessari

A gunfighter is hired to track bandidos.

Place Called Glory (1965) FF—Ger./Sp.

Lex Barker
Pierre Brice
D: Ralph Gideon (Sheldon Reynolds)

Two gunfighters face off over a common love.

The Plainsman (1936) Paramount ★★★⯪

Gary Cooper
Jean Arthur
James Ellison
Charles Bickford
George Hayes
Pat Moriarty
Anthony Quinn
D: Cecil B. DeMille

Buffalo Bill, Wild Bill and Calamity Jane
prevent a gunrunner from supplying rifles
to the Cheyenne. Technical advise by
Joe De Yong. Filmed at the Paramount Ranch
and the Iverson Movie Location Ranch.

Au ★★

S ★★★★

A ★★★⯪

Jean Arthur as Calamity in
The Plainsman (1936).

The Plainsman (1966) Universal

Don Murray
Guy Stockwell
Abby Dalton
Bradford Dillman
D: David Lowell

Calamity Jane

Made for TV remake of the 1937 version.

The Plainsman and the Lady (1946) Republic

William Elliott
Vera Ralston
Gail Patrick
Iron Eyes Cody
D: Joe Kane

A cattle rancher contends with a plot against the Pony Express. Filmed in the Alabama Hills.

Au ★★

S ★★

A ★

—You ring-tailed baboon!
—William Elliott
The Plainsman and the Lady

Plainsong (1982) ESP

Jessica Nelson
Teresanne Joseph
Lyn Traverse
Steve Geiger
D: Ed Stabile

Pioneers seek revenge for range war murders.

The Plunderers (1948) Republic

Rod Cameron
Ilona Massey
Adrian Booth
Forrest Tucker
D: Joseph Kane

A one-armed Civil War veteran faces his town. Filmed at the Iverson Movie Location Ranch.

Au ★

S ★

A ★

—I like women that give off sparks…I have a hunch if somebody roped us together, we'd both make sparks.
—Rod Cameron
The Plunderers (1948)

The Plunderers (1960) AA

Jeff Chandler
John Saxon
Dolores Hart
Marsha Hunt
Jay C. Flippen
Ray Stricklyn
D: Joseph Pevney

Four young drifters terrorize a town.

—…there are none who trespass against us as we trespass against ourselves.
—Jeff Chandler
The Plunderers (1960)

Filmed at Ingram Ranch, California.

Au ★ ⧓

S ★ ⧓

A ★ ⧓

Plunderers of Painted Flats (1959) Republic ⧓

Corinne Calvet
John Carroll
Skip Homeier
D: Albert C. Gannaway

A cattleman and his hired gun
threaten a squatter and his bride.

Au ★

S ⧓

A ⧓

"Coming and Going of the Pony Express."

Poker Alice (1987) HMP/NW ★ ★ ⧓

Elizabeth Taylor
George Hamilton
Tom Skerritt
D: Arthur Allan Seidelman

A prim and proper "bible toter" wins cash and a cat
house. Made for TV movie. Filmed at Old Tucson.

Au ★ ★ ★

S ★ ★ ★

A ★ ★ ★ ⧓

Poker with Pistols (1967) FF—Ital.

George Hilton
George Easton
D: Joseph Warren (Giuseppe Vari)

In order to pay off a gambling debt, a gunfighter investigates a land baron.

*—But, it's how we behave when times are bad
that makes us who we are.*

—Daniel Hugh Kelly
Ponderosa

Ponderosa (2001) PAX-TV ★ ★ ★

Daniel Hugh Kelly
Matt Carmody
Drew Powell
Jared Daperis
D: Simon Wincer

Ben Cartwright and his young sons settle a parcel of scrub
land in the Nevada Territory. Prequel to the original TV series.
Made for TV pilot for the 2001 series.

Au ★ ★ ★ ★

S ★ ★ ★

A ★ ★ ★ ⧓

The Cartwrights

Pony Express (1953) Paramount

Charlton Heston
Rhonda Fleming
Jan Sterling
Forrest Tucker
D: Jerry Hopper

As the pony express establishes a mail rout to the West, Buffalo Bill and Wild Bill Hickok foil a plot to secede California from the Union. Story by Frank Gruber. Filmed at Kanab, Utah.

Au ★★◗
S ★★★
A ★★★◗

—*...ya can't make a racehorse out of a jackass.*
—Forrest Tucker
Pony Express

Pony Express Rider (1976) D-D ★★

Stewart Peterson
Henry Wilcoxon
Buck Taylor
Maureen McCormack
Ken Curtis
Slim Pickens
Jack Elam
Dub Taylor
D: Robert Totten

A goat rancher's son joins the Pony Express while searching for his father's murderer.

Au ★★★
S ★◗
A ★★◗

—*But, it ain't my fault that you forgot who and what you are neither. You're a cowboy, Trevor. A rich one now. But, you ain't no governor—just a cowboy.*
—Ken Curtis
Pony Express Rider

Pony Soldier (1952) 20th C. Fox ★★★◗

Tyrone Power
Cameron Mitchell
Thomas Gomez
Robert Horton
Nipo T. Strongheart
John War Eagle
Chief Brightfire Thundersky
D: Joseph M. Newman

A Mountie and his guide track waring Cree Indians to Montana. Filmed at Sedona, Arizona.

Au ★★★★
S ★★★◗
A ★★★◗

Posse (1975) Paramount ★★★◗

Kirk Douglas
Bruce Dern
Bo Hopkins
James Stacy
D: Kirk Douglas

A marshal forms a posse with outlaws in order to further his political ambitions. Filmed at Tucson, AZ.

Au

S ★★★✦

A ★★★★

Posse (1993) PGF ★★✦

Mario Van Peebles
Stephen Baldwin
Billy Zane
Isaac Hayes
Woody Strode
Nipsey Russell
Blair Underwood
D: Mario Van Peebles

Returning from the Spanish American War with a fortune in gold, black troopers elude their corrupt former commander. Filmed at Old Tucson.

Au

S ★★

A ★★✦

Posse From Heaven (1975) P.M. Films

Fanne Foxe
Todd Compton
Sherry Bain
Ward Wood
D: Philip Pine

A young man is sent by God to save the Old West protected by the Archangel Gabriel posing as a horse.

Posse From Hell (1961) U-I ★★

Audie Murphy
John Saxon
Zohra Lampert
Vic Morrow
Lee Van Cleef
Allen Lane
D: Herbert Coleman

A deputized gunman leads a posse after outlaws. Story by Clair Huffaker. Filmed in the Alabama Hills.

Au ★★

S ★✦

A ★★

Powderkeg (1971) Filmways ★★★✦

Rod Taylor
Dennis Cole
Fernando Lamas

> *—I'll get every God damned one of you if it's the last thing I do!*
> —Kirk Douglas
> *Posse* (1975)

> *—I think we can cut 'em off if we ride at an angle to them.*
> —Audie Murphy
> *Posse From Hell*

Audie Murphy and John Saxon in *Posse From Hell*.

John McIntire
Michael Ansara
Jim Brown
D: Douglas Heyes

A pair of gunfighters drive to Mexico in their Stutz Bearcat in 1914 to free hostages held on a train by bandidos.

Au

S ★★★★

A ★★★★

Powder River (1953) 20ᵗʰ C. Fox

Rory Calhoun
Corinne Calvet
Cameron Mitchell
D: Louis King

A marshal searches for a killer.

Prey of the Vultures (1973) FF—Sp./Ital.

Peter Lee Lawrence
Orchidea De Santis
D: Rafael Romero Marchent

An artist discovers that his lover's father is his father's murderer.

Price of Death (1972) FF—Ital.

John Garko
Kaus Kinski
D: Vincent Thomas (Enzo Gicca Palli)

A bounty hunter tracks the outlaws who robbed the town casino.

Price of Power (1969) FF—Ital./Sp.

Giuliano Gemma
Fernando Rey
D: Tonino Valerii

When President Garfield is assassinated in Dallas and his assassin is murdered in transport between jails, a gunman uncovers a conspiracy.

A Professional Gun (1968) FF—Ital./Sp.

Franco Nero
Tony Musante
Jack Palance
D: Sergio Corbucci

A Polish mercenary becomes entangled in a miners' revolt. Music by Ennio Morricone and Bruno Nicolai.

The Professionals (1966) Columbia

Burt Lancaster
Lee Marvin
Robert Ryan
Jack Palance
Claudia Cardinale
Ralph Bellamy
Woody Strode
D: Richard Brooks

Mercenaries are hired to rescue a man's wife from a bandido. Based on Frank O'Rourke's, *A Mule for the Marquesa*. Oscar nominations for direction, writing: based on material from another medium, and cinematography: color. Filmed in Death Valley. #50 Best of the West.

Au ★★★★

S ★★★★

A ★★★★

Lancaster, Marvin, Ryan and Strode are *The Professionals*.

The Proud and the Damned (1973) FF—U.S./Sp.

Chuck Connors
Aron Kincaid
Cesar Romero
D: Ferde Grofé, Jr.

—Yes sir. [I am a bastard.] In my case an accident of birth. But, you sir, are a self-made man.

—Lee Marvin
The Professionals

Proud Men (1956) 20ᵗʰ C. Fox

Charlton Heston
Peter Strauss
Nan Martin
Alan Autry
Buck Taylor
D: William A. Graham

Made for TV movie.

The Proud Ones (1956) BV

Robert Ryan
Virginia Mayo
Jeffrey Hunter
Walter Brennan
Edward Platt
Jackie Coogan
D: Robert D. Webb

A young gunfighter joins a marshal against a gambler and his gang. Filmed at Tucson, Arizona.

Au ★★

S ★★★

A ★★★

—You know, pride can kill a man faster than a bullet.

—Chico
The Proud Ones

379

The Proud Rebel (1958) BV

Alan Ladd
Olivia de Havilland
David Ladd
Dean Jagger
John Carradine
D: Michael Curtiz

A Civil War veteran searches the country for
a doctor to cure his son's dumbness.

Purgatory (Purgatory, West of the Pecos) (1999) TNT ★★★★

Sam Shephard
Eric Roberts
Randy Quaid
Peter Storemare
R.G. Armstrong
D: Uli Edel

Residents of a Western purgatory
must earn their way to salvation.

Au ★★★★
S ★★★★
A ★★★★

Pursued (1947) WB

Teresa Wright
Robert Mitchum
Judith Anderson
Dean Jagger
Alan Hale
Harry Carey, Jr.
D: Raoul Walsh

A gunman is haunted by his past as he
attempts to discover meaning in his life.

Pursuit (1975) KI

Ray Danton
DeWitt Lee
Troy Nabors
Diane Taylor
D: Thomas Quillen

After he is mauled by a bear, an Army scout is tracked by an Indian.

Pyramid of the Sun God (1965) FF—Ger./Ital./Fr.

Lex Barker
Michele Giardon
D: Robert Siodmak

A man searches for lost treasure. Sequel to *Treasure of the Aztecs*.

Sam Shephard in *Purgatory*.

—Welcome to Refuge, son.
Purgatory

Quantez (1957) U-I

Fred MacMurray
Dorothy Malone
James Barton
Sydney Chaplin
Michael Ansara
D: Harry Keller

Outlaws seek refuge in a ghost town.

Au ★★★◀

S ★★★

A ★★★

Quantrill's Raiders (1958) AA ★★

Steve Cochran
Diane Brewster
Leo Gordon
Gale Robbins
D: Edward Bernds

A Confederate officer helps stop
Quantrill from terrorizing a town.

Au ★◀

S ★★◀

A ★★★

Queen of the West see Cattle Queen

Queen of the Yukon (1940) Mono.

Charles Bickford
Irene Rich
Melvin Long
George Cleveland
D: Phil Rosen

An aging dancehall woman protects her daughter from her way of life.
Story by Jack London.

The Quest (1976) DGP/Columbia ★

Tim Matheson
Kurt Russell
Brian Keith
Keenan Wynn
Will Hutchins
Neville Brand
Cameron Mitchell
Iron Eyes Cody
D: Lee H. Katzin

A white man raised by Indians and his brother
search for their sister. Pilot for the TV series.

William Quantrill

Quantrill's raiders.

Filmed at Tucson, Arizona.

Au

S ★

A ★◗

The Quest: The Longest Drive see The Longest Drive

The Quick and the Dead (1987) JCC/HBO ★★★◗

Sam Elliott
Kate Capshaw
Tom Conti
Matt Clark
D: Robert Day

A plainsman protects a family crossing the frontier in a covered wagon. Based on the Louie L'Amour novel. Filmed at Old Tucson.

Au

S ★★★★◗

A ★★★

> —*The meek ain't gonna inherit nothin' west of Chicago!*
> —Sam Elliott
> *The Quick and the Dead* (1987)

The Quick and the Dead (1995) Tri-Star ★★

Sharon Stone
Gene Hackman
Woody Strode
D: Sam Raimi

A woman gunfighter avenges her father's murder during a gunfighter's tournament. Filmed at Tucson, Arizona.

Au ★

S ★

A ★◗

> —*I'm gonna kill you if I have to ride all the way to hell to do it!*
> —Sharon Stone
> *The Quick and the Dead* (1995)

The Quick Gun (1964) Columbia

Audie Murphy
Merry Anders
James Best
Ted de Corsia
D: Sidney Salko

Upon his return home, a young cowboy is rejected for a past deed. Filmed at the Columbia Studio Ranch.

The Quiet Gun (1957) RF/20th C. Fox ★◗

Forrest Tucker
Mara Corday
Jim Davis
Lee Van Cleef
D: William Claxton

A lawman investigates the source

> —*I don't want anybody around when we start cuttin' fences and changin' brands.*
> —Lee Van Cleef
> *The Quiet Gun*

Belle Starr, cattle thief. Shot from ambush in 1889.

Ella "Cattle Kate" Watson (Maxwell). Lynched for rustling in 1899.

The Rose of Cimarron was George Newcomb's
(Doolin-Dalton gang) sweetheart.

**The
Notorious Women
of the
West**

Pearl Hart serving a five year sentence in an Arizona
prison for the last recorded stagecoach robbery in 1899.

"Big Nose Kate" Fisher was Doc Holliday's sweetheart.

Sharon Stone as a gunfighter in *The Quick and the Dead*.

of rumors responsible for a lynching.

Au

S

A

Quincannon, Frontier Scout (1956) Bel-Air/UA

Tony Martin
Peggie Castle
John Bromfield
D: Lesley Selander

A scout leads an expedition into hostile country to recover stolen rifles.

UNCHARTED
TERRITORY

Quinta: Fighting Proud (1969) FF—Ital./Sp.

Steven Todd
German Cobos
D: Leon Klimovsky

Rare.

UNCHARTED
TERRITORY

Quintana: Dead or Alive (1969) FF—Ital./Sp.

George Stevenson
Femi Benussi
D: Glenn Vincent Davis (Vincenzo Musolini)

A masked freedom fighter must prevent the execution of his friend.

UNCHARTED
TERRITORY

Racing Blood (1954) 20th C. Fox

Bill Williams
Jean Porter
Jimmy Boyd
D: Wesley Barry

Intended to be destroyed at birth because of a split hoof, a colt is raised by a stable boy and his uncle.

UNCHARTED
TERRITORY

Rage at Dawn (1955) RKO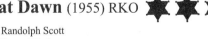

Randolph Scott
Forrest Tucker
Mala Powers
Edgar Buchanan
D: Tim Whelan

A special agent infiltrates the Reno brothers' gang of train robbers. Story by Frank Gruber.

Au

S

A

"A Cayuse."

—You want law and order!
Is this the way to get it with a mob?
—Randolph Scott
Rage at Dawn

The Raid (1954) 20th C. Fox

Van Hefflin
Anne Bancroft
Richard Boone
Lee Marvin
Peter Graves
Claude Akins
D: Hugo Fregonese

Confederates escape from a Union prison
and attempt to overrun a Canadian town.

The Raiders (Riders of Vengeance) (1952) U-I

Richard Conte
Viveca Lindfors
Barbara Britton
Hugh O'Brian
Dennis Weaver
D: Lesley Selander

Miners and homesteaders fight a land-grabber.

The Raiders (1964) Universal

Brian Keith
Robert Culp
Judy Meredith
Harry Carey, Jr.
D: Herschel Daugherty

A host of western legends help Texas stockmen
when they turn raiders and pursue the railroad.

Au ★★
S ★★
A ★★

Raiders of Old California (1957) Republic

Jim Davis
Arleen Whelan
Faron Young
Marty Robbins
Lee Van Cleef
D: Albert C. Gannaway

Following the Mexican War, cavalry officers attempt
to create their own empire in California.

"The Patient Pack-Mule."

Rails Into Laramie (Fort Laramie) (1954) U-I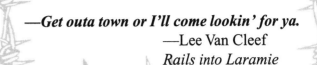

John Payne
Mari Blanchard
Dan Duryea
Lee Van Cleef
D: Jesse Hibbs

A gunfighter stops outlaws from disrupting
the completion of a railroad.

Au

S

A

—Get outa town or I'll come lookin' for ya.
—Lee Van Cleef
Rails into Laramie

Raise Your Hands, Dead Man…You're Under Arrest (1971) FF—Ital./Sp.

Peter Lee Lawrence
Espartaco Santoni
D: Leon Klimovsky

A Texas Ranger investigates a land-grabbing
scheme that is terrorizing local ranchers.

UNCHARTED
TERRITORY

Ramona (1936) 20th C. Fox

Loretta Young
Don Ameche
Kent Taylor
Pauline Frederick
Chief Thunder Cloud
D: Henry King

When a half-breed woman falls in love with an Indian, she experiences
prejudice from white settlers. Story by Helen Hunt Jackson.

UNCHARTED
TERRITORY

Ramon the Mexican (1966) FF—Ital./Sp.

Robert Hundar
Wilma Lindamar
D: Maurizio Pradeaux

A gunman avenges the murder of his lover's brother.

UNCHARTED
TERRITORY

Rampage at Apache Wells (1965) FF—Ger./Yug.

Stewart Granger
Pierre Brice
D: Harald Philipp

Chief Winnetou and a gunfighter
resolve a conflict over oil fields.

UNCHARTED
TERRITORY

Ramrod (1947) Enterprise/UA

Joel McCrea
Veronica Lake
Ian McDonald
D: Andrè de Toth

A rancher starts a range war then expects her foreman to fight it for her. Technical advise by Joe De Yong. André de Toth's first Western. Based on the Luke Short novel. Filmed near Springdale, Utah.

Au ★★

S ★★

A ★★

—Took me about a week to rope that hangover.
—Joel McCrea
Ramrod

The Ramrodder (1969)

Jim Gentry
Kathy Williams
Bobby Beausoleil
D: Ed Forsyth and Van Guilder

A cowboy marries an Indian and is framed for murder.

Ramsbottom Rides Again (1956) JHP

Arthur Askey
Sidney James
Betty Marsden
D: John Baxter

An English publican inherits a Canadian Ranch.

Rancho Notorious (1952) RKO/Fidelity

Marlene Dietrich
Mel Ferrer
Arthur Kennedy
George Reeves
Jack Elam
Russell Johnson
William Frawley
Lloyd Gough
D: Fritz Lang

A former saloon singer operates an outlaw hideout.
The first Western to include a theme song, "Chuck-A-Luck."
Howard Hughs omitted Gough's name from the credits because he defied the McCarthy hearings.

Au ★★

S ★★★★

A ★★★★

—I wish you'd go away and come back ten years ago.
—Marlene Dietrich
Rancho Notorious

Rangers of Fortune (1940) Paramount

Fred MacMurray
Patricia Morison

Betty Brewer
Albert Dekker
Gilbert Roland
D: Sam Wood

A renegade Army officer, a Mexican and
an ex-prizefighter rid a town of outlaws.

Ransom for Alice (1977) NBC-TV

Yvette Mimieux
Gil Gerard
Charles Napier
Gene Barry
D: David Lowell

A Seattle lawman and his partner investigate a white slavery ring.

The Rare Breed (1966) Universal

James Stewart
Maureen O'Hara
Brian Keith
Juliet Mills
Jack Elam
Ben Johnson
Harry Carey, Jr.
D: Andrew V. McLaglen

An English noblelady imports a prize Hereford bull to
the western range in order to cross with Texas longhorns.

Raton Pass (Canyon Pass) (1951) WB

Dennis Morgan
Patricia Neal
Steve Cochran
D: Edwin L. Marin

A husband and wife fight for their New Mexico ranch.
Story by Tom Blackburn. Filmed at Gallup, New Mexico.

Au ★★
S ★★
A ★★

*—Why, Sam always was so woman
shy it took a team just to drag him
into a dance.*

—Ben Johnson
The Rare Breed

Rattler Kid (1968) FF—Ital./Sp.

Richard Wyler
Brad Harris
D: Leon Klimovsky

A priest helps an innocent man escape his execution so that he can track the real killer.

388

Ravenous (1999) FF—U.S./Brit./Mex./Czech./Slov.

Guy Pearce
Robert Carlyle
David Arquette
D: Antonio Bird

In 1847 an army captain investigates a tale of canabalism in the Sierra Nevadas. Filmed in Slovakia and Mexico.

Raw Edge (1956) U-I

Rory Calhoun
Yvonne De Carlo
Mara Corday
Neville Brand
D: John Sherwood

A woman becomes attracted to the gunman out to kill her husband.

Robert Carlyle in *Ravenous*.

Rawhide (Desperate Siege) (1951) 20ᵗʰ C. Fox ★ ★ ★ ★

Tyrone Power
Susan Hayward
Hugh Marlowe
Edgar Buchanan
Jack Elam
D: Henry Hathaway

Outlaws hold hostages at a stagecoach station. Filmed in the Alabama Hills. #41 Best of the West.

Au ★ ★ ★ ★
S ★ ★ ★ ★
A ★ ★ ★ ★ ◖

The Rawhide Trail (1950) AA

Rex (Rhodes) Reason
Nancy Gates
Richard Erdman
D: Robert Gordon

Two men are jailed for leading a wagon train into a Comanche ambush.

Jack Elam in *Rawhide*.

The Rawhide Years (1956) U-I ★ ★

Tony Curtis
Colleen Miller
Arthur Kennedy
William Demarest
D: Rudolph Mate

A riverboat gambler is falsely accused of murder. Story by Norman Fox.

Au ★ ◖

S
A

Reach You Bastard! (1971) FF—Ital.

Hunt Powers
Gordon Mitchell
D: Lucky Dickerson (Demofilo Fidani)

Wild Bill Hickok meets bounty hunter, Django.

A Reason to Live, a Reason to Die (1974) (Massacre at Fort Holman) (1972) FF—Ital./Sp./Fr./

W. Ger.

James Coburn
Telly Savalas
Bud Spencer (Carlo Pedersoli)
D: Tonio Valerii

A dishonored Union officer uses condemned soldiers to
clear his name. Western version of *The Dirty Dozen*.

Au
S
A

—*He was innocent!*
—James Coburn
*A Reason to Live,
a Reason to Die*

The Rebel see The Bushwackers

Rebel in Town (1956) Bel-Air/UA

John Payne
Ruth Roman
J. Carroll Naish
Ben Johnson
D: Alfred Werker

A couple's son is accidently killed by the son of a Confederate.

Rebels of Arizona (1969) FF—Sp.

Charles Quiney
Claudia Gravy
D: Josè Maria Zabalza

Pioneers defend their homes from bandidos and Indians.

Reckoning (2002) LMG

Ramon Becerra
Becky
Kathryn Brucher
Ritchie Copenhaver

D: Jason Rodriguez

Red Blood, Yellow Gold (1968) FF—Ital./Sp.

George Hilton
Edd Byrnes
D: Nando Cicero

A former priest, an explosives expert and a bandit demonstrate
their loyalty to one another during their adventures.

Red Canyon (1949) U-I

Howard Duff
Ann Blyth
George Brent
Edgar Buchanan
John McIntire
Chill Wills
Lloyd Bridges
D: George Sherman

Based on Zane Grey's, *Wildfire*.

Red Coat (1975) FF—Ital.

Fabio Testi
Lionel Stander
D: Joe D'Amato (Aristide Massaccesi)

A Canadian Mountie and his dog, Fang, rescue a boy in
the wilderness. Based on Jack London's characters.

Red Earth, White Earth (1989) C/RP

Timothy Daly
Genevieve Bujod
Ralph Waite
Richard Farnsworth
D: David Greene

Made for TV movie.

The Redhead and the Cowboy (1951) Paramount

Glenn Ford
Edmond O'Brien
Rhonda Fleming
D: Leslie Fenton

A cowboy relies on the testimony of a Confederate spy to
clear himself of murder charges. Filmed in Sedona, Arizona.

Red-Headed Stranger (1986) AF ★★★✦

Willie Nelson
Morgan Fairchild
Katherine Ross
Royal Dano
D: Bill Wittliff

A Philadelphia preacher moves his new bride to a troubled Montana town. Inspired by Nelson's album, "Red Headed Stranger." Filmed in Spiceworld, Texas, at the Luck townsite built specifically for this film.

Au ★★★★

S ★★★

A ★★★✦

> ♪
> —*This is the tale of the red-headed stranger and if he should pass your way, stay out of the path of the ragin' black stallion and don't lay a hand on the bay…*
> —Willie Nelson
> *The Red-Headed Stranger*

The Redhead From Wyoming (1953) U-I ★★

Maureen O'Hara
Alex Nicol
Robert Strauss
Jack Kelly
Dennis Weaver
D: Lee Sholem

A dance hall queen becomes the pawn in a scheme to elect a crook as Governor of Wyoming. Filmed at Agoura, CA.

Au ★★

S ★★

A ★✦

> —*It's high time women took a hand in running this world!*
> —Maureen O'Hara
> *The Redhead From Wyoming*

Red Mountain (1951) Paramount

Alan Ladd
Lizabeth Scott
John Ireland
Arthur Kennedy
Neville Brand
Jay Silverheels
D: William Dieterle

Two men foil Quantrill's plans to build a western empire.

The Red Pony (1949) Republic ★★★

Myrna Loy
Robert Mitchum
Louis Calhern
Shepperd Strudwick
Peter Miles
Beau Bridges
D: Lewis Milestone

A farm boy in circa 1900 California grows to

love his horse. From the John Steinbeck novel.

Au ★★★
S ★★★★⦚
A ★★★★⦚

The Red Pony (1973) Universal/OP ★★★★⦚

Henry Fonda
Maureen O'Hara
Clint Howard
Jack Elam
Clint Howard
D: Robert Totten

Remake of the 1949 version.

Au ★★★★⦚
S ★★★
A ★★★

Red River (1948) Monterey/UA ★★★★★

John Wayne
Montgomery Clift
Joanne Dru
Walter Brennan
Coleen Gray
John Ireland
Noah Beery, Jr.
Chief Yowlachie
Harry Carey, Sr.
Harry Carey, Jr.
Shelley Winters
Pierce Lyden
D: Howard Hawks

A Texas cattleman and his adopted son tangle during the first successful cattledrive on the Chisholm trail. Technical advise by Joe De Yong. Based on Borden Chase's (Frank Fowler) serial written for the *Saturday Evening Post*, "The Blazing Guns of the Chisholm Trail." Oscar nominations for writing: original story and film editing. Filmed in part in Elgin, Arizona, on the lower Verde River near Phoenix. The finest Western ever made. #1 Best of the West, #5 IMDb, #2 LPFF.

Joanne Dru and John Wayne in *Red River*.

Au ★★★★⦚
S ★★★★★
A ★★★★⦚

—...there are only two things more beautiful than a good gun—a Swiss watch or a woman from anywhere. Ya ever had a good Swiss watch?
—John Ireland
Red River

With the branding of their first stock, John Wayne, Walter Brennan and Micky Kuhn begin a cattle empire in *Red River* (1948).

Red River (1988) Catalina P./MGM-UA Television

James Arness
Bruce Boxleitner
Gregory Harrison
Ray Waltson
Guy Madison
D: Richard Michaels

Remake of the 1948 version.

Red Sun (1971) FF—Ital./Fr./Sp.

Charles Bronson
Ursula Andress
Toshiro Mifune
Alain Delon
D: Terence Young

A gunfighter and a Samurai warrior set out
to recover a stolen ceremonial sword intended
for the president. #56 Best of the West.

—A gun, a sword. We all die the same-a-way.
—Toshiro Mifune
Red Sun

Red Sundown (1956) U-I

Rory Calhoun
Martha Hyer
Dean Jagger
D: Jack Arnold

A retired gunfighter must strap on his
guns in order to prevent a range war.
Filmed at Conejo Valley, California.

—Call a man a dog—someone throws a rock at him.
—Rory Calhoun
Red Sundown

Red Tomahawk (1967) Pramount

Howard Keel
Joan Caulfield
Broderick Crawford
Scott Brady
D: R.G. Springsteen

Upon stumbling on Custer's battleground, a man
attempts to warn troops unaware of Custer's fate.

UNCHARTED
TERRITORY

Little Big Horn, "Couriers."

The Red, White and Black (1970) (Soul Soldiers) (Buffalo Soldiers) (1971) HN/NBC-TV

Robert Doqui
Isaac Fields
Barbara Hale
Rafer Johnson
D: John Cardos

Buffalo soldiers of the 10th Cavalry fight Indians. NBC-TV pilot. Filmed at Old Tucson.

Relentless (1948) Columbia

Robert Young
Marguerite Chapman
Willard Parker
D: George Sherman

A girl helps an innocent cowboy chased by a posse.

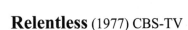

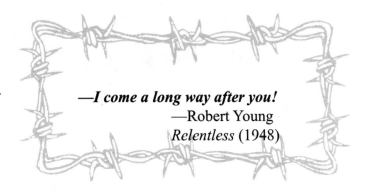

—I come a long way after you!
—Robert Young
Relentless (1948)

Relentless (1977) CBS-TV

Will Sampson
Monte Markham
John Hillerman
D: Lee H. Katzin

Remake of the 1948 version.

Relentless Four (1966) FF—Sp./Ital.

Adam West
Robert Hundar
Dina Loy
D: Primo Zeglio

A bounty hunter frames a marshal for murder.

The Renegades (1946) Columbia

Evelyn Keyes
Willard Parker
Larry Parks
Edgar Buchanan
Forrest Tucker
D: George Sherman

A woman searches for excitement with a gang of outlaws.

Reno (1939) RKO

Richard Dix
Gail Patrick

Anita Louise
Paul Cavanaugh
D: John Farrow

A lawyer turns a mining town into the country's divorce capital.

Reprisal! (1956) Columbia

Guy Madison
Felicia Farr
Kathryn Grant
Edward Platt
D: George Sherman

A half-breed rancher defends local Indians from vigilantes. Filmed at Old Tucson.

Au
S
A

> —*My name is Neola. That part of me that is white, I deny!*
>
> —Guy Madison
> *Reprisal!*

Requiem for a Bounty Hunter (1970) FF—Ital.

Ray O'Connor
Lawrence Bien
D: Mark Welles (Mel Welles)

A rancher hires a bounty hunter to avenge the murder of his family.

Requiem For A Gunfighter (1965) Embassy

Rod Cameron
Stephen McNally
Mike Mazurki
Bob Steele
Boyd "Red" Morgan
D: Spencer G. Bennet

A gunfighter impersonates a judge.

The Restless Breed (1957) Alp./20th C. Fox

Scott Brady
Anne Bancroft
Jay C. Flippen
Jim Davis
D: Allan Dwan

The son of a government agent avenges his father's death. Intended to be a comedy, but not perceived as such.

396

The Return of a Man Called Horse (1976) UA

Richard Harris
Gale Sondergaard
Geoffrey Lewis
Bill Lucking
D: Irvin Kershner

An English nobleman returns to America
and discovers his tribe decimated. Sequel
to *A Man Called Horse*. Filmed at Custer
State Park, Black Hills, South Dakota and
in Mexico. #25 Best of the West.

Au ★★★★┥

S ★★★★┥

A ★★★★┥

Return of Clint the Stranger (1971) FF—Ital./Sp.

George Martin
Klaus Kinski
D: George Martin

Sequel to *Clint the Stranger*.

The Return of Desperado (1988) Mirisch/Universal-TV

Alex McArthur
Robert Foxworth
Billy Dee Williams
D: E.W. Swackhamer

Made for TV movie.

Henry Fonda as Frank James.

The Return of Frank James (1940) 20ᵗʰ C. Fox ★★★★★

Henry Fonda
Gene Tierney
Jackie Cooper
John Carradine
J. Edgar Bromberg
D: Fritz Lang

Frank avenges Jesse's murder. Sequel to *Jesse James*.
Filmed at Bishop and Lone Pine, CA. #11 Best of the West.

Au ★★★

S ★★★★★

A ★★★★★

The Return of Jack Slade (1955) AA ★★┥

John Ericson
Mari Blanchard
Neville Brand
Angie Dickinson
D: Harold Schuster

A gunfighter's son is recruited by the Pinkertons.

Au

The Return of Jesse James (1950) Lippert

John Ireland
Ann Dvorak
Henry Hull
Hugh O'Brian
D: Arthur Hilton

An outlaw poses as Jesse James and leads the remnants of his gang.

The Return of Josey Wales (1986) Multi/Tacar P./RMI

Michael Parks
Raphael Campos
Bob Magruder
Paco Vela
D: Michael Parks

This sequel to *The Outlaw Josey Wales* is the worst domestic Western I've ever seen.

Au

Return of Ringo (1966) FF—Ital./Sp.

Giuliano Gemma
Fernando Sancho
D: Duccio Tessari

Upon his return from the Civil War, a veteran discovers
his town overtaken by bandidos. Sequel to *Pistol for Ringo*.

Return of Rin Tin Tin (1947) PRC/EL

Rin Tin Tin III
Donald Woods
Bobby Blake
Claudia Drake
D: Max Nosseck

When a padre brings a European boy to his western mission,
he takes a dog who must be returned to his master.

Return of Sabata (1972) FF—Ital./Fr./Ger.

Lee Van Cleef
Reiner Schone
D: Frank Kramer (Gianfranco Parolini)

Two gunmen plot to rob a bank. Sequel to *Sabata*.

Lee Van Cleef in *Return of Sabata*.

Filmed in Spain.

Au ★★✦
S ★✦
A ★✦

Return of Shanghai Joe (1974) FF—Ger./Ital.

Klaus Kinski
Chen Lee
D: Bitto Albertini

A vigilante faces off with a town boss.

Return of the Badmen (1948) RKO ★★

Randolph Scott
Robert Ryan
Anne Jeffreys
George "Gabby" Hayes
Jason Robards
D: Ray Enright

A marshal is forced out of retirement
to face a host of legendary badmen.

Au ★✦
S ★★
A ★★

*—But, if our mothers walked the streets,
mine had more customers!*
—Lee Van Cleef
Return of Sabata

*—Now, you don't jerk the trigger, you know.
Ya just squeeze it a leeetle might. Understand?*
—"Gabby" Hayes
Return of the Badmen

Return of the Big Cat (1974) Disney

Jeremy Slate
Pat Crowley
David Wayne
D: Tom Leetch

A cougar threatens a northern California pioneer family in the 1890s.

The Return of the Cisco Kid (1939) 20th C. Fox

Warner Baxter
Lynn Bari
Cesar Romero
Henry Hull
Ward Bond
D: Herbert I. Leeds

The Cisco Kid defends a woman against a crooked lawyer.
Sequel to *The Cisco Kid* (1931).

Return of the Frontiersman (1950) WB

Gordon MacRae
Jack Holt
Rory Calhoun

D: Richard Bare

A sheriff's son is falsely imprisoned for a murder he did not commit.

Return of the Gunfighter (1967) ABC-TV/King Bros./MGM ★◗

Robert Taylor
Ana Martin
Chad Everett
John Crawford
D: James Nielson

Two gunfighters help a Mexican girl avenge the murder of her family. Coscreenplay by Burt Kennedy and Robert Buckner. Filmed at Old Tucson.

Au ★◗

S ★

A ★◗

—Stop trying to prove how good you are. There's always somebody in the next town just a little bit faster.
—Robert Taylor
Return of the Gunfighter

Return of the Lone Ranger (1961)

Tex Hill
D: ?

The Return of the Seven (1966) FF—Sp. ★★★

Yul Brynner
Robert Fuller
Claude Atkins
D: Burt Kennedy

Two survivors of *The Magnificent Seven* are back to help their friend, Chico, protect his people from bandits. Oscar nomination for scoring: adaptation or treatment. Filmed near Alicante, Spain.

Au ★★◗

S ★★◗

A ★★★◗

Return of the Texan (1952) 20th C. Fox

Dale Robertson
Joanne Dru
Walter Brennan
Richard Boone
Robert Horton
D: Delmer Daves

A widower returns to ranching only to be confronted by outlaws.

Return of the Vigilantes see The Vigilantes Return

Return of Wildfire (Black Stallion) (1948) Lippert/Screen Guild

Richard Arlen
Patricia Morison
Mary Beth Hughs
James Millican
D: Ray Taylor

A wrangler confronts an outlaw attempting to monopolize the wild horse trade.

Return to Lonesome Dove (1993) RHIE

Jon Voight
Rick Schroeder
Barbara Hershey
Louis Gossett, Jr.
D: Mike Robe

Sequel to *Lonesome Dove*. TV mini-series.

Au ★★★★★

S ★★★

A ★★★★

—*I'm gonna count to three. You don't drop that shooter in the dirt, I'll put a hole in your heart.*
—Jon Voight
Return to Lonesome Dove

Return to Warbow (1958) Columbia

Phil Carey
Catherine McLeod
Andrew Duggan
Jay Silverheels
D: Ray Nazarro

Three outlaws discover their buried loot is missing.

Revenge for Revenge (1968) FF—Ital.

John Ireland
John Hamilton
D: Ray Calloway (Mario Colucci)

Two gunmen face off over stolen gold.

Revenge of the Wild Bunch see Machismo—40 Graves for 40 Guns

The Revengers (1972) NG ★★★★

William Holden
Ernest Borgnine
Susan Hayward
Woody Strode
D: Daniel Mann

A Colorado rancher hires convicts to help him find the renegade and Comanches who killed his family. Filmed in Mexico.

Au ★★★★

S
A

Reverend Colt (1970) FF—Ital./Sp.

Guy Madison
Richard Harrison
D: Leon Klimovsky

A former bounty hunter turned reverend is suspected of robbing the town bank.

Revolt at Fort Laramie (1957) Bel-Air/UA

John Dehner
Gregg Palmer
Frances Helm
D: Lesley Selander

A cavalry outpost becomes divided when the
Civil War breaks out, but reunites to fight Indians.

Revolt in Canada (1964) FF—Sp.

George Martin
Pamela Tudor
Luis Marin
D: Mando De Ossurio

An outlaw trapper blames Canadian trappers for his deeds. Dubbed.

U.S. 7th Cavalryman.

The Reward (1965) 20th C. Fox

Max von Sydow
Yvette Mimieux
Efrem Zimbalist, Jr.
Gilbert Roland
D: Serge Bourguignon

Bounty hunters disagree about their
reward money. Filmed at Old Tucson.

The Reward's Yours, the Man's Mine (1970) FF—Ital.

Robert Woods
Aldo Berti
D: Edward G. Muller (Edoardo Mulargia)

A bounty hunter agrees to bring his man in alive.

Ride a Crooked Trail (1958) U-I ★ ★ ★

Audie Murphy
Gia Scala
Walter Matthau
Henry Silva

402

D: Jesse Hibbs

An outlaw is mistaken for a U.S. marshal.
Story by Borden Chase. Filmed in part in
Ventura Canyon and Janns Ranch, California.

Au

S ★★★

A ★★★★

Ride and Kill (1964) FF—Ital./Sp.

Alex Nicol
Robert Hundar
D: J.L. Boraw (Josè Luis Borau) and Mario Caiano

Corrupt businessmen hire a gunfighter to kill their sheriff.

Ride a Northbound Horse (1969) BV

Carroll O'Connor
Michael Shea
Ben Johnson
Andy Devine
Jack Elam
D: Robert Totten

A fifteen-year-old orphan is determined to become a Texas cattleman. Disney.

Ride a Violent Mile (1957) RF/20th C. Fox

John Agar
Penny Edwards
John Pickard
D: Charles Marquis Warren

A Union agent and her boyfriend prevent
Confederates from trading cattle with Mexico.

The Ride Back (1957) AAC/UA ★ ★ ★

Anthony Quinn
William Conrad
George Trevino
D: Allen H. Miner

A lawman must deliver an accused murderer for trial.
The only film in which Quinn and Conrad appear together.
Theme song sung by Eddie Albert.

Au ★★★

S ★★★

A ★★★★

♪
*—There's somethin' I must tell you before
I am dead. I didn't bring the prisoner in,
he brought me instead.*

—Eddie Albert
The Ride Back

Ride Beyond Vengeance (1966) Tiger/Sentinal/Fenady

Chuck Connors
Michael Rennie
Joan Blondell
Kathryn Hayes
Bill Bixby
Claude Akins
D: Bernard McEveety

A bartender relates an incident in his town's past involving a branded buffalo hunter.

Au ★★☆
S ★★☆
A ★★★

Ride Clear of Diablo (1953) U-I ★★

Audie Murphy
Dan Duryea
Susan Cabot
Russell Johnson
Jack Elam
D: Jesse Hibbs

A gunfighter helps a cowboy avenge the murder of his father and brother. Filmed in the Alabama Hills and Victorville, California.

Au ★☆
S ★★
A ★★

Audie Murphy in *Ride Clear of Diablo.*

> *—I told you once before, if I ever started feelin' like a human being—I'd shoot myself.*
> —Dan Duryea
> *Ride Clear of Diablo*

Ride in the Whirlwind (1966) Protcus F. (Ride the Whirlwind) (1971) JHHE

Cameron Mitchell
Jack Nicholson
Millie Perkins
Dean Stanton
D: Monte Hellman

Vigilantes mistake two innocent men for outlaws. Originally released in 1966 for television prior to theatrical release. Filmed at Kanab, UT.

Au ★★☆
S ★☆
A ★★

> *—They're gonna hang us. You think that's right?*
> —Jack Nicholson
> *Ride in the Whirlwind*

Ride Lonesome (1959) Columbia

Randolph Scott
Karen Steele
Pernell Roberts
James Best
Lee Van Cleef
James Coburn
Lee Marvin
Donna Reed
D: Budd Boetticher

404

A lawman avenges his wife's murder. Screenplay by Burt Kennedy. Filmed in the Alabama Hills.

Au ★★
S ★★★
A ★★★

Ride Out for Revenge (1957) BP/UA

Rory Calhoun
Gloria Grahame
Lloyd Bridges
D: Norman Retchin

A cavalry scout protects the Cheyenne from a corrupt officer.

UNCHARTED TERRITORY

The Rider of Death Valley (1932) Universal

Tom Mix
Lois Wilson
Fred Kholer
Forrest Stanley
Iron Eyes Cody
D: Albert Rogell

A cowboy protects a woman's hidden mine from outlaws.

UNCHARTED TERRITORY

Rider on a Dead Horse (1962) AA

John Vivyan
Bruce Gordon
Kevin Hagen
D: Herbert L. Strock

One of three prospectors murders a partner then blames the other.

UNCHARTED TERRITORY

Riders in the Storm (1995)

Morgan Brittany
Brett Baxter Clark
Kim Dawson
Bo Hopkins
Doug McClure
D: Charles Biggs

UNCHARTED TERRITORY

Riders of the Purple Sage (1996) TNT

Ed Harris
Amy Madigan
Henry Thomas
D: Charles Haid

A mysterious drifter comes to the aid of a female rancher. Remake of the 1931 and 1941 "B" versions which are based on the Zane Grey novel. Filmed at Moab, Utah. #78 Best of the West.

—Sure beats all, don't it? What a man'll put himself through to get his hands on a woman...Can't says I blame him though.
—Pernell Roberts
Ride Lonesome

—Where I was raised a woman's word was law. I ain't quite outgrowed that yet.
—Ed Harris
Riders of the Purple Sage

Au ★★★★★
S ★★★★◣
A ★★★★

The Riders of Vengeance see The Raiders (1952)

Ride the High Country (Guns in the Afternoon) (1962) MGM ★★★◣

Randolph Scott
Joel McCrea
Mariette Hartley
Edgar Buchanan
Warren Oates
James Drury
John Davis
D: Sam Peckinpah

Two retired gunfighters return a young lady to her father after her gold-camp marriage turns sour. Scott's last film. Filmed at Mammoth Lakes, CA. #25 IMDb.

Au ★★★◣
S ★★★◣
A ★★★★

Randolph Scott and Joel McCrea
in *Ride the High Country.*

Ride the Man Down (1952) Republic ★★

Brian Donlevy
Rod Cameron
Ella Raines
Chill Wills
Forrest Tucker
D: Joseph Kane

When her father dies, a woman and the ranch foreman struggle to save their land. Based on a Luke Short story.

Au ★★
S ★★
A ★★◣

Ride the Whirlwind see Ride in the Whirlwind

Ride to Hangman's Tree (1967) Universal ★★◣

Jack Lord
James Farentino
Don Galloway
Melodie Johnson
D: Al Rafkin

Three outlaws cross paths during stagecoach robberies.

Au ★◣
S ★◣
A ★★

—You wouldn't recognize the truth if it kicked you in the teeth!
—Jack Lord
Ride to Hangman's Tree

Ride, Vaquero! (1953) MGM ★★★¹

Robert Taylor
Ava Gardner
Anthony Quinn
Jack Elam
D: John Farrow

A border town bandido sides with a Texas rancher and his wife. Filmed at Kanab, UT.

Au ★★★¹

S ★★★★

A ★★★★

Ride With the Devil (1999)

Skeet Ulrich
Toby Maguire
Jewel Kilcher
D: Angy Lee

Confederate bushwackers on the Missouri-Kansas frontier seek revenge against northern sympathizers.

Toby Maguire and Jewel Kilcher in *Ride With the Devil.*

Riding Shotgun (1954) WB ★★★

Randolph Scott
Wayne Morris
Joan Weldon
Charles Buchinsky (Bronson)
D: Andrè de Toth

A stagecoach guard is accused of robbing his own coach. Story by Tom Blackburn. Filmed at Bell Ranch, California.

Au ★★¹

S ★★¹

A ★★¹

Ringo: Face of Revenge (1966) FF—Ital./Sp.

Anthony Steffen
Frank Wolff
D: Mario Caiano

Matching halves of a treasure map are tattooed on the backs of two men.

Randolph Scott and Joan Weldon in *Riding Shotgun.*

Ringo and His Golden Pistol (1966) FF—Ital.

Mark Damon
Valeria Fabrizi
D: Sergio Corbucci

A bounty hunter tracks an outlaw boss.

—Looks like you pack all the brains you got in your holster!

—Charles Buchinsky
Riding Shotgun

Ringo, It's Massacre Time (1970) FF—Ital.

Mickey Hargitay
Omero Gargano
D: Mario Pinzauti

Rare.

Ringo, The Lone Rider (1967) FF—Ital./Sp.

Peter Martell
Piero Lulli
D: Rafael R. Marchent

A town hires a gunfighter to protect them from a gang of outlaws.

Ringo's Big Night (1966) FF—Ital./Sp.

William Berger
Adriana Ambesi
D: Mario Maffei

Tombstone stage robberies are blamed on the wrong man.

Rimfire (1949) Lippert/Screen Guild

Jae Millican
Mary Beth Hughs
Henry Hull
Jason Robards
D: B. Reeves Eason

A secret service agent is assigned to recover stolen government gold bullion.

Au
S
A

Rio Bravo (1959) Armada/WB

John Wayne
Dean Martin
Ricky Nelson
Angie Dickinson
Walter Brennan
Ward Bond
John Russell
Claude Akins
Harry Carey, Jr.
Bob Steele
D: Howard Hawks

A sheriff and his deputies must prevent a wealthy rancher from breaking a killer out

♪ —*...Get along home, Cindy, Cindy. I'll marry you sometime.*
—Ricky Nelson, Walter Brennan and Dean Martin
Rio Bravo

Ricky Nelson and John Wayne in *Rio Bravo*.

408

of jail. Filmed at Old Tucson. #12 IMDb.

Au ★★★◤

S ★★★

A ★★★★◤

Rio Conchos (1964) 20th C. Fox ★★◤

Richard Boone
Stuart Whitman
Tony Franciosa
Wende Wagner
Jim Brown
Edmond O'Brien
D: Gordon Douglas

A former Confederate officer supplies guns to Apaches. First film appearance for Jim Brown. Based on Clair Huffaker's, *Guns of the Rio Conchos*. Filmed at White's Ranch, Castle Valley, Professor Valley, Arches National Park, Dead Horse Point State Park, Utah.

Au ★★◤

S ★★★◤

A ★★★

Richard Boone in *Rio Conchos*.

Rio Diablo (1993) CBS-TV ★★◤

Kenny Rogers
Stacy Keach
Travis Tritt
Naomi Judd
D: Rod Hardy

A young farmer receives help from a bounty hunter in tracking the bank robbers who kidnapped his bride. Filmed at Alamo Village, Brackettville, Texas.

Au ★★★★◤

S ★★

A ★★

—…Are you listening? That's good. Now, I want a bottle of whiskey and three glasses sittin' right up here.
—Richard Boone
Rio Conchos

—The question is which one of you lives and which one of you dies where you're standing.
—Kenny Rogers
Rio Diablo

Rio Grande (1950) Argosy/Republic ★★★★

John Wayne
Maureen O'Hara
Claude Jarman, Jr.
Ben Johnson
Harry Carey, Jr.
Chill Wills
Victor McLaglen
Sons of the Pioneers
D: John Ford

A cavalry officer fights Apaches in the shadow of his estranged wife and son. Based on James Bellah's short story, "Mission With No Record." Filmed in Professor Valley's George White Ranch, in Monument Valley, Ida Gulch, CO River, and Onion Creek Narrows, Utah. #48 Best of the West, #31 IMDb.

Au ★★★★◤

John Wayne, Maureen O'Hara and Victor McLaglen in *Rio Grande*.

S ★★★★
A ★★★★

Rio Lobo (1970) NG ★★★★⯪

John Wayne
Jorge Rivero
Jennifer O'Neill
Jack Elam
Jim Davis
George Plimpton
Bob Steele
Red Morgan
Donald (Red) Barry
D: Howard Hawks

An aging Union veteran pursues Union traitors responsible for the death of his adopted son and the theft of a Union payroll. Filmed at Old Tucson and Morelos, Mexico.

Au ★★★
S ★★★⯪
A ★★★

John Wayne, Jorge Rivero and Jack Elam in *Rio Lobo.*

Rita of the West (1967) FF—Ital.

Rita Pavone
Terence Hill
D: Ferdinando Baldi

A woman falls in love with a man who uses her to steal Indian gold.

River Lady (1948) U-I

Yvonne De Carlo
Rod Cameron
Dan Duryea
Jack Lambert
D: George Sherman

A Mississippi gambling queen schemes to win the lumberman she loves.

Robert Mitchum, Marilyn Monroe, Tommy Rettig and Rory Calhoun in *River of No Return.*

River of No Return (1954) 20ᵗʰ C. Fox ★★★⯪

Robert Mitchum
Marilyn Monroe
Rory Calhoun
Tommy Rettig
D: Otto Preminger

A northwest farmer, his boy and a saloon girl escape an Indian attack by rafting down river. Filmed at Devona near Brule east of Jasper and in Banff, Alberta, Canada. Monroe reportedly broke her foot at sixth bridge along the Maligne River. Joe Dimaggio visited her in

♪
—Love is a traveler on the River of No Return.
—Marilyn Monroe
River of No Return

410

Jasper during her recovery.

Au ★★★

S ★★★★

A ★★★★

The River's End (1930) WB

Charles Bickford
Evelyn Knapp
J. Farrell MacDonald
Zasu Pitts
D: Michael Curtiz

An innocent man poses as a dead Mountie.
Remake of the 1920 silent version. Based
on a James O. Curwood story.

River's End (1940) WB

Dennis Morgan
Elizabeth Earl
George Tobias
Victor Jory
D: Ray Enright

Remake of the 1930 version.

The Road to Denver (1955) Republic

John Payne
Mona Freeman
Lee J. Cobb
Lee Van Cleef
D: Joseph Kane

Two brothers love for each other is tested when
they take opposing sides of a new stage line.
Story by Bill Gulick. Filmed at St. George, UT.

Au ★★

S ★

A ★★

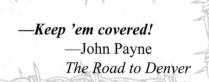

—Keep 'em covered!
—John Payne
The Road to Denver

The Road to Fort Alamo (Arizona Bill) (1966) FF—Ital./Fr.

Ken Clark
Jany Clair
D: Mario Bava

Outlaws rescued by a federal wagon train help protect the train from hostile attack.

Robber's Roost (1955) UA

George Montgomery
Richard Boone
Sylvia Findley

Peter Graves
Boyd "Red" Morgan
D: Sidney Salko

A gunman avenges the murder of his wife and clears his name. Based on the Zane Grey story. Filmed in Durango, Mexico.

Au ✹✹

S ✹✹

A ✹✹

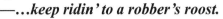

♪
—…keep ridin' to a robber's roost.
—Theme song
Robber's Roost

Robin Hood Of Eldorado (1936) MGM

Warner Baxter
Bruce Cabot
Margo
Ann Lanning
J. Carrol Naish
D: William Wellman

Joaquin Murrieta fights illegal settlers in southern California.

Rock Island Trail (1950) Republic ✮✮✮

Forrest Tucker
Adele Mara
Adrian Booth
Chill Wills
D: Joseph Kane

A railroad builder expands his tracks west of the Mississippi.

Au ✹✹

S ✹✹✹

A ✹✹✮

—You could make more dates with girls by starting arguments with 'em.
—Chill Wills
Rock Island Trail

Rockwell: A Legend of the Wild West (Rockwell) (1994)

Scott Christopher
Michael Flynn
Randy Gleave
Karl Malone
D: Richard L. Dewey

When a pioneer settles in Utah, he discovers the same land grabbers who he left behind in Illinois.

Rocky (1948) Mono.

Roddy McDowell
Gale Sherwood
Nita Hunter
Edgar Barrier
D: Phil Karlson

A young man and his dog experience the frontier.

Rocky Mountain (1950) WB

Errol Flynn
Patrice Wymore
Scott Forbes
Slim Pickens
Yakima Canutt
D: William Keighley

Renegades establish a Confederate outpost in California. Picken's film debut. Story by Alan LeMay.

Rojo (1966) FF—Ital./Sp.

Richard Harrison
Peter Carter
D: Leo Coleman (Leopoldo Savona)

A mysterious gunman avenges the murder of a pioneer family.

The Romance of Rosy Ridge (1947)

Van Johnson
Janet Leigh
Thomas Mitchell
D: Roy Rowland

A mysterious Civil War veteran attempts to resolve postwar unrest amongst Missouri farmers in order to court a farmer's daughter.

Au ★★★★
S ★★★
A ★★★

Romance of the Rio Grande (1941) 20th C. Fox ★

Cesar Romero
Patricia Morison
Lynn Roberts
D: Herbert I. Leeds

The Cisco Kid meets his double while investigating a murder. Based on the character created by O'Henry. Filmed in the Alabama Hills.

Au ★
S ★
A ★★

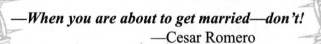

—When you are about to get married—don't!
—Cesar Romero
Romance of the Rio Grande

Rooster Cogburn (And the Lady) (1975) Universal ★★★★

John Wayne
Katharine Hepburn
Anthony Zerbe
Richard Jordan
John McIntire
Strother Martin
D: Stuart Millar

A marshal and the daughter of a murdered minister track outlaws holding a wagon load of nitroglycerine. Sequel to *True Grit*. Filmed in Oregon. #45 Best of the West.

Au

S

A

Rose Hill (1997) CBS-TV/HHFP

Jennifer Garner
Jeffrey D. Sams
Zak Orth
Justin Chambers
D: Christopher Cain

Four young cowboys raise an abandoned child and become a family.

Rose of Cimarron (1952) Alco/20th C. Fox

Jack Buetel
Mala Powers
Bill Williams
Jim Davis
D: Harry Keller

A marshal helps a woman avenge her parents' murder.

Rough Company see The Violent Men

Rough Country see The Violent Men

A Rough Night in Jericho (1967) Universal ★ ★ ★

Dean Martin
Jean Simmons
George Peppard
John McIntire
Slim Pickens
D: Arnold Laven

A former marshal and a gambler help a woman protect her stageline from a town boss. Based on Marvin Alpert's, "The Man in Black."

Au

S

A

Roughshod (1949) RKO ★ ★

Robert Sterling
Claude Jarman, Jr.
Gloria Grahame
John Ireland
D: Mark Robson

Two brothers travel to California with a herd of

Katharine Hepburn and John Wayne in *Rooster Cogburn.*

—Ruben, I have to say it. Livin' with you has been an adventure any woman would relish for the rest of time. Ah, look at you with your burnt out face and your big belly and your bear-like paws and your shining eye. And I have to say you're a credit to the whole male sex and I'm proud to have ya for my friend.
—Katharine Hepburn
Rooster Cogburn

—You said a man had to think enough of ya to walk in the place you were workin' and take ya out of there.
—Robert Sterling
Roughshod

thoroughbreds and a group of dancehall girls.

Au

S ⭐⏐

A ⭐⏐

The Round Up (1941) Paramount ⭐

Richard Dix
Patricia Morison
Preston Foster
Don Wilson
Iron Eyes Cody
D: Lesley Selander

A woman's former sweetheart shows up on her wedding day. Filmed at Lone Pine, CA.

Au ⭐

S ⭐

A ⭐

Rowdy Girls (1999)

Shannon Tweed
Julie Strain
Deanna Brooks
D: Steve Nevius

—I thought it was like the first time you get thrown from a bronc. You gotta get right up on his back again, or the chances are you never will.

—James Cagney
Run for Cover

Roy Colt and Winchester Jack (1970) FF—Ital.

Brett Halsey
Charles Southwood
D: Mario Bava

Two outlaws reunite to face off with a sadistic reverend and his gang.

Run For Cover (1955) Paramount ⭐⭐

James Cagney
Viveca Lindfors
John Derek
Jack Lambert
Ernest Borgnine
D: Nicholas Ray

A sheriff takes on a young deputy who becomes the son he never had. Filmed near Durango, Colorado.

Au ⭐⭐

S ⭐⭐

A ⭐⭐

Run Home Slow (1965) JP/Emerson

Mercedes McCambridge
Linda Gaye Scott
Allen Richards

James Cagney in *Run for Cover.*

D: Tim Sullivan

When their father dies because the local bank failed to loan him money for medicine, the family begins robbing banks. Musical score by Frank Zappa.

Run Man, Run (1967) FF—Ital./Fr.

Tomàs Milian
Donald O'Brien
John Ireland
D: Sergio Sollima

An American adventurer and a bandido search for lost treasure. Sequel to *Big Gundown*.

Running Target (1956) Canyon/UA

Doris Dowling
Arthur Franz
Richard Reeves
D: Marvin R. Weinstein

Run of the Arrow (1957) RKO

Rod Steiger
Sarita Montiel
Brian Keith
Charles Bronson
D: Samuel Fuller

An ex-Confederate joins the Sioux. Filmed at St. George, UT.

—Lee's surrender was not the death of the South, but the birth of the United States.
—Narrator
Run of the Arrow

Au ★★
S ★★
A ★★

Run Simon Run (1970) ABC-TV

Burt Reynolds
Inger Stevens
Royal Dano
D: George McCowan

Upon his release from prison, an Indian avenges the murder of his mother.

Ruthless Colt of the Gringo (1967) FF—Ital./Fr.

Jim Reed (Luigi Giuliano)
Carlo Fabrizi
D: Josè Luis Madrid

When an innocent man is released from prison, he seeks revenge against the town boss who actually committed the murder.

The Ruthless Four (1968) FF—Ital.

Gilbert Roland
Klaus Kinski
Van Heflin
D: Giorgio Capitani

A prospector contends with three undesirable partners.

Sabata (1969) FF—Ital.

Lee Van Cleef
William Berger
D: Frank Kramer

A gunfighter and his partner recover a $60,000 ransom.

Sabata the Killer (1970) FF—Ital./Sp.

Peter Lee Lawrence
Anthony Steffen
D: Tullio Demichelli

A gunman double-crosses his partner and escapes with their bank loot.

The Sabre and the Arrow see The Last Comanches

The Sacketts (Louis L'Amour's "The Sacketts") (1979) NBC-TV/DN/MBSC/Shalako E.

Sam Elliott
Tom Selleck
Glenn Ford
Ben Johnson
Jack Elam
Slim Pickens
Gilbert Roland
D: Robert Totten

Following the Civil War three brothers migrate west
in search of a better life. Two part mini-series based
on two Louie L'Amour stories. Filmed at Old Tucson,
Buckskin Joe, Canon City, CO and Red Hills Ranch, Sonora, CA.
#81 Best of the West.

Sacred Ground (1983) CBPP/PI

Tim McIntire
Jack Elam
L.Q. Jones
Serene Hedin
D: Charles B. Pierce

A frontiersman and his Indian wife settle on sacred Paiute land.

Saddle the Wind (1958) MGM

Robert Taylor
Julie London
John Cassavetes
D: Robert Parrish

A retired gunfighter confronts his younger brother. Screenplay by Rod Serling.

Au ★★★
S ★★★★
A ★★★★

> *—Steve, I had to protect ya. You, you couldn't kill your kid brother, could ya? Steve,…*
> —John Cassavetes
> *Saddle the Wind*

Saddle Tramp (1950) U-I

Joel McCrea
Wanda Hendrix
John Russell
Ed Begley
D: Hugo Fregonese

A drifter takes on four young boys.
Filmed at the Iverson Movie Ranch.

Saddle Tramp Women (Tough Guns) (1972)

John Alderman
Rene Bond
Carl DeJung
D: Stu Segall

Bounty hunters track outlaws who raped a rancher's daughter.

The Sad Horse (1959) 20th C. Fox

David Ladd
Chill Wills
Rex Reason
D: James B. Clark

A young boy befriends a racehorse.

The Saga of Hemp Brown (1959) U-I

Rory Calhoun
Beverly Garland
John Larch
Russell Johnson
Allan Lane
D: Richard Carlson

418

A disgraced cavalry officer must clear his name.
Filmed at Conejo Valley, Thousand Oaks, California.

Au
S
A

Saga of the West see When a Man's a Man

Saguaro (1968) FF—Ital.

Kirk Morris
Larry Ward
D: Amerigo Anton (Tanio Boccia)

A Confederate veteran seeks revenge against the bandidos who murdered his friend.

Sally Fieldgood & Co. (1975) FF—Can.

Vallerie Ambrose
Hagen Beggs
Lloyd Berry
D: Boon Collins

Salome, Where She Danced (1945) Universal

Yvonne De Carlo
Rod Cameron
David Bruce
D: Charles Lamont

A dancer convinces an Arizona outlaw gang to reform.

Sam Hill: Who Killed the Mysterious Mr. Foster? (Who Killed the Mysterious Mr. Foster?) (1971) NBC-TV/Universal

Ernest Borgnine
Stephen Hudis
Will Geer
Bruce Dern
Slim Pickens
D: Fielder Cook

A sheriff investigates the murder of the town preacher.

San Antone (South of San Antone) (Women of Destiny) (1953) Republic

Rod Cameron
Arleen Whelan
Forrest Tucker
Harry Carey, Jr.
Katy Jurado
D: Joe Kane

A Civil War prisoner enters Mexico to trade cattle for
American captives. Filmed at Red Rock Canyon, California.

Au
S
A

San Antonio (1945) WB

Errol Flynn
Alexis Smith
S.Z. "Cuddles" Sakall
D: David Butler

A Texas cattleman avenges the theft of his herd. Based on
the W.R. Burnett story. Screenplay by Alan LeMay and Burnett.
Oscar nomination for art direction-interior decoration: color.
Filmed at Calabasas, California.

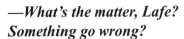

—*What's the matter, Lafe?*
Something go wrong?

—Errol Flynn
San Antonio

Au
S
A

Sand (1949) 20th C. Fox

Mark Stevens
Coleen Gray
Rory Calhoun
Iron Eyes Cody
D: Louis King

A trainer tracks an escaped show horse before he goes wild.
Academy nomination for cinematography: color.

The San Francisco Story (1952) WB

Joel McCrea
Yvonne De Carlo
Richard Erdmann
D: Robert Parrish

When a miner returns to San Francisco,
he confronts a corrupt political boss.

Au
S
A

Santa Fé (1951) Columbia

Randolph Scott
Janis Carter
Jerome Courtland
Peter Thompson
Jock Mahoney
Chief Thunder Cloud
D: Irving Pichel

A Confederate defends the railroad from
his outlaw brother. Filmed at Columbia

Randolph Scott slugging Jock Mahoney in *Santa Fé.*

420

Ranch, Burbank, California.

Au ★★✦

S ★★★

A ★★✦

Santa Fé Passage (1955) Republic ★★✦

John Payne
Faith Domergue
Rod Cameron
Slim Pickens
D: William Whitney

A scout guides a wagon train through hostile country. From the Clay Fisher (Henry W. Allen) novel. Filmed at St. George, UT.

Au ★★✦

S ★★✦

A ★★✦

—We all fought for somethin' we believed in and lost. Now we've got to mend our fences. Hate won't help us any.
—Randolph Scott
Santa Fé

—Ya know, the good book says judge not that ya not be judged…
—Slim Pickens
Santa Fé Passage

The Santa Fe Trail (1940) WB 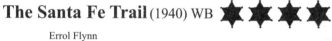 ★★★★

Errol Flynn
Olivia de Havilland
Raymond Massey
Ronald Reagan
Alan Hale
Van Heflin
Ward Bond
D: Michael Curtiz

West Point graduates are assigned to Fort Leavenworth in 1854. Filmed at the Paramount Ranch.
#79 Best of the West.

Au ★★★✦

S ★★★★

A ★★★★✦

Ronald Reagan, Olivia de Havilland and Errol Flynn in *Santa Fé Trail*.

Santee (1973) CP

Glenn Ford
Michael Burns
Dana Wynter
Jay Silverheels
D: Gary Nelson

A rancher turned bounty hunter befriends the son of an outlaw he has killed.

UNCHARTED TERRITORY

Sartana (1968) FF—Ital./Ger.

John Garko
Klaus Kinski
Fernando Sancho
D: Frank Kramer (Gianfranco Parolini)

A gunfighter-vigilante known as the "Angel of Death" sets a trap for gold thieves.

UNCHARTED TERRITORY

Sartana Does Not Forgive (1968) FF—Sp./Ital.

Gilbert Roland
George Martin
Jack Elam
D: Alfonso Balcazar

Vigilante gunfighter, Sartana, avenges the deaths of his brother and his family.

Sartana in the Valley of Death (1970) FF—Ital.

William Berger
Wayde Preston
D: Roberto Mauri

A gunman is hired to break three brothers out of prison.

Sartana Kills Them All (1970) FF—Ital./Sp.

John Garko
William Bogart
D: Rafael Romero Marchent

Vigilante gunfighter, Sartana, tracks gunrunners.

Chief Rain-in-the-Face. When charged with killing Custer, he took refuge in Canada with Sitting Bull.

Saskatchewan (O'Rourke of the Royal Mounted) (1954) U-I ★★★◣

Alan Ladd
Shelley Winters
Robert Douglas
Hugh O'Brian
Jay Silverheels
D: Raoul Walsh

In the aftermath of Custer's defeat, an Indian-raised Mountie prevents a massacre. Filmed in Alberta, Canada.

—*You promised us guns and ammunition. Bring it now so my people can drive the Sioux from our land.*
—Jay Silverheels
Saskatchewan

Au ★★★◣
S ★★★◣
A ★★★◣

The Savage (1952) Paramount ★★◣

Charlton Heston
Susan Morrow
Peter Hanson
D: George Marshall

A white man raised by the Sioux becomes trapped between two cultures. Filmed in the Black Hills, South Dakota.

Au ★★◣
S ★★★
A ★★★

The Savage (1976) see The Great Gundown

Savage Gringo (1966) FF—Ital.

Ken Clark
Piero Lulli
D: Mario Brava with Antonio Romano

A cowboy becomes involved with a plot to murder the town sheriff.

Savage Guns (1961) FF—Ital./Sp./Brit.

Richard Basehart
Paquita Rico
Fernando Rey
D: Michael Carreras

An aging gunfighter teams with an American and his Mexican wife in Sonora to fight a Mexican land baron. The first "modern" Spaghetti Western.

The Savage Horde (1950) Republic

William Elliott
Adrian Booth
Grant Withers
Noah Beery, Jr.
Jim Davis
Bob Steele
D: Joseph Kane

A gunfighter helps ranchers fight a land baron. Filmed at Red Rock Canyon, CA.

Au ★★
S ★
A ★

Savage Land (1994) SLP

Corbin Bernsen
Graham Greene
Vivian Schilling
Martin Kove
D: Dean Hamilton

—All my life I dreamed of seein' the wild West.
—Narrator
Savage Land

Two women and two children outsmart outlaws pursuing their stagecoach. Family film. Filmed at Motion Picture Village, Millarville, Alberta

Au ★
S ★
A ★

Savage Red-Outlaw White see The Great Sundown

Savage Sam (1963) BV

Brian Keith
Tommy Kirk

Kevin Corcoran
Jeff York
Slim Pickens
D: Norman Tokar

A posse uses the son of Old Yeller to track
Apaches who kidnapped two children.
Disney production. Sequel to *Old Yeller*.

Au ★★┫

S ★★┫

A ★★┫

Savage Wilderness (1956) Columbia ★★★

Victor Mature
Guy Madison
Robert Preston
James Whitmore
Anne Bancroft
D: Anthony Mann

A trapper confronts a cavalry colonel
obsessed with destroying Red Cloud.

Au ★★★┫

S ★★★

A ★★★★┫

Scalawag (1970) Paramount ★

Kirk Douglas
Mark Lester
Neville Brand
Danny De Vito
D: Kirk Douglas

A boy and his sister accompany a peg-legged pirate
on a search for buried gold in Baja California.

Au ★

S ★

A ┫

Kea-Boat (Two Hatchet), Kiawa 1898.

The Scalphunters (1968) UA ★★★┫

Burt Lancaster
Shelley Winters
Telly Savalas
Ossie Davis
D: Sidney Pollack

A fur trader and an educated slave fight Kiowas
and scalphunters for the return of stolen furs.
Filmed in Durango, Mexico.

Au ★★★┫

S ★★★┫

A ★★★★

Scalplock (1966) Columbia

Dale Robertson
Robert Random
Diane Hyland
Sandra Smith
D: James Goldstone

A gambler decides to complete the construction of a half-built railroad that he wins in a card game. Pilot for the "Iron Horse" TV series.

Au
S
A

Scalps (1987) FF—Ital./Ger.

Vassili Karis
Mary Galan
D: Werner Knox (Bruno Mattei)

An evil Confederate colonel orders his soldiers to kidnap a Comanche chief's daughter.

UNCHARTED
TERRITORY

Scarlet Angel (1952) U-I

Yvonne De Carlo
Rock Hudson
Richard Denning
D: Sidney Salko

Robbed of his bankroll in New Orleans, a sea captain catches up to a dancehall girl in Fan Francisco.

Au
S
A

Ralph Morrison, hunter. Scalped by Cheyennes in 1868.

Scar Tissue (19??) NBC-TV/Universal

Richard Boone
Kurt Russell
Dick Haymes
D: ?

An aging lawman must prevent a young man from killing the father who deserted him.

UNCHARTED
TERRITORY

Scream (The Outing) (1985) CI/CFL/C-C

Pepper Martin
Hank Worden
Alvy Moore
Ethan Wayne
Julie Marine
Woody Strode
D: Byron Quisenberry

UNCHARTED
TERRITORY

The Sea of Grass (1947) MGM ★ ★ ★

Spencer Tracy
Katharine Hepburn
Melvin Douglas
Phyllis Thaxter
Harry Carey
D: Elia Kazan

When a New Mexico cattle baron enters a
range war, his wife has an affair with a
judge. From the Conrad Richter novel.
Filmed at Gallup, New Mexico.

Au ★ ★ ⯪

S ★ ★ ★

A ★ ★ ★ ⯪

*—He tried to tell me how he felt, how the grass
was somehow godly to him. He tried to tell me
and I didn't hear. And he was right.*
—Katharine Hepburn
The Sea of Grass

The Search (1956) WC

Clayton Moore
Jay Silverheels
Allen Pinson
John Crawford
D: Earl Bellamy

Compilation of three episodes of
"The Lone Ranger" TV series.

The Search (1960)

Joseph Cotton
Jim Davis
Martha Scott
D: Bernard McEveety

UNCHARTED
TERRITORY

*—Whatta ya want me to do, draw you a
picture—spell it out? Don't ever ask me!
Long as you live, don't ever ask me more!*
—John Wayne
The Searchers

The Searchers (1956) CVW/WB ★ ★ ★ ★

John Wayne
Jeffrey Hunter
Vera Miles
Ward Bond
Natalie Wood
Harry Carey, Jr.
Chief Thunder Cloud
D: John Ford

A Confederate veteran searches five years for
a girl captured by Comanches. Based on Alan
LeMay's novel. Filmed in Monument Valley, San
Juan River at Mexican Hat, UT, and Gunnison Valley,
CO. #33 Best of the West, #96 AFI GM, #4 IMDb, #1 LPFF.

Au ★ ★ ★ ⯪

S ★ ★ ★ ★

A ★ ★ ★ ★

John Wayne in *The Searchers*.

The Second Time Around (1961) 20ᵗʰ C. Fox

Debbie Reynolds
Steve Forrest
Andy Griffith
Juliet Prowse
D: Vincent Sherman

The New York widow who becomes
sheriff of a wild Arizona town.

Au

S

A

Secret of Captain O'Hara (1965) FF—Sp.

German Cobos
Marta Padovan
D: Arturo Ruiz Castillo

Rival cavalry officers face off over Indian policy and a woman.

UNCHARTED
TERRITORY

The Secret of Convict Lake (1951) 20ᵗʰ C. Fox

Glenn Ford
Gene Tierney
Ethel Barrymore
Lack Lambert
D: Michael Gordon

Escaped convicts arrive in a town full of women.

UNCHARTED
TERRITORY

Secrets (1933) MPP

Mary Pickford
Leslie Howard
C. Aubrey Smith
Blanche Frederici
D: Frank Borzage

A woman contends with the discovery of her
husband's affair. Pickford's final role.

UNCHARTED
TERRITORY

Seminole Uprising (1955) Columbia

George Montgomery
Karin Booth
William Fawcett
D: Earl Bellamy

The Army chases Florida Indians in Texas.
Filmed in Sedona, Arizona.

Au ★★★

S ★★

A

September Gun (1983) CBS-TV ★ ★ ★

Robert Preston
Patty Duke Astin
Christopher Lloyd
Sally Kellerman
D: Don Taylor

An aging gunfighter helps a nun transport
Apache orphans. Filmed at Old Tucson.

Au ★ ★ ★

S ★ ★ ★

A ★ ★ ★ ◄

—[I plead] not guilty to both charges, Sir.
—Woody Strode
Sergeant Rutledge

Sergeant Rutledge (1960) WB ★ ★ ★ ★

Jeffrey Hunter
Constance Towers
Billie Burke
Woody Strode
Juano Hernandez
D: John Ford

A buffalo soldier is accused of rape.
Filmed at Monument Valley, and San
Juan River at Mexican Hat, Utah.
#37 Best of the West.

Au ★ ★ ★ ◄

S ★ ★ ★ ★

A ★ ★ ★ ★

Woody Strode as Sergeant Rutledge.

Sergeants 3 (1962) UA

Frank Sinatra
Dean Martin
Sammy Davis, Jr.
Peter Lawford
Joey Bishop
D: John Sturges

Three brawling sergeants
establish a frontier outpost.
Filmed at Kanub, Utah.

The Settlers see The New Land

Seven Alone (1974) D-DP

Dewey Martin
Aldo Ray
Ann Coolings
Dean Smith
D: Earl Bellamy

When their parents are killed, seven children
continue their 2000 mile trek to Oregon.

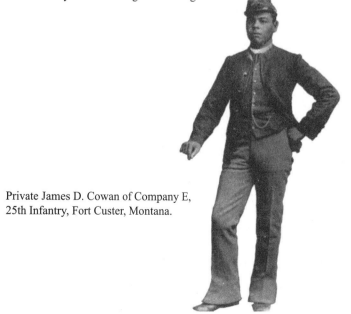

Private James D. Cowan of Company E,
25th Infantry, Fort Custer, Montana.

Seven Dollars on the Red (1968) FF—Ital./Sp.

Anthony Steffen
Elisa Montes
Fernando Sancho
D: Alberto Cardone (Albert Cardiff)

A gunman avenges his wife's murder.

7 Faces of Dr. Lao (1964) MGM

Tony Randall
Barbara Eden
Arthur O'Connell
D: George Pal

A Chinese magician with the ability to transform himself
into seven mythical characters saves a town from a crooked
land baron. Oscar nomination for special visual effects.

Seven for Pancho Villa (1966) FF—Sp.

John Ericson
Nuria Torray
Ricardo Palacios
D: Josè M. Elorrieta

Rescued by a ban of supporters, Pancho Villa is nursed
back to health in order to resume the revolution.

Seven Guns for Timothy (1966) FF—Sp./Ital.

Sean Flynn
Fernando Sancho
D: Rod Gilbert

After being run off by bandidos, a mining foreman
recruits convicts to return with him for revenge.

Seven Guns from Texas (1964) FF—Sp./Ital.

Paul Piaget
Robert Hundar (Claudio Undari)
Fernando Sancho
D: Joaquin Romero Marchent

Three gunmen and a Chinese cook escort a woman to El Paso.

Seven Guns to Mesa (1958) AA

Carles Quinlivan
Lola Albright
James Griffith

Jay Alder
D: Edward Dein

Outlaws hold stagecoach passengers hostage.
Filmed at Chatsworth, California.

Au

S

A

Seven Hours of Gunfire (1964) FF—Sp./Ital.
Rick Van Nutter
Adrian Hoven
D: Josè Hernandez (Joaquin Romero Marchent)

Buffalo Bill, Wild Bill Hickok, and Calamity Jane attempt
to resolve hostilities between settlers and Indians.

Seven Men From Now (1956) Batjac/WB
Randolph Scott
Gail Russell
Lee Marvin
Stuart Whitman
D: Bud Boetticher

A man tracks the outlaws who murdered his wife. Burt
Kennedy's first screenplay. Filmed in the Alabama Hills.

Randolph Scott in *Seven Men From Now.*

Seven Nuns in Kansas City (1973) FF—Ital.
Lea Gargano
Enzo Maggio
D: Marcello Zeanile

Hungry prospectors attempt to overrun a convent.

Seven Pistols for a Gringo (1967) FF—Ital./Sp.
Gèrard Landry
Dan Harrison
Fernando Rubio
D: Juan Xiol Marchel (Ignacio Iquino)

A man is framed for the murder of a card shark.

7th Cavalry (1956) SB/Columbia
Randolph Scott
Barbara Hale
Jay C. Flippen
Harry Carey, Jr.
D: Joseph H. Lewis

In the aftermath of Custer's defeat, a

Jay C. Flippen and Randolph Scott in *7th Cavalry.*

captain volunteers for burial detail.

Au ★

S ★★

A ★★

Seven Ways From Sundown (1960) U-I ★★✦

Audie Murphy
Barry Sullivan
Venetia Stevenson
John McIntire
D: Harry Keller

A green Texas Ranger tracks his brother's murderer.
Story by Clair Huffaker. Filmed near Las Vegas, NV.

Au ★✦

S ★✦

A ★★

> —*Seven, when I pass on to glory, my one wish will be to go with a pocket full of cigars. Where I'm goin' they'll be no problem lightin' 'em.*
> —Barry Sullivan
> *Seven Ways From Sundown*

Shade of Zorro (1963) FF—Ital./Sp.

Frank Latimore
Mary Anderson
Raffaella Carra
D: Francesco De Masi

UNCHARTED TERRITORY

Shadow of Chikara (Wishbone Cutter) 1978 Howco Prod.

Joe Don Baker
Sondra Locke
Ted Kneeley
Slim Pickens
D: Earl E. Smith

Two Confederates search for diamonds protected by a curse.

UNCHARTED TERRITORY

Shadow of Sartana…Shadow of Your Death (1968) FF—Ital.

Jeff Cameron
Dennys Colt
D: Sean O'Neal (Demofilo Fidani)

Wanted for vigilante activities, Sartana, is offered amnesty
for eliminating a corrupt sheriff and two outlaw brothers.

UNCHARTED TERRITORY

Shadow of Zorro (1963) FF—Sp./Ital.

Frank Latimore
Maria Luz Galicia
D: Joaquin Romero Marchent

El Zorro protects the town of San Pueblo from bandidos.

The Shadow Riders (Louis L'Amour's "The Shadow Riders") (1982) CBS-TV

Tom Selleck
Sam Elliott
Ben Johnson
Katherine Ross
Harry Carey, Jr.
D: Andrew McLaglen

Brothers attempt to rescue their sisters from white slavery in Mexico. From the Louie L'Amour novel. Filmed at Columbia, California and Sonora, Mexico.

Au ★★★★
S ★★★
A ★★★★

Shalako (1968) FF—Brit./Fr.

Sean Connery
Brigitte Bardot
Woody Strode
D: Edward Dmytryk

An army scout rescues a French countess from Apaches. Based on the Louie L'Amour novel. Filmed at Almería, Andalucía, Spain.

Au ★★★
S ★★★
A ★★★

Shane (1953) Paramount

Alan Ladd
Jean Arthur
Van Heflin
Brandon De Wilde
Jack Palance
Ben Johnson
Edgar Buchanan
D: George Stevens

A former gunfighter takes up his guns to protect a Wyoming settler from cattlemen. Inspired by the Johnson County War. Technical advise by Joe De Yong. Montgomery Clift (Shane) and William Holden (Joe Starrett) originally cast, but dropped out early from the project. Believing that it would fail at the box office, Paramount tried unsuccessfully to sell the project during production to Howard Hughes. From the Jack Schaefer novel. Oscar nominations for best picture, supporting actor for De Wilde and Palance, direction, and writing: screenplay. Oscar for best cinematography: color. Filmed outside Jackson Hole, Wyoming. Some filming in Big Bear, California. #13 Best of the West, #69 AFI GM, #16 IMDb, #3 LPFF.

Au ★★★★
S ★★★★★
A ★★★★★

—I think he cares alot, he just…He, he don't know how to say it.
—Tom Selleck
The Shadow Riders

Sean Connery and Brigitte Bardot in *Shalako.*

Alan Ladd and Brandon De Wilde in *Shane.*

—Shaaaane, come baaaack!
—Brandon De Wilde
Shane

Shango (1969) FF—Ital.

Anthony Steffen
Eduardo Fajardo
D: Edward G. Muller (Edoardo Mulargia)

Renegade Confederates join border
town outlaws to search for gold.

Shaughnessy (Louie L'Amour's Shaughnessy) (1996) CBS-TV ★ ★ ◖

Matthew Settle
Linda Kazlowski
Tom Bower
Stuart Whitman
D: Michael Rhodes

A young Irishman flees New York City and becomes the marshal
of a Kansas town. Adapted from L'Amour's, *The Iron Marshal*.
Filmed in Tuolumne County, California.

*—Maybe I'm, heh, like an atheist.
Sometimes I've even got doubtin' my
own disbelief.*

—Linda Kazlowski
Shaughnessy

Au ★ ★ ★ ★

S ★ ★

A ★ ★ ◖

She Came to the Valley (1977)

Ronee Blakley
Dean Stockwell
Scott Glenn
Freddy Fender
D: Albert Band

The Sheepman (1958) MGM ★ ★ ◖

Glenn Ford
Shirley MacLaine
Leslie Neilsen
Edgar Buchanan
Pernell Roberts
Slim Pickens
D: George Marshall

A sheep rancher settles in cattle country. Oscar
nomination for writing: original story and screenplay.

Au ★ ★

S ★ ★ ◖

A ★ ★ ★

Shep of the Painted Hills see The Painted Hills

The Sheriff see The Silver Star

Sheriff of Rock Spring (1971) FF—Ital.

Richard Harrison
Cosetta Greco

A 19th century sheepman poses with coyote
pelts taken with his 1876 Winchester.

D: Anthony Green (Primo Zeglio)

A retired gunfighter becomes
the sheriff of a peaceful town.

Sheriff Was a Lady (1965) FF—Ger.

Freddy Quinn
Mamie Van Doran
D: Sobey Martin (Carlo Croccolo)

A gunman avenges the death of his parents.

Sheriff with the Gold (1966) FF—Ital./Sp.

Louis McJulian
Jacques Berthier
D: Richard Kean (Osvaldo Civirani)

A sheriff rescues an outlaw from execution
only to use him in a gold robbery.

John Wayne in *She Wore a Yellow Ribbon*.

Sheriff Won't Shoot (1967) FF—Ital./Fr./Brit.

Mickey Hargitay
Vincente Cashino
D: J. Luis Monter

A sheriff discovers that his
younger brother is an outlaw.

—Never apologize, Mister. It's a sign of weakness
—John Wayne
She Wore a Yellow Ribbon

She Wore a Yellow Ribbon (1949) Argosy/RKO ★ ★ ★ ★ ◖

John Wayne
Joanne Dru
John Agar
Ben Johnson
Harry Carey, Jr.
Victor McLaglen
Chief John Big Tree
Chief Sky Eagle
D: John Ford

In the aftermath of Custer's defeat, a cavalry
officer is reluctant to retire. Based on James
Bellah's short story, "War Party." Oscar for
best cinematography. Filmed in Monument
Valley and San Juan River, Mexican Hat, Utah.
#14 Best of the West, #20 IMDb.

Au ★ ★ ★ ◖
S ★ ★ ★ ★ ★
A ★ ★ ★ ★ ◖

Ben Johnson (left) and John Wayne (center) in *She Wore a Yellow Ribbon*.

434

The Shooter (Desert Shooter) (1997)

Michael Dudikoff
Randy Travis
Valerie Widman
Peter Sherayko
D: Fred Olen Ray

A drifter stands up to the family controlling a town.

Shoot, Gringo…Shoot! see The Longest Hunt

The Shooting (1966) Santa Clara

Warren Oates
Will Hutchins
Millie Perkins
Jack Nicholson
D: Monte Hellman

A woman hires a bounty hunter to lead her through the desert.

The Shooting (1971) JHHE

Jack Nicholson
Millie Perkins
Warren Oates
Will Hutchins
D: Monte Hellman

Three gunmen and a woman run out of water in the desert. Originally televised in 1966 before theatrical release. Filmed at Kanab, UT.

Au ★★
S ★
A ★★

—Lord almighty, I'm so hungry I could chaw off my own lung.
—Will Hutchins
The Shooting

—I won't be wronged, I won't be insulted and I won't be laid a hand on. I don't do these things to other people and I require the same from them.
—John Wayne
The Shootist

The Shootist (1976) Paramount

John Wayne
Lauren Bacall
Ron Howard
James Stewart
Richard Boone
Hugh O'Brian
Bill McKinney
Harry Morgan
John Carradine
Scatman Crothers
D: Don Siegel

A gunfighter insures the dignity of his own death. John Wayne's finest and final performance. Based on Glendon Swarthout's novel. Oscar nomination for art direction-set direction. Filmed in and around Carson City, Nevada, and at the Burbank Studios, California. #3 Best of the West, #33 IMDb, #6 LPFF.

Au ★★★★★

Lauren Bacall and John Wayne in *The Shootist*.

S
A ★★★★★

Shoot Joe, and Shoot Again (1972) FF—Ital.

Richard Harrison
Josè Torres
D: Hal Brady (Emilio P. Miraglia)

A gunman is blinded by outlaws, but regains
his sight in time for a showdown.

Shoot Out (1971) Universal

Gregory Peck
Pat Quinn
Robert F. Lyons
Susan Tyrell
Arthur Hunnicutt
Dawn Lyn
D: Henry Hathaway

An ex-convict seeks revenge against
his back-shooting partner.
Filmed in Chama, New Mexico.

Au ★★
S ★★★
A ★★★★

Shoot Out at Big Sag (1962) Parallel

Walter Brennan
Leif Erickson
Luana Patten
Chris Robinson
D: Roger Kay

A preacher tries to run off settlers and his son.
Unsuccessful pilot for the "Barbed Wire" TV series.

Shoot-Out at Medicine Bend (1957) WB

Randolph Scott
James Craig
Angie Dickinson
Dani Crayne
James Garner
D: Richard L. Bare

A Union veteran discovers who sold
his dead brother faulty ammunition.

Au ★★★
S ★★★
A ★★★

—You are tougher than whang leather.
—Gregory Peck
Shoot-Out

Dawn Lyn and Gregory Peck in *Shoot Out.*

436

Shootout in a One-Dog Town (1974) ABC-TV/H-BP

Richard Crenna
Stephanie Powers
Jack Elam
Michael Ansara
D: Burt Kennedy

A small-town banker stands up to bank robbers.
Filmed at Los Organos, Mexico. From a Larry Cohen story.

Shoot the Living...Pray for the Dead (1971) FF—Ital.

Klaus Kinski
Victoria Zinny
D: Joseph Warren (Giuseppe Vari)

A gunman avenges the murder of his parents.

Shoot the Sun Down (1981) JADFI

Christopher Walken
Geoffrey Lewis
Margot Kidder
Bo Brundin
D: David Leeds

In the 1830s, goldseekers and an indentured
servent search for Montezuma's treasure.

Shoot to Kill (1963) FF—Sp.

Edmund Purdom
Frank Latimore
Fernando Sancho
D: Ramon Torrado

A foreman falls in love with the rancher's daughter.

Short Grass (1950) AA

Rod Cameron
Cathy Downs
Johnny Mack Brown
Alan Hale, Jr.
D: Lesley Selander

A marshal and a cowboy confront an ambitious rancher.
Story by Tom Blackburn.

Shotgun (1955) AA

Sterling Hayden
Yvonne De Carlo
Zachary Scott
D: Lesley Selander

A deputy and a bounty hunter track a marshal's murderer.

Filmed in Sedona, Arizona.

Shotgun (1969) FF—Ital.

Tab Hunter
Erika Blanc
D: Roberto Mauri

A sheriff avenges the murder of his wife.

Shots Ring Out! (1965) FF—Ital./Sp.

Paul Piaget
Fred Canow
D: Augustin Navarro

A gunfighter is falsely accused of a series of murders.

The Showdown (1950) Republic

Bill Elliott
Walter Brennan
Marie Windsor
Henry Morgan
Jim Davis
Yakima Canutt
D: Dorrell and Stuart McGowan

A trail boss joins a cattle drive to
uncover his brother's murderer.

Au ★ ❙

S ★ ❙

A ★ ★

Showdown (1963) Universal

Audie Murphy
Kathleen Crowley
Charles Drake
Harold J. Stone
Skip Homeier
Strother Martin
D: R.G. Springsteen

Two escaped convicts head for Mexico.
Filmed near Lone Pine, California.

Showdown (1973) Universal

Rock Hudson
Dean Martin
Susan Clark
Donald Moffat
Ed Begley, Jr.
D: George Seaton

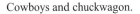

Cowboys and chuckwagon.

*—Look, there's a force or a power, or whatever
you want to call it, that sees that a man gets
what he deserves far better than we can. I once
heard a preacher call it, it retribution.*

—Walter Brennan
The Showdown

Old friends find themselves on opposite sides of the law.
Filmed at Ghost Ranch, New Mexico.

Au

S ★★★

A ★★★✦

Showdown at Abilene (1956) U-I

Jock Mahoney
Martha Myer
Lyle Bettger
David Janssen
D: Charles Haas

A gunshy veteran returns home from the Civil War to discover his girl
is with his friend. Filmed at Morrison Ranch, Agoura, California.

Au ★★

S ★★

A ★★

Showdown at Boot Hill (1958) RF/20th C. Fox

Charles Bronson
Robert Hutton
John Carradine
Carole Matthews
D: Gene Fowler, Jr.

A marshal shoots an outlaw in a town where he is not welcome.

Au ★★✦

S ★★

A ★★

> *—A barber did that to a fella once [cut his nose off]. Stuck it back on, he got it on upside down. Every time the fella sneezed, he blew his hat off. When it rained, he drowned!*
> —John Carradine
> *Showdown at Boot Hill*

Showdown at Williams Creek (1991) Republic

Donnelly Rhodes
Tim Burlinson
D: Allan Kroeker

An Irish officer survives in the Northwest Territory. Based on a true story.

Showdown for a Badman (1972) FF—Ital.

Klaus Kinski
Hunt Powers
Jeff Cameron
D: Miles Deem (Demofilo Fidani)

A gunman avenges the murder of his parents.

UNCHARTED
TERRITORY

The Siege at Red River (1954) Pan.Prod./20th C. Fox

Van Johnson
Joanne Dru

Richard Boone
Milburn Stone
D: Rudolph Mate

A Confederate and a renegade compete for stolen
Gatling guns. Filmed in Professor Valley (Locomotive
Rock), Colorado River, and Castle Valley, Utah

Audie Murphy and Wanda Hendrix in *Sierra*.

Sierra (1950) U-I

Audie Murphy
Wanda Hendrix
Dean Jagger
Burl Ives
Jim Arness
D: Alfred E. Greene

A frontier lawyer sets out to prove the
innocence of an outlaw and his son.
Filmed at Kanub, Utah.

Au ★★◣
S ★★
A ★★◣

Sierra Baron (1958) 20ᵗʰ C. Fox

Brian Keith
Rick Jason
Rita Gam
Mala Powers
D: James B. Clark

A crooked land baron hires gunfighters to steal land.
Story by Tom Blackburn.

Sierra Passage (1951) Mono.

Wayne Morris
Lola Albright
Lloyd Corrigan
Alan Hale, Jr.
D: Frank McDonald

A gunman postpones his marriage in order to avenge his father's murder.
Story by Tom Blackburn.

Sierra Stranger (1957) Columbia ◤

Howard Duff
Gloria McGhee
Dick Foran
D: Lee Sholem

An outlaw turns on the good Samaritan

who saved him from claim jumpers.

Au

S

A

Sign of Coyote (1964) FF—Ital./Sp.

Fernand Canova
Maria Luz Galicia
D: Mario Caiano

A California "Robin Hood" opposes an oppressive governor.

The Sign of Zorro (1960) BV

Guy Williams
Henry Calvin
Gene Sheldon
Romney Brent
D: Norman Foster, Lewis R. Foster

Zorro fights for justice. Compiled from the first 13 Disney TV episodes.
Based on the writings of Johnston McCulley.

Au

S

A

Sign of Zorro (1964) FF—Ital./Sp.

Sean Flynn
Folco Lulli
D: Mario Caiano

Zorro's father is murdered by a dictator.

Signora dell 'Ovest see Girl of the Golden West (1942)

Silent Barriers see The Great Barriers

The Silent Gun (1969) ABC-TV/Paramount

Lloyd Bridges
John Beck
Ed Begley
Pernell Roberts
D: Michael Caffey

After shooting a child, a sheriff carries an unloaded weapon.

Silent Tongue (1993) FF—Fr./Neth./Brit./U.S.

Richard Harris
Sheila Tousey
Alan Bates
River Phoenix

Tantoo Cardinal
D: Sam Shephard

Silverado (1985) Columbia

Kevin Kline
Scott Glenn
Rosanna Arquette
John Cleese
Kevin Costner
Brian Dennehy
Danny Glover
D: Lawrence Kasdan

Four drifters shoot it out with a crooked sheriff
and his gang. Costner's film debut. Oscar nominations
for best sound and scoring: original music. Filmed at
the Cook Ranch (a.k.a. Silverado Set) NM. #49 IMDb.

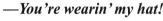

—You're wearin' my hat!
—Kevin Kline
Silverado

Au ★★★★
S ★★★
A ★★★★

Silver City (High Vermilion) (1951) Paramount

Edmond O'Brien
Yvonne De Carlo
Richard Arlen
Edgar Buchanan
D: Byron Haskins

A woman and her father turn to a miner for help when threatened by a gunfighter.
Based on a Luke Short story.

Silver Devil see Wild Horse

Silver Dollar (1932) FN

Edward G. Robinson
Bebe Daniels
Aline MacMahon
Jobyna Howland
D: Alfred E. Green

A Kansas farmer becomes a Colorado prospector.

The Silver Horde (1930) RKO-Radio

Evelyn Brent
Louis Wolheim
Jean Arthur
Joel McCrea
Raymond Hatton
Blanche Sweet
D: George Archainbaud

A saloon girl helps a salmon fisherman keep his business.

442

Filmed on the Alaskan coast.

Silver Lode (1954) RKO

John Payne
Dan Duryea
Jack Hale
Harry Carey, Jr.
Stuart Whitman
D: Allan Dwan

A man has two hours to prove
that he is not a murderer.

Au ★★★⯪

S ★★★★⯪

A ★★★★

Silver Queen (1942) UA

George Brent
Priscilla Lane
Bruce Cabot
D: Lloyd Bacon

A girl gambles to pay off her father's debts.
Oscar nomination for art direction-interior
decoration: B&W, and scoring: drama/comedy.

Lady gambler playing keno.

Silver River (1948) WB

Errol Flynn
Ann Sheridan
Thomas Mitchell
D: Raoul Walsh

A silver magnate pursues a married woman and builds
an empire. Filmed at Bronson Canyon, Griffith Park, CA.

*—A man is only lonely when he depends on
other people, Mr. Beck—I don't.*

—Errol Flynn
Silver City

Au ★★⯪

S ★★★★⯪

A ★★★★

Silver Saddle (1978) FF—Ital.

Giuliano Gemma
Sven Valsecchi
D: Lucio Fulci

A young boy turns gunfighter after the murder of his father.

The Silver Star (The Sheriff) (1955) Lippert

Edgar Buchanan
Marie Windsor
Lon Chaney, Jr.

D: Richard Bartlett

A reluctant sheriff hides from three gunfighters.

The Silver Whip (1953) 20ᵗʰ C. Fox

Dale Robertson
Rory Calhoun
Robert Wagner
D: Harmon Jones

When a green stage driver is deputized, he must choose between two kinds of law and order.

Au ★★

S ★★◀

A ★★★

—Law work's kinda slow sometimes, Jess. It's like fishin'. Nothing we can do except keep the hooks out and keep 'em baited.
—Rory Calhoun
Silver Whip

The Singer Not the Song (1961) FF—Brit.

John Mills
Dirk Bogarde
Mylene Demongeot
D: Roy Baker

An atheistic bandido opposes a priest for control of a village.

Singing Guns (1950) Palomar/Republic

Vaughn Monroe
Ella Raines
Walter Brennan
Ward Bond
D: R.G. Springsteen

A singing outlaw is reformed by a saloon keeper and a doctor.

Au ★★

S ★★◀

A ★★★

—A man is tempered by by his setbacks, not by his victories.
—Walter Brennan
Singing Guns

Sin Town (1942) Universal

Constance Bennett
Broderick Crawford
Patric Knowles
Ward Bond
Andy Devine
D: Ray Enright

Two conmen arrive in a town where the newspaper editor has been murdered.

Siringo (1994) Siringo P.

Brad Johnson
Chad Lowe
Stephen Macht
D: Kevin Kremin

A half-Apache lawman tracks a murderer.

Au ★★★

S ★★

A ★★

—Don't worry. I'll get you back. If I got to carry you up the gallows myself, I'll get you back.
—Brad Johnson
Siringo

Sitting Bull (1954) UA

Dale Robertson
Mary Murphy
J. Carroll Naish
Iron Eyes Cody
John Hamilton
D: Sidney Salko

A cavalry major seeks just treatment for Sitting Bull and his people. Filmed at the Iverson Movie Ranch.

Au ★◖

S ★★

A ★★

J. Carroll Naish as Sitting Bull

Six Black Horses (1962) U-I

Audie Murphy
Dan Duryea
Joan O'Brien
Bob Steele
D: Harry Keller

A widow avenges the murder of her husband. Screenplay by Burt Kennedy. Filmed near Las Vegas, Nevada.

UNCHARTED TERRITORY

Six-Gun Law (1963) BV

Robert Loggia
James Dunn
Lynn Bari
Annette (Funicello)
James Drury
D: Christian Nyby

An English rancher is accused of murder. Compilation of Disney episodes of "The Nine Lives of Elfego Baca" mini-series released theatrically.

UNCHARTED TERRITORY

Sitting Bull

Skipalong Rosenbloom (1951) (The Square Shooter) (1953) ELC/UA

Maxie Rosenbloom
Max Baer
Jackie Coogan
D: Sam Newfield

A gunfighter confronts a badman.

A Sky Full of Stars for a Roof (1968) FF—Ital.

Giuliano Gemma
Mario Adorf
D: Giulio Petroni

Two drifters wander through the West.

Slaughter Trail (1951) RKO

Brian Donlevy
Gig Young
Virginia Gray
Andy Devine
D: Irving Allen

An army officer must prevent an outlaw gang from disturbing the peace with the Navajos. Filmed at Corriganville, CA.

Au ★⚹

S ★⚹

A ★★

Smoke in the Wind (1975) Gamalex Prod.

John Ashley
John Russell
Myron Healey
Walter Brennan
Susan Houston
D: Joseph Kane

A family of mountainmen returning from the Civil War are mistaken for traitors.

Smoke Signal (1955) U-I

Dana Andrews
Piper Laurie
Rex Reason
Milburn Stone
D: Jerry Hopper

Survivors of an Indian attack escape down the Colorado River. Filmed at Big Bend of the Colorado River, Professor Valley, Ida Gulch, and San Juan River, Utah.

Au ★★

S ★★⚹

A ★★⚹

Snowfire (1958) AA

Don Megowan
Molly Megowan

♪
—You could only here the sound of the hoofbeats on the ground and the bandits goin' round the Slaughter Trail.
—Theme song
Slaughter Trail

Panambono and Mitiwara, Mojave guides on the Wheeler Survey.

—I gotta do it. It's gotta be set right about Halliday. It's gotta be set right.
—Milburn Stone
Smoke Signal

446

Claire Kelly
D: Dorrell and Stuart McGowan

When her father captures a stallion, a young girl sets him free.

Soldier Blue (1970) AE

Candice Bergen
Peter Strauss
Donald Pleasence
Bob Carraway
D: Ralph Nelson

The two sole survivors of a Cheyenne attack
must find their way back to civilization.

The Soldiers of Pancho Villa (La Cucaracha) (1958) FF—Mex.

Dolores Del Rio
Mario Felix
Emilio Fernandez
D: Ismael Rodriguez

Two women love a peon follower of Pancho Villa. Dubbed.

Something Big (1971) NG

Dean Martin
Brian Keith
Honor Blackman
Carol White
Ben Johnson
Merlin Olsen
Harry Carey, Jr.
Bob Steele
D: Andrew V. McLaglen

"The Midday Meal."

An inept colonel attempts to prevent an outlaw from pulling off his last big heist.

Something for a Lonely Man (1968) NBC-TV/Universal

Dan Blocker
Susan Clark
John Dehner
Warren Oates
Edgar Buchanan
Iron Eyes Cody
D: Don Taylor

A blacksmith attempts to redeem himself in the eyes of the people he brought west.

Song of the Caballero (1930) Universal

Ken Maynard
Doris Hill
Francis Ford
Frank Rice
D: Harry Joe Brown

A caballero seeks justice in old California.

Sonny and Jed (A Criminal Story of the Far West) (1974) FF—Ital./Sp./Ger.

Tomas Milan
Susan George
Telly Savalas
D: Sergio Corbucci

An escaped convict joins a young girl to rob their way across Mexico.

Son of a Gunfighter (1966) FF—Sp./U.S. ★

Russ Tamblyn
Kieron Moore
Fernando Rey
D: Paul Landres

A gunfighter avenges the death of his mother.

Au ★

S ★

A ✦

Son of Belle Starr (1953) AA ★✦

Keith Larson
Dona Drake
Peggie Castle
D: Frank Mc Donald

An outlaw's son attempts to clear his family name.

Au ★✦

S ★✦

A ★✦

—I never met a lady.
—Keith Larson
Son of Belle Starr

Son of Django (1967) FF—Ital.

Guy Madison
Gabriela Tinti
D: Osvaldo Civirani

A gunman is joined by a reverend to avenge his family's murder.

Son of Jesse James (1965) FF—Ital.

Robert Hundar
Mercedes Alonso
Adrian Hoven
D: A. Del Amo

Jesse James' son is falsely accused of murder.

Son of the Morning Star (1991) ABC-TV/Republic

Gary Cole
Rosanna Arquette
Dean Stockwell
Rodney Grant
D: Mike Robe

General Custer carries on his war against the plains Indians. Two-part mini-series. Filmed at Badlands National, Park, SD. #29 Best of the West.

Au ★★★★⯪

S ★★★★

A ★★★★

—*The Crow called him Son of the Morning Star who attacks at dawn…I remember him. I saw him die.*
—Kimberly Norris (Kate Big Head)
Son of the Morning Star

"A Reconnaissance."

Son of Zorro (1973) FF—Ital./Sp.

Robert Widmark (Alberto Dell'Acqua)
Fernando Sancho
D: Gianfranco Baldanello

Rare.

UNCHARTED TERRITORY

The Sons of Katie Elder (1965) Paramount

John Wayne
Dean Martin
Martha Hyer
George Kennedy
Dennis Hopper
Strother Martin
D: Henry Hathaway

Four brothers reunite at their mother's funeral only to discover the family ranch swindled and their father murdered. Filmed in Durango, Mexico. #91 Best of the West.

Au ★★★⯪

S ★★★★

A ★★★★

John Wayne and Dean Martin in *The Sons of Katie Elder.*

Sons of the Saddle (1930) Universal

Ken Maynard
Doris Hill
Francis Ford
Joe Girard
D: Harry Joe Brown

A ranch foreman and his friend love the boss's daughter.

UNCHARTED TERRITORY

The Soul of Nigger Charley (1973) Paramount

Fred Williamson
D'Urville Martin
Denise Nicholas
Pedro Armendariz, Jr.
Dick Farnsworth

James Beckwourth

The Faces of the African American Frontiersman

Nat Love

Bill Pickett

Fred Williamson and D'Urville Martin in *The Soul of Nigger Charley*

450

Boyd "Red" Morgan
D: Larry G. Spangler

Two freed slaves and a bandido attempt to free slaves
from Confederates living in Mexico. Sequel to
The Legend of Nigger Charley. Filmed at Old Tucson.

Soul Soldiers see The Red, White and Black

South of Heaven West of Hell (2000) MMF

Dwight Yoakam
Vince Vaughn
Bridget Fonda
Billy Bob Thornton
Peter Fonda
D: Dwight Yoakam

A lawman tracks a psychopath and his gang.
Music by Dwight Yoakam. Filmed at Old Tucson
(Mescal), and Sharps Ranch, Arizona.

Au ★★★
S ★
A ★★

*—I don't know if I'm certain of my existence,
Taylor…only my intentions.*
—Dwight Yoakam
South of Heaven West of Hell

South of Hell Mountain (1971) CF

Anna Stewart
Martin J. Kelly
D: William Sachs, Louis Lehman

Three outlaws hold two women hostage in their mountain cabin.

South of San Antone see San Antone

South of St. Louis (1949) WB

Joel McCrea
Alexis Smith
Zachary Scott
Dorothy Malone
Bob Steele
D: Ray Enright

Ranchers avenge the burning of their homes by Union guerrillas.

Southwest Passage (Camels West) (1954) Small/UA

John Ireland
Joanne Dru
Rod Cameron
D: Ray Nazarro

A scout charting a new passage to California is bent on
proving that camels are practical frontier transportation.

Specialists (1969) FF—Ital./Fr./Ger.

Johnny Hallyday
Sylvie Fennec
D: Sergio Corbucci

A gunfighter defends a town against a dope-smoking gang of outlaws.

The Spikes Gang (1974) UA

Lee Marvin
Gary Grimes
Ron Howard
Charlie Martin Smith
Noah Beery (Jr.)
D: Richard Fleischer

When three farm boys nurse a gunshot bank
robber back to health, he teaches them his trade.

Au ★★★
S ★★
A ★★

Spirit of the Wind (1980) RP

Pius Savage
Chief Dan George
Slim Pickens
George Chutesi
D: Ralph Liddle

A young handicapped boy achieves his goals.

The Spoilers (1930) Paramount

Gary Cooper
Kay Johnson
Betty Compson
William "Stage" Boyd
Harry Green
D: Edward Carewe

A crooked gold commissioner and a cheated prospector
fight over a Yukon saloon girl. Remake of the 1914
silent version. Based on Rex Beach's novel.

The Spoilers (1942) Universal ★★★

Marlene Dietrich
Randolph Scott
John Wayne
Harry Carey
D: Ray Enright

Remake of the 1930 version.
Filmed at Lake Arrowhead, CA.

Au ★★★

Randolph Scott, John Wayne and Marlene Dietrich in *The Spoilers.*

S ★★★
A ★★★★⯪

The Spoilers (1956) U-I ✡✡

Ann Baxter
Jeff Chandler
Rory Calhoun
Ray Danton
Wallace Ford
Bob Steele
D: Jesse Hibbs

Remake of the 1942 version.

Au ✡✡

S ✡✡

A ✡✡

—A woman doesn't run out on the man she loves. She sticks with him—win or lose!
—Marlene Dietrich
The Spoilers

Springfield Rifle (1952) WB ✡✡✡

Gary Cooper
Phyllis Thaxter
Lon Chaney, Jr.
Alan Hale, Jr.
Fess Parker
D: Andrè De Toth

A double agent attempts to foil a scheme to steal Union horses. Filmed in the Alabama Hills.

—Men have to do strange things sometimes that they don't like to tell their wives about. It has nothing to do with not trusting them.
—Gary Cooper
Springfield Rifle

Au ✡✡

S ✡✡✡

A ✡✡✡

The Square Shooter see Skipalong Rosenbloom

The Squaw Man (The White Man) (1931) MGM

Warner Baxter
Lupe Velez
Eleanor Boardman
Charles Bickford
D: Cecil B. DeMille

An English Lord heads west and marries an Indian woman.

UNCHARTED
TERRITORY

Stagecoach (1939) UA ✡✡✡⯪

Claire Trevor
John Wayne
Andy Devine
John Carradine
Thomas Mitchell
Louise Platt
George Bancroft
Bill Cody
Yakima Canutt
James Mason

John Wayne in *Stagecoach*.

Chief White Horse
Chief Big Tree
D: John Ford

A stagecoach full of misfits travel through
Apache country. Based on Ernest Haycox's
short story, "Stage to Lordsburg." Nominated
for best picture, direction, film editing, art
direction, and cinematography: B&W. Best
supporting actor Oscar for Mitchell and best
scoring: original song score and/or adaptation.
Filmed in Monument Valley and the Iverson Movie
Location Ranch. The most over rated Western
ever made. #63 AFI GM, #10 IMDb, #5 LPFF.

Au ★★★

S ★★★★

A ★★★★

—Well, there's some things a man just can't run away from.
—John Wayne
Stagecoach

Stagecoach (1966) 20ᵗʰ C. Fox

Ann-Margret
Red Buttons
Mike Connors
Alex Cord
Bing Crosby
Robert Cummings
Van Hefflin
Slim Pickens
Stefanie Powers
Keenan Wynn
D: Gordon Douglas

Remake of the 1939 version. Filmed in Colorado.

Au ★★★

S ★★▪

A ★★★

Stagecoach (1986) RKP/Plantation P./HE/CBS-TV

Willie Nelson
Kris Kristofferson
Johnny Cash
Waylon Jennings
Elizabeth Ashley
Anthony Franciosa
June Carter Cash
Lash LaRue
D: Ted Post

Made for TV remake of the 1939
version. Filmed at Old Tucson.

Au ★★▪

S ★★

A ★★

Stagecoach to Dancer's Rock (1962) U-I

Warren Stevens
Martin Landau
Jody Lawrence

D: Earl Bellamy

When a stage driver discovers smallpox amongst his passengers, he leaves all of them stranded in the desert.

Stagecoach to Fury (1956) Regal/20ᵗʰ C. Fox

Forrest Tucker
Mari Blanchard
Wallace Ford
D: William Claxton

Stage passengers confront their pasts when bandidos hold them captive. Oscar nomination for cinematography: B&W.

Au ★★

S ★★

A ★

Stage to Thunder Rock (1964) Paramount

Barry Sullivan
Marylin Maxwell
Scott Brady
Lon Chaney, Jr.
John Agar
Keenan Wynn
D: William F. Claxton

A lawman must bring in his outlaw foster family. Filmed at Janss Conejo Ranch, Thousand Oaks, CA.

Au ★★

S ★

A ★★

Stage to Tuscon (Lost Stage Valley) (1951) Columbia ★ ★

Rod Cameron
Wayne Morris
Kay Buckley
D: Ralph Murphy

Two Union agents investigate hijacked Arizona stagecoaches. Filmed at the Iverson Movie Ranch and the Alabama Hills.

Au ★★

S ★★

A ★★

—When you're my age ya still won't have sense enough to pound sand down a rat hole.

—Rod Cameron
Stage to Tuscon

The Stalking Moon (1969) NG ★ ★ ★ ★

Gregory Peck
Eva Marie Saint
Robert Forster
Nolan Clay
D: Robert Mulligan

When an Indian scout offers refuge to a white captive and her half-breed son, the boy's father seeks his son's return. Filmed in Nevada. #75 Best of the West.

Au
S ★★★★
A ★★★★

Stallion Canyon (1949) Kanob/Astor

Ken Curtis
Caroline Cotton
Shug Fisher
Forrest Taylor
D: Wallace Fox

A gunman foils rustlers.

Stampede (1949) AA

Rod Cameron
Johnny Mack Brown
Gale Storm
D: Lesley Selander

Two cattle barons feud while the sheriff pursues outlaws who are cheating settlers out of their water rights.

Stampede (1960) see Guns of the Timberland

The Stand at Apache River (1953) U-I ★★

Stephen McNally
Julia Adams
Hugh Marlowe
Jack Kelly
Hugh O'Brian
Russell Johnson
D: Lee Sholem

A genocidal Army officer, a lawman and others are trapped by Apaches at a stage station. Filmed at Red Rock Canyon and Victorville, CA.

Au ★★
S ★
A ★★

Stand Up And Fight (1939) MGM

Wallace Beery
Robert Taylor
Florence Rice
Helen Broderick
D: W.S. Van Dyke II

A stagecoach man and a railroad man attempt

—Can you cook?…I never lived with anybody in my life. But, I've agreed with myself that you're welcome to come—if ya wanna?
—Gregory Peck
The Stalking Moon

"In a Stampede."

—Being loved and not being loved back in the same way is like being alone.
—Julia Adams
The Stand at Apache River

456

to settle their differences with their fists.

Star in the Dust (Lawman) (1956) U-I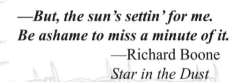

John Agar
Mamie Van Doren
Richard Boone
Clint Eastwood
D: Charles Haas

A sheriff must see that a death sentence is
carried out. Eastwood's Western film debut.

Au ★

S ✦

A ✦

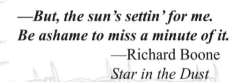

—But, the sun's settin' for me.
Be ashame to miss a minute of it.
—Richard Boone
Star in the Dust

Star of Texas (1953) Westwood/AA

Wayne Morris
Paul Fix
Frank Ferguson
Rick Valin
Jack Larson
John Crawford
D: Thomas Carr

A Texas Ranger poses as a convict to infiltrate an outlaw gang.

Stars in My Crown (1950) MGM

Joel McCrea
Ellen Drew
Dean Stockwell
Alan Hale
Ed Begley
Jack Lambert
Arthur Hunnicutt
James Arness
D: Jacques Tourneur

A new preacher resorts to the use of his gun.

Station West (1948) RKO

Dick Powell
Jane Greer
Agnes Moorehead
Burl Ives
Raymond Burr
D: Sidney Lanfield

An Army officer pursues gold thieves. From the
Luke Short novel. Filmed in Sedona, Arizona.

Agnes Moorehead in *Station West*.

Stolen Women: Captured Hearts (1997) CBS-TV  ★ ★ ★

Janine Turner
Jean Louisa Kelly
Patrick Bergin
William Shockley
Dennis Weaver
D: Jerry London

Two Kansas women are kidnapped by
Lakota warriors. Based on a true story.

Au ★ ★ ★ ★ ◀
S ★ ★ ★
A ★ ★ ★ ★

Stone Fox (1987) H-BP/TEG

Buddy Ebsen
Joey Cramer
Belinda Montgomery
D: Harvey Hart

A boy must win a dog sled race in order to save
his grandfather's ranch. Made for TV movie.

The Storm (1930) Universal

Lupe Velez
Paul Cavanaugh
William Boyd
Alphonse Ethier
D: William Wyler

Snowed in with a woman in the Canadian wilderness, two friends compete
for her affections. Dialogue written by John Huston and Tom Reed.

Janine Turner in *Stolen Women: Captured Hearts*

The Storm Rider (1957) RF/20th C. Fox

Scott Brady
Mala Powers
Bill Williams
John Goddard
D: Edward Bernds

A wealthy rancher hires a gunfighter to stop his competitors.

The Storm Rider (1972) see The Big Gundown

Stormy (1935) Universal

Noah Beery, Jr.
Jean Rogers
J. Farrell MacDonald
Raymond Hatton
D: Louis Friedlander (Lew Landers)

458

A man searches for a lost stallion.

Strange Incident see The Ox-Bow Incident

Strange Lady in Town (1955) WB

Greer Garson
Dana Andrews
Cameron Michell
Nick Adams
D: Mervyn LeRoy

A female physician experiences rejection from
the people of Santa Fé. Filmed at Old Tucson.

Au ★★✦

S ★★

A ★✦

*—Yeh, ya get a trial. Ya get it right out there
in the nearest tree!*

—Cameron Mitchell
Strange Lady in Town

Stranger and the Gunfighter (1973) FF—Ital./Sp./HK

Lee Van Cleef
Lo Lieh
D: Anthony Dawson (Antonio Margheriti)

Two gunmen search for a dead Chinese businessman's fortune.

Stranger At My Door (1956) Republic

Macdonald Carey
Patricia Medina
Skip Homeier
Slim Pickens
D: William Witney

When an outlaw seeks refuge on a farm, a preacher
and his family attempt to reform him.

Au ★✦

S ★

A ★

Stranger in Paso Bravo (1968) FF—Ital./Sp.

Anthony Steffen
Eduardo Fajardo
D: Salvatore Rosso

A drifter avenges the murder of his wife and child.

Stranger in Sacramento (1964) FF—Ital.

Mickey Hargitay
Barbara Frey
D: Serge Bergon

A rancher avenges his family's murder.

Stranger in Town (1966) FF—Ital./U.S.

Tony Anthony
Frank Wolff
D: Vance Lewis (Luigi Vanzi)

A bounty hunter faces the U.S. Cavalry and Mexican
revolutionaries over a treasure of gold.

Stranger on Horseback (1955) UA

Joel McCrea
Miraslava
John McIntire
John Carradine
D: Jacques Tourneur

A circuit judge straps on his guns to enforce his rulings.
Based on a Louie L'Amour story. Filmed in Sedona, Arizona.

Joel McCrea in *Stranger on Horseback.*

Stranger on the Run (Death Dance at Banner) (1967) NBC/Universal

Henry Fonda
Anne Baxter
Michael Parks
Dan Duryea
Sal Mineo
D: Don Siegel

A drifter is falsely accused of murder. Made for
TV movie and released theatrically in Europe.

Stranger Returns (1967) FF—Ital./Sp./U.S.

Tony Anthony
Dan Vadis
D: Vance Lewis (Luigi Vanzi)

A bounty hunter tracks stagecoach robbers. Sequel to *Stranger in Town.*

Stranger That Kneels Beside the Shadow of a Corpse (1971) FF—Ital.

Hunt Powers
Chet Davis
D: Miles Deem (Demofilo Fidani)

An evil mine owner terrorizes a town.

460

The Stranger Wore a Gun (1953) Columbia ★★

Randolph Scott
Claire Trevor
Joan Weldon
Lee Marvin
Ernest Borgnine
D: Andrè de Toth

An ex-Confederate spy protects a stageline from outlaws.
Originally in 3-D. Story by John M. Cunningham. Filmed in
the Alabama Hills and at the Iverson Movie Location Ranch.

Au ★★

S ★★

A ★★◗

Randolph Scott bucks the tiger playing faro
in *The Stranger Wore a Gun.*

Streets of Laredo (1949) Paramount ★★★◗

William Holden
William Bendix
Macdonald Carey
D: Leslie Fenton

Three outlaws reunite when two of them join the
Texas Rangers. Remake of *The Texas Rangers*.
Filmed at Corriganville, Paramount Ranch, CA
and Gallup, New Mexico.

Au ★★

S ★★★

A ★★★◗

*—Wahoo, I figure that a man's friendship
for another man is about as honest as
anything that comes along.*

—William Holden
Streets of Laredo

Streets of Laredo (Larry McMurtry's Streets of Laredo) (1995) dPE/LP/RHIE

★★★★

James Garner
Sissy Spacek
Ned Beatty
Randy Quaid
Wes Studi
George Carlin
All Star Cast
D: Joseph Sargent

A lawman forms an unseasoned posse to pursue
a young Mexican bandito. The final chapter of
Lonesome Dove. From Larry McMurtry's novel.
Filmed at Alamo Village, Brackettville, Texas.
#92 Best of the West.

Au ★★★★★

S ★★★

A ★★★★

William Holden in *Streets of Laredo.*

Stronghold (1952) Lippert

Veronica Lake
Zachary Scott
Arturo de Cordova
Rita Macedo
D: Steve Sekely

A beautiful mine owner is kidnapped by a bandido.

The Substitute Wife (1994) NBC-TV ★ ★

Farrah Fawcett
Lea Thompson
Peter Weller
Karis Bryant
D: Peter Werner

A terminally ill woman arranges for a whore to raise her sodbuster family.

Au ★★★
S ★
A ★★◗

Sugar Colt (1966) FF—Ital.Sp.

Hunt Powers
James Parker
D: Franco Giraldi (Frank Garfield)

A government agent investigates the disappearance of a detachment of Union sharpshooters.

Sugarfoot (Swirl of Glory) (1951) WB

Randolph Scott
Adele Jergens
Raymond Massey
D: Edwin L. Marin

An ex-Confederate officer discovers an old enemy controls the Arizona land he wishes to ranch.

John Hamilton, S.Z. Sakall, Randolph Scott and Robert Warwick in *Sugarfoot.*

Sundance and the Kid see Alive or Preferably Dead

Sundance Cassidy and Butch the Kid see Alive or Preferably Dead

The Sundowners (Thunder in the Dust) (1950) L-T/EL

Robert Preston
John Barrymore, Jr.
Robert Sterling
Chill Wills
D: George Templeton

Two brothers compete for control of the range.
Screenplay by Alan LeMay.

Sunscorched (1966) FF—Sp./Ger.

Mark Stevens
Mario Adorf
D: Alfonso Balcazar

462

A sheriff confronts his former gang.

Surrender (1951) Republic

Vera Ralston
John Carroll
Walter Brennan
Francis Lederer
D: Allan Dwan

Susannah of the Mounties (1939) 20th C. Fox

Shirley Temple
Randolph Scott
Margaret Lockwood
Martin Good Rider
Chief Big Tree
D: William A. Seiter

A young girl befriends a Mountie.
Technical advise by Joe De Yong.

Sutter's Gold (1936) Universal

Edward Arnold
Lee Tracy
Binnie Barnes
Harry Carey
Jim Thorpe
D: James Cruze

Sutter discovers gold in California. A box office disaster.
From the Blaise Cendras novel, *L'Or*. Filmed in the Sandwich
Islands and at various locations in California including at
Barton Flats in the San Bernardino Mountains.

The Sweet Creek County War (1979) IF/KI

Richard Egan
Albert Salmi
Nita Talbot
Slim Pickens
D: J. Frank James

Homesteaders defend themselves against outlaws.

Swirl of Glory see Sugarfoot

Taggart (1965) Universal

Tony Young
Dan Duryea
Dick Foran
David Carradine
Harry Carey, Jr.
Bob Steele
D: R. G. Springsteen

A gunfighter tracks his man into Indian country with
a miner and his wife. Based on the Louie L'Amour novel.

Au

S ★⚔

A ★⚔

Take a Hard Ride (1974) FF—Ital./Brit./Ger.

Jim Brown
Lee Van Cleef
Fred Williamson
Barry Sullivan
Harry Carey, Jr.
D: Anthony Dawson (Antonio Margheriti)

A bounty hunter tracks two black gunmen and an Indian
resembling "Billy Jack." Filmed in Spain's Canary Islands.

Au ★⚔

S ★

A ★⚔

♪
—Oh my darlin', oh my darlin', ooh mmmy daaarlin' Clementine. You are gone a' l'st foreeeverrr. Deadful sorry Clementiiine.
—Harry Carry, Jr.
Take a Hard Ride

Take Me to Town (1953) U-I

Anne Sheridan
Sterling Hayden
Philip Reed
Guy Williams
D: Douglas Sirk

The sons of a backwoods widower bring
a vaudeville artiste as their mother.

Au ★

S ★

A ★

A Talent for Loving (1969) FF—Brit./Sp.

Richard Widmark
Cesar Romero
D: Richard Quine

A bounty hunter inherits a Mexican ranch.

464

Tale of Adventure (1954) CBS-TV/P-A

Lon Chaney
Don DeFore
Rita Moreno
D: Herbert Kline

Comprised of three Jack London stories. Compilation of three 1952 segments of "The Schlitz Playhouse of Stars."

Tale of Gold (1956) WC

Clayton Moore
Jay Silverheels
Harry Lauter
D: Earl Bellamy

Compilation of three episodes of "The Lone Ranger" TV series.

Talion see An Eye for an Eye

Tall in the Saddle (1944) RKO ★★★

John Wayne
Ella Raines
Audrey Long
Ward Bond
George "Gabby" Hayes
D: Edward L. Marin

A cowhand is hired as a regulator and becomes involved in a Western "who–done–it" mystery. Technical advise by Joe De Yong. Filmed in Sedona.

Au ★★

S ★★★

A ★★★

Tall Man Riding (1955) WB ★★★

Randolph Scott
Dorothy Malone
Peggie Castle
D: Lesley Selander

A gunman helps a rancher keep his home during a land rush. Story by Norman Fox.

Au ★★★

S ★★★

A ★★★

The Tall Men (1955) 20th C. Fox ★★★★

Clark Gable
Jane Russell
Robert Ryan
Cameron Mitchell

John Wayne and Ella Raines in *Tall in the Saddle.*

Aaah, he's as stubborn as an ol' mule.
—George "Gabby" Hayes
Tall in the Saddle

Gabby Hayes and John Wayne in *Tall in the Saddle.*

Randolph Scott and William Ching in *Tall Man Riding.*

D: Raoul Walsh

Texans drive longhorns to Montana. From the Clay Fisher novel. Filmed in Durango, Mexico.

Au

S ★★★★

A ★★★★

Clark Gable in *The Tall Men.*

The Tall Stranger (Walk Tall) (1957) AA

Joel McCrea
Virginia Mayo
Barry Kelley
Michael Ansara
D: Thomas Carr

Homesteaders defend their land from outlaws. From Louie L'Amour's, "Showdown Trail."

Au

S ★★

A ★★

The Tall T (1957) Columbia

Randolph Scott
Richard Boone
Maureen O'Sullivan
Arthur Hunnicutt
Skip Homeier
D: Budd Boetticher

A homesteader and a gunfighter can not avoid a confrontation. Based on an Elmore Leonard story. Filmed in the Alabama Hills.

UNCHARTED
TERRITORY

—I just wanted to see if you're the same girl I've been kissin'—you ain't!
—Clark Gable
The Tall Men

Tall Texan (1953) Lippert

Lloyd Bridges
Lee J. Cobb
Marie Windsor
D: Elmo Williams

A lawman and a wagon load of passengers enter sacred Indian land in search of gold. Filmed at Deming and City of Rocks State Park, NM.

UNCHARTED
TERRITORY

Randolph Scott and Richard Boone in *The Tall T.*

Tall Women (1966) FF—Ger./Ital./Sp.

Anne Baxter
Maria Perschy
D: Sidney Pink

Seven women survive a wagon train attack and must endure a long trek across the desert.

UNCHARTED
TERRITORY

466

Tashunga see North Star

Taste of Violence (1961) FF—Fr.

Robert Hossein
Giovanna Ralli
D: Robert Hossein

Rare.

Taza, Son of Cochise (1954) U-I

Rock Hudson
Barbara Rush
Gregg Palmer
D: Douglas Sirk

A son of Cochise attempts to keep peace when his brother
wants war with the cavalry. Filmed at Professor Valley,
Castle Valley, and White's Ranch, Utah.

Au
S
A

Taza

Tell Them Willie Boy Is Here (Willie Boy) (1970) Universal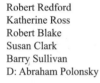

Robert Redford
Katherine Ross
Robert Blake
Susan Clark
Barry Sullivan
D: Abraham Polonsky

A sheriff tracks an Indian through the southern
California desert. Filmed in the Morongo Basin, CA.

Au
S
A

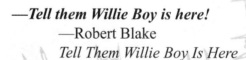

—Tell them Willie Boy is here!
—Robert Blake
Tell Them Willie Boy Is Here

The Tenderfoot (1964)

Brian Keith
Brandon De Wilde
James Whitmore
D: Byron Paul

Tennessee's Partner (1955) RKO-Radio

John Payne
Ronald Reagan
Ronda Fleming
D: Allan Dwan

When a cowboy saves his life, a gold rush gambler
repays the favor. Based on a Bret Harte short story.

Ronald Reagan and John Payne in *Tennessee's Partner.*

Filmed at the Iverson Movie Location Ranch.

Au
S
A

Tension at Table Rock (1956) RKO

Richard Egan
Dorothy Malone
Cameron Mitchell
Angie Dickinson
D: Charles Marquis Warren

An outlaw helps a sheriff control a town overrun by cowboys. Story by Frank Gruber. Filmed at the Iverson Movie Location Ranch.

Ten Thousand Dollars Blood Money (Guns of Violence) (1966) FF—Ital.

Gary Hudson (Gianni Garko)
Fidel Gonzales
D: Romolo Guerrieri

Gunfighter, Django, is hired to return a Mexican land baron's kidnapped daughter. Unauthorized sequel to *Django*.

Ten Wanted Men (1955) S-B

Randolph Scott
Jocelyn Brando
Richard Boone
Skip Homeier
Dennis Weaver
Lee Van Cleef
D: Bruce Humberstone

An Arizona cattleman protects his ranch from a crooked land baron and his gang. Filmed at Old Tucson.

Au
S
A

Ten Who Dared (1960) BV

Brian Keith
John Beal
James Drury
Ben Johnson
D: William Beaudine

John Wesley Powell explores the Colorado River. Disney. Filmed in Professor Valley, Big Bend of the CO River, White's Ranch, Arches National Park, and Dead Horse Point St. Park, UT.

Richard Boone and Randolph Scott in *Ten Wanted Men*.

—*Maybe you were better off in the old days when you took and kept what you wanted with a hard fist and a fast gun.*
—Richard Boone
Ten Wanted Men

468

Terrible Sheriff (1963) FF—Sp./Ital.

Walter Chiari
Lici Calderòn
D: Antonio Momplet

Two brothers become fearless gunfighters after eating a
fighting chicken laced with a "super strength elixir."

Terror At Black Falls (1962) Beckman

House Peters, Jr.
John Alonso
Sandra Knight
D: Robert C. Sarafian

A madman takes hostages that the sheriff must rescue.

Terror in Texas Town (1958) UA

Sterling Hayden
Sebastian Cabot
Carol Kelly
D: Joseph H. Lewis

A land baron swindles Texans out of their oil-rich land.

Terror of Oklahoma (1961) FF—Ital.

Maurizio Arena
Delia Scala
D: Mario Amendola

Rare.

Tex and the Lord of the Deep (1985) FF—Ital.

Giuliano Gemma
William Berger
D: Duccio Tessari

A Yaqui Indian witchdoctor employs a secret weapon against
enemy Aztecs, a glowing green rock which mummifies humans.

The Texan (The Big Race) (1930) Paramount

Gary Cooper
Fay Wray
Donald Reed
Emma Dunn
D: John Cromwell

An outlaw poses as a long lost son in order
to cheat a woman out of her inheritance.
Based on O'Henry's, *The Double-Eyed Deceiver*.

"A Texan Cowboy."

The Texan Meets Calamity Jane (1950) Columbia

James Ellison
Evelyn Ankers
Lee "Lasses" White
D: Andre Lamb

A Texan helps Calamity Jane prove she owns a saloon.

The Texans (1938) Paramount

Randolph Scott
Joan Bennett
May Robson
Walter Brennan
Robert Cummings
D: James Hogan

Ex-Confederates make the first cattle drive
to Abilene. Remake of *North of '36* (1924).
Filmed in Kernville, CA. #65 Best of the West.

Au ★★★★
S ★★★★
A ★★★★⯪

—Women are like horses. Some will take rawhide and some won't.

—Walter Brennan
The Texans

Texas (1941) Columbia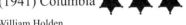

William Holden
Claire Trevor
Glenn Ford
George Bancroft
Edgar Buchanan
D: George Marshall

Two outlaws take separate paths.

Au ★★⯪
S ★★★⯪
A ★★★★

—Why you blankety-blank, hamstrung, hunk of jerky beef!

—Claire Trevor
Texas

Texas (James A. Michener's Texas) (1995) ★★★

Rick Schroder
Patrick Duffy
Stacy Keach
Randy Travis
D: Richard Long

Conflicts develop between settlers and the
Mexican government leading to war. Narrated by
Charlton Heston. Based on James Michener's novel.
Filmed at Alamo Village, Brackettville, Texas.

Au ★★★★⯪
S ★★★
A ★★★

"A Texas Type of Cowboy."

Texas Across the River (1966) Universal ✦

Dean Martin
Alain Delon
Joey Bishop
Rosemary Forsyth
Peter Graves
Michael Ansara
Dick Farnsworth
D: Michael Gorden

A Spanish gentleman joins up with a gunrunner and his Indian sidekick.

Au

S ✦

A ✦

—Wrestlin' longhorns and jumpin' rattlesnakes. Lucky thing there's no elephants around so you can rope 'em—dumb fool!
—Dean Martin
Texas Across the River

Texas, Adios (The Avenger) (1966) FF—Ital./Sp.

Franco Nero
Josè Suarez
D: Ferdinando Baldi

A sheriff and his brother avenge the murder of their father.

UNCHARTED
TERRITORY

Texas Guns see Once Upon a Texas Train

Texas Lady (1955) RKO ✦ ✦

Claudette Colbert
Barry Sullivan
Gregory Walcott
Ray Collins
D: Tim Whelan

A gambler and a newspaper woman tame a frontier town. Filmed at Columbia State Park, California.

Au ✦ ✦

S ✦ ✦

A ✦ ✦

—Well, there go the last of the giants.
—Barry Sullivan
Texas Lady

The Texas Rangers (1936) Paramount ✦ ✦ ✦

Fred MacMurray
Jack Oakie
Jean Parker
Llyod Nolan
George Hayes
D: King Vidor

Three outlaws reunite when they join the Texas Rangers. Oscar nomination for sound recording. Filmed at Santa Fé, New Mexico.

Au ✦ ✦ ✦

S ✦ ✦ ✦

A ✦ ✦ ✦ ◣

Texas Ranger, Samuel Walker.

The Texas Rangers (1951) Columbia

George Montgomery
Gale Storm
Jerome Courtland
Noah Beery, Jr.
D: Phil Karlson

A gunfighter is released from prison in order to help the Texas Rangers. Story by Frank Gruber. Filmed at the Iverson Movie Location Ranch.

Au

S

A

—*Well, nail me up to a barn door to dry!*
—Noah Beery, Jr.
The Texas Rangers

Texas Rangers (2001) DF

James Van Der Beek
Rachael Leigh Cook
Ashton Kutcher
Dylan McDermott
Usher Raymond
Tom Skerritt
Randy Travis
D: Steve Miner

Young gunmen band together to form the Texas Rangers. Based on George Durham's, *Taming of the Neuces Strip: The Story of McNelly's Rangers*. Filmed in Alberta, Canada.

UNCHARTED TERRITORY

Ashton Kutcher, James Van Der Beek, Dylan McDermott and Usher Raymond in *Texas Rangers*.

Texas Rangers Ride Again (1940) Paramount

John Howard
Ellen Drew
Akim Tamiroff
Broderick Crawford
Anthony Quinn
Robert Ryan
D: James Hogan

Texas Rangers investigate the disappearance of cattle. Sequel to *The Texas Rangers* (1936).

UNCHARTED TERRITORY

Texas Ranger circa 1835.

Texican (1966) FF—U.S./Sp.

Audie Murphy
Broderick Crawford
D: Josè A. Espinosa with Lesley Selander

An ex-sheriff avenges the murder of his brother. Filmed near Barcelona, Spain.

Au

S

A

—*Dave, drag the bodies out of the street. It might give the place a bad name.*
—Broderick Crawford
Texican

There Was a Crooked Man (1970) WB

Kirk Douglas
Henry Fonda
Hume Cronyn
Warren Oates
Burgess Meredith
Alan Hale (Jr.)
D: Joseph L. Mankiewicz

A robber in the territorial prison plots to escape in order to recover his buried loot. The only film in which Fonda and Douglas appear together. Filmed at Joshua Tree National Park, California.

Au

S

A

—Like askin' a pack a coyotes to keep quiet about a dead horse.

—Burgess Meredith
There Was a Crooked Man

These Thousand Hills (1959) TFC

Don Murray
Richard Egan
Lee Remick
Patricia Owens
Stuart Whitman
D: Richard Fleischer

A cowboy ruthlessly pursues his political ambitions.

UNCHARTED TERRITORY

They Call Him Cemetery (1971) FF—Ital./Sp.

Gianni Garko
William Berger
D: Anthony Ascott (Giuliano Carmineo)

A bounty hunter teaches two pacifist ranchers how to defend themselves against outlaws.

UNCHARTED TERRITORY

They Call Him Veritas (1972) FF—Ital./Sp.

Mark Damon
Pat Nigro
D: Luigi Perelli

A conman and his partners meet their mentor.

UNCHARTED TERRITORY

They Called Him Trinity (1972) FF—Ital./Sp.

Dean Stratford
Gordon Mitchell
D: Fred Lyon Morris (Luigi Batzella)

A gunman avenges his sister's murder.

UNCHARTED TERRITORY

They Came to Cordura (1959) Columbia ★★★★

Gary Cooper
Rita Hayworth
Van Heflin
Tab Hunter
Richard Conte
Dick York
Carlos Romero
Ed Platt
D: Robert Rossen

Following Pancho Villa's raid in New Mexico, an awards officer returns four citation recipients to Cordura. Filmed at St. George, UT and in Mexico. #87 Best of the West.

Au ★★★⭑
S ★★★★
A ★★★★

They Died With Their Boots On (1941) WB ★★★⭑

Errol Flynn
Olivia de Havilland
Arthur Kennedy
Charley Grapewin
Anthony Quinn
D: Raoul Walsh

General Custer pursues an infamous military career. Filmed in Pasadena and Warner Ranch, Calabasas, CA.

Au ★⭑
S ★★★★
A ★★★★

7th Cavalry Indian scout with lost trooper's horse.

They Passed This Way see Four Faces West

They Still Call Me Amen (1972) FF—Ital.

Luc Meranda
Sydne Rome
D: Alfio Caltabiano

A gunman and his partner track a swindling schoolteacher. Sequel to *A Man Called Amen.*

They Rode West (1954) Columbia ★⭑

Robert Francis
Donna Reed
May Wynn
Phil Carey
Jack Kelly
John War Eagle
D: Phil Karlson

A doctor is determined to prevent the spread of an epidemic on a Kiowa reservation.

474

Filmed at the Iverson Movie Location Ranch.

Au

S

A

Thirteenth is Judas (1971) FF—Ital.

Donald O'Brien
Maurice Poli
D: Joseph Warren (Giuseppi Vari)

A bounty hunter tracks a sadistic outlaw.

UNCHARTED
TERRITORY

Thirty Winchesters for El Diablo (1967) FF—Ital.

Carl Mohner
Topsy Collins
D: Frank G. Carrol (Gianfranco Baldanello)

A cowboy is hired to foil rustlers.

UNCHARTED
TERRITORY

This Is the West That Was (1974) Universal

Ben Murphy
Kim Darby
Jane Alexander
Anthony Franciosa
D: Fielder Cook

Wild Bill Hickok develops an unwanted and unearned reputation.
Made for TV farcical look at three Western legends.

Au

S ★

A ★

This Man Can't Die (1968) FF—Ital.

Guy Madison
Lucienne Bridou
D: Gianfranco Baldanello

A government agent avenges the murder of his parents and rape of his sister.

UNCHARTED
TERRITORY

This Savage Land (1969) Universal

George C. Scott
Barry Sullivan
Kathryn Hays
John Drew Barrymore
Brenda Scott
D: Vincent McEveety

Settlers face Confederate raiders in Kansas.
From "The Road West" TV series.

Au

S

A

Thomasine And Bushrod (1974) Columbia

Max Julian
Vonetta McGee
George Murdock
Glynn Turman
D: Gordon Parks, Jr.

A black gunfighter and his girlfriend run from the law.
Filmed at Eaves Movie Ranch, Santa Fé, New Mexico.

Au

S

A

> *—Good morning folks. My name is Mr. Bushrod. This pretty young lady is Miss Thomasine. We're here to rob this bank.*
> —Max Julian
> *Thomasine And Bushrod*

Thompson 1880 (1966) FF—Ital./Ger.

George Martin
Gian Sandi
D: Albert Moore (Giudo Zurli)

A mysterious stranger takes on the town boss.

Those Dirty Dogs! (1973) FF—Ital./Sp.

John Garko
Stephen Boyd
D: Giuseppe Rosati

A soldier is sent to Texas to end attacks by Mexican revolutionaries.

Those Redheads From Seattle (1953) Paramount

Rhonda Fleming
Gene Barry
Agnes Morrehead
D: Lewis R. Foster

A widow and her four daughters head to the Klondike. Originally in 3-D.

Thousand Pieces of Gold (1991) BV

Rosalind Chao
Dennis Dunn
Michael Paul Chan
Chris Cooper
D: Nancy Kelly

When a Chinese woman is sold into slavery by her family and sent to the American West, she must choose between the three men she loves.

476

Three Bullets for a Long Gun (1970) FF—Ger./South Africa

Beau Brummell
Keith Van Der Wat
D: Peter Henkel

A gunfighter and a bandido search for Confederate treasure.

Three Desperate Men (1951) Lippert

Preston Foster
Jim Davis
Virginia Grey
D: Sam Newfield

Two Texas lawmen free their brother from a California jail.

Three from Colorado (1967) FF—Sp.

George Martin
Luis Dàvila
D: Armando de Ossorio

A retired gunfighter is forced into one last showdown.

Three Godfathers (Miracle in the Sand) (1936) MGM

Chester Morris
Lewis Stone
Walter Brennan
D: Richard Boleslawski

Three fugitives promise a dying woman to safely deliver her baby out of the desert. Remake of *Hell's Hero* (1930) From Peter Kyne's novel.

—I'm sorry I called ya a chili-dippin' horse thief back there.

—John Wayne
Three Godfathers

3 Godfathers (1948) Argosy/MGM ★★★⯪

John Wayne
Pedro Armendariz
Harry Carey, Jr.
Ward Bond
Harry Carey, Sr.
Ben Johnson
D: John Ford

Remake of the 1936 version. Filmed in Death Valley.

Au ★★★⯪

S ★★★★⯪

A ★★★

John Wayne, Harry Carey, Jr. and Pedro Armendariz.

Three Graves for a Winchester (1966) FF—Ital.

Gordon Mitchell
Mickey Hargitay
D: Erminio Salvi

Rare.

Three Guns for Texas (1968) Universal

Neville Brand
Peter Brown
William Smith
Martin Milner
Philip Carey
D: David Lowell Rich, Paul Stanley, Earl Bellamy

The Texas Rangers deliver law and order. Lighthearted stories of the
Texas Rangers taken from three episodes of the "Larado" TV series.

Au ★

S ★

A ★★

Three Hours to Kill (1954) Columbia

Dana Andrews
Donna Reed
Dianne Foster
Carolyn Jones
D: Alfred Werker

A stagecoach driver has three
hours to clear himself of murder.
Filmed at Lake Sherwood, CA.

Au ★★

S ★

A ★

*—What's the matter, Ben? Can't you shoot me
lookin' me in the face? Easier in the back isn't it?*
—Dana Andrews
Three Hours to Kill

The Three Outlaws (1956) AFRC

Neville Brand
Alan Hale, Jr.
Bruce Bennett
D: Sam Newfield

A lawman chases Butch Cassidy
and his gang into Mexico.
Filmed at Corriganville, CA.

Au

S

A ★

*—Didn't you always say the Wild Bunch
made its own luck?*
—The Sundance Kid (Alan Hale, Jr.)
The Three Outlaws

Three Rogues (Not Exactly Gentlemen) (1931) Fox

Victor McLaglen
Fay Wray
Lew Cody
Eddie Gribbon
D: Ben Stoloff

When three outlaws raid a wagon train, they

478

abduct a girl with her father's goldmine map.

Three Silver Dollars (1968) FF—Ital.

Charles Southwood
Alida Chelli
D: Irving Jacobs (Mario Amendola)

A dying Confederate soldier gives a cowboy a clue to locate a treasure.

Three Swords of Zorro (1963) FF—Ital./Sp.

Guy Stockwell
Gloria Milland
Michaela Wood
D: Ricardo Blasco

Zorro passes the freedom-fighting torch to his son and daughter.

3:10 to Yuma (1957) Columbia

Glenn Ford
Van Heflin
Felicia Farr
D: Delmer Daves

A rancher attempts to take an outlaw to Yuma for the reward.
Filmed in Sedona, Arizona, and at Old Tucson.

Three Violent People (1957) Paramount

Charlton Heston
Anne Baxter
Gilbert Roland
Forest Tucker
D: Rudolph Mate

Two brothers quarrel while protecting their Texas
ranch from carpetbaggers. Filmed at Phoenix, AZ.

Au ★★★★
S ★★★★
A ★★★★

*—The glow of true beauty in a woman's face
is kindled only by first love.*
—Gilbert Roland
Three Violent People

Three Warriors (1978) UA/FFl

Randy Quaid
Byron Patt
Charlie White Eagle
Lois Red Elk
D: Keith Merrill

While learning the ways of his people, an Indian boy meets an Indian agent.

Three Were Renegades see Tumbleweed

Three Young Texans (1954) 20ᵗʰ C. Fox

Mitzi Gaynor
Jeffrey Hunter
Keefe Brasselle
D: Henry Levin

When outlaws attempt to force his father to
commit a crime, a young man covers for him.

Thundercloud see Colt .45

Thunderhoof (1948) Columbia

Preston Foster
Mary Stuart
William Bishop
D: Phil Karlson

A rancher and his family pursue a wild stallion into Mexico.

Thunder in the Dust see The Sundowners

Thunder in the Sun (1959) Paramount

Susan Hayward
Jeff Chandler
Jacques Bergerac
D: Russell Rouse

A scout leads Basque farmers to Napa Valley, California
to begin a wine industry. Filmed in the Alabama Hills.

General George Crook (left), the U.S.
Army's most effective Indian fighter.

Thunder Mountain (1935) Atherton/Fox

George O'Brien
Barbara Fritchie
Frances Grant
Morgan Wallace
George Hayes
D: David Howard

A prospector is swindled by a saloon keeper.
From a Zane Grey story.

A Thunder of Drums (1961) MGM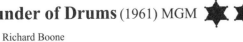

Richard Boone
George Hamilton
Luana Patten
Charles Bronson
Richard Chamberlain
Slim Pickens
D: Joseph Newman

*—Bachelors make the best soldiers. All they
have to lose is their loneliness.*
—Richard Boone
A Thunder of Drums

A seasoned cavalry captain force feeds Arizona Indian war strategy on a green lieutenant. Filmed in Old Tucson.

Au

S ★★

A ★★

Thunder Over Arizona (1956) Republic ★

Skip Homeier
Kristine Miller
George Macready
Wallace Ford
D: Joe Kane

Mistaken for a gunfighter, a cowboy helps guard a silver mine. Filmed at the Iverson Movie Ranch.

Au ★

S ★

A ★

Thunder Over the Plains (1953) WB ★★★

Randolph Scott
Lex Barker
Phyllis Kirk
Fess Parker
Lane Chandler
D: Andrè de Toth

An Army captain is ordered to protect carpetbaggers in postwar Texas.

Au ★★★

S ★★★

A ★★★⸸

Randolph Scott and Lane Chandler in *Thunder Over the Plains*.

Thunder Over El Paso (1972) FF—Ital./Sp.

Antonio Sabàto
Chris Avram
D: Roberto Montero

A bounty hunter is robbed of his reward by a bandido.

Thunder Pass (1954) Lippert ★★⸸

Dane Clark
Dorothy Patrick
Raymond Burr
Andy Devine
John Carradine
D: Frank McDonald

White settlers attempt to escape hostile Indians via Thunder Pass. Filmed at Bronson Canyon, Griffith Park, CA.

Au ★ ★ ⸗

S ★ ★ ★

A ★ ★

Timberjack (1955) Republic ✶ ✶

Sterling Hayden
Vera Ralston
David Brian
Adolphe Menjou
Chill Wills
Jim Davis
D: Joseph Kane

Two lumberjacks face off over timberland.
Filmed in Glacier National Park and western Montana.

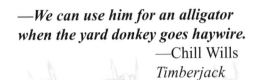

—We can use him for an alligator
when the yard donkey goes haywire.
—Chill Wills
Timberjack

Au ✶ ✶

S ✶ ✶

A ✶ ✶

Time and Place for Killing (1968) FF—Ital.

Anthony Ghidra
Jean Sobieski
D: Vincent Eagle (Enzo Dell'Aquila)

A lawman avenges the murder of his sister.

UNCHARTED
TERRITORY

A Time For Dying (1982) Fipco P./Corinth F.

Audie Murphy
Ann Randall
Victor Jory
Richard Lapp
Bob Random
D: Budd Boetticher

A gunfighter and a woman are involuntarily married by Judge
Roy Bean and encounter Jesse James. Murphy's last film originally
scheduled for a 1969 release, but delayed for more than a decade
following his death.

UNCHARTED
TERRITORY

Judge Roy Bean saloon and courthouse, Langtry, Texas.

A Time for Killing (The Long Ride Home) (1967) Columbia ✶✶

Glenn Ford
Inger Stevens
Paul Peterson
George Hamilton
Max Baer
Harrison J. Ford
D: Phil Karlson

A Union officer's fiancèe is abducted
by Confederates. Filmed at Old Tucson.

Au ✶✶

S ✶✶✶✦

A ✶✶

*—I can see men die for their country. That's
my duty. But, I can't see men die for your
honor—or mine!*

—Glenn Ford
A Time for Killing

Time of Vultures (Last of the Badmen) (1967) FF—Ital.

George Hilton
Frank Wolff
D: Nando Cicero

A vaquero is beaten and branded when he is caught with his employer's wife.

Timerider: The Adventures of Lyle Swann (Timerider) (1983) JF

Fred Ward
Belinda Bauer
Peter Coyote
Richard Masur
D: William Dear

While competing in a motocycle race, a man is transferred back in time to the Old West.

The Tin Star (1957) Paramount ✶✶✶✦

Henry Fonda
Anthony Perkins
Betsy Palmer
Neville Brand
John McIntyre
Lee Van Cleef
Russell Simpson
D: Anthony Mann

A young lawmen and a bounty hunter attempt
to tame a town. Oscar nomination for
writing: original story and screenplay.

Au ✶✶✶

S ✶✶✶✦

A ✶✶✶✶

*—You got nothin' more to learn. Maybe I learned
from you—a man can't run away from his job.*

—Henry Fonda
The Tin Star

To Hell and Back (1968) Ital./Sp.

George Hilton
Paul Stevens
D: Giovanni Fago

A gunman avenges the murder of his parents.

Today It's Me...Tomorrow You (1968) FF—Ital.

Brett Halsey
Bud Spencer
Tatsuya Nakadai
D: Tonino Cervi

A gunfighter recruits gunmen to avenge the murder of his wife.

Tomahawk (Battle of Powder River) (1951) U-I

Van Heflin
Yvonne De Carlo
Preston Foster
Jack Oakie
Rock Hudson
D: George Sherman

Following the Fetterman massacre, Jim Bridger works for peace. Filmed in the Black Hills, SD.

Au ★★

S ★★★

A ★★★

Captain William J. Fetterman recklessly led his men into an ambush by Crazy Horse.

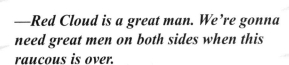

—*Red Cloud is a great man. We're gonna need great men on both sides when this raucous is over.*
—Jim Bridger (Van Heflin)
Tomahawk

Tomahawk Trail (1957) Bel-Air/UA ★

Chuck Connors
John Smith
Susan Cummings
D: Robert Perry

Apaches surround a fort seeking the return of the chief's daughter.

Au ★

S ★

A ★★

—*You know somethin', I'm not letin' you go anywhere. Those big towns, they're not safe for a girl alone.*
—Chuck Connors
Tomahawk Trail

Tombstone (The Tombstone Wars) (1993) Cinergi P. ★★★★

Kurt Russell
Val Kilmer
Michael Biehn
Powers Booth
Sam Elliott
Charlton Heston
Harry Carey, Jr.
Billy Bob Thornton
Peter Sherayko
Buck Taylor
D: George P. Cosmatos

Friction between the Earps and the Clantons leads to the shoot-out at the OK Corral. Narrated by Robert Mitchum. Script rewritten by Russell during filming.

Kurt Russell and Val Kilmer in *Tombstone*.

Filmed at Old Tucson. #52 Best of the West, #41 IMDb.

Au ★ ★ ★ ★ ★ ⟩

S ★ ★ ★ ★

A ★ ★ ★ ★

Tombstone—The Town Too Tough to Die (Tombstone) (1942) Paramount

Richard Dix
Kent Taylor
Edgar Buchanan
D: William McGann

The Earps deliver law and order to a frontier mining town.

The Tombstone Wars see Tombstone

Steve McQueen as Tom Horn

Tom Horn (1980) WB ★ ★ ★ ★ ⟩

Steve McQueen
Linda Evans
Richard Farnsworth
Billy Green Bush
Slim Pickens
D: William Wiard

During the last years of his
legendary life, Horn is hired
by Wyoming cattlemen to
"regulate" their rangeland.
"Working title" during
filming was, I, Tom Horn.
Filmed at Old Tucson (Mescal),
Empire Ranch, and Mackenzie Ranch, AZ.
#20 Best of the West.

Au ★ ★ ★ ★ ★

S ★ ★ ★ ★ ⟩

A ★ ★ ★ ★ ⟩

Tom Horn

—Well, if I'd a killed that kid, it a been the best shot I ever made—and the dirtiest trick I ever done.

—Steve McQueen
Tom Horn

Tonka (A Horse Called Comanche) (1958) BV/Disney ★ ★ ⟩

Sal Mineo
Phillip Carey
Jerome Courtland
Rafael Campos
John War Eagle

D: Lewis Foster

A Sioux brave's horse is bound as a Seventh Cavalry
mount to Custer's last stand. Filmed at Bend, Oregon.

Little Big Horn, "A Wounded War-Pony."

Au

S ★

A

Too Much Gold for One Gringo (1974) FF—Ital.Sp.

Anthony Steffen
Daniel Martin
Fernando Sancho
D: Juan Bosch (Ignacio Iquino)

A Yankee gunfighter and a bandido
compete for a hidden treasure.

*—The horse known as Commanche, being the only
living representative of the bloody tragedy of the Big
Horn, Montana, June 25, 1876, his kind treatment
and comfort should be a matter of special pride and
solicitude on the part of the 7th Cavalry…*
—1878 General Orders No. 7
Tonka

Top Gun (1955) Fame Pict./UA

Sterling Hayden
William Bishop
Karen Booth
Rod Taylor
D: Ray Nazarro

A town shuns the gunman who can save them from an outlaw.

El Topo (1971) FF—Mex.

Alexandro Jodorowsky
Brontis Jodorowsky
David Silva
D: Alexandro Jodorowsky

A mystic gunfighter pursues enlightenment
by shooting the four masters of the desert.

The Torch (1950) EL

Paulette Goddard
Pedro Armendariz
Gilbert Roland
D: Emilio Fernandez

When a small Mexican village is overrun by a rebel
and his army, they fall for a nobleman's daughter.

Torrejón City (1961) FF—Sp.

Tony Le Blanc
May Hetherly
D: Leon Klimovsky

A lawman delivers justice to a boom town.

Toughest Gun in Tombstone (1958) UA

George Montgomery
Beverly Tyler
Don Beddoe
Jim Davis
D: Earl Bellemy

A Texas Ranger poses as an outlaw in order to capture Johnny Ringo.

The Toughest Man in Arizona (1952) Republic

Vaughn Monroe
Joan Leslie
Walter Brennan
Victor Jory
Harry Morgan
D: R.G. Springsteen

A singing lawman tracks
an escaped gunrunner.

Au ★★
S ★★
A ★★

♪ —Oh, a man's best friend is his horse. But of course. But of course. Oh, what a girl's nice to hold, but they don't want your gold. So a man's best friend is his horse.

—Vaughn Monroe
The Toughest Man in Arizona

Tough Guns see Saddle Tramp Women

To the Last Drop see Bury Them Deep

To The Last Man (1933) Paramount

Randolph Scott
Esther Ralston
Noah Beery
Jack LaRue
Larry "Buster" Crabbe
Shirley Temple
D: Henry Hathaway

A family feud erupts when one family begins rustling. Story by Zane Grey.

A Town Called Bastard see A Town Called Hell

A Town Called Hell (A Town Called Bastard) (1971) FF—Brit./ Sp.

Telly Savalas
Robert Shaw
Stella Stevens
Fernando Rey
Martin Landau
D: Robert Parish

A bounty hunter tracks a Mexican revolutionary.

Town Tamer (1965) Paramount

Dana Andrews
Terry Moore

Pat O'Brien
Lon Chaney
D: Lesley Selander

A gunfighter avenges his wife's murder.
Story by Frank Gruber. Produced by A.C. Lyles.

The Tracker see Dead or Alive

Trackers (1956) WC

Clayton Moore
Jay Silverheels
Mary Ellen Kay
D: Earl Bellamy, Oscar Rudolph

Compilation of three episodes of "The Lone Ranger" TV series.

The Trackers (1971) ASP

Sammy Davis, Jr.
Ernest Borgnine
Julie Adams
Jim Davis
Arthur Hunnicutt
D: Earl Bellamy

A black tracker helps a white rancher search for
his kidnapped daughter. Made for TV movie.

Au ★★

S ★★

A ★★★⯪

*—An Apache can see better in the
dark than a mountain lion.*
—Sammy Davis, Jr.
The Trackers

Track of the Cat (1954) WB

Robert Mitchum
Teresa Wright
Diana Lynn
Tab Hunter
D: William Wellman

A California rancher obsessively tracks a black cat.
Based on Walter Van Tillburg Clark's novel.
Filmed at Mt. Ranier National Park, WA. #67 Best of the West.

Au ★★★★

S ★★★★

A ★★★★⯪

Trail of the Falcon (1968) FF—Ger./U.S.S.R.

Gojko Mitic
Hannjo Hasse
D: Gottfried Kölditz

488

Dakota Indians battle settlers and speculators.

Trail of the Vigilantes (1940) Universal

Franchot Tone
Warren William
Broderick Crawford
Andy Devine
D: Allan Dwan

An undercover investigator pursues rustlers.

Trail of the Yukon (1949) Mono.

Kirby Grant
Suzanne Dalbart
D: William X. Crowley

A mountie investigates a bank robbery. Based on James O. Curwood's, *The Gold Hunters*.

Trail Street (1947) RKO Radio

Randolph Scott
Robert Ryan
Anne Jeffreys
George "Gabby" Hayes
D: Ray Enright

Bat Masterson settles a dispute between farmers and cattlemen.

Au ★★

S ★★

A ★★✦

—Well, I've had women from Arkansas to Zanzibar. No matter what they're thinkin', I'm just a jack rabbit hop ahead of 'em!
—Gabby Hayes
Trail Street

Train for Durango (1967) FF—Ital./Sp.

Anthony Steffen
Mark Damon
D: William Hawkins (Mario Caiano)

Gunfighters and bandidos fight over a stolen safe full of gold with missing keys.

The Train Robbers (1973) WB

John Wayne
Ann-Margret
Rod Taylor
Ben Johnson
Bobby Vinton
Richardo Montalban
D: Burt Kennedy

John Wayne in *The Train Robbers*.

A widow hires a Civil War veteran to recover gold that her late husband robbed from Wells Fargo. Screenply by Burt Kennedy. Filmed near Durango, Mexico, at Los Organos.

Au

S ★★★

A ★★★★

Tramplers (1965) FF—Ital.

Gordon Scott
Joseph Cotten
James Mitchum
D: Albert Band (Alfredo Antonini)

A Confederate rebel's sons turn against him.

John Wayne and Ann-Margret in *The Train Robbers*.

Trap On Cougar Mountain (1972) SI

Keith Larsen
Karen Steele
Eric Larsen
D: Keith Larsen

A young boy and a mountain lion experience the wilderness together.

Treasure of Lost Canyon (1952) U-I

William Powell
Julia Adams
Rosemary DeCamp
D: Ted Tetzlaff

A medic and an orphan search for a treasure chest. Based on a Robert Louis Stevenson story.

The Treasure of Pancho Villa (1955) RKO ★★★

Rory Calhoun
Shelley Winters
Gilbert Roland
D: George Sherman

An American mercenary and a Mexican rebel steal gold for the revolution. Filmed in Mexico.

Au ★★★★

S ★★★

A ★★★★

Treasure of the Ruby Hills (1955) AA

Zachary Scott
Carole Mathews
Dick Foran
Lee Van Cleef
D: Frank McDonald

A rancher fights corrupt ranchers. Based on
Louie L'Amour's, *Rider of the Ruby Hills*.

The Treasure of Silver Lake (1962-3) Columbia/FF—Ger./Yug.

Lex Barker
Herbert Lom
Pierre Brice
D: Harald Reinl

"Old Shatterhand" and Winnetou track stagecoach robbers.
First of the "Winnetou" films. Based on Karl May's characters.
Filmed in Germany.

Au ✦

S ✦✦

A ✦

*—His scalp belongs to me, but I don't
want it! I'm a friend of the red-man!*
—Lex Barker (Old Shatterhand)
The Treasure of Silver Lake

Treasure of the Aztecs (1965) FF—Ger./Ital./Fr.

Lex Barker
Gerard Barray
D: Robert Siodmak

Two men search for Aztec treasure.

Trespasses (1987) XITP/Shapiro Ent.

Robert Kuhn
Van Brooks
Ben Johnson
Mary Pillot
Adam Roarke
Lou Diamond Phillips
D: Loren Bivens, Adam Roarke

Tribute to a Bad Man (1956) MGM ✦✦✦✦

James Cagney
Don Dubbins
Stephen McNally
Vic Morrow
Lee Van Cleef
D: Robert Wise

A self–made Wyoming horse rancher
confronts his own callousness.

Au ✦✦✦✦

S ✦✦✦✦

A ✦✦✦✦

Trigger Fast (Floating Outfit: Trigger Fast) (1993) Libra P./Trimark Pict.

Christopher Atkins
Corbin Bernsen
Jurgen Prochnow

Martin Sheen

D: David Lister and Peter Edwards

A cattle rancher fights land barons in post-Civil War Texas.

Trinity and Sartana Are Coming (1972) FF—Ital.

Robert Widmark
Harry Baird
D: Mario Siciliano

Two bank robbers become heroes.

Trinity Is Still My Name (1974) FF—Ital.

Terence Hill (Mario Girotti)
Bud Spencer (Carlo Pedersoli)
Harry Carey, Jr.
D: E.B. Clucher (Enzo Barboni)

Two gunmen become involved with gun runners.

Trinity Plus the Clown and a Guitar (1975) FF—Ital./Austria/Fr.

George Hilton
Rinaldo Talamonti
D: Francois Legrand (Franz Autel)

An acrobat and a minstrel join a gunfighter
in a border town struggle against bandidos.

Trinity Sees Red (1971) FF—Ital./Sp.

Terence Hill (mario Girotti)
Maria Grazia Buccella
Fernando Rey
D: Mario Camus

A gunfighter escapes to Mexico where he becomes involved in the revolution.

Trippa Joe (1968) FF—Ital./Sp.

Aldous McNice
Guy MacJeanne
Tony Spanish
D: Alberto Spanish

—The Sioux nation must live on!
—Richard Harris
Triumphs of a Man Called Horse

Triumphs of a Man Called Horse (1983) JF/Paramount

Richard Harris
Michael Beck
Ana DeSade
Buck Taylor

D: John Hough

The half-breed son of an English nobleman carries on his father's quest to protect his tribe's life-style from encroaching settlers. Second sequel of *A Man Called Horse.* Filmed in Montana and Arizona.

Au

S ★✦

A ★

Trooper Hook (1957) UA ★ ★

Joel McCrea
Barbara Stanwyck
Earl Holleman
John Dehner
D: Charles Marquis Warren

A cavalry officer is assigned to return a white woman held captive by Apaches to her white husband. Filmed at Kanab, UT.

Au ★★

S

A ★★

"Dismounted—The Troopers Moving the Led Horses."

—Soldierin's the only thing I know.
—Joel McCrea
Trooper Hook

Trouble in High Timber Country (1980) ABC-TV

Eddie Albert
Joan Goodfellow
Martin Kove
D: Vincent Sherman

A corporation schemes to take over a family's lumber and mining operations.

True Grit (1969) Paramount ★★★★

John Wayne
Glen Campell
Kim Darby
Jeremy Slate
Robert Duvall
Strother Martin
Dennis Hopper
Jay Silverheels
D: Henry Hathaway

A one-eyed marshal and a Texas Ranger help a girl track her father's killer. Based on Charles Portis's novel. Oscar nomination for best song. Best actor Oscar for Wayne. Filmed in San Miguel and Ouray counties (Ridgeway), Colorado. #51 Best of the West, #40 IMDb.

Au ★★★★

S ★★★★✦

A ★★★★

John Wayne in *True Grit.*

—You can't serve papers on a rat. You've gotta kill'em or let'em be.
—John Wayne
True Grit

True Grit (:A Further Adventure) (1978) ABC-TV

Warren Oates
Lisa Pelikan
Lee Meriwether
Jeff Osterhage
D: Richard T. Heffron

A teenage girl is bent on reforming a crusty old marshal.
Sequel to *True Grit* and *Rooster Cogburn*.
Filmed at Buckskin Joe, Canon City, Colorado.

Au

S ★★

A ★★◗

The True Story of Jesse James (1957) 20ᵗʰ C. Fox

Robert Wagner
Jeffrey Hunter
Hope Lange
Agnes Moorehead
Alan Hale
John Carradine
D: Nicholas Ray

Remake of the 1939 *Jesse James.*

UNCHARTED
TERRITORY

True Women (1997) CBS-TV

Dana Delany
Annabeth Gish
Angelina Jolie
Tina Majorino
Michael York
Irene Bedard
Powers Boothe
D: Karen Arthur

In the aftermath of the Alamo, pioneer women contribute
to the settling of Texas. Two-part mini-series. Based on
Janice Woods Windle's historical novel. Filmed in Texas.

Au ★★★

S ★★

A ★★

Dana Delany and Annabeth Gish in *True Women.*

*—Whoever said you were safe if you
weren't on the battlefield, sure as hell
wasn't a woman.*

—Dana Delany
True Women

The Trumpet Blows (The Trumpet Calls) (1934) Paramount

George Raft
Adolphe Menjou
Frances Drake
Sidney Toler
D: Stephen Roberts

A younger brother of a bandido wishes to become a bullfighter.

UNCHARTED
TERRITORY

The Truth (1956) WC

Clayton Moore
Jay Silverheels
Claire Carleton
Slim Pickens
D: Earl Bellamy, Oscar Rudolph

Compilation of three episodes of "The Lone Ranger" TV series.

Tumbleweed (Three Were Renegades) (1953) U-I

Audie Murphy
Lori Nelson
Chill Wills
Russell Johnson
Lee Van Cleef
D: Nathan Juran

A cowboy is blamed for an Indian raid on a wagon train.
Filmed at Red Rock Canyon, southern California.

"Unhorsed."

20 Mule Team (1940) MGM

Wallace Beery
Leo Carrillo
Marjorie Rambeau
Anne Baxter
Noah Berry, Jr.
D: Richard Thorpe

Two borax miners defend their claim.
Filmed in Death Valley.

Twenty Paces to Death (1970) FF—Ital./Sp.

Dean Reed
Albert Farley
D: Ted Mulligan (Manuel Esteba)

Two men compete for the affections of an Indian woman.

Twenty Thousand Dollars for Seven (1968) FF—Ital.

Brett Halsey
Herman Lang
D: Albert Cardone (Albert Cardiff)

Rare.

495

Twice a Judas (1968) FF—Sp./Ital.

Klaus Kinski
Antonio Sabàto
D: Nando Cicero

A crooked land baron runs illegal workers across the Mexican border.

The Twinkle In God's Eye (1955) Republic

Mickey Rooney
Coleen Gray
Hugh O'Brian
Joey Foreman
Touch (Mike) Connors
D: George Blair

A preacher brings religion to a frontier town.

Au

S ⭐︎

A ⭐

Twins for Texas (1964) FF—Ital./Sp.

Walter Chiari
Raimondo Vianello
D: Steno (Stefano Vanzina)

Twin brothers confront their enemies.

Two Against the Wind see The Avenging

Two Crosses at Danger Pass (1968) FF—Ital./Sp.

Peter Martell
Anthony Freeman
D: Rafael R. Marchent

A gunfighter avenges the murder of his family.

Two Flags West (1950) 20th C. Fox

Joseph Cotton
Linda Darnell
Jeff Chandler
Cornel Wilde
Dale Robertson
Noah Beery, Jr.
D: Robert Wise

Confederate prisoners fight Indians in New Mexico.

Two for Texas (1998) TNT ★★★✦

Kris Kristofferson
Scott Bairstow
Peter Coyote
Irene Bedard
Tom Skerritt
D: Rod Hardy

Louisiana penal colony escapees join Sam Houston's army and avenge the Alamo. Filmed in Texas.

Au ★★★★★
S ★★★
A ★★★✦

—They called themselves Texicans. Some wanted a fresh start. Some figured to make their fortune. Some just craved a good fight. But, all of them expected to be free.
—Scott Bairstow
Two for Texas

The Two From Rio Bravo (Guns Don't Argue) (1963) FF—Ital.

Rod Cameron
Horst Frank
Vivi Bach
D: Manfred Rieger

UNCHARTED TERRITORY

Two-Gun Lady (1956) AFR Co. ✦

Peggie Castle
William Talman
Marie Windsor
D: Richard Bartlett

A lawman helps a gunwoman avenge her father's murder.

Au ★
S ✦
A ✦

Two Gunmen (1964) FF—Sp./Ital.

Alan Scott
George Martin
D: Anthony Greepy (Primo Zeglio)

A Texas Ranger must track down an old friend.

UNCHARTED TERRITORY

Two Guns and a Badge (1954) Westwood/AA

Wayne Morris
Morris Ankrum
Beverly Garland
D: Lewis Collins

An exconvict is mistaken for a hired gun hired to rid the Arizona Territory of outlaws. Compilation of B series episodes released as a feature film.

Two In Revolt (1936) RKO

John Arledge
Louise Latimer
Moroni Olson
Emmett Vogen
D: Glenn Tyron

A dog and a horse help a man fight outlaws.

Two Mules for Sister Sarah (1970) Universal

Clint Eastwood
Shirley McLaine
Manolo Fabregas
Armando Silvestre
D: Don Siegel

A gunfighter teams up with a whore disguised as a nun to fight the French. Elizabeth Taylor turned down McLaine's role. Filmed in Mexico.

Au ★★★☆

S ★★★☆

A ★★★★

—*This is no cat house. This is the best whore house in town!*
—Shirley McLaine
Two Mules for Sister Sarah

Two Pistols and a Coward (1967) FF—Ital.

Anthony Steffen
Richard Wyler
D: Calvin J. Padget (Giorgio Ferroni)

A cowardly circus sharpshooter must face outlaws.

Two Rode Together (1961) Columbia ★★★☆

James Stewart
Richard Widmark
Shirley Jones
Linda Crystal
Andy Devine
John McIntire
Harry Carey, Jr.
Ken Curtis
Woody Strode
D: John Ford

A marshal and Army officer pair up to rescue Comanche captives. Filmed at Alamao Village, Brackettville, Texas.

Au ★★☆

S ★★★☆

A ★★☆

—*Nobody wants their past tattooed across their forehead.*
—James Stewart
Two Rode Together

Two Sides of the Dollar (1967) FF—Fr./Ital.

Monty Greenwood
Jacques Herlin
D: Roberto Montero

Three men and a whore plot to
rob gold from a territorial fort.

Two Sons of Ringo (1967) FF—Ital.

Franco Franchi
Ciccio Ingrassia
Gloria Paul
D: Giorgio Simonelli

—Ben, I saw blue butterflies down by the crik this mornin'. About a million of 'em. They were flyin' in twos like sweethearts with four wings apiece. That ain't a ladylike thing to say. Is it?

—Audrey Hepburn
The Unforgiven

Two Thousand Dollars for Coyote (1965) FF—Sp.

James Philbrook
Nuria Torray
D: Leon Klimovsky

A freedom-fighter battles a corrupt southern California governor. Sequel to *Coyote*.

Ugly Ones see The Bounty Killer (1966)

Ulzana's Raid (1972) Universal ★★★★

Burt Lancaster
Bruce Davison
Richard Jaeckel
Jorge Luke
Richard Farnsworth
D: Robert Aldrich

An Indian scout tracks renegade
Apaches. Filmed in Nevada.
#68 Best of the West.

Au ★★★★
S ★★★★
A ★★★★

—Lieutenant, a horse will run so far, so fast, for so long. Then he'll lie down on ya. Horse lies down on an Apache, he puts a fire under his belly, gets him back up on his feet. When the horse dies, he gets off, eats a bit of it—steals another. Ain't no way you can better that.

—Burt Lancaster
Ulzana's Raid

The Undefeated (1969) 20ᵗʰ C. Fox ★★★★

John Wayne
Rock Hudson
Antonio Aguilar
Roman Gabriel
Lee Meriwether
Merlin Olsen
(Jan) Michael Vincent
Ben Johnson
Harry Carey, Jr.
D: Andrew V. McLaglen

Following the Civil War, a
Union and Confederate officer
team up in Mexico. Some 3000

Rock Hudson and John Wayne in *The Undefeated*.

horses were used for filming, the most utilized in any film. Filmed at Durango, Mexico. #88 Best of the West.

Au ★★★⯪

S ★★★★

A ★★★★

The Unforgiven (1960) UA ★★★★⯪

Burt Lancaster
Audrey Hepburn
Audie Murphy
Lillian Gish
Doug McClure
John Saxon
Charles Bickford
D: John Huston

A rancher and her sons fight Kiowas over an adopted Indian daughter. Story by Alan LeMay. Filmed in Durango, Mexico. #22 Best of the West.

Au ★★★★

S ★★★★★

A ★★★★⯪

Audie Murphy and Burt Lancaster in *The Unforgiven*.

Unforgiven (1992) WB ★★★★

Clint Eastwood
Gene Hackman
Morgan Freeman
Richard Harris
D: Clint Eastwood

An aging gunfighter is lured back to his former profession. Oscar nominations for best actor (Eastwood), writing: directly for the screen, cinematography, art direction-set direction, and sound. Oscars for best picture, supporting actor (Hackman), and director. Filmed at the E.P. Ranch in Alberta, Canada. #60 Best of the West, #98 AFI GM, #13 IMDb.

Au ★★★★⯪

S ★★★★

A ★★★★⯪

Clint Eastwood in *Unforgiven*.

Uninvited (Ghoul's Gold) (1993)

Jack Elam
Christopher Boyer
Bari Buckner
Jerry Rector
D: Michael D. Bohusz

An evil man lures eight people to a mysterious mountain in search of gold.

UNCHARTED TERRITORY

500

Union Pacific (1939) Paramount

Barbara Stanwyck
Joel McCrea
Akim Tamiroff
Robert Preston
Brian Donlevy
Anthony Quinn
Lon Chaney, Jr.
Iron Eyes Cody
D: Cecil B. DeMille

Railroad men do their part to connect the western
portion of the transcontinental railroad with the East.
Technical advise by Joe De Yong. Story by Ernest
Haycox. Oscar nomination for special effects.
Filmed in Utah.

Au ★★★

S ★★★★

A ★★★★

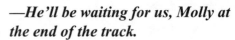

*—He'll be waiting for us, Molly at
the end of the track.*

—Joel McCrea
Union Pacific

Building the Central Pacific circa 1867.

The building of the transcontinental railroad in *Union Pacific*.

Unknown Valley (1933) Columbia

Buck Jones
Cecilia Parker
Bret Black
Carlota Warwick
Ward Bond
D: Lambert Hillyer

Lost in the desert, an ex-Army scout is rescued by a religious sect.

The Untamed Breed (1948) Columbia

Sonny Tufts
Barbara Britton
George Hayes
D: Charles Lamont

A rancher crosses Texas cattle with his Bramha bull.

Untamed Frontier (1952) U-I

Joseph Cotten
Shelley Winters
Scott Brady
Lee Van Cleef
Fess Parker
D: Hugo Fregonese

Conflict arises between a cattleman's nephew and his son. Filmed at Agoura, CA.

Au ★★
S ★★
A ★★

Up the MacGregors! (1967) FF—Ital./Sp.

David Bailey
Agata Flori
D: Frank Garfield

Two families go after bandidos. Sequel to *Seven Guns for the MacGregors.*

Utah Blaine (1957) Columbia

Rory Calhoun
Susan Cummings
Max Baer
D: Fred F. Sears

When a cowboy rescues a man from a lynching, he receives half title to a ranch.

Valdez is Coming (1971) UA

Burt Lancaster
Susan Clark
Jon Cypher
Barton Heyman
D: Edwin Sherin

A constable helps a widow whose husband is wrongfully killed. Filmed at Almería, Andalucía, Spain. #49 Best of the West.

Au ★★★★
S ★★★★
A ★★★★

Valley of Fury see Chief Crazy Horse

Valley of the Dancing Widows (1974) FF—Sp./Ger.

Judith Stephen
Audrey Allen
D: Volker Vogeler

Upon their return from the Civil War, Texans are taught a "lesson" by their women.

Valley of the Giants (1938) WB

Wayne Morris
Claire Trevor
Frank McHugh
Alan Hale
Charles Bickford
D: William Keighley

A religious homesteader prevents a timber boss from clear-cutting the California redwoods. Based on Peter Kyne's novel.

Valley of the Sun (1942) RKO

Lucille Ball
James Craig
Sir Cedric Hardwicke
Iron Eyes Cody
Jay Silverheels
D: George Marshall

—Every girl expects to be married sooner or later.
—Lucille Ball
Valley of the Sun

A military fugitive investigates corruption in the Indian agency. Filmed Taos, New Mexico.

Au ★
S ★┃
A ★┃

The Vanishing American (1955) Republic

Scott Brady
Audrey Totter
Forrest Tucker
Jim Davis
Lee Van Cleef
Jay Silverheels
D: Joseph Kane

A young Indian protects his home from land grabbers. Remake of the 1926 silent version. Story by Alan LeMay.

Standing Bear, Omaha sub-chief 1883.

The Vanishing Frontier (1932) Paramount

John Mack Brown
Evalyn Knapp
Zasu Pitts
Ben Alexander
D: Phil Rosen

An American stops military corruption in old California.

Vendetta at Dawn (1971) FF—Ital.

George Eastman
Ty Hardin
D: Willy S. Regan (Sergio Garrone)

A doctor avenges the murder of his family.

Vengeance (1964) BAP/CIP

William Thourlby
Melora Conway
Owen Pavitt
D: Dene Hilyard

When a Civil War veteran avenges his brother's murder,
he in turn is hunted by the family of the man he killed.

Vengeance (1968) FF—Ital./Ger.

Richard Harrison
Claudio Camaso
D: Anthony Dawson (Antonio Margheriti)

A gunman avenges the murder of his friend.

Vengeance Is a Dish Served Cold (1971) FF—Ital./Sp.

Leonard Mann
Ivan Rassimov
Klaus Kinski
D: William Redford (Pasquale Squittieri)

The sole survivor of an Indian attack avenges the deaths of his family.

Vengeance Valley (1951) MGM

Burt Lancaster
Robert Walker
Joanne Dru
John Ireland
D: Richard Thorpe

A cowboy protects his foster brother's
secret regarding an unwed mother.
From the Luke Short novel.

Au ★★★
S ★★★★
A ★★★★

—When you're loyal to a man, Hewie, you're loyal to everything about him—even his faults. Even his son.

—Burt Lancaster
Vengeance Valley

Vengeance Vow (1956) WC

Clayton Moore
Jay Silverheels
Jim Bannon
D: Earl Bellamy

Compilation of three episodes of "The Lone Ranger" TV series.

Vera Cruz (1954) H-L/UA

Gary Cooper
Burt Lancaster
Denise Darcel
Cesar Romero
Charles Bronson
Ernest Borgnine
Jack Elam
Jack Lambert
D: Robert Aldrich

Two adventurers escort a gold shipment to Vera Cruz.
Story by Borden Chase. Filmed at Cuernavaca, Morelos, Mexico.

Au ★★
S ★★★◀
A ★★★★

The Vigilantes Return (Return of the Vigilantes) (1947) Universal

Jon Hall
Margaret Lindsay
Andy Devine
Paula Drew
Jack Lambert
D: Ray Taylor

A lawman goes undercover in order to investigate a crooked saloon operator.

Villa! (1958) 20ᵗʰ C. Fox

Brian Keith
Cesar Romero
Margia Dean
D: James B. Clark

An American gunrunner supplies Pancho Villa with weapons for the revolution.

Villa Rides (1968) Paramount

Yul Brynner
Robert Mitchum
Charles Bronson
Fernando Rey
John Ireland
D: Buz Kulik

An American aviator assists Pancho
Villa during the revolution.
Filmed in Spain.

Au ★★★
S ★★★◗
A ★★★★

—Go outside and die!
Where are your manners!
—Charles Bronson
Villa Rides

Wallace Berry in *Viva Villa!*

The Faces of Pancho Villa

Yul Brynner in *Villa Rides.*

Pancho Villa (fourth from the left) poses with his revolutionaries in 1911.

The Violent Men (Rough Company) (1955) Columbia ★★★

Glenn Ford
Barbara Stanwyck
Edward G. Robinson
Brian Keith
Jack Kelly
D: Rudolph Matè

A rancher fights a land-grabbing cattle baron.
Filmed in the Alabama Hills and at Old Tucson.

Au ★★★

S ★★★

A ★★★★◗

*—Here in Anchor we don't pay, eh, much
attention to this hogwash about the meek
inheritin' the earth.*
—Edward G. Robinson
The Violent Men

Virginia City (1940) WB ★★★◗

Errol Flynn
Miriam Hopkins
Randolph Scott
Humphrey Bogart
Frank McHugh
Alan Hale
George Reeves
D: Michael Curtiz

Union and Confederate spies compete with a bandido
for a Nevada gold shipment. Filmed in Arizona.

Au ★★★

S ★★★★◗

A ★★★★◗

George Regas, Paul Fix, Humphrey Bogart, Moroni
Olsen and Randolph Scott in *Virginia City*.

The Virginian (1929) Paramount ★★★◗

Gary Cooper
Walter Huston
Richard Arlen
Mary Brian
Chester Conklin
James Mason
Randolph Scott
D: Victor Fleming

A cowboy hangs his friend,
courts a schoolteacher and
confronts a rustler. From
the Owen Wister novel. The
first sound feature-length
Western. Randolph Scott's
film debut. Filmed at
Sonora, California

Au ★★★◗

S ★★★★

A ★★★★◗

—If you wanna call me that— smile.
—Gary Cooper
The Virginian

—When you call me that, smile!
—Owen Wister
The Virginian (novel)

Gary Cooper as the Virginian.

The Virginian (1946) Paramount ★★★

Joel McCrea
Brian Donlevy
Ward Bond
D: Stuart Gilmore

Remake of the 1929 version. Technical advise by Joe De Yong. Filmed at Paramount Ranch.

Au ★★★◗
S ★★★
A ★★★★

Joel McCrea as the Virginian.

The Virginian (2000) TNT ★★★

Bill Pullman
Diane Lane
John Savage
James Drury
Dennis Weaver
D: Bill Pullman

Remake of the 1929 version. Filmed in Alberta, Canada.

Au ★★★★◗
S ★★★
A ★★★

—When you call me that, smile!
—Joel McCrea
The Virginian (1946)

Viva Cisco Kid (1940) 20th C. Fox

Cesar Romero
Jean Rogers
Chris-Pin Martin
D: Norman Foster

The Cisco Kid is accused of robbing an express office.

UNCHARTED TERRITORY

—It's not for my friends' or enemies' benefit that I do this. I owe it to my own honesty.
—Bill Pullman
The Virginian (2000)

Viva Villa! (1934) MGM ★★★

Wallace Beery
Leo Carrillo
Fay Wray
Donald Cook
D: Jack Conway and Howard Hawks

A bandido joins the Mexican Revolution.

Au ★★★
S ★★★★◗
A ★★★◗

Wallace Berry (left) in *Viva Villa!*

508

Viva Zapata! (1952) 20th C. Fox ★★★

Marlon Brando
Jean Peters
Anthony Quinn
Joseph Wiseman
D: Elia Kazan

A peon leads his people during the Mexican
Revolution. Oscar nominations for Brando for
best actor, writing: screenplay, art direction-set
direction, and scoring: drama/comedy. Best supporting
actor Oscar for Quinn. Filmed at Durango, Colorado.

Au ★★★
S ★★★
A ★★★

Waco (1966) Paramount

Howard Keel
Jane Russell
Brian Donlevy
Wendell Corey
John Agar
D: R.G. Springsteen

A gunman is hired to clean up a town.

Wagonmaster (1950) Argosy/RKO ★★★

Ben Johnson
Harry Carey, Jr.
Joanne Dru
Ward Bond
James Arness
Jim Thorpe
D: John Ford

A Mormon wagon train is kidnapped by outlaws. Johnson's
first leading role. Filmed in Professor, Spanish, and
Monument Valleys, Utah, and at the Colorado River.

Au ★★★
S ★★◗
A ★★★◗

Wagons West (1952) Mono.

Rod Cameron
Peggie Castle
Noah Berry, Jr.
D: Ford Beebe

A wagon master discovers that someone
on his train is selling guns to Indians.

Marlon Brando as Zapata.

Zapata

Harry Carey, Jr., Ben Johnson and Ward Bond in *Wagonmaster*.

Wagons Westward (1940) Republic

Chester Morris
Anita Louise
Buck Jones
Ona Munson
George Hayes
D: Lew Landers

A twin is mistaken for his brother by the woman he promised to marry.
Filmed in the Alabama Hills and the Iverson Movie Location Ranch.

Walk Like a Dragon (1960) Paramount

Jack Lord
Nobu McCarthy
James Shigeta
Mel Torme
D: James Clavell

A rancher returns from San Francisco with a Chinese slave
girl and a Chinaman intent on becoming a gunfighter.

Walk Tall see The Tall Stranger

Walk the Proud Land (1956) U-I

Audie Murphy
Anne Bancroft
Pat Crowley
Jay Silverheels
D: Jesse Hibbs

Indian agent, John Clum, vows to return
Geronimo to the San Carlos Reservation.
Filmed at Old Tucson.

Au

S

A

Wanda Nevada (1979) Pando/UA

Brooke Shields
Peter Fonda
Fiana Lewis
Luke Askew
Henry Fonda
D: Peter Fonda

When a gambler wins a girl in a poker game, they prospect on sacred Indian land.

Wanderer of the Wasteland (1935) Paramount

Dean Jagger
Larry "Buster" Crabbe
Gail Patrick
Raymond Hatton
Jim Thorpe
D: Otto Lovering

510

A drifter encounters outlaws. Remake of the 1924 silent version. Based on a Zane Grey story.

Wanderer of the Wasteland (1945) RKO ⭐

James Warren
Richard Martin
D: Edward Killy and Wallace Grissell

Remake of the 1935 version bears little resemblance to Grey's story or either of the previous versions. Filmed in the Alabama Hills.

Au ⭐

S ⭐⭐

A ⭐

Wanted (1968) FF—Ital./Fr.

Giuliano Gemma
Teresa Gimpera
D: Calvin J. Padget (Giorgio Ferroni)

A sheriff is framed for rustling.

Wanted Johnny Texas (1971) FF—Ital.

James Newman
Fernando Sancho
D: Erminio Salvi

The Army hires a scout to guide a wagon train.

Wanted Sabata (1970) FF—Ital.

Brad Harris
Vassili Karis
D: Robert Johnson (Roberto Mauri)

Rare.

"A Government Scout."

Wanted: The Sundance Woman see Mrs. Sundance Rides Again

Wanted Women see Jessi's Girls

War Arrow (1954) U-I ✡ ✡ ✡

Maureen O'Hara
Jeff Chandler
Noah Berry, Jr.
Dennis Weaver
Jay Silverheels
D: George Sherman

An Army officer trains a Seminole cavalry to fight Kiowas in Texas. Filmed at Agoura, California.

Au ★★★

S ★★★

A ★★★★◖

Warden of Red Rock (2001)

James Caan
David Carradine
Rachel Ticotin
D: Stephen Gyllenhaal

The warden of an Arizona territorial prison encounters an inmate who is an old friend. Made for TV movie.

War Drums (1957) Bel-Air/UA

Lex Barker
Ben Johnson
Joan Taylor
D: Reginald Le Borg

An Indian chief is forced into war when his treaties with the whites are broken.

Warlock (1959) 20th C. Fox ★★★★

Richard Widmark
Henry Fonda
Anthony Quinn
Dorothy Malone
Wallace Ford
D: Edward Dmytryk

A marshal is hired to clean up the town of Warlock. Filmed at Professor Valley, Dead Horse Point St. Park, Kings Bottom, White's Ranch, Arches and Sand Flats, UT. #94 Best of the West.

Au ★★★◖

S ★★★★

A ★★★★

Anthony Quinn in *Warlock.*

War Paint (1953) K-B/UA ★

Robert Stack
Joan Taylor
Charles McGraw
Peter Graves
D: Lesley Selander

An officer leads his cavalry patrol through

—Any man starts a shootin' scrape
I'll kill 'less he kills me first.
—Henry Fonda
Warlock

Death Valley to deliver a peace treaty on time.

Au ★

S ★

A ★◗

War Party (1965) 20ᵗʰ C. Fox

Michael T. Mikler
Davey Davison
Donald Barry
D: Lesley Selander

A rescue party must reach an Army patrol under attack by hostiles.

UNCHARTED
TERRITORY

Warpath (1951) Paramount ★ ★ ★

Edmond O'Brien
Dean Jagger
Forrest Tucker
Harry Carey, Jr.
Chief Yowlachie
D: Byron Haskin

John Vickers enlists in Custer's 7th Cavalry
to avenge a murder. Story by Frank Gruber.
Filmed at the Crow Indian Reservation, MT.

Au ★ ★ ★ ◗

S ★ ★ ★

A ★ ★ ★ ◗

—We're gonna take that wagon.
—John Wayne
The War Wagon

The War Wagon (1967) MS/Batjac/Universal ★ ★ ★ ◗

John Wayne
Kirk Douglas
Howard Keel
Keenan Wynn
Bruce Cabot
Bruce Dern
Emilio Fernandez
D: Burt Kennedy

An ex-convict attempts to take back his
gold–rich land. From a Marvin H. Albert novel.
Filmed near Durango, Mexico, at Los Organos.

Au ★ ★ ◗

S ★ ★ ★ ◗

A ★ ★ ★ ◗

Kirk Douglas and John Wayne in *The War Wagon*.

Wasser für Canitoga see Water for Canitoga

Watch Out Gringo! Sabata Will Return (1972) FF—Ital./Sp.

George Martin
Victor E. Richelmy
D: Alfonso Balcazar

A rambling gunfighter seeks adventure in the Old West.

Water For Canitoga (Wasser für Canitoga) (1939) FF—Ger.

Hans Albers
Charlotte Susa
Hilde Sessak
Peter Voss
Hans Mierendorff
D: Herbert Selpin

Pioneers pipe water to a Canadian
mining company. Shatterhand film.

Waterhole #3 (1967) Paramount

James Coburn
Carroll O'Connor
Margaret Blye
Claude Akins
Bruce Dern
James Whitmore
D: William Graham

A gunfighter attempts to recover stolen
bullion with a sheriff who's daughter he
seduced. Filmed in the Alabama Hills.

Au ★★➤

S ★

A ★★➤

*—You show me an honest sheriff and
I'll show you a man without money.*
—James Coburn
Waterhole #3

Carroll O'Connor in *Waterhole #3.*

The Way West (1967) UA ★★★★➤

Kirk Douglas
Robert Mitchum
Richard Widmark
Lola Albright
Sally Field
Harry Carey, Jr.
Jack Elam
D: Andrew V. McLaglen

A trail guide leads a wagon train west to the
Willamette Valley via the Oregon Trail.
Filmed in Oregon and at Old Tucson.

Au ★★★★➤

S ★★★★➤

A ★★★★➤

*—Well, I've got me a few dim years left. After
that I'll get myself a couple of wives, a fishing
pole and make camp along the waterfall.*
—Robert Mitchum
The Way West

Welcome to Hard Times (Killer on a Horse) (1967) MGM ★★

Henry Fonda
Janice Rule
Keenan Wynn
Janis Page
Warren Oates

514

Edgar Buchanan
Lon Chaney, Jr.
D: Burt Kennedy

A mayor reluctantly confronts a sadistic gunfighter
bent on destroying his town. Based on E.L.
Doctorow's novel. Screenplay by Burt Kennedy.
Filmed at Janss Conejo Ranch, Thousand Oaks, CA.

Au ★★

S ★✦

A ★★★

*—Like you said, Blue, there's a spirit of
life around here. Yes sir, a spirit of life!*
—Denver Pyle
Welcome to Hard Times

Wells Fargo (1937) Paramount

Joel McCrea
Bob Burns
Frances Dee
Lloyd Nolan
Robert Cummings
D: Frank Lloyd

The legendary express company develops into the West's
most noteworthy stageline. Technical advise by Joe De Yong.
Oscar nomination for sound recording. Filmed at the
Paramount Ranch. #89 Best of the West.

Au ★★★★

S ★★★✦

A ★★★★

Westbound (1959) WB

Randolph Scott
Virginia Mayo
Karen Steele
D: Budd Boetticher

A Union officer guards gold shipments on
the Overland stageline from California.

Au ★★★

S ★★★★

A ★★★✦

The Westerner (1940) UA ★★★★

Gary Cooper
Walter Brennan
Fred Stone
Doris Davenport
Forrest Tucker
Chill Wills
D: William Wyler

Judge Roy Bean regrets
sparing a drifter from hanging.
Oscar nomination for writing:
original story and art direction.
Best supporting actor for Brennan.
#98 Best of the West.

*—When I was a kid I had a pet rattlesnake and I
was fond of it. But, I wouldn't turn my back on it.*
—Gary Cooper
The Westerner

Western Union (1941) 20th C. Fox ★ ★

Robert Young
Randolph Scott
Dean Jagger
Barton MacLane
Virginia Gilmore
John Carradine
Chill Wills
Chief Big Tree
Chief Thunder Cloud
Iron Eyes Cody
D: Fritz Lang

A former outlaw scouts for the Western Union construction crew. Story credited to Zane Grey. The studio later claimed that only Grey's title was used, but there are significant similarities between Grey's 1939 novel and the screenplay. Filmed at Old Pariah, Utah.

West of Montana see Mail Order Bride

West of the Pecos (1934) RKO-Radio

Richard Dix
Martha Sleeper
Samuel S. Hinds
Fred Kholer
D: Phil Rosen

A gunman delivering law and order to postwar Texas rescues a woman disguised as a boy. Story by Zane Grey.

West of the Pecos (1945) RKO

Robert Mitchum
Barbara Hale
Richard Martin
Thurston Hall
D: Edward Killy

Remake of the 1934 version. Story was creditied to Zane Grey, but only the title resembles Grey's work. Filmed in the Alabama Hills.

Westward Ho the Wagons! (1957) Disney/BV ★ ★ ★

Fess Parker
Jeff York
Kathleen Crowley
Karen Pendleton

Randolph Scott in *Western Union.*

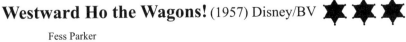

—We can't go on this way any longer. It's got to be either you or me.
—Randolph Scott
Western Union

George Reeves
John War Eagle
Iron Eyes Cody
D: William Beaudine

A frontier doctor leads a wagon train on the Oregon Trail.
Story by Tom Blackburn. Filmed at Janss Conejo Ranch, CA.

Au ★★★

S ★★★

A ★★★

Westward the Women (1952) MGM ★★⭒

Robert Taylor
Denise Darcel
John McIntire
D: William A. Wellman

A trail boss guides a wagon train of mail-order
brides to California. Filmed at Kanab, Utah.

Au ★★

S ★★⭒

A ★★⭒

*—See, you overlooked one thing…the will of
a woman when there's a weddin' ring in sight.*
—John McIntire
Westward the Women

What Am I Doing in the Middle of the Revolution (1973) FF—Ital.

Vittorio Gassman
Paolo Villaggio
Eduardo Fajardo
D: Sergio Corbucci

Two Italians wandering through Mexico become involved in the
revolution when one of them assumes the identity of Zapata.

UNCHARTED TERRITORY

When A Man's A Man (Saga of the West) (1935) Atherton/Fox

George O'Brien
Dorothy Wilson
Paul Kelly
Harry Woods
D: Edward Cline

A cowboy helps recover a rancher's water supply from outlaws.

UNCHARTED TERRITORY

When the Daltons Rode (1940) Universal ★★

Randolph Scott
Kay Francis
Brian Donlevy
George Bancroft
Broderick Crawford
Andy Devine
D: George Marshall

A young lawyer befriends the Daltons.
Bears little resemblance to the book
written by Emmett Dalton, *When the
Daltons Rode.*

*—You don't have to worry about me, Honey.
I'm a one woman man.*
—Andy Devine
When the Daltons Rode

Au ★

S ★★★◗

A ★★★◗

Where the Hell's That Gold ?!!? (1988) WNP/Brigade P./K-S/CBS-TV ★★★

Willie Nelson
Jack Elam
Delta Burke
Gerald McRaney
D: Burt Kennedy

Two gunmen pursue hidden treasure south of
the border. Filmed in Chama, NM, and Alamosa, CO.

Au ★★◗

S ★★★◗

A ★★★★◗

Whirlwind (2001)

Mark Atienza
Scott M. Rudolph
Mikael Paul
D: Frank Robak

Two outlaw brothers are on the run in 1877.

UNCHARTED TERRITORY

Whispering Smith (1949) Paramount ★★◗

Alan Ladd
Robert Preston
Brenda Marshall
William Demarest
D: Leslie Fenton

A railway detective pursues an outlaw gang.
Remake of the 1916 and 1926 versions.
Based on the Frank H. Spearman novel.
Filmed at Paramount Ranch, Agoura, CA.

—The only cards I had were the ones you dealt me.
—Alan Ladd
Whispering Smith

Au ★★

S ★★★◗

A ★★★

White Apache (1984) FF—Ital./Sp.

Sebastian Harrison
Lola Forner
D: Vincent Dawn (Bruno Mattei)

An Irish baby is raised by Apaches.

UNCHARTED TERRITORY

The White Buffalo (Hunt to Kill) (1977) UA

Charles Bronson
Jack Warden
Will Sampson
Kim Novak
Clint Walker
Stuart Whitman
Slim Pickens
John Carradine
D: J. Lee Thompson

Wild Bill Hickok and Crazy Horse
hunt a mythical white buffalo.
Filmed at Buckskin Joe, Canon City, CO.

*—Now, now, sonny boy, didn't your ma never tell
you yer mouth wasn't made for breakin' wind?*
—Jack Warden
The White Buffalo

Au
S
A

White Comanche (1967) FF—Ital./Sp./U.S.

William Shatner
Joseph Cotten
D: Gilbert Lee Kay (Josè Briz)

Two half-breed brothers feud.

White Fang (1936) Fox

Michael Whalen
Jean Muir
John Carradine
Lightning (a dog)
D: David Butler

A young Klondike prospector develops a bond
with a wolf. From the Jack London novel.

White Fang (1947) FF—Rus.

Oleg Giakov
Nina Ismailova
D: Alexander Sguridi

Remake of the 1936 version.

White Fang (1974) FF—Ital./Sp.

Franco Nero
Virna Lisi
Fernando Rey
Harry Carey, Jr.
D: Lucia Fulci

Remake of the 1936 version.

White Fang (1991) BV/SSP

Klaus Marie Brandauer
Ethan Hawke
Seymour Cassel
Susan Hogan
D: Randall Kleiser

Remake of the 1936 version.

Au ★★★★★
S ★★★
A ★★★

White Fang 2: Myth of White Wolf (1994) Disney ★★

Scott Bairstow
Charmaine Craig
Al Harrington
D: Ken Olin

An Alaskan miner and his wolf-dog uncover a scheme to cheat
Indians of their land. Sequel to Jack London's *White Fang*.

Au ★★★
S ★★
A ★★

White Feather (1955) Pan. Prod./20th C. Fox

Robert Wagner
John Lund
Debra Paget
Noah Beery, Jr.
Hugh O'Brian
Milburn Stone
D: Robert Webb

A cavalry officer resettles plains Indians.

The White Man see The Squaw Man

The White Squaw (1956) Columbia ★

David Brian
May Wynn
William Bishop
D: Ray Nazarro

A Swedish settler begins a war when he attempts
to drive Sioux Indians off their reservation.

Au ★
S ★
A ★

Longhorn, a Sauk and Fox.

520

Whitewater Sam (1977)

Keith Larson
D: Keith Larson

The first white mountain man adapts to life in the Rockies.

Whity (1971) FF—Ger.

Günther Kaufmann
Ron Randell
Hanna Schygulla
D: Rainer W. Fassbinder

In 1878 a dysfunctional southwestern family employs
a mulatto butler to murder other family members.

Who Killed Johnny R.? (1966) FF—Ital./Sp.

Lex Barker
Joachim Fushsberger
D: Josè Luis Madrid

A gun salesman is mistaken for an outlaw.

Who Killed the Mysterious Mr. Foster? see Sam Hill: Who Killed the Mysterious Mr. Foster?

Wichita (1955) AA

Joel McCrea
Vera Miles
Lloyd Bridges
Edgar Buchanan
Peter Graves
Jack Elam
D: Jacques Tourneur

Wyatt Earp establishes law and order in a Kansas cowtown.
Filmed at Melody Ranch, California.

Au ★★
S ★★★
A ★★★

The Wicked Die Slow (1968)

Gary Allen
Steve Rivard
Jeff Kanew
D: William K. Hennigar

Wild Bill Hickok

The Wild and the Innocent (1959) U-I ★★◗

Audie Murphy
Joanne Dru
Gilbert Roland
Jim Backus
Sandra Dee
Strother Martin
D: Jack Sher

A young trapper and a mountain girl discover
the complexities of frontier "civilization."
Filmed in Big Bear, California.

Au ★★

S ★★◗

A ★★◗

The Wild and the Sweet see Lovin' Molly

Wild and Wooly (1978) ABC-TV/ASP ★★◗

Sandra Dee and Audie Murphy in *The Wild and the Innocent.*

Chris DeLisle
Susan Bigelow
Elyssa Davalos
Doug McClure
Ross Martin
Vic Morrow
Jessica Walter
D: Philip Leacock

Four women escape from a women's prison in Yuma
and prevent the assassination of Teddy Roosevelt.
Filmed at Old Tucson.

Au ★★★

S ★★◗

A ★★★

—A place ain't what one man makes it.
—Audie Murphy
The Wild and the Innocent

Wild Bill (1995) UA ★★★◗

Jeff Bridges
Ellen Barkin
John Hurt
Diane Lane
David Arquette
Bruce Dern
Keith Carradine
Marjoe Gortner
Robert Peters
D: Walter Hill

The legendary gunfighter administers
law and order to frontier towns.
Filmed at Melody Ranch, California.

Au ★★★★★

S ★★★

A ★★★◗

Robert Peters and Jeff Bridges in *Wild Bill.*

522

Wild Bill Hickok Rides (1942) WB

Constance Bennett
Bruce Cabot
Warren William
Ward Bond
D: Ray Enright

Hickok and a gambling queen confront a Chicago
land grabber running settlers off their homesteads.

Au ★★☆
S ★
A ★

Wild Bill's duel.

Wild Bunch (1969) WB ★★★

William Holden
Ernest Borgnine
Robert Ryan
Edmond O'Brien
Warren Oates
Ben Johnson
Strother Martin
D: Sam Peckinpah

Aging outlaws enter Mexico at the turn of the century for
one last job. Oscar nominations for best writing: story
and screenplay not previously published or produced and
original score. Filmed at Durango, Mexico.
#80 AFI GM, #69 AFI MHPM, #6 IMDb.

Au ★★★★☆
S ★★★★
A ★★★★

Ernest Borgnine in *Wild Bunch*.

The Wild Country (The Newcomers) (1971) BV ★★★

Steve Forrest
Jack Elam
Ronny (Ron) Howard
Frank de Kova
D: Robert Totten

A family suffers the hardships of settling
the Wyoming Territory. Disney.

Au ★★★★
S ★★★
A ★★★★

The Wild Dakotas (1956) Assoc. ★

Bill Williams
Coleen Gray
Jim Davis
Iron Eyes Cody
D: Sam Newfield

A frontiersman prevents a wagonmaster
from stirring up trouble with hostiles.
Story by Tom Blackburn.

Au

S

A

Wilderness Mail (1935) Ambassador

Kermit Maynard
Fred Kohler
Paul Hurst
D: Forrest Sheldon

A Canadian Mountie tracks the murderers
of a trapper. Story by James O. Curwood.

UNCHARTED
TERRITORY

Wild Heritage (1958) U-I

Will Rogers, Jr.
Maureen O'Sullivan
Rod McKuen
Casey Tibbs
Troy Donahue
Gary Gray
D: Charles Haas

Two families travel west by covered wagon.
Filmed at Janss Ranch, California.

Au

S

A

Gary Gray, Rod McKuen and Casey Tibbs in *Wild Heritage*.

Wild Horse (Silver Devil) (1931) Allied

Hoot Gibson
Alberta Vaughn
Stepin Fetchit
D: Richard Thorpe, Sidney Algier

A bronc buster is falsely accused of murder.

UNCHARTED
TERRITORY

Wild Horse Mesa (1932) Paramount

Randolph Scott
Sally Blaine
James Bush
George ("Gabby") Hayes
Jim Thorpe
D: Henry Hathaway

A wrangler confronts rustlers and is accused of murder. Remake
of the 1925 silent version. Based on the Zane Grey novel.

UNCHARTED
TERRITORY

The Wild North (The Big North) (1952) MGM

Stewart Granger
Wendell Corey

Cyd Charisse
John War Eagle
D: Andrew Marton

A Canadian trapper is falsely accused of murder.
Filmed in Idaho.

Au ★★★◣

S ★★

A ★★

The Wild Pony (1983) HF/KFE/FF—Can.

Marilyn Lightstone
Art Hindle
Josh Byrne
D: Kevin Sullivan

A young boy tames a wild pony which unites
his mother and stepfather. Made for TV movie.

Wild Rovers (1971) MGM

William Holden
Ryan O'Neal
Karl Malden
Lynn Carlin
Tom Skerritt
Joe Don Baker
Boyd "Red" Morgan
D: Blake Edwards

An aging cowboy and a green gunman team up
to rob a bank. Filmed in Sedona, AZ, Arches
National Park and Monument Valley, Utah,
and at Old Tucson. #69 Best of the West.

*—Hell, Frank, you show me a young cowboy
or an old cowboy or an in between cowboy
that's got more than a few dollars in his poke,
an' I'll show you a cowboy who's stopped
being a cowboy and started robbin' banks!*
—William Holden
Wild Rovers

Au ★★★★

S ★★★★

A ★★★★

Wild Stallion (1952) Mono. ★★◣

Ben Johnson
Edgar Buchanan
Martha Hyer
D: Lewis Collins

An orphan raised by a cowboy at a
cavalry post pursues a wild horse.

Au ★★

S ★◣

A ★◣

Wild Stampede (1962) FF—Mex.

Luis Aguilar
Christiane Martel
Augustine de Anda
D: Raul de Anda

Outlaws and revolutionaries fight over wild horses.

Wild Times (1980) GC

Sam Elliott
Leif Erickson
Bruce Boxleitner
Penny Peyser
Ben Johnson
Cameron Mitchell
Harry Carey, Jr.
Dennis Hopper
D: Richard Comton

A dime-novel hero becomes a Wild West showman. Two-part mini-series. Filmed at Eaves Movie Ranch, Santa Fé, New Mexico.

Au ★★★★
S ★★
A ★★★

The Wild Westerners (1962) Columbia

James Philbrook
Nancy Kovack
Duane Eddy
D: Oscar Rudolph

A lawman and his wife transport Union gold across the desert. Filmed in the Alabama Hills.

Au ★
S ★
A ★

—You know, if I thought you wouldn't get any fool ideas about runnin' off again, well, I'd ask you to come back.
—James Philbrook
The Wild Westerners

Wild Wild West (1999) WB ★★★

Will Smith
Kevin Kline
Kenneth Branagh
Salma Hayek
Buck Taylor
D: Barry Sonnenfeld

Two Secret Service agents protect President Grant from another Dr. Loveless. Based on the TV series. Filmed in northern New Mexico and Monument Valley.

Au ★★
S ★★★
A ★★★

Will Smith in *Wild Wild West.*

The Wild Wild West Revisited (1979) CBS-TV

Robert Conrad
Ross Martin
Harry Morgan

Paul Williams
Skip Homeier
D: Burt Kennedy

Two government agents investigate a plot to
replace European royalty with clones.
Made for TV movie based on the series.
Filmed at Old Tucson.

Au ★★◗

S ★★◗

A ★

Wild Women (1970) ABC-TV ★ ★

Hugh O'Brian
Anne Francis
Marylin Maxwell
D: Don Taylor

Army surveyors disguise themselves as a
wagon train using convicts as their wives.

Au ★★★

S ★◗

A ★★◗

Willie Boy see Tell Them Willie Boy Is Here

Montana cowboy, E.H. Brewster, circa 1880.

Will Penny (1968) Paramount ★ ★ ★ ★ ★

Charlton Heston
Joan Hackett
Donald Pleasence
Lee Majors
Bruce Dern
Ben Johnson
Slim Pickens
D: Tom Gries

An aging cowboy confronts his future. From a
character introduced in *The Bushwackers* (1952).
Filmed in the Inyo National Forest, California.

Charlton Heston as Will Penny.

#4 Best of the West, #4 LPFF.

Au

S ★ ★ ★ ★ ★

A ★ ★ ★ ★ ★

Winchester Does Not Forgive (1968) FF—Ital.

Dean Reed
Monika Brugger
D: Adelchi Bianchi

A gunman avenges the murder of his father.

Winchester for Hire see Blake's Marauders

Winchester '73 (Montana Winchester) (1950) U-I

James Stewart
Shelley Winters
Dan Duryea
Will Geer
Rock Hudson
Tony Curtis
Chief Yowlachie
John War Eagle
D: Anthony Mann

A man tracks his prize Winchester
to the man who stole it. Screenplay
by R.L. Richards and Borden Chase.
Filmed at Old Tucson. #18 IMDb.

—Some things a man has to do, so he does it.
—James Stewart
Winchester '73

Au ★ ★ ◖

S ★ ★ ★ ◖

A ★ ★ ★ ★

Winchester '73 (1967) NBC-TV/Universal

Tom Tyron
John Saxon
Dan Duryea
John Drew Barrymore
D: Herschel Dauherty

Remake of the 1950 version.

Wind from the East (1969) FF—Ital./Sp.

Gian Maria Volenté
Anne Wiazemsky
D: Jean-luc Godard

Filmed near the Cinecitta Studio in Spain.

Wind River (1998)

Blake Heron
A. Martinez
Russell Means
Wes Studi
D: Tom Shell

Based on Tom Shell's adaptation of a Pony Express rider's memoirs.

The Winds of Autumn (1976) Howco Prod.

Jack Elam
Jeanette Nolan
Andrew Prine
Dub Taylor
D: Charles B. Pierce

A boy and his foster father avenge the murder of his family.

Au ★★★★✦

S ★★★

A ★★

Wings of the Hawk (1953) U-I

Van Heflin
Julia Adams
Abbe Lane
Noah Beery, Jr.
D: Budd Boetticher

An American miner becomes entangled with
Mexican rebels in 1911. Originally in 3-D.
Filmed at Corriganville, California.

Au ★★

S ★★★

A ★★★

—Why did you do it, Irish?
The mine was all you had.
—Julia Adams
Wings of the Hawk

Winnetou and Shatterhand in the Valley of Death (1968) FF—Ger./Yugo./Ital.

Lex Barker
Pierre Brice
D: Harald Reinl

Chief Winnetou and his bloodbrother are left for dead.
The final "Winnetou" film.

Winnetou: Last of the Renegades (1964) FF—Fr./Ital./Ger./Yugo.

Lex Barker
Pierre Brice
D: Harald Reinl

Chief Winnetou and his bloodbrother work towards avoiding an Indian war.

Winnetou: The Desperado Trail (1965) FF—Ger./Yugo.

Lex Barker
Pierre Brice
D: Harald Reinl

Chief Winnetou and his bloodbrother attempt to keep
the peace by proving the chief is innocent of murder.

Winnetou the Warrior (Apache Gold) (1963) FF—Fr./Ital./Ger./Yugo.

Lex Barker
Pierre Brice
D: Harald Reinl

Chief Winnetou and his bloodbrother fight the railroad.
The second of the "Winnetou" films. Based on Karl May's
19th century, *Winnetou I.*

Winnetou: Thunder at the Border (1967) FF—Ger./Yugo.

Rod Cameron
Pierre Brice
D: Alfred Vohrer

Chief Winnetou and his bloodbrother defend a border town from outlaws.

Winterhawk (1975) Howco Prod.

Michael Dante
Leif Erickson
Woody Strode
Denver Pyle
Dawn Wells
D: Charles B. Pierce

A Blackfoot chief looks to a white
settlement for a cure for small pox.
Filmed in Montana.

Red Plume, Siouan Blackfoot 1852.

Wishbone Cutter see Shadow of Chikara

With Friends, Nothing Is Easy (1971) FF—Sp./Ital.

Richard Harrison
Fernando Sancho
D: Steve MacCohy (Ignacio Iquino)

A bounty hunter returns three gun runners from Mexico.

Without Honors (1932) Artclass

Harry Carey
Mae Bush
Gibson Gowland
George ("Gabby") Hayes
D: William Nigh

The Wolf Hunters (1950) Mono.

Kirby Grant
Jan Clayton
Helen Parrish
D: Oscar "Bud" Boetticher

A Mountie tracking fur thieves stumbles on a lost gold mine.
Based on a James O. Curwood story.

Woman for Ringo (1966) FF—Ital./Sp.

Pili
Mili
Sean Flynn
D: Rafael R. Marchent

Twin sharpshooters inherit the deed to a ranch.

The Woman of the Town (1943) UA

Claire Trevor
Albert Dekker
Barry Sullivan
Henry Hull
D: George Archbainbaud

Bat Masterson falls for Dodge City's leading woman.

Au ★ ✦

S ★ ★

A ★ ★

The Woman They Almost Lynched (1953) Republic

John Lund
Brian Donlevy
Joan Leslie
Jim Davis
D: Allan Dwan

A woman risks her life for a Confederate spy
in a Missouri border town. Western parody.

Au ★

S ✦

A ✦

Women of Destiny see San Antone

Woman of the North Country (1952) Republic

Ruth Hussey
Rod Cameron
John Agar
Gale Storm
Jim Davis
D: Joseph Kane

A mining engineer encounters a ruthless female miner.

The Wonderful Country (1959) DRMP

Robert Mitchum
Julie London
Gary Merrill
Jack Oakie
Leroy "Satchel" Paige
D: Robert Parrish

A Texan gunfighter is hired by Mexican gunrunners.

The Wooden Gun (2000)

Jon Jacobs
Dawn Kapatos
Michael Kastenbaum
D: Jon Jacobs and Michael Kastenbaum

An outlaw uses a special wooden gun to escape from the law.

Wrath of God (1968) FF—Ital./Sp.

Brett Halsey (Montgomery Ford)
Dana Ghia
D: Alberto Cardone

A gunman avenges the murder of his fiancèe.

Wyatt Earp (1994) WB ★★★★

Kevin Costner
Dennis Quaid
Gene Hackman
Jeff Fahey
Mark Harmon
D: Lawrence Kasden

A brokenhearted gunman becomes a legendary lawman. Oscar nomination for best cinematography. Filmed at the Eaves Movie Ranch, Ghost Ranch, and at the Cumbres & Toltec Railroad, NM. #62 Best of the West.

Au ★★★★★
S ★★★★
A ★★★★

—Throw up your hands. I want your guns!
—Michael Madsen (Virgil Earp)
Wyatt Earp

—Give up your arms!
—Virgil Earp

Wyatt Earp: Return to Tombstone (1994) CSTF/CBS-TV ★★

Hugh O'Brian
Bruce Boxleitner
Jay Underwood
Harry Carey, Jr.
Martin Kove
Don Meredith
Bob Steele
D: Frank McDonald, Paul Landres and Jim Roberson

Wyatt Earp returns to Tombstone in 1914 in order to fulfill a promise. Wonderful use of a series of flashbacks utilizing colorized scenes from "The Life and Times of Wyatt Earp" TV series. Theme song by Johnny Cash.

Au ★★
S ★★
A ★★

Hugh O'Brian as Wyatt Earp.

Wyoming (Bad Man of Wyoming) (1940) MGM ★★★

Wallace Beery
Leo Carrillo
Ann Rutherford
Lee Bowman
Chill Wills
Chief Thunder Cloud
D: Richard Thorpe

A reformed outlaw becomes entangled in a dispute between rustlers and ranchers.

Au ★★★
S ★★★
A ★★★★

—It's not about shootin' fast, Mr. Montgomery. It's about shootin' straight.
—Hugh O'Brian
Wyatt Earp: Return to Tombstone

Kevin Costner (third from the left) as Earp in *Wyatt Earp.*

**Law and Order
on the
Silver Screen**

Burt Lancaster (second from the left) as Earp in *Gunfight at the O.K. Corral.*

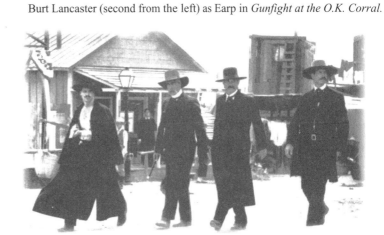

Kurt Russell (third from the left) as Earp in *Tombstone.*

Walter Huston (right) as Earp in *Law and Order* (1932).

Wyoming (1947) Republic ⭐🌙

William Elliot
Vera Ralston
John Carroll
George ("Gabby") Hayes
Ben Johnson
D: Joseph Kane

A rancher defends his self-made empire from homesteaders. Filmed at Kernville, California.

Au ⭐🌙

S ⭐🌙

A ⭐🌙

The Wyoming Kid see Cheyenne

Wyoming Mail (1950) U-I ⭐

Stephen McNally
Alexis Smith
Howard DeSilva
James Arness
D: Reginald LeBorg

A postal investigator poses as a bank robber in order to save a mail franchise.

Au ⭐

S ⭐

A ⭐

"The Cowboy."

Wyoming Renegades (1955) Columbia ⭐🌙

Phil Carey
Martha Hyer
Gene Evans
D: Fred F. Sears

Butch Cassidy's gang stands in the way of an ex-convict and his girlfriend reforming.

Au ⭐🌙

S ⭐🌙

A ⭐🌙

—...a woman can't bite ya, but she sure can gnaw.

—Gene Evans
Wyoming Renegades

Yankee (1967) FF—Ital./Sp.

Philippe Leroy
Adolfo Celi
D: Tinto Brass

A gunfighter enters Mexico to defend the town of Pueblo.

UNCHARTED
TERRITORY

Yankee Dudler (1973) FF—Ger./Sp.

Geraldine Chaplin
William Berger
D: Volker Vogeler

A family of Bavarian woodcutters settle in the American West.

Yaqui Drums (1956) AA ★

Rod Cameron
Mary Castle
J. Carrol Naish
D: Jean Yarbrough

A cowboy fights to save his dead brother's ranch from a crooked land baron.

Au ★ ★

S ★

A ★

Yellow Dust (1936) RKO ★

Richard Dix
Leila Hyams
Moroni Olson
Jesse Ralph
D: Wallace Fox

A saloon girl saves a prospector's gold.

Au ★ ★

S ◀

A ★

The Yellow Mountain (1954) U-I

Lex Barker
Mala Powers
Howard Duff
William Demarest
D: Jesse Hibbs

Two men fight over a girl and a gold claim.

Yellow Sky (1948) 20ᵗʰ C. Fox ★ ★ ★

Gregory Peck
Ann Baxter
Richard Widmark
Henry Morgan
Jay Silverheels
Chief Yowlachie
D: William A. Wellman

Bank robbers escape to a desert ghost town and encounter a prospector and his granddaughter. Based on the W.R. Burnett story. Filmed in the Alabama Hills.

Au ★ ★ ◀

S ★ ★ ★

A ★ ★ ★ ★

—If that don't suit ya, you gotta fight on your hands and you'd better get at it quick!
—Gregory Peck
Yellow Sky

Yellowstone Kelly (1959) WB

Clint Walker
Edward Byrnes
John Russell
Claude Akins
Warren Oates
D: Gordon Douglas

A mountain man attempts the return of an injured
Indian woman to her people. Based on the life of
Luther "Yellowstone" Kelly and on the Clay Fisher
novel. Screenplay by Burt Kennedy. Filmed in Sedona, AZ.

Au ★★

S ★★★★⧫

A ★★★

Clint Walker as Yellowstone Kelly.

The Yellow Tomahawk (1954) Bel-Air/UA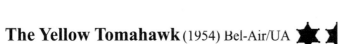

Rory Calhoun
Peggie Castle
Noah Beery, Jr.
Peter Graves
Lee Van Cleef
Rita Moreno
D: Lesley Selander

A massacre and a broken treaty complicate a scout's
association with the cavalry and the Cheyenne.
Filmed at the Kanab Movie Ranch, Utah.

Au ★★

S ⧫

A ★

Yellowstone Kelly circa 1878.

Young and Free (1979)

Ivy Angustain
Eric Larsen
Keith Larsen
D: Keith Larsen

A young man and an Indian girl survive in the wilderness.

*—Got any idea what it's like to spend
a winter in Montana high country?
See nobody white. Talkin' to yourself.
All the time lonesome.*

—Clint Walker
Yellowstone Kelly

Young, Billy Young (1969) UA

Robert Mitchum
Angie Dickinson
Robert Walke
David Carradine
Jack Kelly
D: Burt Kennedy

A young man is accused of murder after a gunfight.
From the Will Henry novel, *Who Rides With Wyatt?*
Screenplay by Burt Kennedy. Kennedy considered this,

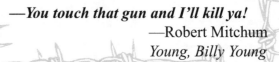

—You touch that gun and I'll kill ya!
—Robert Mitchum
Young, Billy Young

"a bad picture." Filmed near Florence, Arizona and at Old Tucson.

Au ★★★⚊

S ★★★⚊

A ★★★★

The Young Country (1970) ABC-TV/Universal ★ ★ ★

Walter Brennan
Joan Hackett
Roger Davis
Wally Cox
D: Roy Huggins

A young gambler attempts to return a saddlebag of money.

Au ★★★

S ★★★

A ★★★

—*Show me a man who plays poker for fun and I'll show you a loser.*
—Roger Davis
The Young Country

The Younger Brothers (1949) WB

Wayne Morris
Janis Paige
Bruce Bennett
Geraldine Brooks
Alan Hale
D: Edwin L. Marin

The Youngers must avoid trouble for two weeks in order to gain their freedom.

Young Fury (1965) Paramount

Rory Calhoun
Virginia Mayo
Lon Chaney
John Agar
William Bendix
D: Chris Nyby

Young gunfighters take over the town of Dawson.

UNCHARTED TERRITORY

The Young Guns (1956) AA ★★⚊

Russ Tamblyn
Gloria Talbott
Perry Lopez
D: Albert Band

The son of a gunfighter must live up to his reputation.

Au ★★⚊

S ★★

A ★★⚊

Young Guns (1988) 20th C. Fox

Emilio Estevez
Kiefer Sutherland
Lou Diamond Phillips
Charlie Sheen
Brian Keith
Jack Palance
Patrick Wayne
D: Christopher Cain

Billy the Kid leads a band of young
gunfighters during the Lincoln County Wars.
Filmed in New Mexico.

Au ★★★

S ★★★⯪

A ★★★★

Emilio Estevez (lower center) and his gang of outlaws in *Young Guns*.

Young Guns II (1990) MCP

William Petersen
Emilio Estevez
Kiefer Sutherland
Lou Diamond Phillips
Christian Slater
D: Geoff Murphy

Following the Lincoln County Wars, Pat Garrett and his
posse chase Billy and his gang into Mexico. Sequel to
Young Guns. Filmed at White Sands National Monument
and at Old Tucson.

Au ★★★★

S ★★

A ★★★

Rufus Buck (center) and his gang of outlaws were hanged in 1896.

Young Guns of Texas (1963) 20th C. Fox ★★⯪

James Mitchum
Alana Ladd
Jody McCrea
Chill Wills
D: Maury Dexter

A father tracks his daughter and her suitor.
Features the offspring of noted film stars.
Filmed at Old Tucson.

Au ★⯪

S ★⯪

A ★⯪

*—When the good Lord decides that one
man's gonna run this human race, he's
gonna come down here and get that job
done himself.*

—Chill Wills
Young Guns of Texas

Young Jesse James (1960) 20th C. Fox

Ray Stricklyn
Willard Parker
Merry Anders
D: William Claxton

Jesse joins Quantrill's Raiders.

The Young Land (1959) Columbia

Pat Wayne
Yvonne Craig
Dennis Hopper
Ken Curtis
D: Ted Tetzlaff

An American is tried for murdering a Mexican in the new state of California.

Young Maverick: Dead Man's Hand (1979) WB ★★ ◤

Charles Frank
Susan Blanchard
Howard Duff
John Dehner
Donna Mills
John McIntire
Harry Carey, Jr.
D: Hy Averback

Beau Maverick's son takes over a dead man's hand.
Made-for-TV movie based on the "Young Maverick" series.

Au ★◤

S ★◤

A ★★

––If we do ride together, I just want you to understand. I go where I want to, do what I want to and that's how I want to.
—Charles Frank
Young Maverick: Dead Man's Hand

Young Pioneers (1976) ABC-TV/CF

Roger Kern
Linda Purl
Robert Hayes
D: Michael O'Herlihy

Teenage newlyweds head west for
the Dakotas. Filmed at Old Tucson.

Young Pioneers' Christmas (1976) ABC-TV/CF ★

Linda Purl
Roger Kern
Robert Hayes
D: Michael O'Herlihy

Upon losing their infant son, a frontier couple celebrate the holidays.
Made for TV sequel to *Young Pioneers.* Filmed at Old Tucson.

Au ★★

S ★

A ★

You're Jinxed, Friend, You Just Met Sacramento (1970) FF—Ital./Sp.

Ty Hardin
Christian Hay
D: Giorgio Cristallini

A cowboy is forced to face a town boss.

Yuma (1970) ABC-TV/ASP ★ ★

Clint Walker
Barry Sullivan
Kathryn Hays
Edgar Buchanan
D: Ted Post

A marshal investigates corrupt townsmen who are cheating the Indians. Filmed at Old Tucson.

Au ★ ★

S ★ ★

A ★ ★

—He's my prisoner, King. One of us will have to die for him.

—Clint Walker
Yuma

Zachariah (1970) ABC Pictures

John Rubinstein
Pat Quinn
Don Johnson
Country Joe and the Fish
D: George Englund

A gunman must decide between a life of violence or harmony with his environment. Cameos from various rock groups.

Zandy's Bride (For Better, for Worse) (1974) WB ★ ★ ★ ★ ★

Gene Hackman
Liv Ullmann
Eileen Heckert
Harry Dean Stanton
Sam Bottoms
D: Jan Troell

A rough-and-tumble cattle rancher adjusts to a strong-willed mail-order bride. Filmed in Big Sur, California.

Au ★ ★ ★ ★ ★

S ★ ★ ★ ★ ★

A ★ ★ ★ ★ ★

Liv Ullmann as Zandy's bride.

El Zorro see Zorro the Fox

Zorro (1974) FF—Ital./Fr.

Alain Delon
Stanley Baker
D: Duccio Tessari

Zorro leads the people of southern California in a plot to overturn the military rule.

Zorro at the Spanish Court (1962) FF—Ital.

Giorgio Ardisson
Alberto Lupo
Nina Marlowe
D: Luigi Capuano

Zorro opposes a corrupt governor.

Zorro, Rider of Vengeance (1971) FF—Sp./Ital.

Charles Quincey
Malisa Longo
D: Josè Luis Merino

Zorro avenges the death of his friend and rescues his bride from an imposter.

Zorro Rides Again (1959) Republic

John Carroll
Helen Christian
Reed Howes
Noah Beery
Yakima Canutt
D: William Witney, John English

Zorro helps a family whose railroad is threatened.
Feature-length version of the 1937 serial.

Zorro the Avenger (1960) WD/BV

Guy Williams
Henry Calvin
Gene Sheldon
Don Diamond
D: Charles Barton

Zorro fights for justice. Compiled from
episodes 27-39 of the Disney TV series.

Au ★ ◗

S ★ ★

A ★ ★

Zorro the Fox (El Zorro) (1968) FF—Ital./Sp.

George Ardisson
Spartaco Battisti
Femi Benussi
D: Guido Zurli

Zorro the Rebel (1966) FF—Ital.

Howard Ross
Dina De Santis
Charles Borromel
D: Pierro Pierotti

Zorro saves a girl from a forced marriage.

"A Montana Type."

✦ EPILOG. ✦

Ihave spent countless hours researching and preparing this guide for your journey through the Western genre. My journey is complete and yours is about to begin. If you discover that you've been led astray and detect any errors or oversights, I would appreciate hearing from you. You may reach me through the publisher. Be assured that your input will be considered during the preparation of future editions. Best of luck and enjoy.

David F. Matuszak

THE NEXT 100 YEARS.

The golden age of the Western genre rode into the sunset in the 1960s. It's gone forever. Several reasons explain why it will never return. The further we move in time away from the 19th century, the more removed we become from the events that shaped the genre. When the first Western was released in 1903, the frontier had yet to close. Tom Horn was hung that year. Butch and Sundance were on the run and Wounded Knee was a fresh scar. At the beginning of the 20th century the frontier was closing in the West. By the end of the century, the pioneer spirit shifted its focus to the skies. Space travel and *Star Wars* became the new frontier. The marketing of Crockett's "Betsy" was replaced with the sales of "light sabers." The pioneer spirit, however, remained unchanged. What did change was the contemporary events. The first moon landing in 1969 occurred at the same time that the Western genre was fading. Space exploration made the marketing of *Star Wars* timely and hugely successful. Children in the '70s, '80s and '90s rarely, if ever, saw a Western. Consequently, they never fostered an appreciation for the genre. Instead, they watched *Star Wars* and "Power Rangers." I suggest that given the opportunity, today's kids will often react as enthusiastically to the TV Westerns of the '50s.

I happened upon an opportunity to test my hypothesis. While watching my first "Power Ranger" episode with my own son, it hit me like a Sioux war club. The stories, the moral lessons, the clear division between good and evil—even the secret identities were right out of a "Lone Ranger" script. Why then, I theorized, wouldn't my son enjoy my "Lone Ranger" as much as his "Power Rangers?" So, we watched several episodes of "The Lone Ranger." I was surprised at its immediate and overwhelming acceptance. That was nearly two years ago. He is now 13 and rarely watches the "Power Rangers." Instead, he enjoys "The Lone Ranger" with the same enthusiasm that he once demonstrated for his "Power Rangers." Simple and anecdotal proof that youngsters will likely react to whichever frontier is marketed to them. Without the development of a young audience to develop a new generation of Westerns viewers, the popularity of "A" Westerns will never be as widespread as it was during the golden age of Westerns.

The golden age of "A" Westerns, roughly between 1940 and 1965, relied on "Bs" and TV series to cultivate its audience. Viewers were developed much the same way that the minor leagues develop baseball players. How long would major league baseball survive without the minors? During the '30s, '40s and '50s, the "Bs" and TV series developed within rookie viewers a taste for and appreciation of the Western genre. They became the target audience for feature-length filmmakers. That target audience is rapidly graying and populating Boot Hill.

Another factor will prevent a second golden age. The decades of "Bs" and TV Westerns served not only to develop a target audience, but they also developed stars and character actors that will never again ride the range. The sheer number of Westerns of all types created unforgettable personalities on the silver screen. Stars like John Wayne, Clint Eastwood, Randolph Scott, Charlton Heston, Burt Lancaster, Jimmy Stewart, Joel McCrea, etc., created distinctive characters with whom we associated. They created a bond with us—part hero worship and part fantasy association. When the Duke rode into the sunset, we sat in the saddle. In order to recreate that following, hundreds of new Westerns must be made. And, of course, that is not likely.

However, new Western stars can be developed. Kevin Costner continues to demonstrate a passion for Western filmmaking. Tom Selleck too. Selleck is perhaps our best hope in this regard. His enthusiasm for Westerns has been instrumental in keeping the genre alive. Selleck in association with TNT continues to turn out one fine Western after another. Selleck may be our best hope in the near future for producing the perfect Western as well. His presence on screen is sufficient. But, he can not go it alone. What the genre is missing more than any other single factor is a pool of great character actors. Walter, Ben, Slim, Chill and Dick are gone. Only two of the top ten character actors are still working, Dern and Palance. Every effort must be made to include them in the perfect Western.

Wilford Brimley was excellent in Westerns during the '90s. He is developing the sort of recognition necessary for a classic role in the perfect Western. For it is recognition that made the great character actors. Each of them appeared in hundreds of Westerns—good and bad. Brennan, Pickens and Johnson became household names. Others like Jack Elam and Strother Martin simply became household faces. Their very appearance in a film put us in a comfort zone—almost like sitting around the campfire with friends and family. They were the constants in "A" Westerns. With their support many leading actors cut their teeth in the genre. It should be noted that leading actors in the "Bs" built their careers on recognition as well. During the 1940s and 1950s the silver screen and television were flooded with the images of Gene, Roy and Hoppy. The extensive marketing of their images developed them into cultural icons all perpetuated by recognition.

The arrival of a second golden age of Westerns will rely largely on the development of a new generation of Western character actors. It will be no easy task to develop recognition for these actors given the minuscule number of Westerns produced in recent years. Searching for those actors should begin on the rodeo circuit, not in Hollywood. Although Jack Elam's background was in accounting and Edgar Buchanan was a dentist, much of the fresh talent of yesteryear developed their style and charisma on horseback. Ben Johnson, Slim Pickens, Wilford Brimley and Dick Farnsworth are the best examples.

Without a sufficient number of Westerns to develop familiar character actors, the answer may lie in converting many of our finest leading actors to character actors during the twilight of their careers. Robert Duval, Charlton Heston, and Tommy Lee Jones are but a few who have well established recognition. The challenge to filmmakers will be salaries and egos. An epic Western the likes of *How the West Was Won* need not be the goal. The finest Western to date, *Red River*, had a relatively small cast. The same was true of *Dances With Wolves*. *Red River's* greatest strengths were its powerful story and well defined characters. *Dances With Wolves* greatest strength was its portrayal of the western landscape.

At the turn of the 21st century, authenticity in Westerns has never been better. Filmmakers appear to be genuinely concerned about getting the facts right. Revisionist history discussed earlier in the text continues to find its way onto the silver screen. For example, a new film about the Alamo staring Dennis Quaid and Billy Bob Thornton (Crockett) and filmed on location in Texas completed shooting last week. Nearly fifty years after Fess Parker went down swinging Betsy, Davy Crockett's death will be depicted accurately according to the de la Peña diary.

With all the attention to detail and concern for historical accuracy you'd think that Hollywood would finally get one thing right—hats! Period accurate cowboy hats are the last holdout to making a perfect Western completely authentic. Even the most recent Westerns are still holding on to the visual image of the cowboy perpetuated by both silent and golden age Westerns. I suspect that the egos of the stars themselves play some part in selecting a cowboy hat that was not prevalent on the frontier. The hat is the most important aspect of a cowboy's image and perhaps the stars are more concerned with their own image than with authenticity. Fortunately, the "ten gallon" style hat worn by Tom Mix and the "telescope" style hats so prevalent in Westerns during the fifties have been abandoned. However, they have been replaced in recent Westerns by hat styles such as the Montana peak (Gus) and the centerfire. These style hats have traditional Hollywood style brims, but crowns prevalent at the turn of the 20th century. They offer the appearance of the "Marlboro man" with a touch of authenticity. For Westerns set in the early 1900s they are perfect. However, they are commonly worn in Westerns set in the 1870s and 1880s. Plenty of photographic evidence and the works of Frederic Remington and Charles Russell suggest that plain old open crown hats and the "Montana pinch" were most often worn by cowboy's during that period. Variations of the "plainsman" and "sombrero" hats made by hatters like John B. Stetson should fill the silver screen in the perfect Western.

These three elements: story, characters, and landscape are the remaining critical ingredients for producing a perfect Western. Story and landscape have been discussed in previous sections. Character development in a Western need not be in great depth, but it must be well defined. Such was the case in *Red River*. One point should be emphasized. Few Westerns include any of these elements—no Western has done them all well.

The filming of the western landscape in recent years has turned north, north to Canada. The American film industry discovered favorable production conditions in Canada. Along with financial incentives the landscape in Alberta proved to be ideal for Western filmmaking— in particular the Canadian Rockies and the great plains. Conditions have been so good that the genre faces a new dilemma. Most American Westerns are now filmed in Canada. These "Canadian Westerns" are not truly foreign films, unless they are filmed by Canadian production companies. They are for the most part American films that are filmed on location in Canada. Locations such as the E.P. Ranch in Alberta are as convincing as any location here in the states.

Canadian filming is not new. Many fine Westerns such as *Saskatchewan* (1954), *River of No Return* (1954), *Harry Tracy—Desperado* (1982) *Unforgiven* (1992) , were filmed in Alberta, Canada. Canada offers landscapes virtually identical to our own mountains, plains and Pacific Northwest. However, Canadian landscapes lack sufficient diversity to film all Westerns and that is where we are headed. Case in point—Texas Rangers (2001). At no time as I watched that film did I ever feel I was in Texas! Canada does not have a Monument Valley, Grand Canyon, Yellowstone, Death Valley, Alabama Hills or desert southwest. Western film locations must be specific to the story!

Ironically, spaghetti Westerns lacked landscape diversity as well. Virtually all spaghetti Westerns appear to be situated in the desert southwest. The single most unique aspect of the West is the land. Nowhere else on earth offers such diversity in landscape. Western filmmaking must be shot on location either in the West or at locations which are identical in appearance to the story's setting.

At the turn of the 21st century Western filmmaking has taken on a new look—a Canadian look. Canadian Westerns are, for the most part, far better than European Westerns. But, the dilemma is the same. Just as spaghetti Westerns seem to all look and feel the same, so goes it with Canadian Westerns. Two characteristics are beginning to emerge within the Canadian "sub genre" of Westerns. The first is the landscape and the second is the development of its characters. With some noteworthy exceptions, i.e., *Unforgiven, The Jack Bull, Johnson County War*, the lead roles are often written as caricatures—not characters.

Where the trail meets the horizon marks the end of the first century of Western filmmaking. What lies beyond is yet to be seen. The Western is a cinematic portrait of American culture—our only truly American art form. So, we must continue to make Westerns. The first edition of this book ended with a challenge to the film industry to produce the first perfect Western. Four years later it still hasn't been done. However, at the conclusion of the first century of Western filmmaking there are encouraging signs that the industry is again on the right path. Hollywood must shoot films—not budgets. One day all the necessary elements will come together: a great story, great characters, great acting, great use of the landscape and producers who will give a director free reign to create the *Casa Blanca* of the Western genre. I intend to live long enough to see it. Until then be assured that I will continue to roam the genre searching for that Western.

"Dissolute Cow-Punchers."

APPENDIX I.

BEWARE!

Occasionally I have ridden trails terminating in a box canyon. Many films may appear to be Westerns, but in fact are not. The following films which do not meet the criteria established in the introduction of this guide are *not* true Westerns.

Adam's Woman (1970)
Adios Amigos (1974)
Advance to the Rear (1964)
Africa—Texas Style! (1967)
Alias Jesse James (1959)
Allegheny Uprising (1939)
Alvarez Kelly (1966)
The Americano (1955)
Annie Oakley (1935)
The Apple Dumpling Gang (1974)
The Apple Dumpling Gang Rides Again (1979)
Arena (1953)
Arizona Wildcat (1939)
Arkansas Judge (1941)
The Awakening Land (1978)
Back to the Future, Part III (1990)
Back to the Woods (1937)
Bad Day at Black Rock (1954)
The Beast of Hollow Mountain (1956)
Beguiled (1971)
Belizaire the Cajun (1986)
Belle of the Nineties (1934)
Big Country (1994)
The Big Sky (1952)
Bill Tilghman (You Know My Name) (1999)
Billy Jack (1971)
Black Gold (1963)
Black Noon (1971)
Black Rodeo (1972)
The Black Stallion (1979)
Blazing Saddles (1974)
Bloody Trail (1972)
Bobbi Jo and the Outlaw (1976)
Boiling Point (1932)
Bordello (1979)
Born Reckless (1959)
Brave Warrior (1952)
Bronc Buster (1952)
Bronco Billy (1980)
Brothers of the Frontier (1995)
The Brothers O'Toole (1973)
Buffalo Bill Rides Again (1947)
Calamity Jane (1953)

California Country (1973)
Callaway Went Thataway (1951)
Campbell's Kingdom (1957)
Can't Help Singing (1944)
Canyon Crossroads (1954)
The Capture (1950)
Carolina Cannonball (1955)
Carry On Cowboy (1965)
The Castaway Cowboy (1974)
Cat Ballou (1965)
Cathouse Callgirls (1975)
Cavalry Command (1963)
Class of '61 (1993)
Climb an Angry Mountain (1972)
The Cockeyed Cowboys of Calico County (1970)
The Comeback Trail (1982)
Come On, Cowboy! (1948)
Comes a Horseman (1978)
Convict Cowboy (1995)
Coogan's Bluff (1968)
Cotter (1973)
Cowboy (1983)
The Cowboy and the Ballerina (1984)
The Cowboy and the Blonde (1941)
The Cowboy and the Lady (1938)
Cowboy From Brooklyn (1938)
The Cowboy Millionaire (1935)
Cowboys Don't Cry (1988)
Curse of the Undead (1959)
Curtain Call at Cactus Creek (1950)
Dakota (1988)
Dark Before Dawn (1988)
The Dark Power (1985)
Davy Crockett: Rainbow in the Thunder (!988)
Deadly Reactor (The Reactor) (1989)
Death Hunt (1981)
Deep Valley (1947)
Deerslayer (1943)
Desperado (1995)
The Deerslayer (1957)
The Deerslayer (1978)
The Devil and Miss Sarah (1971)
The Devil's Mistress (1966)

The Devil's Rain (1975)
Devil Wolf of Shadow Mountain (1964)
Dirty Dingus Magee (1970)
A Dirty Western (1975)
Disciples of Death (1975)
Distant Drums (1951)
Doc Hooker's Bunch (1976)
Double-Barrelled Detective Story (1965)
Drango (1957)
Dream Chasers (1982)
Dr. Quinn, Medicine Woman: The Heart Within (2001)
Drum (1976)
Drums Along the Mohawk (1939)
Drums in the Deep South (1951)
Drylanders (1963)
The Duchess and the Dirtwater Fox (1976)
The Dude Goes West (1948)
Dust (2001)
Edge of Eternity (1959)
The Electric Horseman (1979)
The Emigrants (1971)
The Enchanted Valley (1948)
Enter the Devil (1972)
Escape Through Time (1993)
Escape to Grizzly Mountain (2000)
Evil Roy Slade (1972)
Female Artillery (1973)
The Female Bunch (1969)
The Fighting Kentuckian (1949)
The Fighting Westerner (1935)
First Traveling Saleslady (1956)
A Fistful of 44s (1975)
A Fistful of Fingers (1994)
Flame of the Barbary Coast (1945)
Flame of the West (1945)
Flap! (The Last Warrior) (1970)
Forbidden Fruit (1984)
Forbidden Trail (1932)
Fort Ti (1953)
Foxfire (1955)
Friendly Persuasion (1956)
The Frisco Kid (1979)
From Dusk Till Dawn 3: The Hangman's Daughter (2000)
The Further Adventures of the Wilderness Family (1978)
Fury River (1962)
The Gambler from Natchez (1954)
The Gay Desperado (1936)
The Gentleman from Arizona (1939)
Get Mean (1975)
Ghost Dancing (1983)
The Ghost of Edendale (2002)
Ghost Town (1988)
Giant (1956)
Glory (1989)
Godmonster of Indian Flats (1973)
Goin' to Town (1935)
The Golden Stallion (1949)
Go West (1940)

Go West, Young Lady (1941)
The Great American Cowboy (1974)
The Great Bank Robbery (1969)
The Great Locomotive Chase (1956)
The Great Meadow (1931)
The Great Scout and Cathouse Thursday (1976)
Green Grass of Wyoming (1948)
Grim Prairie Tales (1990)
Grizzly (Killer Grizzly) (1976)
Guns for San Sebastian (1967)
Gun Smoke (1931)
Gypsy Colt (1954)
Hard Rock Harrigan (1935)
Harpoon (1948)
The Harvey Girls (1946)
Headin' East (1937)
Heart of the North (1938)
Hearts of the West (Hollywood Cowboy) (1975)
Heaven Only Knows (1947)
High, Wide and Handsome (1937)
Hi-Lo Country (1998)
The Honkers (1971)
Hope Ranch (2002)
Horse (1965)
Horse Opera (1993)
The Horse Soldiers (1959)
Hot Lead and Cold Feet (1978)
Hud (1963)
Hung Riders II, The Heat Is On (1997)
Hurricane Smith (1941)
In Old Oklahoma (War of the Wildcats) (1943)
In Pursuit of Honor (1995)
Inside Straight (1951)
The Iron Mistress (1952)
The Jackals (1967)
Jesse James Meets Frankenstein's Daughter (1966)
Jesse James' Women (1954)
Joe Panther (1976)
Journey Through Rosebud (1972)
Justin Morgan Had a Horse (1972)
J.W. Coop (1971)
Kate Bliss and the Ticker Tape Kid (1978)
The Kentuckian (1955)
The Kid From Texas (1939)
Kiss of Fire (1955)
A Knife for the Ladies (1973)
A Lady Takes a Chance (1943)
Lakota Woman: Siege at Wounded Knee (1994)
Last of the Redmen (1947)
The Last Tomahawk (1965)
The Law of the Wild (1934)
The Legend of Earl Durand (1974)
Legends of the Fall (1994)
Life in the Raw (1933)
Light in the Forest (1958)
The Littlest Horse Thieves (1977)
Lonely Are the Brave (1961)
Lone Star Moonlight (1946)

Lone Wolf McQuade (1983)
The Long Rifle and the Tomohawk (1964)
Lucky Luke (1991)
Lust in the Dust (1985)
The Lusty Men (1952)
Mad at the Moon (1992)
Mad Dog Morgan (Mad Dog) (1976)
The Man From Dakota (1940)
A Man From Boulevard Des Capucines (1987)
The Man From Snowy River (1982)
Man in the Shadow (Pay the Devil) (1958)
Many Rivers to Cross (1955)
Mark of the Renegade (1951)
Marshal of Madrid (1972)
The Mc Masters (1970)
Men of America (1932)
The Misfits (1961)
The Missouri Traveler (1958)
Mother Lode (1982)
Mountain Justice (1930)
Mustang (1959)
Mustang Country (1976)
My Friend Flicka (1943)
The Naked Dawn (1956)
Naked in the Sun (1957)
Nakia (1974)
Natchez Trace (1960)
Navajo (1951)
Ned Kelly (1970)
Nightwing (1979)
North Beach and Rawhide (1985)
Northwest Outpost (1947)
Northwest Stampede (1948)
Oklahoma! (1955)
Once Upon a Horse (1958)
Outlaws (1986)
The Outlaws is Coming (1965)
The Outlaw Stallion (1954)
Paint Your Wagon (1969)
The Paleface (1948)
The Palomino (1950)
Pardners (1956)
Pathfinder (1953)
Petticoat Planet (1996)
The Phantom Stockman (1953)
Pocket Money (1972)
The Prairie (1947)
Promise the Moon (1997)
The Proud and the Damned (1972)
The Proud Rebel (1958)
Quigley Down Under (1990)
Rachel and the Stranger (1948)
The Rainmaker (1956)
Rancho Delux (1974)
The Rangers (1974)
Rangle River (Men with Whips) (1936)
Raw Deal (1977)
Red Badge of Courage (1951)

Red Garters (1954)
Red Rock West (1993)
Red Skies of Montana (1952)
The Red Stallion (1947)
Red Stallion in the Rockies (1949)
Renegade Girl (1946)
Revenge of Billy the Kid (1991)
Revolution (1985)
Richochet Romance (1954)
Ride a Crooked Mile (1938)
Ride a Wild Pony (1976)
Ride 'em Cowboy (1942)
Riding High (1943)
Robbery Under Arms (1985)
Romance of the Redwoods (1939)
Rose Marie (1936)
Rose Marie (1954)
Rose of the Rancho (1936)
Rough Riders (1997)
The Rounders (1965)
Ruggles of Red Gap (1935)
Running Wild (Deliver Us From Evil) (1973)
Rustler's Rhapsody (1985)
Rythem on the Range (1987)
Sagittarius Mine (1972)
Samurai Cowboy (1993)
Sam Whiskey (1969)
San Francisco (1936)
Saratoga Trunk (1945)
Savage Pampas (1966)
Savages (1974)
Scandalous John (1971)
The Scavengers (1969)
Scream (The Outing) (1985)
The Second Greatest Sex (1955)
Secret of Navajo Cave (1976)
Seminole (1953)
Sequoia (1934)
Seven Angry Men (1955)
Seven Brides for Seven Brothers (1954)
Seven Cities of Gold (1955)
Seven Guns for the McGregors (1965)
Shadow of the Hawk (1976)
The Shakiest Gun in the West (1968)
Shanghai Noon (2002)
Shark River (1953)
Shenandoah (1965)
The Shepherd of the Hills (1941)
The Shepherd of the Hills (1964)
The Sheriff of Fractured Jaw (1959)
Sidekicks (1974)
The Silver Burro (1963)
Sioux City (1994)
The Skin Game (1971)
Sky Full of Moon (1952)
Slim Carter (1957)
The Slowest Gun in the West (1963)
Smith! (1969)

Smoky (1933, 1946, 1966)
Sodbusters (1994)
Squanto: A Warrior's Tale (1994)
Squares (Riding Tall) (1971)
The Sundowners (1960)
Support Your Local Gunfighter (1971)
Support Your Local Sheriff (1968)
Stageghost (2000)
Standing Tall (1978)
Starbird And Sweet Williams (1978)
Stardust (2000)
Stars in My Crown (1950)
Straight to Hell (1987)
Stranger on My Land (1988)
The Sugerland Express (1974)
Sunset (1988)
Sweet Savage (1979)
Take It Big (1944)
Tall Tale (1995)
Tap Roots (1948)
Tecumseh: The Last Warrior (1995)
Ten Days to Tulara (1958)
The Tenderfoot (1932)
13 Fighting Men (1960)
This Gun for Hire (1942)
Three Amigos! (1986)
The Three Cabelleros (1945)
Three Faces West (1940)
Thunderhead, Son of Flicka (1945)
A Ticket to Tomahawk (1950)
Timerider (The Adventures of Lyle Swann) (1983)
Timestalkers (1987)
Tin Star Void (Death Collector) (1988)
Tomboy and the Champ (1961)
Traveling Saleswoman (1950)
Treasure at Matecumbe (1976)
Treasure of the Sierra Madre (1948)
Trespasses (1987)
Trouble at Midnight (1938)
Tulsa (1949)
The Two From Rio Bravo (1963)
Two Guys From Texas (1948)
Unconquered (1948)
Under a Texas Moon (1930)
Under Colorado Skies (1947)
Under the Pampas Moon (1935)
Untamed Heiress (1954)
Uphill All the Way (1985)
Valerie (1957)
The Valley of Gwangi (1969)
The Vanquished (1953)
The Villain (Cactus Jack) (1979)
The Virgin Cowboy (1975)
Viva Maria (1965)
Viva Max! (1969)
The Wackiest Wagon Train in the West (1976)
Wagons East! (1994)
War Party (1988)

Way of a Gaucho (1952)
Way Out West (1930)
Way Out West (1936)
Welcome to Blood City (1977)
Westworld (1973)
When the Legends Die (1972)
When the Redskins Rode (1951)
Whispering Smith Speaks (1935)
White Hunter, Black Heart (1990)
Wild and Woolly (1937)
Wild Card (1992)
Wild Gals of the Naked West (1962)
Wild Horses (1983)
Wild Horses (1985)
Wild Horse Hank (1979)
The Wild Women of Chastity Gulch (1982)
Windwalker (1981)
Winter Kill (1974)
The Wistful Widow of Wagon Gap (1947)
Wolf Song (1929)
Wrangler (1989)
The Yearling (1946)
Yellowneck (1955)
The Young Country (1970)
Zachariah (1971)
Zorro the Gay Blade (1981)

APPENDIX II.

THE 100 BEST OF THE WEST.

In the first edition of this book I attempted to compile a list of the top ten Westerns of all time. However, I found that list far too exclusive and ultimately expanded the list to twenty. A centennial edition must include a top 100 list. Of the nearly 900 hundred Westerns reviewed in this guide nearly thirty received four and a half or five star ratings—a mere three percent. From these came my original top twenty selections. They remain unchanged. Expanding that list to fifty was relatively easy. However, filling out the balance of the top one hundred was more difficult than I imagined. It should be noted that there is one very obvious omission—*Stagecoach*. It was not an oversight. Stagecoach is without question the most over rated Western ever made. Not a bad Western, simply over rated. My own rating system guided me through the selection process. Ultimately, the determining factor became this thought, "Hell, I'd like to see that one again!"

1. **Red River** (Howard Hawks)
2. **Dances with Wolves** (Kevin Costner)
3. **The Shootist** (Don Siegel)
4. **Will Penny** (Tom Gries)
5. **Jeremiah Johnson** (Sidney Pollack)
6. **The Grey Fox** (Philip Borsos)
7. **Lonesome Dove** (Simon Wincer)
8. **The Good Old Boys** (Tommy Lee Jones)
9. **Zandy's Bride** (Jan Troell)
10. **The Outlaw Josey Wales** (Clint Eastwood)
11. **The Return of Frank James** (Fritz Lang)
12. **The Missouri Breaks** (Arthur Penn)
13. **Shane** (George Stevens)
14. **She Wore a Yellow Ribbon** (John Ford)
15. **Jesse James** (Henry King)
16. **Fort Apache** (John Ford)
17. **A Man Called Horse** (Elliott Silverstein)
18. **McCabe and Mrs. Miller** (Robert Altman)
19. **Pat Garrett and Billy the Kid** (Sam Peckinpah)
20. **Tom Horn** (William Wiard)
21. **How the West Was Won** (Ford,Hathaway&Marshall)
22. **The Unforgiven** (John Huston)
23. **Old Gringo** (Luis Puenzo)
24. **Butch Cassidy and the Sundance Kid** (Hill)
25. **Return of a Man Called Horse** (Irvin Kershner)

26. **The Culpepper Cattle Company** (Richards)
27. **Monte Walsh** (William A. Fraker)
28. **Dream West** (Dick Lowry)
29. **Son of the Morning Star** (Mike Robe)
30. **The New Land** (Jan Troell)
31. **Buffalo Girls** (Rod Harty)
32. **The Bear** (Jean-Jacques Annaud)
33. **The Searchers** (John Ford)
34. **The Gunfighter** (Henry King)
35. **Harry Tracy—Desperado** (William A. Graham)
36. **My Darling Clementine** (John Ford)
37. **Sergeant Rutledge** (John Ford)
38. **High Noon** (Fred Zinnemann)
39. **One-Eyed Jacks** (Marlon Brando)
40. **The Man Who Shot Liberty Valance** (Ford)
41. **Rawhide** (Henry Hathaway)
42. **Cheyenne Autumn** (John Ford)
43. **The Magnificent Seven** (John Sturges)
44. **The Good, the Bad, and the Ugly** (Sergio Leone)
45. **Rooster Cogburn** (Stuart Millar)
46. **The Life&Times of Judge Roy Bean** (Huston)
47. **The Far Country** (Anthony Mann)
48. **Rio Grande** (John Ford)
49. **Valdez is Coming** (Edwin Sherin)
50. **The Professionals** (Richard Brooks)

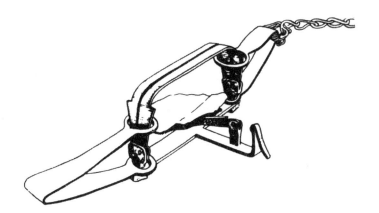

51. **True Grit** (Henry Hathaway)
52. **Tombstone** (George P. Cosmatos)
53. **Broken Arrow** (Delmer Daves)
54. **The Cowboys** (Mark Rydell)
55. **High Plains Drifter** (Clint Eastwood)
56. **Red Sun** (Terence Young)
57. **Goin' South** (Jack Nicholson)
58. **Arrowhead** (Charles Marquis Warren)
59. **Big Jake** (George Sherman)
60. **Unforgiven** (Clint Eastwood)
61. **Major Dundee** (Sam Peckinpah)
62. **Wyatt Earp** (Lawrence Kasden)
63. **The Deadly Trackers** (Barry Shear)
64. **El Dorado** (Howard Hawks)
65. **The Texans** (James Hogan)
66. **Firecreek** (Vincent McEveety)
67. **Track of the Cat** (William Wellman)
68. **Ulzana's Raid** (Robert Aldrich)
69. **Wild Rovers** (Blake Edwards)
70. **Heaven's Gate** (Michael Cimino)
71. **Billy the Kid** (William A. Graham)
72. **The Jack Bull** (John Badham)
73. **Breakheart Pass** (Tom Gries)
74. **Last Train from Gun Hill** (John Sturges)
75. **The Stalking Moon** (Robert Mulligan)

76. **Last Stand at Sabre River** (Dick Lowry)
77. **Crazy Horse** (John Irvin)
78. **Riders of the Purple Sage** (Charles Haid)
79. **Santa Fe Trail** (Michael Curtiz)
80. **The Last Hard Men** (Andrew V. McLaglen)
81. **The Sacketts** (Robert Totten)
82. **Billy Two Hats** (Ted Kotcheff)
83. **Gold Is Where You Find It** (Michael Curtiz)
84. **Calamity Jane** (James Goldstone)
85. **The Mask of Zorro** (Martin Campbell)
86. **Pale Rider** (Clint Eastwood)
87. **They Came to Cordura** (Robert Rossen)
88. **The Undefeated** (Andrew V. McLaglen)
89. **Wells Fargo** (Frank Lloyd)
90. **Blood on the Moon** (Robert Wise)
91. **The Sons of Katie Elder** (Henry Hathaway)
92. **Streets of Laredo** (Joseph Sargent)
93. **The Bounty Hunter** (André de Toth)
94. **Warlock** (Edward Dmytryk)
95. **Dead or Alive** (John Guillermin)
96. **The Man from Laramie** (Anthony Mann)
97. **Dead Man's Walk** (Yves Simoneau)
98. **The Westerner** (William Wyler)
99. **The Hired Hand** (Peter Fonda)
100. **Johnson County War** (David S. Cass, Sr.)

APPENDIX III.

MORE BEST OF THE WEST.

Upon the completion of my top 100 list of films, I could not resist the temptation to compile five more lists: Best Directors, Best Actors, Best Character Actors, Best Actresses, and Best Native American Actors. During the course of the development of the top 100 films it became evident that certain names appeared over and over. Beside each name is a list of the top 100 film rankings of the films in which they worked. Few made the lists without contributing to at least two of the top 100 films.

The pioneer directors of Western filmmaking are discussed in detail in the "Directors" chapter. Because the bulk of their work was in silent films, they are not fairly represented in the top ten list. However, those directors who made the list owe much to directors like Walsh, Lang, Dwan and Lewis. John Ford heads the list having directed nearly ten percent of the top 100 films.

The best actors list includes actors in staring roles in, again, at least two of the top 100 films. The ultimate criteria for making the list was to be convincing and is described in detail in the "Acting" chapter. Apologies go out to legendary Western actors like Randolph Scott, Kirk Douglas, Joel McCrea, Alan Ladd, Anthony Quinn, Robert Mitchum, Glenn Ford and Gary Cooper. The body of their work speaks for itself. However, for whatever reason, their contributions to the great Western films were limited. In regards to the best contemporary actors, such as Tom Selleck, Kevin Costner, Tommy Lee Jones, and Robert Duvall, I expect that their names will appear on the top ten lists of the second century of Western filmmaking. During the first century one name will stand alone in connection with Westerns—John Wayne. He appeared in a whopping 15% of the top 100 Westerns.

The best character actors list includes actors in supporting roles. As I discussed in the "Acting" chapter, outstanding supporting roles ultimately determined the quality of a film. The deciding factor was the ability to convey the look and feel of the Old West.

Compiling these lists often felt like grabbing a rattler by the tail. I reckon they'll generate plenty of discussion the next time we're out on the trail. So, please don't take offense if your favorites don't appear on my lists…

THE 1ˢᵀ CENTURY'S TOP TEN

DIRECTORS

1. **John Ford** (14, 16, 21, 33, 36, 37, 40, 42, 48)
2. **Henry Hathaway** (21, 41, 51, 91)
3. **Clint Eastwood** (10, 55, 60, 86)
4. **Jan Troell** (9, 30)
5. **Henry King** (15, 34)
6. **Howard Hawks** (1, 64)
7. **Tom Gries** (4, 73)
8. **Sam Peckinpah** (19, 61)
9. **Dick Lowry** (28, 76)
10. **William A. Graham** (35, 71)

ACTORS

1. **John Wayne** (1,3,14,16,21,33,40,45,48,51,54,59,64,88,91)
2. **Henry Fonda** (11, 15, 16, 21, 36, 66, 94)
3. **Clint Eastwood** (10, 44, 55, 60, 86)
4. **James Stewart** (3, 21, 40, 42, 47, 53, 66, 96)
5. **Charlton Heston** (4, 52, 58, 61, 80)
6. **Gregory Peck** (21, 23, 34, 75, 82)
7. **Richard Harris** (17, 25, 60, 61, 63)
8. **Burt Lancaster** (22, 49, 50, 68)
9. **Robert Redford** (5, 24)
10. **Lee Marvin** (27, 40, 50)

CHARACTER ACTORS

1. **Walter Brennan** (1, 21, 36, 47, 65, 90, 98)
2. **Ben Johnson** (4, 13, 14, 16, 28, 39, 42, 48, 61, 73, 81, 88)
3. **Slim Pickens** (4, 19, 20, 39, 54, 61, 81)
4. **Richard Farnsworth** (6, 10, 20, 27, 46, 54, 68)
5. **Jack Elam** (19, 38, 41, 47, 66, 81, 96)
6. **Harry Carey, Jr.** (1, 14, 33, 42, 48, 52, 59, 88, 90)
7. **John Carradine** (3, 11, 15, 40, 42)
8. **Jack Palance** (13, 27, 31, 50, 58)
9. **Chill Wills** (19, 48, 98)
10. **Strother Martin** (24, 40, 51, 91)

ACTRESSES

Because the Western is a male dominated genre, the selection of my top ten actresses was very difficult. The early frontier was scarcely populated with women. For example in 1850, just 10% of the California Gold Rush population was female. Women gradually went west during the following decades. But, their roles in the settlement of the West reflected the male dominated culture of the times.

The Western genre reflected this scarcity of women on the frontier. Few substantial roles were written for women. Those roles that were offered to women were written from a 20th century male's view of what pioneer women should have been—not the way they actually were.

Making my selection even more difficult was Hollywood's pattern of casting the genre with female "eye candy." Which is to say, actresses were chosen largely for their appeal to the eyes of a 20th century male dominated audience. These actresses seldom bore any resemblance either physically or emotionally to the hearty female pioneers of the real frontier. Consequently, Western actresses were seldom convincing. As I discussed in the acting chapter, to be convincing is paramount. Two other criteria were considered: presence and career contributions to the genre. These are my selections:

1. Joanne Dru (1, 14)
2. Liv Ullman (9, 30)
3. Katy Jurado (19, 38, 39. 58)
4. Anjelica Huston (7, 31)
5. Maureen O'Hara (48, 59)
6. Barbara Stanwyck
7. Marie Windsor (93)
8. Claire Trevor
9. Yvonne De Carlo
10. Dorothy Malone (94)

NATIVE AMERICAN ACTORS

The "Acting" chapter of the first edition of this book contained an unforeseen error. I discovered the mistake while preparing this top ten list in which I originally placed Iron Eyes Cody at the top. Iron Eyes Cody did more than any other actor to portray Native Americans in a fair and noble manner. Perhaps Cody is best remembered as the Indian with the tear in his eye during the 1970s anti-litter TV commercial. Iron Eyes Cody dedicated his life both on and off the screen to portraying an authentic Indian life. No other man did more to further the Native American cause—no other white man! Iron Eyes Cody was Sicilian American, not Cree-Cherokee as he claimed all his life.

In 1996, Cody's half sister confessed to a New Orleans newspaper the true origin of his life. But, the story was not widely reported and Cody denied it to his grave. Today, over 4,000 websites contain information about Cody. Only a few confirm his well documented Italian ancestry.

Given the substantial and credible documentation, I can not with good conscience include Cody in my list. I have removed his name from the Acting chapter as well. Regardless of his ancestry, he was the most notable Indian actor. Let him be remembered not for what he wasn't, but for what he did and for what he wanted to be.

With some reservation, I offer my top ten picks in this category. I have painstakingly researched the ancestry of each man. Like Cody, some of them were born near the turn of the last century making their birth dates and origins difficult to document. I will trust these men to have told the truth which is a sign of a true Native American.

1. Jay Silverheels (51, 53)
2. Graham Greene (2)
3. Chief Dan George (10)
4. Chief Yowlachie (1)
5. Chief Thundercloud (33)
6. Chief John Big Tree (14)
7. John War Eagle (53, 96)
8. Wes Studi (2, 92)
9. Will Sampson (10)
10. Irene Bedard (77)

BIBLIOGRAPHY.

Adams, Les & Rainey, Buck. *Shoot-Em-Ups: The Complete Reference Guide to Westerns of the Sound Era.* New Rochelle: Arlington House, 1978.

"AFI's 100 Greatest Movies." *American Film Institute.* Online. Available http://www.afionline.org. 17 June 2001.

"AFI's 100 Most Heart Pounding Movies." *American Film Institute.* Online. Available http://www.afionline.org. 17 June 2001.

Barr, Amelia. *Remember the Alamo.* New York: Dodd, Mead and Co., 1898.

Blake, Michael F. "Happy Ending for an Underdog." *Los Angeles Times/Calender,* (June 4, 2003): 2.

Bogdanovich, Peter. *Who the Devil Made It.* New York: Alfred A. Knopf, 1997.

Brown, Dee. *Fort Phil Kearny: An American Saga.* Lincoln: University of Nebraska Press, 1962.

Brown, Dee. *Hear That Lonesome Whistle Blow: Railroads in the West.* New York: Holt, Rinehart & Winston, 1977.

Buck, Solon J. *The Granger Movement.* Lincoln: University of Nebraska Press, 1963.

Buscombe, Edward. *The BFI Companion to the Western.* New York: Da Capo Press, Inc., 1988.

Carson, Kit. *Kit Carson's Autobiography.* Lincoln: University of Nebraska Press, 1966.

Cary, Diana Serra. *The Hollywood Posse.* Boston: Houghton Mifflin Company, 1975.

Chisholm, James. *South Pass, 1868.* Lincoln: University of Nebraska Press, 1960.

Clappe, Louise A.K.S. *The Shirley Letters.* Santa Barbara: Peregrine Smith, Inc., 1970.

Cody, William F. *The Life of Hon. William F. Cody. Lincoln*: University of Nebraska Press, 1978.

Connell, Ed. *Reinsman of the West.* North Hollywood: Wishire Book Co., 1964.

Coyner, David H. *The Lost Trappers.* Albuquerque: University of New Mexico Press, 1970.

Cozad, W. Lee. *Those Magnificent Mountain Movies.* Lake Arrowhead: Rim of the World Historical Society, 2002.

Crook, George. *General George Crook: His Autobiography.* Norman: University of Oklahoma Press, 1960.

Derr, Mark. *The Frontiersman: The Real Life and Many Legends of Davy Crockett.* New York: William Morrow & Co., 1993.

Ellis, Richard N. *General Pope and the U.S. Indian Policy.* Albuquerque: University of New Mexico Press, 1970.

Emory, W.H. *Lieutenant Emory Reports.* Albuquerque: University of New Mexico Press, 1951.

Gagliasso, Dan. "Joe De Yong and Hollywood." *Montana 50*, No. 3 (Autumn 2000): 2.

Gard, Wayne. *Sam Bass.* Lincoln: University of Nebraska Press, 1936.

Garrett, Pat F. *The Authentic Life of Billy the Kid.* Norman: University of Oklahoma Press, 1954.

Gertner, Richard. *International Television Almanac.* New York: Quigly Publications, 1961-82.

Gossett, Sue. *The Films and Career of Audie Murphy.* Madison: Empire Publishing, 1996.

Gowans, F.R. & Campbell, E.E. *Fort Bridger: Island in the Wilderness.* Provo: Brigham Young University Press, 1975.

Hamilton, Wilson. *The New Empire and Her Representative Men.* Oakland: Pacific Press Publishing House, 1886.

Hardy, Phil. *The Western: The Overlook Encyclopedia. Woodstock*: The Overlook Press, 1991.

Henry, Will. *I, Tom Horn.* Philadelphia: J.B. Lippencott Co., 1975.

Heston, Charlton. *In the Arena: An Autobiography.* Simon & Schuster: New York, 1995.

Holliday, J.S. *The World Rushed In.* New York: Simon & Schuster, 1981.

Horn, Tom. *Life of Tom Horn: A Vindication.* Denver: The Louthan Book Co., 1904.

"Internet Movie Data Base Top 50 Westerns." *IMDb.* Online. Available http://us. imdb. com/charts/votes/western. 5 September 2002.

Kennedy, Burt. *Hollywood Trail Boss: Behind the Scenes of the Wild, Wild Western.* New York: Boulevard Books, 1997.

Kittrell, William H. *The Banditti of the Plains: Or the Cattleman's Invasion of Wyoming in 1892.* Norman: University of Oklahoma Press, 1954.

Krakel, Dean. *The Saga of Tom Horn: The Story of a Cattleman's War.* Laramie: Powder River Publishing, 1954.

Laubin, Reginald & Gladys. *The Indian Tipi: Its History, Construction and Use.* New York: Ballantine Books, 1957.

Lathrop, George. *Memoirs of a Pioneer Stagecoach Driver*: Unpublished.

Lummis, Charles R. *General Crook and the Apache Wars.* Flagstaff: Northland Press, 1966.

Margaret Herrick Library. Film Archive files. Academy of Motion Picture Arts and Sciences Center for Motion Picture Study.

Marill, Alvin H. *Movies Made for Television: 1964-1986.* New York: Baseline, 1987.

Monaghan, Jay. *Last of the Badman: The Legend of Tom Horn.* Indianapolis: 1946.

Monosh, Barry. *International Television and Video Almanac.* New York: Quigly Publications, Inc., 1996.

"Movies and Television Specials Filmed in Moab Area." *Moab to Monument Valley Film Commission*. Online. Available http://filmmoab.com. 7 June 2001.

"Movies Filmed in Monument Valley." *Moab to Monument Valley Film Commission*. Online. Available http://filmmoab.com. 7 June 2001.

Murray, John A. Cinema Southwest: *An Illustrated Guide to the Movies and Their Locations*. Flagstaff: Northland Publishing Co., 2000.

Nasatir, Abraham P. *Borderland in Retreat*. Albuquerque: University of New Mexico Press, 1976.

Ogle, Ralph H. *Federal Control of the Western Apaches*. Albuquerque: University of New Mexico Press, 1970.

Old Tucson. *Old Tucson Studios*. Tucson: Terrell Publishing, 1998.

Paine, Lauran. *Tom Horn: Man of the West*. Barre: Barre Publishing Co., 1963.

Phares, Ross. *Bible in the Pocket, Gun in the Hand: The Story of Frontier Religion*. Lincoln: University of Nebraska Press, 1964.

Pitts, Michael R. *Western Movies: A TV and Video Guide to 4200 Genre Films*. Jefferson, N.C.: McFarland and Co., 1986.

Rainey, Buck. *The Shoot-Em-Ups Ride Again: A Supplement to Shoot-Em-Ups*. Waynesville, N.C.: The World of Yesterday, 1990.

Ridge, Martin. "The Life of an Idea: The Significance of Frederick Jackson Turner's Frontier Thesis." *Montana* 41, No. 1 (Winter, 1991): 2.

Riley, Glenda. "The Spector of a Savage: Rumors and Alarmism on the Overland Trail." *Western Historical Quarterly* 15 (October, 1984): 443.

Roosevelt, Theodore. *The Winning of the West*. New York: The Current Literature Publishing Co., 1905.

Roosevelt, Theodore. *Cowboys and Kings*. New York: Kraus Reprint Co., 1969.

Schell, Terri K. *Video Scource Book, Vol. 1-2*. New York: Gale Research, Inc., 1996.

Sherman, Robert G. *Quiet on the Set!: Motion Picture History at the Iverson Movie Location Ranch*. Chatsworth: Sherway Publishing, 1984.

Siewart, Elinore P. *Letters of a Woman Homesteader*. Lincoln: University of Nebraska Press, 1961.

Slide, Anthony. *The American Film Industry: A Historical Dictionary*. New York: Greenwood Press, 1986.

Slide, Anthony. *Nitrate Won't Wait: Film Preservation in the United States*. Jefferson, N.C.: McFarland & Co., Inc., 1992.

Spring, Agnes W. *The Cheyenne and Black Hills Stage and Express Routes*. Lincoln: University of Nebraska Press, 1948.

Steele, James W. *Frontier Army Sketches*. Albuquerque: University of New Mexico Press, 1969.

Taylor, Morris F. *First Mail West: Stagecoach Lines on the Santa Fe Trail* Albuquerque: University of New Mexico Press, 1971.

Thrapp, Dan L. *Al Sieber Chief of Scouts*. Norman: University of Oklahoma Press, 1964.

Turan, Kenneth. "John Ford's Monument." *Los Angeles Times/Calender,* (June 20, 1993): 9.

UCLA Film and Television Archive. Files.

USC Cinema-Television Library. Archive files.

Variety and Daily Variety Reviews, (Vol. 12-18). New York: Garland Publishing, Inc.

Weber, David J. *Foreigners in Their Native Land: Historical Roots of the Mexican Americans*. Albuquerque: University of New Mexico Press, 1973.

Weber, David J. *The Mexican Frontier, 1821-1846: The American Southwest Under Mexico*. Albuquerque: University of New Mexico, 1982.

Weisser, Thomas. *Spaghetti Westerns—the Good, the Bad and the Violent: 558 Eurowesterns and Their Personnel, 1961-1977*. Jefferson, N.C.: McFarland & Company, Inc., 1992.

Williams III, George. *The Red-Light Ladies of Virginia City, Nevada*. Dayton: Tree by the River Publishing, 1984.

Wilmington, Michael. "Elegy for a Not-So-New Frontier." *Los Angeles Times/Calender,* (December 16, 1990): 38.

Winther, Oscar O. *The Transportation Frontier: Trans-Mississippi West, 1865-1890*. Albuquerque: University of New Mexico Press, 1964.

Witzleben, Donna. *BIB Telivision Programming Source Books: 1996-97*. Philadelphia: North American Publishing Co., 1997.

Womack, John, Jr. *Zapata and the Mexican Revolution*. New York: Vintage Books, 1968.

Wyman, Walker D. *The Wild Horse of the West*. Lincoln: University of Nebraska Press, 1945.

ORDER FORM

_____

CENTENNIAL EDITION
THE COWBOY'S TRAIL GUIDE TO WESTERNS
$29.95 Postpaid

Please send me _____ copies of *The Cowboy's Trail Guide to Westerns* @ $29.95 each postpaid.
California residents add 7.75%, or $2.32 per copy, for state sales tax.
Enclosed is my check for $_____, payable to Pacific Sunset Publishing.

NAME_____

COMPANY NAME_____

ADDRESS_____

CITY_____STATE_____ZIP_____

DAYTIME TELEPHONE_____

EMAIL_____

Send check or money order to:
Pacific Sunset Publishing
30320 Live Oak Canyon Road
Redlands, CA 92373

www.pacificsunset.com

Discounts for quantity orders. Please inquire.
If this is a library book, please photocopy this page.

Thank you!